THE LOS
IS KNOWN AROUND THE WORLD

"An adventurer cuts loose...a cut above most of its genre."
—The Oakland Tribune

"One long tale of quest and adventure, of chance meetings and
inevitable partings, meals relished and hotels endured, camel
caravans caught and buses missed–spun through with his
ecclectic gleanings from obscure works of archaeology,
history and explorers' diaries. Also woven throughout the books,
in a crazy-quilt jumble of innocent awe and hard bitten savvy,
are reflections on the people and places he encountered...
...There is a disarming casualness and a kind of festive,
footloose fancy to his tales that are utterly beguiling."
–The San Francisco Chronicle

"...a tonic...experiences in exotic places the rest of us think
only Indiana Jones visits...it will whet your appetite
and leave you chomping at the bit."
—The Missoulian

"...an offbeat travel guide that is fun to read even if you
don't have plans to duplicate author David Hatcher Childress'
remarkable journey. A thoughtful young man, Childress tells
a good story and his book is lively and interesting."
—The Washington Post

"Explore for lost treasure, stone monuments
forgotten in jungles...and hair-raising terrain
from the safety of your armchair."
—Bookwatch

"A fascinating series of books, written with humour,
insight, depth and an astonishing knowledge
of the ancient past."
—Richard Noone, author of 5/5/2000

Other books in the **Lost Cities Series**:

Lost Cities of China, Central Asia & India
Lost Cities & Ancient Mysteries of Africa & Arabia
Lost Cities of Ancient Lemuria & the Pacific
Lost Cities & Ancient Mysteries of South America
Lost Cities of North & Central America

LOST CITIES OF ATLANTIS ANCIENT EUROPE & THE MEDITERRANEAN

DAVID HATCHER CHILDRESS

ADVENTURES UNLIMITED PRESS

I dedicate this book to the "New Atlantis."

"As above, so below." —Hermes Trismegistis

I would like to thank the many researchers who have helped me write this book, whether they know it or not. Thanks especially to Charles Berlitz, Thor Heyerdahl, John Michell, Christine Rhone, Bob Rickard, Nigel Pennick, Leo Duel, John Anthony West, David Zink, William Corliss, Janet & Colin Bord, Bill Donato, Hugh Lynn Cayce, Tim Wallace-Murphy, Kathy Collins, Ranney Moss, Harry Osoff, Carl Hart, and many others.

**Lost Cities of Atlantis,
Ancient Europe & the Mediterranean**
©Copyright 1996
David Hatcher Childress

Printed in the United States of America

First Printing

February 1996

ISBN 0-932813-25-9

Published by
Adventures Unlimited Press
Stelle, Illinois 60919 USA

Maps by John Moss, Paul Barker, J.F. Horrabin, Carl Hart and many others. Thank you all for your help.

Cover photo of Hagar Qim in Malta

The **Lost Cities Series**:
Lost Cities of China, Central Asia & India
Lost Cities & Ancient Mysteries of Africa & Arabia
Lost Cities of Ancient Lemuria & the Pacific
Lost Cities & Ancient Mysteries of South America
Lost Cities of North & Central America
Lost Cities of Atlantis, Ancient Europe and the Mediterranean

TABLE OF CONTENTS

1. ANCIENT ATLANTIS:
Civilization's Legendary Beginning   9

2. TURKEY: Atlantis & the Hittite Empire   51

3. CRETE & THE AEGEAN:
The Sunken Cities of Osiris   91

4. GREECE: The Cyclopean Walls Of Olympus   133

5. ITALY: Etruscans & the Legacy of Rome   163

6. MALTA: Ancient Gods of Osiris   189

7. TUNISIA & MOROCCO:
Carthage & the Lost Cities ofAtlas   221

8. SPAIN & PORTUGAL: The Lost Cities of Hercules   257

9. FRANCE: Atlantis & the Priory of Zion   295

10. GERMANY, HOLLAND & EASTERN EUROPE:
The Northern Atlantis   323

11. ENGLAND & WALES: Stonehenge & The Holy Grail   343

12. SCOTLAND: The Vitrified Forts of Atlantis   383

13. IRELAND: The Lost Land Of Tir-Na-n'Og   423

Bibliography and Footnotes   475

The **New Science Series**:
- THE FREE ENERGY DEVICE HANDBOOK
- THE FANTASTIC INVENTIONS OF NIKOLA TESLA
- THE ANTI-GRAVITY HANDBOOK
- ANTI-GRAVITY & THE WORLD GRID
- ANTI-GRAVITY & THE UNIFIED FIELD
- VIMANA AIRCRAFT OF ANCIENT INDIA & ATLANTIS
- THE COSMIC CONSPIRACY
- TAPPING THE ZERO POINT ENERGY
- THE HARMONIC CONQUEST OF SPACE
- THE ENERGY GRID
- THE BRIDGE TO INFINITY

The **Lost Cities Series**:
- LOST CITIES OF ATLANTIS, ANCIENT EUROPE
  & THE MEDITERRANEAN
- LOST CITIES OF NORTH & CENTRAL AMERICA
- LOST CITIES & ANCIENT MYSTERIES OF SOUTH AMERICA
- LOST CITIES OF ANCIENT LEMURIA & THE PACIFIC
- LOST CITIES & ANCIENT MYSTERIES OF AFRICA & ARABIA
- LOST CITIES OF CHINA, CENTRAL ASIA & INDIA

The **Mystic Traveller Series**:
- IN SECRET TIBET by Theodore Illion (1937)
- DARKNESS OVER TIBET by Theodore Illion (1938)
- IS SECRET MONGOLIA by Henning Haslund (1934)
- MEN AND GODS IN MONGOLIA by Henning Haslund (1935)
- DANGER MY ALLY by Mike Mitchell-Hedges (1957)
- MYSTERY CITIES by Thomas Gann (1925)
- IN QUEST OF LOST WORLDS by Byron de Prorok (1937)

The **Atlantis Reprint Series**:
- ATLANTIS IN SPAIN by Elena Whishaw (1929)
- THE HISTORY OF ATLANTIS by Lewis Spence (1926)
- RIDDLE OF THE PACIFIC by John MacMillan Brown (1924)
- THE SHADOW OF ATLANTIS by Col. A. Braghine (1940)
- SECRET CITIES OF OLD SOUTH AMERICA by H. Wilkins (1952)

LOST CITIES OF
ATLANTIS
ANCIENT EUROPE
& THE MEDITERRANEAN

Observatory in Alexandria, Egypt
From Camille Flammarion, *Les Etoiles*.

Chapter 1

ANCIENT ATLANTIS:
Civilization's Legendary Beginning

...in those days the Atlantic was navigable; and there was an island situated in front of the straits which you call the Columns of Herakles ...the island was larger than Libya and Asia put together, and was the way to other islands, and from the islands you might pass though the whole of the opposite continent which surrounded the true ocean; for this sea which is within the Straits of Herakles is only a harbour, having a narrow entrance, but that other is a real sea, and the surrounding land may be most truly called a continent. Now, in the island of Atlantis there was a great and wonderful empire...
—Solon as quoted in Plato's *Timaeus*

Atlantis. The name has come to mean many things. It evokes images of advanced ancient civilizations, cataclysmic destruction, and the mysterious past. Atlantis is many things to many people, a glorious civilization before history officially begins, a cataclysmic warning to the world today, an allegory and myth meant to stimulate the human mind.

For over 2,000 years, Atlantis has been the subject of countless history and philosophical books. Films, television shows and comic books have all used the familiar subject of Atlantis.

There are wines named after Atlantis, hotels, rental companies, engineering companies, and bookstores. Nearly every educated person in the world today has heard of Atlantis; it is a subject which has increased in popularity over the last 100 years. But did Atlantis really exist?

Critics of the Atlantis theory point out that Atlantis is only an allegory created by the Greek philosopher Plato and that little or no evidence for Atlantis actually exists. Yet proponents of the Atlantis theory claim that an abundance of evidence exists for an ancient civilization in the past that we could call "Atlantis."

My own interest in Atlantis began many years ago when I began a worldwide quest for ancient civilizations, megalithic remains, and evidence of advanced ancient science. My travels took me across the Pacific Ocean, through Asia, and to the Middle East. For several years I travelled in Africa, returning to India and China for another year.

Eventually I was to travel in South and Central America for several years, gathering further evidence for advanced ancient civilizations and attempting to construct a coherent view of the past that took into account what I had learned.

I not only concluded that ancient man had attained a high state of scientific advancement and travelled regularly around the world but also that a lost civilization called Atlantis did at one time exist. My travels then led me back to North America and from there to Europe and the Mediterranean, where I hoped to learn more about this ancient civilization that we call "Atlantis."

As I looked into Atlantis, I was to find a subject fraught with intrigue and amazing implications. There were archaeological cover-ups and frauds, secret societies and political movements, with millions of dollars often involved in one way or another.

Science seems to have taken two divergent paths over the last 120 years or so, in all its various disciplines. For instance, in philosophy there is the well-known split of "sophists" versus "Platonists;" while in anthropology there is the "diffusionism" versus "isolationism" split; and in modern geology there is "cataclysmic" geology versus the "uniformitarian" geology that is generally taught in school. All these "isms" play a part in the acceptance or denial of the Atlantis theme.

Until recently, historians generally taught that civilization started in Sumeria approximately 7,000 years ago. Prior to this man, it is often taught, lived in a primitive state, often in caves.

On the other hand, Atlantists believe that many civilizations quite similar to our own have come and gone on this planet *several* times over. In popular literature, one of these advanced civilizations is called *Atlantis*. The word is Greek and means "Daughter of Atlas." It has come to mean the world before history, outside of history, a time of legend before "official" history began, the Antediluvian world.

Atlantists view history as a rollercoaster ride over tens of thousands of years with the rise and fall of civilizations as part of that rollercoaster ride. Yet, Atlantists need not necessarily believe in a lost continent in the Atlantic Ocean. Many may believe in ancient civilizations before Sumeria, and for lack of a better word, call them "Atlantis."

The well-known author and presenter of the television

documentary *Mystery of the Sphinx*, John Anthony West, says, "Egyptian science, medicine, mathematics and astronomy were all of an exponentially higher order of refinement and sophistication than modern scholars will acknowledge. The whole of Egyptian civilization was based upon a complete and precise understanding of universal laws. And this profound understanding manifested itself in a consistent, coherent and interrelated system that fused science, art and religion into a single organic *Unity*. In other words, it was exactly the opposite of what we find in the world today.

"Moreover, every aspect of Egyptian knowledge seems to have been complete at the very beginning. The sciences, artistic and architectural techniques and the hieroglyphic system show virtually no signs of a period of 'development'; indeed, many of the achievements of the earliest dynasties were never surpassed, or even equaled later on. This astonishing fact is readily admitted by orthodox Egyptologists, but the magnitude of the mystery it poses is skillfully understated, while its many implications go unmentioned.

"How does a civilization spring full-blown into being? Look at a 1905 automobile and compare it to a modern one. There is no mistaking the process of 'development,' but in Egypt there are no parallels. Everything is right there at the start.

"The answer to the mystery is of course obvious, but because it is repellent to the prevailing cast of modern thinking, it is seldom seriously considered. *Egyptian civilization was not a 'development,' but a legacy.*"[4]

In his highly rated NBC special of November, 1993, *Mystery of the Sphinx*, West and his researchers sought to prove that the Sphinx had been severely waterworn and was over 9,000 years old!

The Destruction of Knowledge

As our technology has gotten more advanced, we are able to look into the future and into outer space with a view different from that of scientists and thinkers earlier in this century. Similarly, we are now able to look at the past with greater insight and technological know-how. Just as our minds have been able to imagine a future different than our grandfathers could envision, we are also able to see a past different from that of the scientists and experts of the turn of the century.

Just as our scope of the universe has been pushed back to the farthest reaches of space, we are now in a position to push back to the farthest reaches of history. And many researchers are doing just that.

Atlantis is named in ancient texts. To begin with, it is mentioned in Plato's dialogues (taken from ancient Egyptian records according to the text), and nearly every ancient culture in the world has myths and legends of an ancient world-before and the cataclysm that destroyed it.

The Mayans, Aztecs and Hopis believed in the destruction of four or more worlds before our own. The destruction of Atlantis may not even be the most recent cataclysm to befall the earth.

The most widely known books in the world such as the *Bible*, the *Mahabharata*, the *Koran* and even the *Tao Te Ching* all speak of cataclysms and ancient civilizations that were destroyed. Ancient civilizations and stories about them filled thousands, even hundreds of thousands of volumes of books that were kept in libraries around the world in ancient times. Many ancient libraries were so huge that they were famous among local historians. The library at Alexandria is a well-known example.

Sadly, it is a fact that throughout history huge archives and libraries have been purposely destroyed. According to the famous astronomer Carl Sagan, a book entitled *The True History of Mankind Over the Last 100,000 Years* once existed and was housed in the great library in Alexandria, Egypt. Unfortunately, this book, along with thousands of others, was burned by fanatical Christians in the third century A.D. Any volumes which they might have missed were burned by the Moslems to heat baths a few hundred years later.

All ancient Chinese texts were ordered destroyed in 212 B.C. by Emperor Chi Huang Ti, the builder of the famous Great Wall. Vast amounts of ancient texts—virtually everything pertaining to history, philosophy, and science—were seized and burnt. Whole libraries, including the royal library, were destroyed. Some of the works of Confucius and Mencius were included in this destruction of knowledge.

Fortunately, some books survived because people hid them in various underground caves, and many works were hidden in Taoist temples where they are even now religiously kept and preserved.

The Spanish conquistadors destroyed every Mayan codex that they found. Out of many thousands of Mayan books found by the Spanish, only three or four are known to exist today. Like the fanatical Christian sects of the third century and Emperor Chi Huang Ti in the second century B.C., they wanted to erase all knowledge of the past and the records that they contained.

Europe and the Mediterranean were plunged into the infamous Dark Ages when the Christian church first split after a series of church councils beginning with the council of Nicaea in 325 A.D. The last Patriarch of the early Christian church, Nestorius, was deposed at the Council of Ephesus in 431 A.D. He was banished to Libya and the Nestorian church moved eastward. Their dispute concerned the early Christian doctrine of reincarnation and the idea that Jesus was a Master while Christ was the Archangel Melchizedek.

All books in the Byzantine Empire were ordered destroyed except for a newly edited version of the Bible that the Catholic church was issuing. The library at Alexandria was destroyed at this time, and the great mathematician and philosopher Hypatia was dragged from her chariot by a mob and torn to pieces. The mob went on to burn the library. Thus the suppression of science and knowledge, particularly of the ancient past, began in earnest.

Knowledge has been suppressed throughout the last 2,000 years, and it is sometimes said that history is written by the winners of wars, rather than the losers. Considering the amount of known war-oriented political propaganda in this century, we should consider much of ancient history in the same light.

Given this suppression, it is then, astonishing that the few ancient texts that have survived do indeed speak of ancient civilizations and the cataclysms that destroyed them. Similarly, they talk of wise people who lived in harmony with the earth and the natural workings of all things. But at some time in the distant past, man fell out of harmony with nature and a catastrophe struck the whole earth.

We can see here a startling parallel in the ancient Atlantis "myth" and the situation that modern man now finds himself in. Will modern man survive his own technology and tribalism or will he destroy himself in the natural workings of his destructive practices and disharmony with the earth?

> *If we human beings want to feel humility, there is no need to look at the starred infinity above. It suffices to turn our gaze upon the world cultures that existed thousands of years before us, achieved greatness before us, and perished before us.*
> —C.W. Ceram, *Gods, Graves, & Scholars*

The Rama Empire of India

In an archaeological sense, the idea that civilization began in Sumeria is fairly recent, beginning with the British and German excavations in the mid-1800s. At this time it was established that Sumeria was the oldest civilization in the world, and that all others must be more recent. Science essentially held that man lived in unorganized chaos for tens or hundreds of thousands of years until the Sumerians, circa 9,000 B.C.

For a long time, historians agreed that the civilization of the Indian subcontinent did not go back further than about 500 B.C., which is only a few hundred years prior to Alexander the Great's invasion of the subcontinent. In the past century, however, the extremely sophisticated cities of Mohenjo Daro ("Mound of the Dead") and Harappa have been discovered in the Indus Valley of what is today Pakistan.

Once called Brahminadad, Harappa was brought to light by two brothers, John and William Brunton, who were engineers for the East Indian Railway. In 1856, they were looking for ballast on which to lay the railway tracks; locals told them that not far away was an ancient ruined city. They looted the ancient city and obtained 93 miles of good kiln-fired brick ballast at little expense from the ruins (This has been the unfortunate fate of many ancient cities—they are looted of their building materials to build other cities). Eventually, the Director-General of the Indian Archaeological Survey became aware of the site, stopped the looting and began to excavate it.

Another similar example of the looting of one ancient city to build a new one is that of Tiahuanaco on the high altiplano of Bolivia near Lake Titicaca. Tiahuanaco was systematically looted of its finely cut andesite (a type of granite) blocks to build the original capital of La Paz, closer to Tiahuanaco than modern La Paz is today. Furthermore, large blocks and even four-meter high statues were used to build much of the local town of Tiahuanaco. Today, what is left at the archaeological site are only those blocks that were either buried or were too large and heavy for the Spanish to lift. Yet the builders had clearly moved the blocks into place in ancient times, often a distance of twenty miles or more.

That many ancient cities have been dismantled in the past will no doubt frustrate modern man's attempts to recreate history. When the past has been purposely destroyed, we have precious little evidence to help us create a plausible scenario. Is it any wonder that Atlantis is not a *proven* fact?

Unlike other ancient nations such as Egypt, China, Brittany or Peru, the ancient Hindus did not have their history books all ordered destroyed, and therefore we have one of the few true links to an extremely ancient and scientifically advanced past.

India's own records of its history claim that its culture has existed for literally tens of thousands of years. Yet, until 1920, all the "experts" agreed that the origins of the Indian civilization should be placed within a few hundred years of Alexander the Great's expedition to the subcontinent in 327 B.C. However, that was before another similar city, Mohenjo Daro, was discovered 350 miles south, and eventually other cities with the same plan were found and excavated, including Kot Diji, near Mohenjo Daro, Kalibangan and Lothal, a port in Gujerat, India. Lothal is a port city that is now miles from the ocean.

The discoveries of these cities forced archaeologists to push the dates for the origin of Indian civilization back thousands of years, just as Indians themselves insisted. A wonder to modern-day researchers, the cities are highly developed and advanced. The way that each city is laid out in regular blocks, with streets crossing each other at right angles, and with the entire city laid out in sections, causes archaeologists to believe that the cities were conceived as a whole before they were built—a remarkable early example of city planning. Even more remarkable is that the plumbing-sewage system throughout the large city is so sophisticated that it is superior to that found in many Pakistani (and other) towns today. Sewers were covered, and most homes had toilets and running water. Furthermore, the water and sewage systems were kept well separated.[62, 93, 94]

This advanced culture had its own writing, never deciphered, and used personalized clay seals, much as the Chinese still do today, to officialize documents and letters. Some of the seals found contain figures of animals that are unknown to us today!

Modern scholars value ancient Hindu texts, as they are one of the last tenuous connections to the ancient libraries of the past. The super-civilization known as the Rama Empire will be discussed along with other ancient civilizations in the chapters to come. I hope the reader will become familiar with such great ancient civilizations as Osiris, Poseid, Rama, and Atlan.

Rama ruled the earth for 11,000 years.
He gave a year-long festival
In the very Naimisha Forest.
All of this land was his kingdom then;
One age of the world ago;
Long before now, and far in the past.
Rama was king from the center of the world,
To the Four Oceans' shores.
—the beginning chapter of the
Ramayana by Valmiki

Atlantean Construction

The modern skeptic asks, well, if Atlantis existed then where are the giant megalithic remains that should exist? The answer is that such gigantic ruins do exist; moreover, legends of ancient civilizations and their cataclysmic destruction are part of nearly every culture in the world.

The idea that man was primitive in the past and that the present represents the highest civilization our planet has achieved is fairly accepted in the West, while other cultures see our current society as a decline from a golden age. Yet, out of the past we find megalithic cities built to last for thousands of years. How primitive must we suppose these people were?

Throughout the world, there exists a type of megalithic construction that is called "Atlantean" by Atlantists. This is typically a type of construction which used gigantic blocks of stone, often crystalline granite. Huge blocks are fitted together without mortar in a polygonal style which tends to interlock the heavy blocks in a jigsaw fashion. These interlocked polygonal walls resist earthquake damage by moving with the shock wave of the quake. They momentarily jumble themselves and move freely but then fall back into place. These interlocked jigsaw walls will not collapse with an earthquake shock wave as with brick wall construction.

Such "Atlantean style" construction can be found all over the world. Classical examples of such construction are at Mycenae in the Peloponnesse and the temples of Malta, along with the gigantic megalithic walls of Tiahuanaco, Ollantaytambo, Monte Alban and Stonehenge, as well as the pre-Egyptian structures of the Osirion at Abydos and the Valley Temple of the Sphinx.

Atlantean architecture is often circular, and uses the most exact rock cutting techniques to fit blocks together. Atlantean-type architecture often uses what is known as "keystone cuts"—a metal clamp that is fitted into cut rock on both sides of a joint. These keystone cuts are typically an hourglass shape or a double-T shape. The clamps that went inside them may have been copper, bronze, silver, electrum (a mixture of silver and gold) or some other metal. In nearly every case where keystone cuts can be found, the metal clamp has been already removed—many thousands of years ago!

Readers of this book will discover that many well-known, and not-so-well-known, ruins of the world contain the remains of even earlier cities within them. Such sites as Ba'albek in Lebanon, the Acropolis of Athens, Lixus in Morocco, Cadiz in Spain and even the Temple Mount of Jerusalem are built on gigantic remains of earlier ruins.

Where then is Atlantis? Atlantis is all around us, asserted British scholar John Michell in his book *The View Over Atlantis*.[13] Michell further showed that amazing ancient ruins are a worldwide phenomenon in his *Megalithomania*.[80] Many authors have attempted to show how the worldwide distribution of megaliths points to an advanced civilization in an antediluvian sense, including such scholarly works as *Megaliths & Masterminds*[7] by Peter Lancaster Brown, *The God-Kings & the Titans*[8] by James Bailey, *Mysteries From Forgotten Worlds*[9] by Charles Berlitz and many others.

Their thesis was that the ancient world was remarkably advanced for its so-called Stone-Age inheritance and argued that an advanced civilization called "Atlantis" preceded the dawn of history. The prehistoric civilization not only ranged worldwide but built impressive monuments and buildings as well.

The idea that man has only recently invented such things as electricity, generators, steam and combustion engines, or even powered flight does not necessarily hold true for a world that rides the rollercoaster of history.

Indeed, when we see how quickly inventions are absorbed into today's society we can imagine how quickly a highly scientific civilization may have arisen in remote antiquity. Just as today there are still primitive tribes in New Guinea and South America who live a Stone-Age existence, so could Atlantis have existed during a period where other areas of the world lived in various states of development.

The ancient world of Atlantis may have been a lot like the modern world of today—juxtaposed between various factions in the government and military, while international discontent rises in various client colonies of an economic system set up by large business interests. According to the mythos that has built up around Atlantis, it was destroyed because of the wars that it had fought around the world, including the Mediterranean region. Today the world is again teetering on the brink of wholesale Armageddon because of political, religious and ethnic differences. Does modern man have something to gain by studying the past? Students of Atlantis believe so.

The Past Repeats Itself

Believers in Atlantis and the rollercoaster of history look for evidence of advanced science in ancient history. One form of science that may help prove the existence of Atlantis is the use of ancient electricity. We think of electricity as a modern convenience, though science tells us that electricity was used in the ancient world as well.

That the Egyptians and Babylonians electroplated objects is generally considered scientific fact. Many books on mysteries of the past mention the first century B.C. clay batteries found in Baghdad. The first report of the "Baghdad batteries" in the popular press was in the 1940 science book *The Birth & Death of the Sun* by the American astronomer George Gamow. In a subchapter entitled "Ancient Arabian Electrogilding" Gamow says, "The first practical use of electricity and electric current takes us back to the distant past. In recent excavations at Khujut-Rabua, not far from Baghdad, a very strange type of vessel has been found among the relics that probably belong to the first century B.C. It consists of a vase, made of clay, inside of which is fastened a cylinder of pure copper. Through a thick asphalt cover on its top is driven a solid iron rod, the lower part of which has been eaten away, probably by the action of some acid.

"This assembly could hardly have been used for any other purpose than that of generating a weak electric current, and was most probably used by Arabian silver-smiths, long before the reign of the fabulous Harun al Rashid, for electrogilding their wares. In the backs of little shops in colourful oriental bazaars, electric currents were depositing uniform layers of gold and silver on earrings and bracelets almost 2000 years before the phenomenon of electrolysis was rediscovered by the Italian Dottore Galvani and made widely known to humanity."[112]

Yet, the knowledge of electrical devices was not limited to electroplating. Authors such as Jerry Ziegler in his books *YHWH* [113] and *Indra Girt by Maruts*[114] claim that electrical devices of various sorts were used in temples and often utilized as oracles or impressive manifestations of deities. Ziegler cites a wealth of ancient sources on ancient lights, sacred fires and oracles in his books. The famous Ark of the Covenant is often described as an electrical device and several passages in the Old Testament describe how unfortunate people who touch the relic are killed, seemingly by electrocution.

In the myths and legends of many cultures around the world are found tales of electricity and advanced science, and artifacts relating to ancient electricity have been found all over the world. For instance, an aluminum belt fastener believed to be at least 1,700 years old was discovered in China. Aluminum was discovered by the West in 1803 and not refined until fifty years later, because the process requires electricity! Ancient Hebrew legends tell of a glowing jewel that Noah hung up in the Ark to provide a constant source of illumination and of a similar object in the palace of King Solomon about 1000 B.C.[104]

One of the early proponents of electricity in ancient Egypt was Denis Saurat in his 1957 book *Atlantis & the Giants.*[21] Saurat suggests that the flashes in the eyes of Isis in her temples throughout Egypt were made with an electrical apparatus. Like many other authors, Saurat saw Atlantis as linked to the sciences of the ancient world.

In the basement of the Temple of Hathor in southern Egypt there is an incised petroglyph in the room designated No. XVII that depicts a strikingly unusual scene with what appears to be electrical objects. The famous British scientist Ivan T. Sanderson discusses ancient Egyptian electricity in his book *Investigating the Unexplained.*[103] In the petroglyph, attendants are holding two "electric lamps" supported by *Djed-Osiris* pillars and connected via cables to a box.

Djed columns are always associated with Osiris, being the temple column in which Isis discovered her husband Osiris (see below, page 28). They are held like torches by devotees and the odd "condenser" design at the top of the columns makes them seem strikingly like electrical devices.

Sanderson tells how an electrical engineer named Alfred Bielek explained the petroglyph to Sanderson as depicting some sort of projector with the cables being a bundle of many multi-purpose conductors, rather than a single high voltage cable.[103]

Another depiction from a papyrus scroll showing a Djed column with an ankh with hands holding up an orb was thought to be a static electricity generator commonly known as a Van de Graff machine, named after the inventor (or re-inventor, as the case may be). In such a device, static electricity builds up in the orb, and, says electrical engineer Michael Freedman, "...what better 'toy' for an Egyptian priest of ancient times? ...such an instrument could be used to control both the Pharaoh and fellahin (peasant), simply by illustrating, most graphically, the powers of the gods; of which, of course, only the priests knew the real secrets. Merely by placing a metal rod or metal-coated stave in the general vicinity of the sphere, the priest could produce a most wondrous display, with electric arcs and loud crashes. Even with nothing more elaborate than a ring on his finger, a priest could point to the 'life-symbol,' be struck by a great bolt of lightning, but remain alive and no worse for wear, thus illustrating the omnipotent powers of the gods—not to mention himself—in preserving life for the faithful."[103]

Sanderson also mentions how electroplating was used by the Egyptians. Part of the circumstantial evidence for ancient Egyptian electrics is the fact that tombs and underground passages are highly painted and decorated, yet there is no smoke residue or evidence of torches on the ceilings! It is usually assumed that the artists and workers would have to work by torchlight, just as early Egyptologists did in the 1800s. However, no smoke is found on the ceilings. Did the Egyptians use electric lighting? One ingenious theory is that the tombs were lit by a series of mirrors, bringing sunlight from the entrance. Yet many tombs, it is said, are far too elaborate, with deep and twisting turns, for this to work. Even more interesting is the suggestion by some people that the ankh was also a device similar to an electrified tuning fork which was used to "acoustically levitate" stones!

Ancient electrics in many cases were apparently only used by special priesthoods and not by the masses. In Ziegler's *Indra Girt by Maruts*[114] it is maintained that many of the ancient Vedas also describe electrical devices, and these were typically used in religious ceremonies. Legends of lost cities with legendary "eternal glowing lights" can be found in my other books.[16, 57, 58, 59]

Behind the Temple of Hathor in Dendera is a Temple of Isis. According to the esoteric book *The Ultimate Frontier*,[105] the Ark of the Covenant was a simple electrical device known as a condenser and was first kept in the Temple of Isis in lower Egypt for many thousands of years before it was moved into the so-called King's Chamber of the Great Pyramid. The Ark of the Covenant was said to be a relic of Atlantis, and in the days of ancient Egypt (1,000 to 5,000 B.C.) the identity of the Ark was well known and it was an important relic.[105]

Is it possible that the Biblical Ark of the Covenant was at one time kept in the Isis Temple at Hathor, and could the underground crypt depict a portion of the electrical system that was used in the ancient temples? Jerry Ziegler argues that the Ark of the Covenant as well as the sacred flames of Mithraic and Zoroastrian oracles were ancient electrical devices used for impressing the congregation.[113, 114]

In his book *We Are Not the First*,[22] Australian Atlantis researcher Andrew Tomas has an entire chapter entitled "Electricity In the Remote Past." According to Tomas, classical authors have made many statements in their works testifying to the reality of ever-burning lamps in antiquity. Some of these ever-burning lamps may have used ancient electrical devices of various design.

Tomas mentions that Lucian (A.D.120-180), the Greek satirist, gave a detailed account of his travels. In Hierapolis, Syria, he saw a shining jewel in the forehead of the goddess Hera which brilliantly illuminated the whole temple at night. Nearby, the Roman temple of Jupiter at Ba'albek was said to be lit by "glowing stones."[22]

A beautiful golden lamp in the temple of Minerva, said to burn for a year at a time, was described by the second-century historian Pausanias. Saint Augustine (A.D. 354-430) wrote of an ever-burning lamp which neither wind nor rain could extinguish found in a temple to Isis.

Tomas relates that when the sepulchre of Pallas, son of Evander, immortalized by Virgil in his *Aeneid*, was opened near Rome in 1401, the tomb was found to be illuminated by a perpetual lantern which had apparently been alight for hundreds of years. [22]

Other mysterious lights and "glowing stones" have been reported in lost cities around the world. Tomas relates the strange story of a South African missionary who reported at a 1963 conference that he had seen a strange village in the highlands of Papua New Guinea that was lit by round glowing stones mounted on pillars. [22]

Tibet is said to have such glowing stones and lanterns mounted on pillars in towers. Tomas relates that Father Evariste-Regis Huc (1813-1860), who travelled extensively in Asia in the 19th century, left a description of ever-burning lamps he had seen, while the Russian Central Asian explorer Nicholas Roerich reported that the legendary Buddhist secret city of Shambala was lit by a glowing jewel in a tower.

Atlantis and ever-lasting stone lamps were featured in the beliefs of the famous British explorer Colonel Percy Fawcett, who vanished in the Brazilian jungles in 1925 while searching for a lost city which he believed was lit by glowing stones on pillars. Tomas quotes a letter sent by Fawcett to British Atlantis authority Lewis Spence about the lost city in the jungle and what the natives had told him about the glowing stones. "These people have a source of illumination which is strange to us—in fact, they are the remnant of a civilization which has gone and which has retained old knowledge."[22, 57, 126]

Spence was a popular Scottish mythology writer who wrote such books as *The Problem of Atlantis*[6] (1924), *The History of Atlantis*[12] (1926) and *The Occult Sciences In Atlantis*[14] (1943) among others. Colonel Fawcett disappeared with his oldest son in 1925 but his youngest son published a book of his father's material in 1953 entitled *Expedition Fawcett*[126] (called *Lost Trails, Lost Cities* in the U.S. edition).

Tomas, probably quoting from Harold Wilkins' books on South America,[124,125] relates that in 1601 the Spanish author Barco Centenera wrote of the discovery of the lost city of Gran Moxo near the source of the Paraguay River in the Mato Grosso. In the center of the island city he says "on the summit of a 20 foot pillar was a great moon which illuminated all the lake, dispelling darkness."[22] More can be found on Colonel Fawcett and his search for Atlantis in the Amazon jungles in my book *Lost Cities & Ancient Mysteries of South America*.[57]

‰‰‰‰‰‰‰‰‰≈◈≈‰‰‰‰‰‰‰‰‰

Cataclysms of the Earth

The famous 19th-century French naturalist George Cuvier, associated with the Museum of Natural History in Paris and widely acknowledged as the founder of vertebrate paleontology, once said, "Life on earth has often been disturbed by terrific events. Numberless living beings have been the victims of these catastrophes, such violent sweeps that entire races of living beings have been extinguished forever and have left no other memorial of their existence than some fragments which the naturalist can scarcely recognize."[178]

Cuvier once described a disaster that had apparently occurred in a far northern part of the Pacific Ocean in an area off Siberia today known as the Laptev Sea. The earliest scientific exploration of these areas in 1805 and 1806 surprisingly uncovered evidence of a cataclysm.

At a site on the Liahknov Islands, a deposit was discovered: a layer of broken trees 200 feet deep. It appeared that millions of trees had been wrenched out by the roots in one violent blow of nature. Encased in the mud beneath the splintered wood were found the broken and frozen bodies of millions of animals. Some belonged to extinct species, like the woolly mammoth, and some were of contemporary species, such as bison. Ivan Liahknov, discoverer of the islands, reported, "Such was the enormous quantity of mammoths' remains that it seemed that the island itself was actually composed of the bones and tusks."[24]

Greed and avarice turned these paleontological finds for the most part into billiard balls and piano keys. Indeed, for a time, the area supplied half the world's ivory, and twelve-thousand-year-old ivory at that!

Scientists agreed that vegetable-eating creatures such as bison could not have existed in the polar climate present today on the Liahknov Islands. Yet, in the stomachs of frozen animals they found undigested food currently not grown anywhere in the area for hundreds of miles around. Fractured bones and other evidence indicated a sudden, violent shock.[178]

Cuvier surmised that at some time in the remote past, a huge wave had swept these creatures up from some distant spot and dragged them through the forest, tearing them apart and burying them.

Native Russian and Atlantis author Andrew Tomas says that when a carbon-14 test was made on a mammoth discovered in the northern part of Siberia, the result was 12,000 years before present (B.P.) That the mammoths died suddenly, apparently by freezing to death, is evidenced by grasses in their mouths and stomachs plus the fact that they are sometimes found standing upright in the frozen tundra.

Says Tomas, "It must be noted here that the mammoth was not a polar animal. In spite of longer hair, in structure and thickness its skin is similar to that of the tropical Indian elephant. The skin of these frozen animals is congested with red blood corpuscles. This is said to be proof of death due to suffocation by water or gases.

"For centuries ivory from the mammoths' tusks has constituted an item of trade. According to Richard Lydekker, approximately 20,000 pairs of tusks in perfect condition were sold in the few decades preceding 1899. This figure gives some idea as to the great number of frozen mammoths unearthed. It is important to emphasize here that ivory for carving can be used only from freshly killed animals, or those which have been frozen. Exposed tusks dry out and become valueless. Tens of thousands of mammoths have been discovered in northern areas of America and Asia. Since the mammoth ivory traded was of the best quality, there is no doubt that the beasts perished suddenly."[24]

The well-known American archaeologist Frank C. Hibben (who coined the term *clovis point* for a certain type of flint spearhead) estimated that 40 million animals were exterminated in North

America alone at the close of the Ice Age. "This death was catastrophic and all-inclusive," he writes.[179, 180]

What incredible geological event could create such massive destruction? Whatever it might have been, it is the event generally credited as being the cause of the extinction of the woolly mammoths and other Ice Age mammals. Evidence of cataclysmic events in geology are responsible for the division of the science of geology into two main schools of thought during the 19th century.

These two schools are known as Uniformitarianism and Catastrophism. Uniformitarianism, for years the prevailing school of thought, holds that earth changes are gradual in nature, happening slowly over thousands if not millions of years. Geological strata then build up over millions of years creating the familiar geologic "Ages" such as Jurassic or Permian that science assures us have built up over eons of slow geological change.

Nearly all dating of fossils and geological strata is done according to this theory. Carbon-14 cannot accurately date anything older than about 30,000 years. Fossil dating is done by stratification —that is, depending on the strata of the earth that it has been found in. The strata is dated, as previously said, by guess-timating the age in millions of years. It is sometimes said that "fossils are dated by the strata and the strata is dated by the fossils."

While Uniformitarianists will admit that volcanoes occasionally erupt suddenly and earthquakes do happen, they maintain that the general workings of nature are gradual and easily observable. Mountain ranges inch their way up or down over millions of years, continents inch their way around the globe over millions of years and occasionally glaciers creep down from the poles and cause mass extinction. Most people will recognize this school as being in alignment with the geology that they were taught in high school or on television documentaries.

The other school, catastrophism, holds that major earth changes can happen very suddenly, much like Cuvier's destructive wave. In a violent wrenching of the earth's crust or a sudden slamming of two continental plates, mountain ranges can be created in a few days, oceans can spill out of their basins, large lakes can be created and continents can sink!

Though different from what is taught in schools today, this explanation of earth changes is more in line with ancient myths, legends, and traditions. More and more geology is moving toward a catastrophic view of the past. For instance, catastrophism fits perfectly into the presently accepted plate tectonic theory.

Why is there resistance to catastrophism in academic fields? There are several reasons: It is not a very pleasant thought that everything we hold as stable today could be destroyed overnight when Mother Earth has the hiccoughs! The very notion itself could send Wall

Street into a spin.

Also, for the past 200 years or so, the modern age of "science" and "reason" has been at odds with the traditional wisdom and cosmology of religion. Cataclysmic changes in the earth are part of nearly every religion and mythology in the world.

In Nietzschean philosophy, Man is the measure of all things, and the master of his destiny. Mother Nature is subjugated by the Nietzschean man. Curiously, this is just the lesson of Atlantis according to Plato and Solon: that man reaches such a height of technology and power that he no longer lives in harmony with the earth and his fellow man. The high technology of civilization inevitably leads to ever more sophisticated ways of waging war on his fellow man. In Plato's story Atlantis wages war on the Mediterranean and Asia and then shortly afterward the world is destroyed in cataclysmic earth changes, with Atlantis being sent to the ocean bottom for its arrogance.

Were Plato and Solon alive today, one wonders if they would have the same warning for us. Are we about to repeat the mistakes of the ancient past and reap similar consequences?

The Roman poet Ovid also wrote about the Great Flood and continued the unfinished chronicle of Plato thusly:

> There was such wickedness once on earth that Justice fled to the sky, and the king of the gods determined to make an end of the race of men... Jupiter's anger was not confined to his province of the sky. Neptune, his sea-blue brother, sent the waves to help him. Neptune smote the earth with his trident and the earth shivered and shook... Soon there was no telling land from sea. Under the water the sea nymphs Nereides were staring in amazement at woods, houses and cities. Nearly all men perished by water, and those who escaped the water, having no food, died of hunger.

Legends and prophecies concerning cataclysms occur on the other side of the Atlantic as well. The Native American scholar Frank Waters in his book *Mexico Mystique*[167] states that the Mayas, Aztecs and Hopi Indians all believed that the world had been destroyed several times before in cataclysmic changes.

Waters says that by Mayan and Aztec calculation, we are now in the Fifth World or Fifth Sun. The previous worlds had all been destroyed in cataclysms. Waters says that the Mayans have calculated the present Fifth Sun as beginning in 3113 B.C. and whose cataclysmic end is predicted for 2011 A.D. After this the Sixth World or Sixth Sun will begin.[178]

In Aztec mythology the first sun was *Ocelotonatiuh*, Sun of the Tiger, whose sign was *4 Ocelotl* (ocelot, jaguar, tiger). The world was inhabited by giants and was destroyed by wild animals. It was an era of dark earth-bound matter.

The second sun, with the sign of 4 *Ecatl*, was the Sun of Air, *Ecatonatiuh*, represented as Quetzalcoatl in his aspect of the god of wind. In a single day most of the inhabitants were destroyed by wind, and the survivors turned into monkeys.

The third sun was *Quiauitonatiuh*, sun of the Rain of Fire, under the sign 4 *Quiauitl* (fiery rain). Its inhabitants were turned into birds (turkeys).

The fourth sun was *Chalchiuhtlicue*, its sign 4 *Atl* (water). It was destroyed by a flood, and the people turned into fish. We are now in the present fifth sun, *Tonatiuh*, whose sign is 4 *Ollin* (movement).[178]

Waters points out that in Hopi Indian cosmology, we are presently in the fourth sun, not the fifth sun. Each world has been similarly destroyed in a catastrophe and another is looming on the near horizon—the next "Sun."

Andrew Tomas says that the Dresden Codex of the Mayas shows the destruction of the earth in pictorial form. The Popul Vuh, the sacred book of the Quiché Maya of Guatemala, speaks of the last disaster. While survivors went underground, roaring fires were heard above. The earth shook and things revolted against man. It rained hot tar with water. The trees were swinging, houses crumbling, caves collapsing. Then day became black night.[24]

Another Mayan epic preserved orally is the Chillam Balam of the Yucatan Maya. It asserts that the Motherland of the Mayas was swallowed up by the sea amid earthquakes and fiery eruptions in a very distant epoch.

Giving witness to this statement is the astonishing frieze that once decorated the main Mayan temple at Tikal. This frieze shows a man in a boat escaping from a land that is sinking into the water. A drowning man can be seen and a volcano erupts as a Mayan-style pyramid collapses into the water.

This frieze was discovered and photographed by the great German archaeologist Teobert Maler (1842-1917). Unfortunately he removed the frieze from the pyramid at Tikal and shipped it to the Berlin Museum. The museum and much of what it contained, including the Mayan frieze, was destroyed during World War II.

This amazing bit of ancient art screams out cataclysmic earth changes and is one of the great works of art of all time—possibly showing the destruction of Atlantis. The great American architect Robert Stacy-Judd's classic book *Atlantis: Mother Of Empires*[190] was the first, but not the last, volume on Atlantis to use this amazing photo. Stacy-Judd was a wealthy architect whose unusual buildings in California are still studied for their artistic Mesoamerican look. *Atlantis: Mother Of Empires* belongs in every library on Atlantis.

~~~~~~~~🪬~~~~~~~~

Ancient Seafaring and the Atlantean League

Part of the solution to the mysteries of Atlantis lies in the way we see the ancient world and the seafaring that was part of ancient trade. For instance, many of the early Atlantis theorists believed that evidence of bearded men in armor in ancient Mexico is supportive of Atlantis when, in my opinion, it is really only evidence of early seafarers crossing the ocean.

Early Atlantists reasoned that since there was a great deal of obvious similarity in Old World and New World artifacts—everything from stepped pyramids to small wax seals—a continent in the middle of the Atlantic for their common origin made perfect sense.

Just as today, historians at the turn of the century believed neither in Atlantis nor ancient seafarers, so all such evidence or discussion is doubly damned. Today the evidence for early maritime discovery voyages is becoming overwhelming. This coupled with other discoveries may help us to prove "Atlantis."

The first step in proving Atlantis is to first prove that ancient man has had an advanced civilization and travelled the world for many thousands of years. The size and sophistication of many of the early Phoenician, Egyptian and Greek ships are amazing. Maritime scholar Gardner Soule in *Men Who Dared the Sea*[140] says that under Ptolemy IV, Philopator of Egypt (220-204 B.C.), a 420-foot-long ship was built that required 4,000 rowers.

In order to show the public what went on at sea, the Romans staged mock naval battles in the amphitheaters specially flooded for the purpose around 70-90 A.D. Some of the amphitheaters were 1,800 feet long and 1,200 feet wide while as many as 30 ships and 3,000 fighting men took part.[140]

Circa 1500 B.C. the Mediterranean was full of large double-oared ships that could ram and sink an enemy ship if necessary. According to Soule, the earliest depiction of a large trading ship is a bas-relief from the Abusir Pyramids near Cairo—2950 B.C.[140]

Yet, seafaring must surely go back many thousands of years further than this date! Archaeologists currently struggle with a date of human settlement of 30,000 years B.P. on the island of New Ireland to the east of New Guinea. Yet geologists say that there was no land bridge. Therefore, anthropologists are forced to say that early man came to New Ireland via boat 30,000 years ago.

If man was sailing about in the Pacific Ocean 30,000 years ago, then we might imagine that man was sailing about in the Mediterranean and Atlantic 15,000 years ago. There is only one good reason to think that man was not sailing large ships in the Mediterranean at that time—it was not a sea!

According to ancient tradition associated with Atlantis, the Mediterranean area was once a huge fertile valley with lakes, while large areas of the Sahara Desert were part of a large sea of which Lake Chad is the last vestige. This ancient civilization is most typically identified with the Osirian civilization.

~~~~~~~~~~~🜨 ~~~~~~~~~~~

The Osirian Civilization

The Osirian Civilization, according to esoteric tradition, was an advanced civilization contemporary with Atlantis. In the world of about 15,000 years ago, there were a number of highly developed and sophisticated civilizations on our planet, each said to have a high degree of technology. Among these fabled civilizations was Atlantis, while another highly developed civilization existed in India. This civilization is often called the Rama Empire.

What is theorized is a past quite different from that which we have learned in school. It is a past with magnificent cities, ancient roads and trade routes, busy ports and adventurous traders and mariners. Much of the ancient world was civilized, and such areas of the world as ancient India, China, Peru, Mexico and Osiris were thriving commercial centers with many important cities. Many of these cities are permanently lost forever, but others have been or will be discovered!

It is said that at the time of Atlantis and Rama, the Mediterranean was a large and fertile valley, rather than a sea as it is today. The Nile River came out of Africa, as it does today, and was called the River Styx. However, instead of flowing into the Mediterranean Sea at the Nile Delta in northern Egypt, it continued into the valley, and then turned westward to flow into a series of lakes, to the south of Crete. The river flowed out between Malta and Sicily, south of Sardinia and then into the Atlantic at Gibraltar (the Pillars of Hercules). This huge, fertile valley, along with the Sahara (then a vast fertile plain), was known in ancient times as the Osirian civilization.

The Osirian civilization could also be called "Pre-Dynastic Egypt," the ancient Egypt that built the Sphinx and pre-Egyptian megaliths such as the Osirion at Abydos. In this outline of ancient history, it was the Osirian Empire that was invaded by Atlantis, and devastating wars raged throughout the world toward the end of the period of Atlantis's warlike imperial expansion.

Solon relates in Plato's dialogues that Atlantis, just near the cataclysmic end, invaded ancient Greece. This ancient Greece was one that the "ancient" Greeks knew nothing about. This "unknown ancient Greece," we shall see, is closely connected to the Osiris-Isis civilization.

~~~~~~~~~~👁~~~~~~~~~~

The Story of Osiris

The story of Osiris himself, as related by the Greek historian Plutarch, is revealing in our search for Atlantis and other vanished civilizations. According to Egyptian mythology Osiris was born of the Earth and Sky, was the first king of Egypt and the instrument of its civilization. He weaned the inhabitants from their barbarous ways, taught agriculture, formulated laws and taught the worship of the gods. Having accomplished this, he set off to impart his knowledge to the rest of the world.

During his absence, his wife Isis ruled, but Osiris' brother and her brother-in-law, Typhon (Set, known to us as Satan) was always ready to disrupt her work. When Osiris returned from civilizing the world (or attempting to, at least), Set/Typhon decided he would kill Osiris and take Isis for himself. He collected 72 conspirators to his plot and had a beautiful chest made to the exact measurements of Osiris. He threw a banquet and declared that he would give the chest to whomever could lie comfortably within the chest. When Osiris got in, the conspirators rushed to the chest and fastened the lid with nails. They then poured lead over the box and dumped it into the river where it was carried out to sea. When Isis heard of Osiris' death, she immediately set out to find her beloved.

The box with Osiris in it came aground at Byblos in present day Lebanon, not too far from the massive slabs at Ba'albek. A tree grew where the box landed, and the king of Byblos had it cut down and used it as a pillar in his palace, Osiris still being inside the chest. Isis eventually located Osiris and brought him back to Egypt, where Typhon (Set/Satan) broke into the box, chopped Osiris into fourteen different pieces, and scattered him about the countryside.

The loving Isis went looking for the pieces of her husband, and each time she found a piece she buried it—which is why there are temples to Osiris all over Egypt. In another version, she only pretends to bury the pieces, in an attempt to fool Set/Typhon, and puts Osiris back together, bringing him back to life. Eventually she found all the pieces, except the phallus, and Osiris, one way or another, returned from the underworld and encouraged his son Horus (the familiar hawk-headed god) to avenge his death. Scenes in Egyptian temples frequently depict the hawk-headed Horus spearing a great serpent, Typhon or Set, in a scene that is identical to that of St. George and the dragon, though depicted thousands of years earlier.

In the happy ending, Isis and Osiris get back together, and have another child, Harpocrates. However, he is born prematurely and is lame in the lower legs as a result.[147,148]

There are many important themes in the legend of Osiris, including resurrection and the vanquishing of evil by good, and perhaps a key to the ancient Osirian civilization. Were the 14 pieces of Osiris the 14 vestiges of the now flooded land? I have already mentioned the theory that the Mediterranean was once a fertile valley with many cities, farms and temples.

A key to the megalithic society of Osiris can be found in the curious buried ruins of the Osirion (the megalithic, pre-dynastic ruins at Abydos in southern Egypt). The British archaeologist Naville noted in a *London Illustrated News* article that "here and there on the huge granite blocks was a thick knob... which was used for moving the stones. The blocks are very large—a length of fifteen feet is by no means rare; and the whole structure has decidedly the character of the primitive construction which in Greece is called cyclopean. An Egyptian example of which is at Ghizeh, the so-called temple of the Sphinx."

Naville is directly relating the Osirion to the gigantic and prehistoric construction in Greece and also to the temple of the Sphinx. Other such sites around the Mediterranean are on the island of Malta, Ba'albek, and other areas of the Mediterranean. (In fact, virtually every Mediterranean island of any size has prehistoric megaliths on it.) Furthermore, the knobs, which may or may not be for moving the stones, are the same sort of knobs that occur on the gigantic stones that are used on the massive walls to be found in the vicinity of Cuzco, Peru.

The lack of inscriptions indicates that the Osirion, like the valley temple of the Sphinx, was built before the use of hieroglyphics in Egypt! The Osirion is evidently a relic from the civilization of Osiris itself.

Who was Osiris really? According to esoteric legend, he was not an Egyptian but a king of Atlantis who was tricked and murdered by a group of infiltrators (72 of them?) who sought to use Atlantean higher knowledge for their own nefarious purposes. Osiris attempted to stop them, but it was too late. Atlantis went on to wage war on the world and was destroyed shortly afterward.

It is important to note that archaeological evidence for this Osiris-Isis civilization is often confused with evidence for Atlantis. Sunken cities and evidence of cataclysmic earth changes in various areas of the Mediterranean may seem like evidence of Atlantis when it may actually be evidence of a parallel civilization, such as Crete.

Similarly, evidence for ancient diffusion of cultures, such as ancient Egyptians or Phoenicians in the Americas, was often used in early Atlantis books as proof of Atlantis. It was reasoned that since historians told us that ancient man was incapable of traveling over the oceans, therefore the evidence suggests that there was a continent between Europe and North America from which the diffusion of ideas originated.

I believe this evidence was rather evidence of ancient contact with such sophisticated seafaring nations as ancient Egypt, Phoenicia, Persia, Celts and Greeks. But what did the ancient Mediterranean have to do with the legend of Atlantis?

> *The present and the past are*
> *perhaps both present in the future*
> *and the future is contained in the past.*
> —T.S. Eliot

~~~~~~~~~~ 𓂀 ~~~~~~~~~~

Sunken Cities of the Mediterranean

According to tradition, Atlantis was destroyed in a cataclysmic upheaval that ultimately submerged the mini-continent in the Atlantic. With this cataclysmic change in the ocean, the Osirian civilization was apparently hit by a giant wave of water. Great cities were flooded, and only Osirians on higher ground survived. Portions of Egypt may have been spared, but apparently a huge wave washed across the entire Middle East causing the flood of Sumerian legends.

In such a scenario, we can see a Biblical Noah building, or already possessing a giant boat which he then loads with domesticated animals, food and his immediate relatives. He closes the top of his huge boat and rides out the flood that had been predicted to him. He ultimately comes aground in the high mountains of Ararat in eastern Turkey.

He leaves his boat and walks down the mountain as the waters eventually subside. Today his ice-bound ship from "before the Flood" is legendary.

The theory of a huge wave striking the Mediterranean and the Middle East helps explain the strange megalithic remains all over the Mediterranean, especially on the islands of Malta, Sardinia, Corsica, Sicily, Crete and the Balearic Islands of Spain. Sunken structures of megalithic proportions have been found off Morocco and Cadiz in Spain.[3]

It is an archaeological fact that there are more than 200 known sunken cities in the Mediterranean. Egyptian civilization, along with the Minoan and Mycenaean in Crete and Greece are, in theory, remnants of this great, ancient culture. The subject of the Osirian Empire is a fascinating, little-known topic. (For more information on the war between Atlantis and the Rama Empire of India see also my book *Lost Cities of China, Central Asia & India*[16].)

If one postulates an advanced and ancient civilization in the

Mediterranean, the mystery of some of the awesome and inexplicable sites around this area does not seem quite so mysterious after all. Yet, most researchers, even those who write books about Atlantis or ancient astronauts, have never even heard of the theory of the Osirian Empire.

〜〜〜〜〜〜〜〜👁〜〜〜〜〜〜〜〜

Ba'albek and Osiris

One of the most astonishing ancient ruins in the world is the megalithic base of Ba'albek, the pre-Roman ruins upon which a Roman-era temple sits.

The archaeological site of Ba'albek is 44 miles east of Beirut and consists of a number of ruins and catacombs. 2,500 feet long on each side, it is one of the largest stone structures in the world. A portion of it consists of gigantic cut stone blocks from some ancient time, with a Roman temple built on top of it. The Roman temple to Jupiter and Venus was built on top of the earlier temples dedicated to the corresponding ancient deities—Ba'al and his partner, the goddess Astarte.[94]

While it is quite likely that Jupiter and Venus correspond to Ba'al and Astarte, the temple may actually have been built as a prehistoric Sun Temple, and even then on the ruins of an even more ancient structure, its purpose unknown.

The Roman architecture, largely destroyed by an earthquake in 1759, does not pose any archaeological problems, but the massive cut stone blocks beneath it certainly do. One part of the enclosure wall, called the Trilithon, is composed of three blocks of hewn stone that are the largest stone blocks ever used in construction on this planet, so far as is known (underwater ruins may reveal larger constructions); an engineering feat that has never been equaled in history. The blocks, which are over 60 feet long and 13 feet high, are so large that even their weight cannot be accurately calculated.

The temple was first excavated by German archaeologists just prior to World War I. In an article written in 1914 for the journal *Art and Archaeology* entitled "The German Excavations at Ba'albek," the author Lewis Bayles Paton says, "One of the chief results of excavation has been the disclosure of the original ground-plan of the temple-complex. The buildings stood upon a readied platform that was enclosed with a massive retaining wall. Instead of filling in this area with earth, arched vaults were constructed that were used as shops and storehouses. The sacred enclosure was reached by a grand staircase at the eastern end, at the head of which stood the Propylaea, consisting of a portico flanked by two towers. Within this

31

was an hexagonal Forecourt from which three doors led into the great Court of the Altar. In the center of this court over the altar one sees the ground-plan of the later Basilica of Theodosius. On the west side of this court a flight of steps and a single portal led up to the Temple Court. Here, in line with the axis of the sanctuary, stood the Great Temple, traditionally called 'the Temple of the Sun,' but now known to have been dedicated to Jupiter and all the Gods of Heliopolis. South of this lay a smaller temple, traditionally called 'the Temple of Ba'al' but now known to have been dedicated to Bacchus.

"The lowest course of the outer retaining wall consisted of moderate-sized stones. Above these came three courses of stones, each about thirteen feet in length. The middle courses remain only on the western side, and these consist of three of the largest stones ever used by builders. One is sixty-four feet long, another sixty-three feet and one-half and the third sixty-two and one-half. All are about thirteen feet high and ten feet thick. The inner surface of one of these stones has been exposed by the excavations on the west side of the Temple Court. From these remarkable stones the temple probably received its ancient designation of Trilithon. A similar stone seventy by fourteen by thirteen feet and weighing at least one thousand tons remains in the quarry from which the other stones were obtained. How these gigantic blocks were transported and raised to a height of twenty-six feet in order to rest upon the lower courses, is an unsolved problem. The method of quarrying by which they were cut out like columns from the native rock and then split off may still be studied in situ."[17]

The above article is interesting, but the author fails to recognize several important points. One is that the structure is several structures in one, constructed over various ages, thousands of years apart. Therefore the different names are all correct, for the Roman temple was dedicated to Roman gods, while the earlier construction was dedicated to earlier gods, and most probably in prehistory it was a temple to the sun.

Ba'albek is a good example of what happens to large, well-made ancient walls—they are used again by other builders who erect a new city or temple on top of the older one, using the handy stones that are already to be found at the site. This is exactly what has been going on at many sites, in the Old World and in the Americas. Examples of very ancient stonework (3,000 to 6,000 years old) mixed with more recent ancient stonework (500 to 2,500 years ago) can be seen at Monte Alban in Mexico and at such Andean sites as Chavin, Cuzco and Ollantaytambo.

According to an article by Jim Theisen in the *INFO Journal*,[102] the Greeks called the temple "Heliopolis" which means "Sun Temple" or "Sun City." Even so, the original purpose of the gigantic platform may have been something else entirely.

The weight and even size of the stones is open to controversy. According to the author Rene Noorbergen in his fascinating book *Secrets of the Lost Races*,[92] the individual stones are 82 feet long and 15 feet thick and are estimated to weigh between 1,200 and 1,500 tons each (a ton is 2000 pounds, which would make the blocks weigh an estimated 2,400,000 to 3,000,000 pounds each, slightly less in kilograms). While Noorbergen's size may be incorrect, his weight is probably closer to the truth. Even conservative estimates say that the stones weigh at least 750 tons each, which would be one and a half million pounds. [94]

It is an amazing feat of construction, as the blocks have been raised more than 20 feet in order to lie on top of smaller blocks. The colossal stones are fitted together perfectly, and not even a knife blade can be fitted between them.[92] Even the blocks on the level below the "Trilithons" are incredibly heavy. At 13 feet in length, they probably weigh about 50 tons each, an extremely large-sized bunch of stones by any other estimate, except when compared to the "Trilithons." Yet, even these are not the largest of the stones!

The largest hewn block, 13 feet by 14 feet and nearly 70 feet long and weighing at least 1,000 tons (both Noorbergen and Berlitz give the weight of this stone at 2,000 tons [3, 102]), lies in the nearby quarry which is half a mile away. 1,000 tons is an incredible two million pounds! The stone is called *Hadjar el Gouble,* Arabic for "Stone of the South." Noorbergen is correct in saying that there is no crane in the world that could lift any of these stones, no matter what their actual weight is. The largest cranes in the world are stationary cranes constructed at dams to lift huge concrete blocks into place. They can typically lift weights up to several hundred tons. 1,000 tons, and God forbid, 2,000 tons are far beyond their capacity. How these blocks were moved and raised into position is beyond the comprehension of engineers.

Large numbers of pilgrims came from Mesopotamia as well as the Nile Valley to the Temple of Ba'al–Astarte. It is mentioned in the Bible in the Book of Kings. There is a vast underground network of passages beneath the acropolis, which were possibly used to shelter pilgrims.

Who built the massive platform of Ba'albek? According to ancient Arab writings, the first Ba'al–Astarte temple, including the massive stone blocks, was built a short time after the Flood, at the order of the legendary King Nimrod, by a "tribe of giants."[94]

Ancient astronaut theorists have frequently suggested that Ba'albek was built by extraterrestrials. Not such a wild conclusion, considering the facts. This makes more sense than saying that it was all built by the Romans. Charles Berlitz says that a Soviet scientist named Dr. Agrest suggests that the stones were originally part of a landing and takeoff platform for extraterrestrial spacecraft.[3]

Like Buddha seeking the "middle-path," the Atlantist seeks middle ground in this intriguing mystery of the past. While ancient astronauts may well have visited earth in the past, it seems unlikely that they would have arrived here in rockets. They would have mastered the art of anti-gravity and their spaceships would be electric solid-state models, at the very least. Such aircraft could land and take off in a pleasant grassy field, and would not need a gigantic platform.

What then was Ba'albek and who built it? The theory of Ba'albek being some remnant of the Osirian Empire, along with some of the other megalithic sites in the Mediterranean, fits in well with the Arab legend mentioned previously: that the massive stone blocks were built a short time after the Flood, at the order of King Nimrod, by a "tribe of giants."[94]

Yet, even if Ba'albek is a remnant from the Osirian civilization, how were such huge blocks transported and lifted? One clue is the massive block that still remains at the quarry a half mile away. This stone was apparently meant to take its place on the platform with the other stones, but for some reason never made it to the site. According to the *INFO* article,[102] the largest stones used in the Great Pyramid of Egypt only weigh about 400,000 pounds (these are several large granite blocks in the interior of the pyramid). They also point out that until NASA moved the gigantic Saturn V rocket to its launch pad on a huge tracked vehicle, no man had transported such a weight as the blocks at Ba'albek.

In his book *Baalbek*[154] archaeologist Friedrich Ragette devotes the last chapter to how Ba'albek was built and how the stones were moved into place. Explaining Ba'albek is no easy task, Ragette admits, but he does his best.

Ragette first explains that there are two quarries, one about 2 km north of Ba'albek and a closer quarry where the largest stone block in the world still lies.

He then makes this interesting remark about the quarries: "After the block was separated on its vertical side, a groove was cut along its outer base and the piece was felled like a tree on to a layer of earth by means of wedging action from behind. It seems that the Romans also employed a sort of quarrying machine. This we can deduce from the pattern of concentric circular blows shown on some blocks. They are bigger than any man could have produced manually, and we can assume that the cutting tool was fixed to an adjustable lever which would hit the block with great force. Swinging radii of up to 4 m (13 ft) have been observed."[154]

Ragette goes on to theorize that moving an 800-ton stone on rollers would be possible "if we assume that the block rested on neatly cut cylindrical timber rollers of 30 cm (12 in) diameter at half-metre distances, each roller would carry 20 tons. If the contact surface of the roller with the ground were 10 cm (4 in) wide, the pressure would be 5 kg/cm² (71 lbs/in²), which requires a solid stone paving on the ramp. The theoretical force necessary to move that block horizontally would be 80 tons. Another possibility is that the whole block was encased in a cylindrical wrapping of timber and iron braces." Ragette dismisses this second idea as unlikely and cumbersome. "Also there remains the question of how the block would have been unwrapped and put in place, which brings us to the even more perplexing problem of lifting great weights."[154]

There is, however, no evidence of an ancient road, which would have to have been paved, says Ragette. According to the *INFO* article, "one sees no evidence of a road connecting the quarry and Temple. Even if a road existed, logs employed as rollers would have been crushed to a pulp. But, obviously, someone way back then knew how to transport million-pound stones."[102]

There is not a contractor today that would attempt to move or lift these stones. It is simply beyond our modern machine technology. I find it interesting that there is no discernible road between the quarry and the massive Sun Temple. This indicates one or both of two possibilities: the building of the lower platform occurred at such an ancient time in antiquity that the road is long gone, or a road was never needed for transporting the block. As the *INFO* article points out, a road would have been of little use anyway.

Ragette cannot solve the problem of lifting such a block into place, saying that it is impossible to lift a huge block such as this completely off the ground by the use of levers. He says that we know that the stone had to be lifted so that the log rollers could be removed from underneath the block and then the block lowered into place. In order to fit perfectly, the stone probably had to be lowered and lifted into place several times at least.

His suggestion is that a giant lifting frame was built around the block and then at least 160 "Lewis" stones—wedge-shaped keystones with metal loops—were inserted into the top of the block. Then a system of pulleys and tackles were used with thousands of manual workers to raise and lower the gigantic blocks a few inches.

Ragette makes no suggestion as to why the Romans, or anyone else, would go through so much immense trouble, a virtually impossible engineering feat, in order to lay the foundation for a temple to Jupiter. If they had cut the stone into, say, 100 pieces, they would still be of unusually large size, larger than a man, but at least could have been stacked into a wall much more easily. One is left with the unsettling thought that the reason they used these huge stones was because they *could* use them—and do it relatively easily, though today we have no idea how.

Ragette makes one final interesting comment on Ba'albek: "The real mystery of Baalbek is the total absence of written records on its construction. Which emperor would not have wanted to share the fame of its creation? Which architect would not have thought of proudly inscribing his name in one of the countless blocks of stone? Yet, nobody lays claim to the temples. It is as if Heliopolitan Jupiter alone takes all the credit."[154]

Osirian Remains in Egypt

Other vestiges of Osiris still exist in the eastern Mediterranean. The foundation ashlars of the Wailing Wall at Jerusalem are also gigantic blocks said to be similar to those at Ba'albek. Megalithic ruins can be found underwater at Alexandria, Egypt, and at Abydos is the Osirion, a structure which, like the Sphinx and Valley Temple next to it, are believed to predate the dynastic Egypt of the Pharaohs. In fact, it is from the Osirion that we get the name for this lost civilization from the time of Atlantis.

The submerged megalithic ruins at Alexandria are another clue to ancient Osiris. Alexandria is not really an Egyptian city, it is Greek. As one might easily guess, Alexandria is named after Alexander the Great, the Macedonian king who first conquered the city-states of Greece and then set out to conquer the rest of the world, starting with Persia. Persia was also Egypt's traditional enemy, and so Egypt fell willingly into Alexander's hands. He went to Memphis near modern-day Cairo and then descended the Nile to the small Egyptian town of Rhakotis. Here he ordered his architects to build a great port city, what was to be Alexandria.

Alexander then went to the temple of Ammon in the Siwa Oasis where he was hailed as the reincarnation of a god, which is to say, some great figure from ancient Osiris or Atlantis. Which god, we do not know. He hurried on to conquer the rest of Persia and then India. Eight years after leaving Alexandria, he returned to it, in a coffin. He never saw the city, though his bones are said to rest there to this day (though no one has ever found the tomb).

Of all the mysteries of Alexandria, however, none is more intriguing than the prehistoric harbor which lies to the west of the Pharos lighthouse near the promontory of Ras El Tin. Discovered at the turn of the century by the French archaeologist M. Jondet and discussed in his paper "Les Ports submerges de l'ancienne Isle de Pharos,"[152] the prehistoric port is a large section of massive stones that today is completely submerged. Near it was the legendary Temple of Poseidon, a building now lost, but known to us in literature.[152]

The Theosophical Society, upon learning of the submerged harbor of megaliths, quickly ascribed it to Atlantis. M. Jondet theorized that it might be of Minoan origin, part of a port for Cretan ships. E.M. Forster theorizes, in his excellent guide to Alexandria,[152] that it may be of ancient Egyptian origin, built by Ramses II circa 1300 B.C. Most of it lies in 4 to 25 feet of water and stretches for 70 yards from east to west, curving slightly to the south.

Probably the true origin of the massive, submerged harbor, which was definitely at least partially above water at one time, is a blend of M. Jondets theory of Minoan builders and the Theosophical Society's belief that it is from Atlantis.

In theory, with the Mediterranean slowly filling up with water, the sea would have stabilized after a few hundred years, and then the remnants of the Osirians, using a technology and science similar to that of Atlantis, built what structures and ports they could. Later, in another tectonic shift, the port area, probably used by what we would call "pre-dynastic Egyptians" (like those who built Abydos and the Temple of the Sphinx), was submerged, and was then essentially useless.

It is interesting to note, in accord with this theory, that a temple to Poseidon was located at the tip of Ras El Tin. Atlantis was known to the ancients as Poseid, and Poseidonis or Poseidon was a legendary king of Atlantis. Similarly, Poseidonis and Osiris are thought to be the same person. The main temple at Rhakotis, the Egyptian town which Alexander found at the ancient harbor, was naturally dedicated to Osiris.

In his book, *The Alexandria Project*, author Stephan Schwartz describes several scuba dives into the eastern harbor. In the last dive, Schwartz's team discovered huge cut-stone blocks, including what they believed to be "The Crown of Osiris," part of a statue of Osiris that was located in about 20 feet of water. They also discovered huge pedestals, presumably for statues, cut out of massive granite blocks with sockets in them. Says Schwartz in his book, which is largely about experimental psychic archaeology, "Like everything else in the Pharos area, this pedestal is on a very large scale."[151]

Therefore, as the reader of this book is to find, the study of Atlantis is more than research into Plato's sunken island. The search for Atlantis is the search for mankind's past and the ancient civilizations that may have existed before our history began.

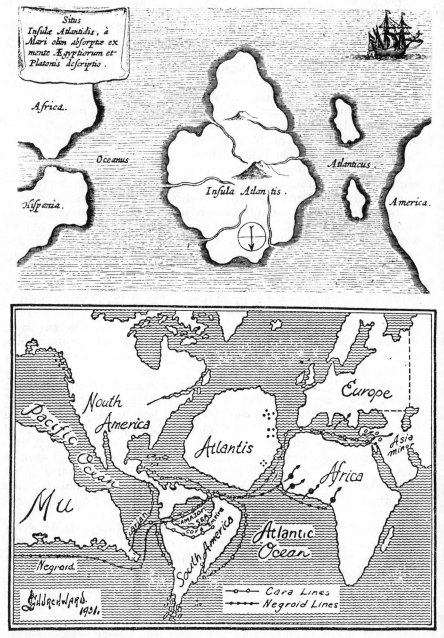

Top: A 1678 map of Atlantis from the book *Mundus Subterraneus* by
Athanasius Kircher. North is at the bottom of the page. Bottom: James
Churchward's 1931 map showing his concepts of Mu, Atlantis and
ancient South America.

Top: An 18th-century depiction of the Biblical Flood. Bottom: James Churchward's drawing of a cataclysmic wave destroying a colony of Atlantis in the Yucatan. From his 1926 book, *The Lost Continent of Mu*.

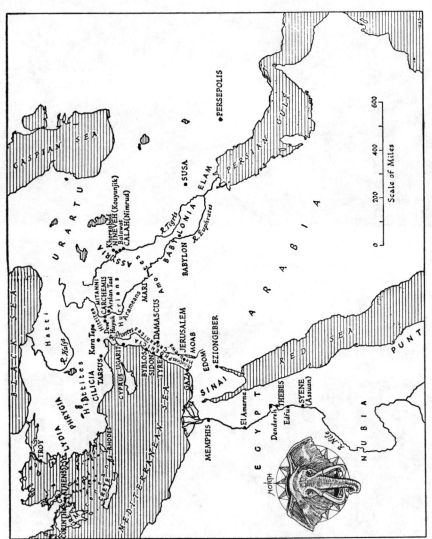

The ancient Middle East.

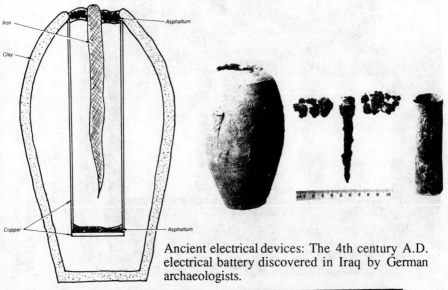

Ancient electrical devices: The 4th century A.D. electrical battery discovered in Iraq by German archaeologists.

Apparent electrical devices depicted at the Temple of Hathor, Egypt.

Gateway at Tiahuanaco

Gateway at Persepolis

Pierre Honoré's comparison of two similar megalithic gateways: one from Persepolis in Persia and one from Tiahuanaco in the Andes.

RIGHT: This massive block of stone has sharp-edged grooves that could not have been made with stone axes or wooden wedges.

BOTTOM LEFT: This statue from Tiahuanaco, carved out of a single block, stands in La Paz (Bolivia) today. Who made such huge monuments? Are they likenesses of extraterrestrial beings?

BOTTOM RIGHT: Fragment of a Tiahuanaco statue of a quite different kind. Today it, too, is in La Paz (Bolivia).

Pierre Honoré's photos of the stones of Tiahuanaco, including two unusual statues. A Hittite connection?

Colossal heads

La Venta Colossal Head 1. Ht 2.4 m.

Colossal stone head found at Tres Zapotes in the early 1860s.

San Lorenzo Colossal Head 1, during excavation.

Giant stone heads like these have been found buried in Mexico and Guatemala. Are they relics of Atlantis?

Isis is seen here protecting Osiris. From Karnak Temple, Egypt (c.700 B.C.)

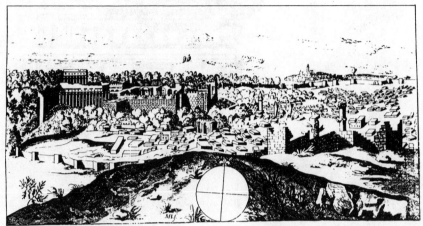

Baalbek as seen by Henry Maundrell in 1697

A reconstruction of the Roman north gate

A reconstruction of a corner of Ba'albek showing one of the three massive blocks
in relation to the rest of the structure. The Roman Temple of Jupiter sits on top of
the earlier platform.

Ba'albek, Lebanon. Above: the three massive stones that are part of the foundation of the Roman Temple to Jupiter. Placed there before the Romans, these stones are among the largest in the world. Below, the largest block, still at the quarries a few miles away.

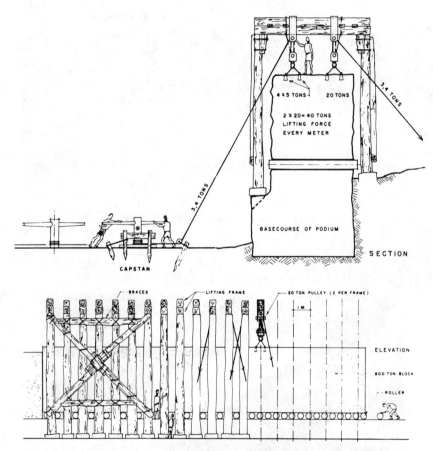

4 × 5 TONS   20 TONS

2 X 20 = 40 TONS
LIFTING FORCE
EVERY METER

3.4 TONS

3.4 TONS

BASECOURSE OF PODIUM

SECTION

CAPSTAN

BRACES   LIFTING FRAME   20 TON PULLEY (2 PER FRAME)

1 M

ELEVATION

800 TON BLOCK

ROLLER

A hypothetical procedure for lifting an 800 ton block into place, such as at Ba'albek.

Chapter 2

TURKEY
& the EASTERN
MEDITERRANEAN:

Atlantis & the Hittites

...in mind you are all young; there is no old opinion handed down among you by ancient tradition, nor any science that is hoary with age. And I will tell you the reason... there have been many destructions of mankind arising out of many causes...
> —Plato, *Critias*

My first stop in the search for ancient Atlantis was to the eastern Mediterranean. I wanted to find out what I could about the gigantic ruins and reports of sunken cities.

On a breezy spring afternoon I stepped off a plane in Istanbul and looked out at the city of two continents. I wondered what secrets of Atlantis might be kept along the eastern shore of the Mediterranean. At the Pudding Shop, a traveller's hangout in the Sultanamet region of Istanbul, I had a dinner of rice pilaf and gazed at the bustling street outside the window.

As in many of my journeys, Istanbul became the starting point for a long series of adventures. It is the crossroads of the east and west, the nexus of the modern world and the old world, the meeting point of the Islamic and Christian worlds.

I had been to Turkey and Istanbul several times before, but I found that I had missed a great deal. Turkey is a large country that holds as much in terms of ancient history, cultural attractions and lost cities as any other, and my previous journeys had only scratched the surface (see *Lost Cities of China, Central Asia & India*). The underground cities and volcanic cone houses of Cappadocia had fascinated me in the past, as had the mysteries of Noah's Ark and Mount Ararat. But this time I was after the lost Hittite cities in north-central Turkey. It was at these huge megalithic complexes that my search for Atlantis was to begin.

I had heard a great deal about the Hittites, how they built huge megalithic cities, how they controlled the early iron industry in the Middle East and how their cities were destroyed in a horrific war that left portions of the capital literally vitrified from the heat. Did the Hittites have something to do with Atlantis? I was convinced they did!

I left Istanbul on a day bus for Ankara, the modern capital of Turkey. It was dusk when I found a cheap hotel in the old city. Looking out from my window I could see the Tomb of Kemal Ataturk lit up on a hill above the capital.

When Ataturk was born in 1881, Turks normally had but one name, and Ataturk's was Mustafa, but he earned the nickname of Kemal (excellence) from his teachers for his work at school. In World War I he was a lieutenant colonel of infantry and became a hero by successfully defending Gallipoli from the British.

Though Turkey was defeated in WWI, Ataturk led the War of Independence in May of 1919 when the Greek army invaded the Aegean coast at Izmir (Smyrna). The Turkish War of Independence lasted from 1920 to 1922. In September 1921 the Greeks very nearly reached Ankara, Ataturk's nationalist headquarters, but the Turks held them off and began a counter-offensive a year later and drove the Greek armies back to Izmir by September of 1922.

Mustafa Kemal was now fully in control of Turkey; the Sultanate was abolished along with the Ottoman Empire. The Turkish Republic was born and Mustafa was proclaimed Ataturk or "Father Turk." Ethnic Greeks in Turkey and ethnic Turks in Greece were required to leave their ancestral homes and move to their respective nation-states. Entire Greek cities in Turkey became ghost towns, and a mass movement of people began, similar to the partition of India and Pakistan twenty years later.

I looked at the squared columns and large mausoleum that shone in the darkness. Even though Ataturk had died on November 10, 1938, he seemed everywhere in modern Turkey. A bust or statue of him is in every park and quotations from his speeches and writings are on every public building. His picture is in every office, shop and hotel lobby. He was a forward-looking man who separated church and state, changed the written script to a Latin-based one and turned the backward Ottoman state into a forward-thinking Western nation.

As I drew the curtains and turned out the light, I said a quiet prayer for Kemal Ataturk, a man of great intelligence, energy and daring. A man who almost single-handedly created the modern Turkish state.

~~~~~~~~≈⚓≈~~~~~~~~

The next day I headed for Ankara's premier museum, the Museum of Anatolian Civilizations. A spacious building on a hill, it is a converted covered market built in 1471. Entering the museum, one is first confronted with an impressive display of one of the buildings excavated at Catal Huyuk, a town built in 7500 B.C. and often said to be one of the oldest cities in the world.

Of interest at the Catal Huyuk display are the bull motifs and the leopards facing each other. Catal Huyuk is evidence that cattle have been an extremely important symbol of wealth for many millennia. Similarly, in Plato's story of Atlantis, the bull and its worship plays an important part.

Leopards and lions no longer live in the Middle East owing to hunting and probably climatic change. Curiously, the same motif of two leopards, or jaguars, can be found at such ancient South American sites as Tiahuanaco and Samaipata.

Walking past the Catal Huyuk display one enters the several halls of Hittite artifacts. There were metallic statues and daggers, cylinder seals and ring seals as used in Sumeria and the Indus Valley, and bull statues.

One hall was full of huge granite rock slabs, often covered in Hittite hieroglyphs or with a large sphinx carved into the face of the rock. The similarity to Egyptian monuments was striking and it was interesting to note that the Egyptian god Bes, popular among Phoenician sailors as well, was apparently a common Hittite statuette depiction.

Bes is typically depicted as a dwarf with a thick beard and often an erect phallus. He was a god of good luck for sailors and of fertility. He was sometimes depicted with a hunchback and is therefore similar to the hunchbacked flute player called Kokopelli who is found on rock paintings throughout the American Southwest. Images of Bes can be found in Egypt, Phoenicia, Greece, Central America and other far-flung areas.

The museum was impressive, piquing my interest in the origin of the Hittites and their strange culture. Like Egypt, they appeared to arrive as a full-blown megalithic culture without a gradual rise from a primitive state. Had the Hittites come originally from Atlantis?

Back at the hotel that evening I decided to go into the new city of Ankara. I got into a taxi outside the hotel, but was not sure where to tell the driver my destination was. I then remembered that I had read that there was a McDonald's restaurant in the new city. Reasoning that the McDonald's would probably be in the busy center of the new city I used it as my landmark for Ankara. The taxi driver nodded in recognition and put the Turkish-made Fiat into gear. I mused to myself whether Kemal Ataturk would have approved. Perhaps Turkey had become too Western!

I soon found myself on a crowded street with leather shops, jewelry shops, department stores and, yes, a McDonalds. I strolled among the busy shoppers and businessmen, stopping for a bite to eat in a café. As the signs became lit in the evening, I noticed an entire street of beer halls.

Choosing a pub with some live music, I pushed past the front tables and took a seat at the bar next to a foreign-looking man sitting on a stool. He noticed my American accent as I ordered a beer and introduced himself as Roger.

Roger was a middle-aged British expatriate who had taught English in Saudi Arabia, Abu Dhabi and Sri Lanka. I told him that I had taught English in Taiwan years ago and over a few drinks he told me what he was doing there in Turkey.

He had seven children by two wives and was now divorced. Roger worked on his small bottle of vodka and suddenly told me about his penchant for young boys. "I'm here in Turkey to find a young boy to be my permanent lover," he said. "I like teaching English here in Ankara, but it's the young boys I'm really after."

I may have travelled all over the world, but I am still shocked by some things. "You're an admitted pedophile then?" I asked.

"Sure," he said. "I've got my children, they're mostly grown. I've got no use for women anymore. It's young boys that I desire. I'd like a steady relationship."

"Is it common to have such a relationship here in Turkey?" I asked. "I mean, what would the family say?"

"Oh, you must make arrangements with the family," he said. "That's very important. Currently I'm still negotiating. It takes time." With that he sipped his vodka. "Don't be shocked," he went on. "It's relatively common here. Most of the men here have such experiences when they are young. Women are still very much forbidden to men until marriage. Most men must save for ten or fifteen years to have the dowry amount necessary for marriage. Therefore there is a great deal of homosexual activity."

I told him I was in Turkey searching for Atlantis.

"That is strange," he said. "You are a strange person, aren't you?"

"Well, it is all in one's taste," I said as I finished my beer, and said I had to be going. At least he was honest, I thought to myself as I left. My search for Atlantis would bring me into contact with a wide variety of people, I was to find out.

The Mystery of the Hittites

Atlantis was on my mind when I awoke the next morning. I checked out of the hotel and took a bus from the central terminal to Sungurlu, several hours east. A mini-bus ride later I was in the town of Bogazkale.

Bogazkale was a small Turkish village along a gorge in the central Anatolian mountains. It was early spring and it had snowed among the mountains the night before. People were dressed warmly, I noticed as I got off the bus in the town plaza. In front of me was one of Bogazkale's several hotels, the Hattusas Pension and Restaurant.

I dumped my pack on the bed of my room and decided to use what was left of the afternoon. The museum was nearby and the friendly hotel staff directed me to the office. As the only tourist in town, I had the museum to myself, and enjoyed the small rooms of cylinder seals, cuneiform tablets, amphorae, and iron weapons.

As at the museum in Ankara, the ancient sphinx motifs were present as well as the winged discs. Looking at some of the photos from the excavation, I noticed several remaining foundation walls with the perfectly cut, polygonal walls that are characteristic of construction at Mycenae and Peru, a type of cyclopean construction often associated with Atlantis.

Back at the pension I met two young Turks, Amil and Mustafa. Both were married with young children, but they spent their time watching the Hattusas Pension, owned by Mustafa's father. Amil's father worked in Germany. Amil had lived for awhile in Germany and spoke excellent English. He twirled the keys to a Turkish-made Fiat that was parked on the road outside the hotel and asked me if I wanted to go for a ride with him up to the gorge to inspect his family's irrigation project.

I accepted and without further ado we were soon driving up a steep hill on the edge of town and along the high road that headed for a pass over the southern mountains. Overlooking the ancient city of Hattusas, we walked to a rushing mountain stream that suddenly dropped through a gorge forming a natural rock wall. The ancient Hittite capital used this vertical wall and rushing stream as part of its defense wall.

Amil showed me where he was planning to build a dam across the stream and flood a portion of the mountains near Hattusas. He had already begun, and I was impressed by the partially constructed log wall.

"Isn't this irrigation project great?" he asked me, his arms and hands out wide to show me the scope of his vision.

"Sure, it's great," I said. "But what would the Archaeological Institute in Ankara say?"

"Oh, I don't think that they would care," he replied, climbing over

55

his log dam.

I cast a look across the river at the ruined city wall of Hattusas. Amil, I thought, had something to learn about national historical sites.

I had arranged to have Amil meet me the next morning to be my guide around Hattusas. He met me after breakfast and we began a driving tour through the city, which covered several square miles.

We stopped first at the so-called Temple Complex, megalithic foundation walls with the remains of a huge gate into which lions were carved. Although the buildings were once several stories high only the foundations remained and all other stones had been removed.

We continued on to the massive Lion Gate on the west side of the gigantic wall that once surrounded all of the city. Hattusas, like many ancient cities, was a series of massive fortifications, each leading to a higher citadel, like in some J.R.R. Tolkien novel. The Hittite world was one of mighty armies, magic spells, sorcerers, and massive fortresses.

In Robert E. Howard's fictional world of Conan the Barbarian, the action takes place about 7000 B.C. after the sinking of Atlantis. Various kingdoms fought for power and the world was one of swordplay, strange ruined cities and savage armies that roamed the countryside for conquest and pillage.

Why would anyone want to go through the tremendous amount of effort it must have taken to make these 60-foot-high megalithic walls and gates? Clearly, a lot of organized effort went into building fortifications on a gigantic scale, utilizing local cliffs and gorges. As in Conan's time, they apparently had a lot to be afraid of.

The Hittites are one of the most fascinating and little-known of all the great ancient empires of the Middle East. The heart of the Hittite empire was the river Halys which makes a huge bend through central Turkey on its way to the Black Sea. In the middle of this bend was built the cyclopean city of Hattusas, the later capital of the Hittites.

In 1905 this virtually unknown civilization came to light when the German Assyriologist Professor Hugo Winckler discovered a number of cuneiform texts along with a curious ancient form of hieroglyphics. These discoveries aroused a great deal of interest among archaeologists around the world.

The Hittites were declared by German archaeologists to be an Indo-Germanic tribe, the "Sons of Heth" of the Bible. Translations of the cuneiform texts began immediately and cross-references to Egyptian texts and the Bible were made to ascertain the role of the Hittites in the history of the ancient Near East and eastern Mediterranean.

There are few books available on the Hittites. One of the more readable scholarly works is *The Secret of the Hittites*[68] by the famous German archaeologist C.W. Ceram. This 1955 book gives a good overview of the Hittites and describes in detail the chronology of the discoveries and Middle Eastern scholars' attempts to decipher Hittite texts.

Ceram mentions how no less than eight different languages were found in the clay texts at Hattusas. These languages encompassed a wide range of trading languages from India. These languages were Sumerian, Akadian, the language now known as Hittite, Proto-Indic, Hurrian, Proto-Hattian, Luvian, and Palaic. Hattusas was a very cosmopolitan place with obviously large numbers of foreign traders and diplomats. Other Hittite stelae were written in Phoenician and Hittite and it was these stone tablets that provided the modern key for deciphering ancient Hittite hieroglyphs.

Hittite text is read in a boustrophedon pattern, which is "as the ox plows," or left to right and then right to left. Such unusual scripts as the Rongo Rongo writing of Easter Island and Doric Greek were written in a boustrophedon pattern.

Ceram quotes from the work of the Swiss epigrapher Emil Forrer who assumes that the Hittites had migrated into Asia Minor from Eastern Europe since they were an Indo-European people. The question of who the previous population was arises, and since nothing could be found about them for a long time they were simply called "proto-Hattians."

They spoke a *non*-Indo-European language which appeared in several of the clay tablets found at Hattusas and was always preceded by the word *hattili* ("in Hattian"). This term "was undoubtedly derived from *Hatti,* the name of the country. Hatti, then, where Hattian (Hittite) had been spoken, had existed as a kingdom before the Indo-European ruling class invaded Asia Minor. Evidence for this was contained in three inscriptions of King Anitta of Nesa in which a successful war against the 'King of Hatti' is mentioned."[68]

Therefore, Ceram says, Hattians (Hittites) should then be the proper name for the original inhabitants, not for the Indo-European conquerors. Their language was called "Kanisic" by Forrer but today the term "Hittite" for the official language has stuck.

Ceram says that Hittite came from the "centrum" group of European languages such as Greek, Celtic, Latin and Germanic. This is opposed to the "satem" group of eastern languages such as Slavic, Iranian and Indic. Therefore the conquering "Hittites" (we do not know their real name) must have come by way of the Balkans and the Bosphorus. Yet Ceram says a mystery is associated with this because of the beginning of a prayer by the Hittite king Muwatallis

(c. 1300 B.C.):

> *Sun God of Heaven, shepherd of man!*
> *You rise out of the sea, Sun of Heaven.*
> *Up to Heaven you move in your course.*
> *Sun God of Heaven, my Lord! To children of men,*
> *To dogs, to swine, to the wild beasts of the field,*
> *You give justice, O divine Sun, day after day!*

Ceram asks, how did the Hittites know that the sun rises out of the sea? In Anatolia (Turkey) or anywhere in Europe, the sun would not rise up out of the sea. Ceram suggests that the Black Sea or the Caspian Sea was to the east during their migration.

A possible answer to this question would be that such a prayer to the ancient monotheistic sun god may have originated in Atlantis. If Atlantis was an island in the Atlantic, then the sun would have risen up out of the sea. Otherwise, one would have to be on the east coast of the Americas, or India or Asia.

Indeed, there are many links between the Hittites and Atlantis. A look at Hittite portraits shows that they have a high bridged nose that goes to the middle of the forehead, much like the Mayans of Central America. Hittites also used a hieroglyphic script as did the Mayans and like the Mayans made important political announcements on stone stelae which were placed at the entrances or plazas of a city.

The Hittites also used personal seals, a stone "chop" as is still used in China today to officialize any document or letter. Such seals were used by the Indus Valley civilization at Mohenjo Daro and Harappa, as well as by the Mayans and proto-Mayans. Seals virtually identical to Hittite seals can be seen at the Mayan museums in Guatemala!

Similarly, many Hittite motifs show a Hittite carrying a strange purse-like box or satchel. This same odd package with a handle is seen in a number of the Olmec statues in Mexico.

The Hittites are said to be the inventors of the chariot and horses were of great importance to them. However, it seems unlikely that horsemanship and wheeled chariots were first invented by the Hittites. It is with the ancient Hittite stelae that we first see the chariot being used. It is highly likely, for instance, that chariots were in use in ancient China at the same time.

The Hittites used the unusual double-headed eagle motif, a symbol Germany still uses today. Like the Egyptians and other Mediterranean cultures, the sphinx was a popular artistic subject and most of the gigantic city gates were guarded either by huge stone sphinxes or lions.

The Hittites used the gigantic megalithic construction known as cyclopean—huge odd-shaped polygonal blocks perfectly fitted together. The massive walls and gates of Hattusas are eerily similar in construction to those in the high Andes and other megalithic sites around the world. Such construction is the most sophisticated building technique known, being able to withstand powerful earthquakes and last for thousands of years.

Mankind has been in this area and nearby northern Iraq for a long time. Excavations at a cave in Kurdistan, northern Iraq, in the '50s and '60s demonstrated that man had been living in the "Shanidar Cave" up to 100,000 years ago.

In his book *Shanidar: The First Flower People*,[72] author Ralph Solecki relates that excavations in the cave revealed that Neanderthal man was living in this cave, and burials of dead men, women and children dated 50,000 or more years old while artifacts on the floor were dated to 100,000 years.

Furthermore, Solecki says that the Neanderthals of this cave cared for their aged, nursed their wounded, and buried their dead with flower ceremonies—hence his title characterizing them as the first 'flower people.' Not only has the Middle East been occupied for millennia, but huge armies have passed through the valleys and civilizations have risen and fallen to dust.

The Hittites are also related to the amazing world of ancient India. Proto-Indic writing is found at Hattusas and scholars now admit that the civilization of ancient India, as the ancient Indian texts like the Ramayana have said, goes back many millennia. The ancient civilization of India that allegedly existed at the time of Atlantis was called the Rama Empire.

The country between Mesopotamia and the Hittites was an Indic-Hindu state known as Mittani. Mittani retained its ancient links to India, including the age-old Hindu-Dravidian beliefs in reincarnation, cremation, karma and avatars. Such an Indic-Middle Eastern state must have had strong effects on the religion and beliefs of the countries around it.

One such historical case is that of Nefertiti, the wife of the Egyptian Pharoah Akhenaton. Nefertiti, who was not an Egyptian, is now known to have come from Mittani. The German archaeologist Philip Vandenburg claims that it was Nefertiti who was behind the Atonist religious revolution in Egypt, rather than her husband Akhenaton, who, however, clearly went along with her beliefs.

That Mittani was closely allied with the Hittites can be seen through the so-called Amarna letters in which the Queen Nefertiti asks the king of the Hittites to send a son to be her husband, so that she could continue to rule Egypt after Akhenaton had died from poisoning by the priests they fought against.

Did the Hittites hold the same beliefs as the Hindus of Mittani? It would be a fascinating turn of history if it was proven that they too were believers in reincarnation, just as were Atonists, the Essenes and the Greeks. For more information on the fascinating Atonist rebellion in Egypt and the religious wars over mummification and reincarnation see my book *Lost Cities & Ancient Mysteries of Africa & Arabia*.[58]

In his 1965 book, *The Bible As History*,[100] the German historian Werner Keller cites more of the mysteries concerning the Hittites. According to Keller, the Hittites are first mentioned in the Bible in connection with the Biblical patriarch Abraham who (in *Genesis* 23) acquires from the Hittites a burial place in Hebron for his wife Sarah.

Conservative classical scholar Keller is confused by this, because the time period of Abraham was circa 2000-1800 B.C. while the Hittites are classically said to have appeared in the 16th century B.C.

Even more confusing to Keller is the Biblical statement that the Hittites are the founders of Jerusalem (*Numbers* 13:29-30).[100] This is a fascinating statement, as it would also mean that the Hittites also occupied Ba'albek, which lies between their realm and Jerusalem. The Temple Mount at Jerusalem is also built on a foundation of huge ashlars like Ba'albek.

It also means that the ancient Hittite empire existed for several thousand years with frontiers with Egypt. Indeed, the Hittite hieroglyphic script is undeniably similar to Egyptian hieroglyphs, probably more so than any other language.

Just as Egypt goes back many thousands of years B.C. and is ultimately connected to Atlantis, so does the ancient Hittite empire. Like the Egyptians, the Hittites carved massive granite sphinxes, built on a cyclopean scale, and worshiped the Sun. The Hittites also used the common motif of a winged disc for their Sun God, just as the Egyptians did. The Hittites were well known in the ancient world, because they were the main manufacturer of iron and bronze goods. The Hittites were metallurgists and seafarers.

In many ways the Hittites and the Egyptians were the last holdovers from the civilizations that arose right after the "flood" and the time of Atlantis.

Some histories of Atlantis assert that Atlanteans wore pointed shoes and turbans. Well, the Hittites wore pointed shoes and long conical caps. Many Hittites look very Mayan in their facial features, with the long nose bridge coming high to the forehead.

The Hittites were also very warlike. Their mountain fortresses with their megalithic gates and fortifications give the foreboding sense of armies besieging a city. Dark warriors with iron swords and spears patrolled a strange world that was similar to Conan the Barbarian's. It was a time of mighty warriors, marauding armies and dark sorcerers. Exotic cults ruled by priests and priestesses could be found in any major Egyptian, Hittite or Sumerian city.

Did the Hittites exist in 7,000 B.C.? Apparently so, with Catal Huyuk and Jericho being two cities inhabited by them. Other Hittite cities like Jerusalem and Hebron are modern cities today.

The Hittites were also great seamen and were the first to repopulate the island centers of Cyprus and Crete after the Mediterranean had been flooded. The Hittites controlled all of coastal Turkey, present day Lebanon and southward probably as far as Gaza. They also controlled Cyprus and were probably strongly allied with ancient Crete and Mycenae.

These ancient seafarers, I believe, were the survivors of Atlantis who became the early seafarers sometimes known as the 'Atlantean League.' These early sailors of 6,000 B.C. ultimately became the Phoenicians. These pre-Phoenician sailors ventured beyond the Mediterranean from their ports at Ugarit (modern Ras Sharma in Lebanon), Mersin near Adana and the ports in Cyprus. They sailed to northern Europe and controlled the important tin trade from England.

I believe that they crossed the Atlantic to the Americas. They traded for metals and voyaged up rivers. This was by at least 3000 B.C. and probably many thousands of years earlier. They mined the pure copper formations in northern Michigan and Lake Superior. They traded iron weapons to the Maya and Toltecs. They made their way to the ends of the earth: the civilizations of the high Andes like Tiahuanaco.

Hittite Relics in North America

Amil called for me to come back to the car. I looked again at the huge stones with the carved lions. They must weigh over 100 tons each, I thought. Amil told me that the lion gate was designed "to protect the city from evil." Other gates in the city were guarded by a pair of sphinxes or a "warrior-god."

Amil then drove me up the winding dirt road to the very top of the city. Here there were still large sections of the 50-foot wall left. I looked out over the city that was now rubble. A great deal of effort had been made to protect this sprawling city, center for the ironworks of Asia Minor. Blue-green stains of copper-laden soil could be seen on the nearby hills.

"Look over here," said Amil, showing me a 70-meter tunnel that was wide enough for two men abreast to walk through. The tunnel was a secret tunnel, though huge, that cut under the wall at the highest part of the city. We walked through, using our small flashlights. Out the back side was a steep hill sloping down to a river. Hattusas had been built at a naturally fortified site.

Back at my hotel I sat at a table looking over some books and wondering if there was proof that the Hittites had been to North America. According to Frank Edwards in his second collection of mysteries, *Strange World,*[51] the Hittites are among the many ancient cultures who voyaged across the Atlantic to the Americas. In a chapter entitled "Who Was First In America," Edwards tells the following story of an object found in 1921 by a Pennsylvania fisherman named Elwood D. Hummel.

"He was fishing along the Susquehanna River near his home at Winfield, Pennsylvania. Elwood was a fly fisherman and he frequently waded the shallows of the Susquehanna. One day he chanced to glance down in the clear water and, as he did so, he noticed a small flat stone which appeared to have some markings on it. He picked it up and recognized it as some kind of baked clay, covered with tiny figures which were unintelligible to him. Odd, but not important to him at the moment, so Elwood dropped it into the pocket of his fishing coat.

"For 37 years Mr. Hummel kept that curious little stone rattling around in his fishing gear. Then one day one of his grandchildren found it and began using it for a toy. The handling and wear polished the stone and made the markings more distinct. The youngsters asked what the markings meant—and their grandfather decided that it was time he learned the answer to that question for himself. So he sent it to the curator of the Field Museum in Chicago.

"Experts there promptly identified and translated the odd little markings. They spelled out the details of a small loan made by an Assyrian merchant in Cappadocia about 1800 years before Christ."[51]

This out-of-place artifact (Ivan T. Sanderson coined the term "oopart") matches perfectly with the many cuneiform tablets that constituted the Hittite state archives at Hattusas, discovered shortly after 1905 when German archaeologists began their excavations of the megalithic city thought to have been the last capital of the Hittites.

These archives consisted of thousands of clay tablets written in cuneiform and the subject was largely of a commercial nature, detailing loans, sales of goods, etc. These tablets were written in cuneiform by Assyrian merchants who came up the river from Mesopotamia to trade. Nearly everything that archaeologists have surmised about the Hittites (right and wrong) has come from these clay tablets.

The Hittites, however, had their own script, which was hieroglyphic in nature and remarkably similar to the Linear A and Linear B hieroglyphic scripts used in ancient Crete and Mason. Like these other hieroglyphic scripts, the Hittite script and language remain undeciphered, lost in the mists of history like many other languages.

An even more amazing discovery was made on a farm near Newberry, Michigan, in November of 1896. Two woodsmen clearing land on a farm uprooted a tree and discovered three statues and a clay tablet written in Hittite-Minoan.

The Michigan *Newberry News* carried this article on November 20, 1896:

"Last week we called attention, briefly, to a curious find said to have been made in this county a few miles north of Newberry. Since then we have examined more closely into the matter and find that the discovery is likely to turn out to be of great historical value and importance. Three figures of stone have been unearthed. They are made of soft sandstone and resemble human beings in a stooping position. They are supposed to be heathen idols or images, as they bear a close resemblance to similar specimens found in other countries. Along with the images was a stone slab or tablet measuring about 19 x 26. This tablet is divided into 140 squares by lines cut into the stone. In each of the spaces is a letter or character, which in all probability record the history or religious creed of some prehistoric people. Some of the characters are very much like letters of the Greek alphabet, others resemble Egyptian hieroglyphics.

"A party consisting of Dr. H.C. Farrand, Messrs. W.T. Crocker, D.N. McLeod, Wm. Trueman and Charles Brebner, drove out to the place where the find was made with the intention of doing a little exploring. They found the upturned hemlock root where the figures and tablet were dug out, but owing to the recent thaw the hole was filled with water and the surrounding territory also covered with water to the depth of several inches and digging was out of the question. However several test pits were sunk and struck rock every time and the party were of the opinion that further important discoveries would yet be made.

"Just what the explorers' pick and shovel may reveal is hard to surmise. Some are of the opinion that the site of some religious edifice belonging to some prehistoric people will be brought to light. The work on the tablet is too artistic to be ascribed to any of the Indian tribes. It must have been done by some people of a higher order of intelligence. The tablet is remarkably well preserved, every square stands out clearly and only three letters or characters are missing. With the aid of a magnifying glass these may yet be made out.

"The find may turn out to be a rich prize to the antiquarian and the archaeologist. The tablet no doubt contains the key to the mystery and until that is deciphered only wild guesses can be made."[140]

Historian Betty Sodder devotes large chapters of her books, *Michigan Prehistory Mysteries*[140] and *Michigan Prehistory Mysteries II*,[141] to the Newberry Tablet.

According to Sodder and her detailed researches, the tablet and statues, though typically described in the old newspaper articles as being made of sandstone, are actually of unbaked clay. Unfortunately, neither the University of Michigan nor the Smithsonian Institution showed any interest in the amazing discovery at the time, or at any later period.

Photos of the tablet and statues were sent to the Smithsonian where they "disappeared." When contacted fifty years later, the Smithsonian had no idea where the only photos of the tablet could be located. They never made any comment on the writing or possible origin of the unusual artifact. Later, nearly 100 years after the discovery, one rare photo of the tablet was discovered. It is reprinted at the end of this chapter.

The Smithsonian Institution has been accused of ignoring and even covering up important archaeological finds. In my book *Lost Cities of North & Central America* I relate several important cases where the Smithsonian has apparently not only "lost" important artifacts that would prove that ancient seafarers came to America, but has actually suppressed their own astonishing excavations of Egyptian finds in the Grand Canyon area of northern Arizona.

In the case of the Newberry Tablet, now known to be written in ancient Hittite, one wonders if the Smithsonian simply has no interest in this historical line of thinking or if it is actively suppressing this evidence? No one took much interest in the Newberry Stone except the locals. Eventually the statues and the tablet with the strange writing were relegated to a woodshed on the McGruer farm, near a water hole that the children would swim in during the summer.

The statues and tablet crumbled away from exposure to the environment, while the curious teenage visitors from the swimming hole would stop by the shed to see them.

In the '40s, when some interest in the Tablet and its writings were revived, many older folk could still remember seeing the articles and all the ruckus they caused at the turn of the century. It was during this same period of the '40s that the Smithsonian said that it had lost all the photos and information.

Eventually, the well-known Chicago patent lawyer, Dr. Henrietta

Mertz, published an article in the Epigraphic Society's 1981 *Occasional Publications* (Vol. 9, June, 1981) on the fascinating topic of the Newberry Stone.

In the next publication, the late president of the Epigraphic Society, Dr. Barry Fell, wrote an article on his decipherment of the tablet. Fell said the tablet was written in "Hittite-Minoan." He immediately compares it with the Phaistos Disk from Crete.

Says Fell, comparing the two, "Both tablets are magic quadrangles, to be read both vertically and horizontally, in the alternate directions; both are magical charms, apparently copied from an import from the eastern Mediterranean, not later than Hellenistic times."

Therefore, this text was read in a boustrophedon pattern, an unusual pattern (at least for modern readers) of reading successive lines in alternating directions.

But the Newberry Tablet is a magic square and is therefore read twice! Once across, as the ox plows, across the tablet and then again up and down. Says Fell, "The tablet is composed as an acrostic, to be read vertically as well as horizontally."

Unfortunately, it was not the definitive record from a lost civilization; it contained instructions for obtaining favorable omens from birds by enticing them to peck at offered grain. It is also a magical charm and invocation to the gods for good luck.

Though the University of Michigan refused to look at the stone when it was first discovered in 1896 on the grounds that it was too unusual to be authentic, it would now seem that it is virtually impossible for even the most diabolical back-country farmer to have faked an early Hittite inscription. Since the Hittites themselves were essentially "discovered" in 1905, it would have been highly improbable that a "faked" Hittite tablet would appear nine years earlier.

Do we finally have an iron-clad demonstration that ancient man travelled across the many oceans of the world in search of metals, spices and other trade items? It would appear so, as even an expert on Hittite could not have made such a forgery without a time machine. It is logical that great ancient empires like the Hittites would journey in search of that which they found: pure copper from the Lake Superior open-pit mines.

The early newspaper article quoted above mentions that other probing done around the statues with a steel rod indicated that there were more sandstone and clay objects buried on the farm.

Does a lost Hittite city lie buried on a farm outside of Newberry, Michigan? If in the future we excavated such a city, would we find a megalithic gateway guarded by stone lions and a sphinx or perhaps just imitations of the huge structures back in Asia Minor, both cities now buried in the dust of time.

Cuneiform Texts Mention Atlantis

One interesting theory on Atlantis comes from British science writer George Michanowsky who wrote in his 1977 book *The Once & Future Star*[162] that Sumerian tablets recorded the burst of a supernova some 7,000 years ago. Michanowsky believes these cuneiform tablets record the gigantic stellar explosion that occurred in the southern constellation of Vela. He terms the supernova Vela X.

He also claims that Atlantis is mentioned in these texts as NI-DUK-KI. This, he explains, means Dilmun, the legendary Isle of the Blest from before the flood. Michanowsky theorizes that NI-DUK-KI, or Dilmun, was an island in the southern sea and that Sumerian legend relates that seven sages came to Sumeria from the southern sea. Their Sumerian name was AB-GAL, meaning 'Masters of Knowledge'. Says Michanowsky, "The word read as AB-GAL is actually written NUN-ME in cuneiform. As is evident, the palm tree-derived NUN sign is its principal component. We thus have the same basic cuneiform symbol for the Vela star and for the master-of-knowledge figure. And this same palm was the sacred tree of the Isle of the Blest, the ocean-circled garden of E-A and NIN-MAH."[162]

Michanowsky theorizes that the supernova explosion of Vela X sometime before 4000 B.C. affected the climate of the earth by raising the temperature. A global warming may have broken up the Antarctic ice cap and raised the level of the oceans, thereby submerging NI-DUK-KI or Dilmun/Atlantis.

Michanowsky's theories are interesting but not without some serious problems. Dilmun is more typically identified with the island of Bahrain, and Bahrain was definitely not Atlantis (see my book *Lost Cities & Ancient Mysteries of Africa & Arabia* for a complete discussion of Bahrain and Dilmun). However it is interesting to think that Dilmun may be from a farther "Island of the Blest" such as Ceylon, a lost south sea island (Mu?) or even from an Atlantic island (Atlantis).

Undoubtedly there have been many climatic changes over the tens of thousands of years of mankind's history and it seems quite possible that there was one six or seven thousand years ago. However, Michanowsky makes a common mistake among non-climatographers: a warming of the earth does not necessarily melt the poles!

As the earth heats up from global warming the equatorial ocean areas heat up first. This causes condensation of water from the oceans which then flows via the air currents to the polar areas where it freezes and snows. Polar ice caps actually become larger during global warming, not smaller as often predicted. Vela X would more likely have created an ice age and a lowering of sea levels rather than a raising of them.

Vela X is a fascinating theory with its ancient supernova and cuneiform tablets. However, Atlantis was said by Plato to be of an earlier period and it sank in a sudden cataclysm, not by the slow rising of sea levels.

Particularly interesting is Michanowsky's mention of the seven "Masters of Wisdom" who have a great deal in common with the legend of Osiris who went around the world teaching the wise arts of civilization. Curiously, on Easter Island there is the unusual platform of "Seven Masters" which has seven statues looking out to sea. This is unusual on Easter Island as all the other statues around the edge of the island look away from the ocean toward the center of the island, allegedly protecting it from further earth changes that had sunk the lost land of "Hiva"—the legendary sunken land of which Easter Island was once a part, according to their own legends.

It is interesting to think of these emissaries from Atlantis or "Mu" as being the civilizers of Sumeria. Zechariah Sitchin in his book *The 12th Planet*[77] theorizes that the ancient Sumerians were actually genetically created by extraterrestrials from a "12th Planet" with an errant elliptical orbit outside of Pluto.

These extraterrestrial "Nefilim" not only genetically engineered mankind to work as slave labor in their gold mines, but were the gods of the Sumerians as well. Sitchin has these aliens from the 12th planet, "Marduk," using giant rocketships that take off from Ba'albek and a spaceport in the Sinai somewhere (Sitchin never identifies this site). The Great Pyramid of Egypt is their space-beacon.

In standard translations of Assyrian and Sumerian books such as *The Babylonian Genesis*[67] by Alexander Heidel, Marduk is a "god" such as Osiris. Sitchin admits to Marduk as a god, but according to Sitchin he is also a planet and, paradoxically, the creator of Earth.

Who's Who In Non-Classical Mythology[192] by Egerton Sykes gives this definition of Marduk: "Babylonian god of the spring sun, the Bel of the Old Testament, and head of the Babylonian pantheon. He was the son of El and Damkina and was the champion of the gods in their fight against Tiamat. To this end he was made king of the gods, and given the power that his commands, whatever they might be, would be effected immediately. After the great battle he defeated Tiamat and her husband, Kingu, and cut her body into two parts, one of which he made into the dome of heaven and the other into the abode of the father El. This victory was celebrated at the new year's feast. After arranging heaven and earth he caused Kingu to be sacrificed, and from his blood El created man. Another version says that he decapitated himself and from his own blood man was formed. Marduk had fifty ceremonial names, in a similar manner to the seventy-five praises of Ra and the ninety-nine names of God mentioned in the Koran. He appears to have been originally a vegetation god, similar to Baal and Tammuz. The battle with Tiamat was one stage in the ousting of the mother goddesses. He is equated with Tagtug and with Merodach."

Was Marduk some king-hero of the warlike "gods" who defeated the the peaceful "mother-goddess" civilizations? The cutting up of the body of Marduk is also similar to the Egyptian god Osiris being chopped into pieces and scattered over the Mediterranean. However, in Sitchin's books, Marduk and Tiamat are planets in a Velikovsky-type catastrophe.

In *The 12th Planet*,[77] Sitchin describes a scenario where the planet Marduk comes close to earth and one of its moons, called in the Sumerian texts (according to Sitchin) "the North Wind," strikes the Earth and carves out the Pacific Ocean. However, according to tectonic plate geology, the Pacific continental plate (tectonic plate) is where it should be, and is merely "lower" or "submerged" in relation to surrounding plates.

Sitchin dates the Sumerian city of Nipur back to 400,000 B.C. and the primitive slave-worker man is created by the Nefilim about 300,000 B.C. Sitchin has his 12th-planet spacemen building rocket-centers as well as seaports for metal trade with Africa. The Nefilim watch over earth and eventually vow to let mankind perish, which he simply refuses to do.

I like Sitchin's "Earth Chronicle" books, and they make fascinating reading. But as far as ancient Hindu, Egyptian or Greek records are concerned, Sitchin's 12th-planet scenario is the history of some other solar system, not ours. There doesn't seem to be a place in Sitchin's hypothesis for such beliefs as advanced ancient civilizations like Atlantis, Rama, Hyperborea or "Mu." Besides, according to Sitchin all early civilizations are derived from "Marduk" and centered around the Middle East.

There may well be another planet with an elliptical orbit beyond Pluto. Mankind may be genetically engineered as well, but it seems unlikely that the entire history of the world has revolved around Nipur in Sumeria for the last 400,000 years.

The lesson to be learned here is that ancient histories and texts are highly subjective and open to wild interpretation. It is often easy to find supporting evidence for a wide variety of conflicting theories. The theory of historical isolationism demonstrates how outmoded concepts, such as oceans being "barriers" between civilizations, can actually be the conventional wisdom of the well-educated. Similarly, it is easier for some to believe that the many unusual megalithic structures around the world must be the work of extraterrestrials rather than the ancient works of an industrious mankind.

≋≋≋≋≋👁≋≋≋≋≋

There's no such thing as a goodie or a baddie anymore.
Just people... standing in the dusk of history.
—John Gardner, *Amber Nine*

The Mystery War of 1200 B.C.

The Hittite empire, one of the last remnants of the Atlantean world, was destroyed through conquest by a mysterious group of astonishingly sophisticated seafarers known historically only as the Sea Peoples. In the 12th century B.C. an invasion of the entire eastern Mediterranean occurred which altered history. During this period the Sea Peoples captured Cyprus and all of coastal Asia Minor.

Two ancient Hittite cities, Ugarit on the Syrian coast and Byblos on the Lebanese coast, were both conquered and occupied by a mysterious group of seafarers who are believed to have been the ancestors of the Phoenicians and Carthaginians.

Ugarit has been dated to the 7th millennium B.C., which is an astonishing 9,000 years ago.[13] Considering that ancient Sumeria is only dated from about 3100 B.C.[14] and is still generally considered as the oldest known civilization, this is an astonishingly old date, making the city one of the oldest authenticated cities in history.

The lost city of Ugarit was excavated by the French in the 1930s (who were controlling both Syria and Lebanon at the time by League of Nations mandate). It is situated only a few miles (12 km) north of the modern Syrian port of Latakia, and had its own ancient harbor, Minet-el-Beida.

Ugarit was well placed for Mediterranean trade to the west, as well as for trading with the civilizations on the Tigris and Euphrates. Many of the caravan routes from China, Central Asia, India and the southern Arabian kingdoms ended here or at other nearby ports.

The French archaeologist Claude Schaeffer directed the excavations and published *Statigraphie comparée et chronologie de l'Asie occidentale* in 1948, which compared all the information collected from the Ugarit excavations with the surrounding area. Schaeffer was a respected archaeologist, but his beliefs about cataclysmic geology and the relevance of earthquakes to absolute chronology were not then and are not now accepted by mainstream archaeology.

Schaeffer's principal discovery at Ugarit was cuneiform texts written in Ugaritic-Hittite. These give historians a better understanding of the development of the alphabet, and help support the Greek tradition that the modern alphabet was invented by the Phoenicians.[18]

Trilingual texts in Hittite, cuneiform and Phoenician have been important in deciphering what little we know of these early languages. Not much is known about the early millennia of Ugarit, but the later city of the second millennium B.C. (just prior to its destruction by the Sea Peoples) was a magnificent one with stone blocks of massive proportions. There were two temples in the city, the temple of Ba'al on the west side and the temple of Dagan at the summit of the central mound of the city. The temple of Dagan was built out of gigantic blocks of cut stone, much like the Hittite cities to the north.

But, alas, after its destruction by the mysterious Sea Peoples in approximately 1170 B.C., the city was not to rise again. It was left to await the French archaeologist in 1929.

One of the mysteries surrounding the demise of the Hittites is how it was that some of the ruins became vitrified. Vitrification is the fusing of brick or stone with a glass-like glaze. It requires such an extreme heat that modern scholars are at a loss to explain the phenomenon and attempts to recreate vitrification have failed totally. Vitrified forts have been found in Scotland, Ireland, France, Turkey (the Hittite cities), Iraq, India and even Peru. (See the chapter on Scotland for more on this subject.)

The fusing of brick and stone takes such a tremendous amount of heat that a simple fire just will not suffice. Nuclear weapons do a very good job of vitrification, though that is not necessarily the answer in this case. A mysterious substance known in history as "Greek fire" is reportedly responsible, a substance used in naval warfare that when flung from catapults on the ships would set the target ships on fire, and could not be put out with water, as it would actually burn underwater! Obviously it was some chemical fire, and though we can make some guesses as to its composition, its actual contents remain a mystery. How such a substance might be used against brick and stone forts and actually vitrify the walls is even more of a mystery, and suggests that this was a different type of "Greek fire" (for more information on vitrification in the Middle East and India see my book, *Lost Cities of China, Central Asia & India*[15]).

The many ships of the Sea Peoples lay siege to the Hittite cities of Ugarit, Byblos and other cities along the eastern Mediterranean coast while an inland army apparently swept from the north to Hattusas and its mountain strongholds. At Ugarit, the city army and navy had already gone north, attempting to help the Hittite capital.

A tablet was discovered by Schaeffer, still in the oven where it was baked. When deciphered, it proved to be from the last king of Ugarit, Ammurapi, to the king of Alashia (Cyprus). It said:

"My father, behold, the enemy's ships came here, my cities were burned and they did evil things in my country. Does not my father know that all my troops and chariots (?) are in the Hittite country and all my ships are in the Lukka land? Thus the country is abandoned to itself. May my father know it: the seven ships of the enemy that came here inflicted much damage upon us...."[18]

The identity of these attackers is highly confusing, and they appear to have actually been a number of groups working together who therefore had a number of names. Egyptian texts call them the Thekel, the Shekelesh, the Weshesh and Peleset. The Peleset are generally thought to have been the Philistines of the Bible. Goliath was a Philistine (or at least a mercenary working for them), and when he was slain by David in the famous Bible story, the Philistines became subjects of Israel. A race of men of unusually large stature, they became King David's palace guard and were known as the Cherethites and Pelethites. Martin Luther introduced them into the German language as the "Krethi and Plethi," a term which in German (and also obscurely in English) has the same general usage as the phrase "Tom, Dick and Harry."[153]

Yet, historians still argue as to who these attackers were and where they came from. This huge, unknown army swept into the wealthy and powerful port cities of the eastern Mediterranean and defeated them. Powerful military empires such as the Hittites fell under the mystery onslaught wrought by the Sea Peoples.

Logic tells us that these people came from some other area of the Mediterranean, or perhaps beyond. Their arrival and subsequent conquest of the eastern Mediterranean ports was baffling and a total surprise, if ancient texts are being read correctly.

The Egyptians were also attacked by the Sea Peoples, but defeated them, forcing them out of Egypt in a decisive sea battle. However, the Sea Peoples succeeded in capturing and later colonizing along the coast an area that was to be called Phoenicia.

Still, where had these people originally come from? It must have been a great empire with a navy that was sophisticated and daring. The western Mediterranean naturally comes to mind, with the known megalithic ports in Spain and Morocco.

A maritime empire based at the gates of Hercules would be well based for trade with northern Europe, England and Ireland. Could the huge forts in the Aran Islands of Ireland, as well as in Scotland and the Shetlands, have something to do with an Atlantic sea empire that spanned the entire Atlantic coast of Europe and Morocco? It is quite possible that portions of this army came from now-sunken cities in the North Sea and between England and France. More on that will come in later chapters.

Many scholars see the Sea Peoples as coming from Greece and Crete. Minoan and Mycenaean sailors were apparently part of the invasion of the Sea Peoples, as Egyptian reliefs of captured prisoners shows. Yet these people are not generally thought to have been the origin of the Phoenicians, who are unmistakably intertwined with the Sea Peoples.

Some scholars have even tried to equate the invasion of the Sea Peoples with the invasion from Atlantis that Solon mentions in Plato's account. The logic is that the 12th century B.C. had a great war and an invasion from the west occurred, as Plato had said. Therefore Plato was embellishing on early Greek history and had his dates wrong. This would place the war with Atlantis at only 1000 years before Plato rather than 9000 years.

It seems to me that the Greeks of Plato's time had a pretty good idea of their own history of a thousand years earlier—witness the *Iliad* and the *Odyssey*, Homer's epics of Troy, and the early adventures of seafarers like Jason and the Argonauts. The Greeks were familiar with this heroic period of their history, while Atlantis was of a time many thousands of years earlier, or so the Egyptian priests told the Athenean statesman Solon.

Vitrified Remains and Escape Tunnels

Amil and I walked through the ruins of the Great Castle, or King's Residence, on the east side of the city. Amil suddenly bent down and picked up some blackened, fused brick chunks.

"Here's where the vitrification took place," he said. "This was the king's main palace structure, built of stone and brick. A great fire took place here that fused the bricks and stones together. It is a mystery that a fire should burn so hot."

I bent down and picked up the crumbling, blackened mass of clay and stone. What could have made such a building "melt" like this? Was I on the trail of some early chemical warfare? Was Greek fire some sort of ancient napalm recipe?

Greek fire was thought to be a mixture of crude oil, sulfur, pitch and quicklime. If saltpeter were added to the mixture, it would spontaneously combust when it hit. Catapults were used to bombard ships or cities with Greek fire bombs. Was Greek fire part of the reason for the vitrification of Hattusas?

Nearby was the King's Gate with a large warrior-god guarding the entrance. Next to it a huge tomb was cut out of solid rock. Kings and gods seem interchangeable in the archaeologists' confusing world of the Hittites. What were originally thought to be depictions of kings were later said to be carvings of gods. Yet, no one is sure of the Hittites' religious beliefs (probably quite varied) and there is the common thought that dead kings became gods to be worshiped. On the other hand, the Hittites may have had a more sophisticated metaphysical view, much like the ancient Hindus of Dravidian India.

We walked downhill among the fallen walls and fused stone of the palace. Amil showed me secret escape tunnels beneath the ruins in spots where the ceilings had collapsed. Did a vast network of ancient tunnels still run beneath this strange city? It seemed so.

Secret tunnel systems in Tibet, South America, Mexico and Arizona had caught my interest on previous trips and here was another ruined megalithic city with a tunnel system. How far beneath this city did it run? Could some lost gold treasure be hidden in a sealed vault beneath the city? I looked at my small flashlight and its worn batteries. I wouldn't be crawling into that Stygian darkness on this afternoon...

The Sea Peoples Become the Phoenicians

The ultimate result of the mystery invasion was the creation of the eastern Mediterranean state of Phoenicia. The ancient port city-states of Byblos, Tyre and Sidon were the harbors of the Mediterranean that were closest to the goods of the east.

The German historian Gerhard Herm in his book *The Phoenicians*[153] says that the Phoenicians originated from Bedouin tribes of the Sinai desert who settled along the Levant, or mountains and coastal areas of the eastern Mediterranean, and became seafarers. When they were conquered by the Sea Peoples and merged with them, they became the seed of the Phoenician peoples and empire.

While ancient tribes of Arabia may be linked to the Phoenicians, these resourceful traders were apparently always linked to the sea, with important manufacturing centers in Lebanon and Turkey. This area of the Mediterranean was particularly significant because it was located at one of the only sources of good wood for shipbuilding. Most of the Middle East was a treeless desert, nor did Egypt have any shipbuilding wood to speak of. The mighty cedars of Lebanon were the main source of wood, even for the Egyptians. Only in Greece and the forests of the Adriatic were there other abundant sources of wood nearby.

This source of wood, plus good trading skills and a bold, fearless attitude toward sea travel made the Phoenicians masters of the seas, as far as the North Sea and across the Atlantic. They controlled all of

Spain and much of North Africa. Their buildings and ports were made of large, well-cut stones, their roofs were thatched, their ships were large with battering rams. They wore purple clothes and the sails of their ships had purple stripes in them. The purple dye came from a species of shellfish that was kept secret by the Phoenicians though also harvested, curiously, by the Mayans on the Caribbean coast.

My day with Amil came to an end with a visit to the rock frescoes at the "Open-Air Temple" of Yazilikaya. Here were magnificent rock reliefs of Hittite kings, priests and gods in their curled shoes, conical hats, and flowing dresses.

Back in town I made the obligatory visit to a relative's carpet shop and then played backgammon in the town tearoom with Mustafa and Amil in the evening. As a full moon rose over the citadel of Hattusas I wondered again at these amazing people and their ancient capital that had thrived from 7000 B.C. to 1200 B.C. Then a devastating war by a mystery people wiped them out, leaving only fused brick and the foundations of megaliths behind.

Who were these people?

Another fascinating theory about the origin of the Sea Peoples is the "Atlantis of the North" theory which postulates that now submerged areas of Holland, Denmark and Germany had large port cities and navies. It was from this submerged coastal area that the Sea Peoples migrated by the thousands to the eastern Mediterranean and the mountains of Turkey. More on this theory will be found in a later chapter.

The next morning Amil and Mustafa volunteered to take me back to the main town of Sungurlu on the Ankara highway. We stopped at another Hittite megalithic city in the mountains north of Hattusas called Alacahoyuk. Here in rolling hills on the edge of a small village was an unpretentious museum and the remains of the megalithic city.

The most impressive sight was the beautiful red granite gates carved into two gigantic sphinxes. There were finely fitted polygonal foundation stones and a tunnel which ran from inside the city to outside the megalithic stone walls. The official dating at the site is 4,000 B.C., at least 6,000 years ago.

I thanked Amil and Mustafa as they dropped me off at the bus station for my journey back to Ankara. I waved to them from my seat on the bus. They had been friendly and helpful guides. I congratulated myself for doing the nearly impossible—I had visited his relative's carpet shop and had gotten away without buying anything. To the west, the sun was setting over the fields. For the Hittites, the sun had set a long, long time ago.

≈≈≈≈≈≈≈𝔞≈≈≈≈≈≈≈

For this saith the Lord God:
I shall make thee a desolate city.
Like the cities that are not inhabited.
I shall bring the deep upon you
and great water shall cover thee.
—Ezekiel 27:1

Having now seen the Hittite cities in central Turkey, I was ready to head for the coast, where the sun always shone and the ancient ports of Asia Minor had been turned into tourist resorts.

It was an all-day bus ride from Ankara to the coastal city of Izmir. I sat next to a young soldier from the Black Sea who insisted on practicing his English on me for much of the journey. He showed me photos of his young wife and newborn child. I was interested for awhile, looking politely at each blurry photo and teaching him a few new English words.

By late afternoon we arrived in Izmir, Turkey's third largest city and major port. Izmir was a Greek city called Smyrna until the Turkish War of Independence when Ataturk took it on September 9, 1922. The Greek army retreated to ships waiting at Smyrna and pulled out of Turkey for good. A disastrous fire swept through the city, completely destroying it. Modern Turkey was born and the city was rebuilt.

Izmir has had a long history. The city goes back at least 5,000 years to a Hittite port of 3,000 B.C. Conservative archaeologists have said that the Hittite empire did not extend this far west, but a Hittite bas-relief was found carved into a cliff at Kemalpasa, a small village in the Karabel Pass only 20 kilometers from Izmir.

Smyrna/Izmir has been destroyed several times over by earthquakes, armies and fires. There isn't a great deal for the tourist anymore, so I headed by bus south to Selçuk, the nearest Turkish town to the ancient city of Ephesus.

As the bus left Izmir, I looked at the modern palm-lined streets of the city and its busy port. Turkey had repelled the Greek "invaders" but it was hard to say who were the real invaders and who were the "legitimate" occupiers of the land. Asia Minor was only occupied by the Turks in the late 11th and 12th centuries.

The Turks had been nomads in central Asia for thousands of years and were eventually pushed into the Middle East by the expanding empire of Ghengiz Khan and the Mongol hoards. The Turks had already worked as mercenaries in the Baghdad Abbasid Caliphate. Soon the invading Turkish armies took control of Baghdad and formed the Great Seljuk Turkish Empire and began to invade Anatolia, defeating the Byzantines in 1071.

So we see how the Turks came to Turkey only a thousand years ago and in 1922 succeeded in finally expelling the Greeks, who had inhabited the western coastal areas for thousands of years before that. Armenian kingdoms had existed in the East for thousands of years.

Yet the history of the Middle East, and the entire world for that matter, is one of invasion and counter-invasion. The Hatti had been invaded by an unknown Indo-European group who became the historical Hittites. These people were later invaded by the mysterious Sea Peoples who became the Phoenicians and ancient Greeks. Later there were invasions by the Goths and Arabs. The Mongols swept through Asia Minor in 1243, leaving a wake of destruction in their path.

With such a record of constant invasion, war and genocide, the overall karmic outlook for the Middle East is one of constant war and destruction. Though occasional prophets and philosophers have appeared to preach peace and brotherly love, the ethnic violence continues. Will it ever end? Perhaps only Armageddon, the final war, will bring peace to this unsettled part of the world.

Human Sacrifice to Dinosaurs In Babylon

In the exciting world of Robert E. Howard's "Conan", evil sorcerers ruled from tall fortresses, many men were giants and prehistoric monsters still threatened mankind. Saber-tooth tigers and huge cave bears lived in the forests, mastodons and war-elephants were commonplace, and the occasional monster such as a pterodactyl or dinosaur was encountered.

Incredibly, the world of 4000 B.C. was a lot like a Conan story, if we believe the ancient Biblical book of Daniel, chapter 14, which is now part of the Apocrypha (an appendix to the Old Testament). *Bel and the Dragon* is the name given to Daniel, chapter 14, and it tells the story of Daniel's attempts to free his people from bondage in the sixth century B.C.

The Israelites are in captivity by King Nebucanezzar in Babylon. Daniel has been impressing the king with his prophetic powers and the king is trying to impress Daniel. The king takes Daniel to a great pit where people can worship and view for themselves the horrible "dragon" that is part of some priestly cult. This monster appears to have been some sort of giant saurian, possibly a carnivorous one like an allosaurus. The famous Ishtar gate at the entrance to Babylon was plastered with dragon motifs.

Nebucanezzar says to Daniel, "Wilt thou also say that this is of brass? Lo, he liveth, he eateth and drinketh. Thou canst not say that he is no living god: therefore worship him." Daniel boasts to the king that he is not afraid of this saurian monster and that he shall slay the dragon.

Nebucanezzar regretfully accepts his dare. Daniel then takes pitch-tar, fat and hair, sews it up with meat and throws it down into the pit. The dragon eats it and then dies of indigestion.

The king is unhappy with the death of his expensive toy (dragons weren't cheap in those days either!) and has Daniel thrown to the lions. But Daniel escapes that one too. Apparently, the Babylonians (at least some of them) worshiped what was a virtual dinosaur.

Cryptozoologists like Ivan T. Sanderson and Bernard Heuvelmans like to compare the dragon on the famous Ishtar gate at Babylon with the Chipekwe, a rumoured dinosaur from Central Africa.

The Babylonian animal was called a Sirrush and kept in a dark cavern in the temple and was worshiped by the Babylonians. The relief on the Ishtar gate is of a real animal with a single horn, scales, feet like a bird or lizard and a snake's head on a long neck. A forked tongue darts from its mouth. Depicted on the gate is the Sirrush alternated with the giant extinct ox called an *auroch*. There are also lions on part of the gate.

The famous Swiss zoologist Bernard Heuvelmans says that the Babylonian Sirrush is not an accurate picture of an Iguanadon or a Ceratosaurus, but it's a good stylized likeness. "The Sirrush could have lived in Central Africa, where it has been proved that the Chaldeans went, and where they could have seen a giant lizard (and captured it). When Hans Schomburgh came back to Europe with native tales about the Chipekwe, he also brought back several glazed bricks of the same type as those on the Ishtar Gate!"[105]

A lost Babylonian city in the jungles of Central Africa from 3,000 B.C.? Dinosaurs for sale in the ancient world? As the promoter of King Kong figured, oddball prehistoric monsters left over from the last cataclysm can draw quite a crowd and media blitz. Even in ancient times!

Rural Turkey still looked like something out of a fantasy movie. As I looked out the window of the bus I saw a sign on the highway for camel wrestling. I laughed to myself. Now that was a sport for Conan the Barbarian!

The Lost Cities of Coastal Turkey

No touring along coastal Turkey is complete without a visit to the ancient city of Ephesus, so I soon found myself looking for a hotel in Selçuk, the modern town near ancient Ephesus, the Paris of the ancient world.

This area of Turkey was ancient Ionia, a Greek colony founded at the time of the invasion of the Sea Peoples. The original inhabitants were said to be "Lelegers and Karers" who would have been affiliated with the Hittites. According to historians, on the western slope of the castle hill above Ephesus stood an ancient temple to the old Anatolian earth goddess Cybele.

Under the influence of the Ionians, Cybele became Artemis, the virgin goddess of the hunt and the moon. A fabulous temple was built for Artemis and the city became a prosperous trading city centered around the goddess. When the Romans took over the eastern Mediterranean, they made Ephesus the provincial capital of the province of Asia. Artemis became the Roman goddess Diana.

During Greek and Roman times the temple to Artemis was so sacred, even to the various conquering armies that transited Asia Minor, that when the Lydian king Croesus attacked Ephesus in 550 B.C., a city without a defensive wall or army, the citizens could think of no better defense than to fasten a rope around the Artemis Temple and have the entire population take refuge in the sacred temple precinct. Croesus spared the population and donated building material to the as yet unfinished temple. He still insisted on plundering the city however.

It was a bright sunny day as I walked around Ephesus, one of the best preserved of ancient Greek cities. I had gotten to the site just before the large tour groups arrived and had much of the city to myself for awhile.

Walking through the wide city streets, I was impressed by the splendor that these people lived in. It was an elegant life, with hot and cold running water (thanks to hot springs nearby) and public toilets. Americans, me included, always judge other cultures by their plumbing!

I was disappointed that the famous amphitheater had been closed a few years before. This is ostensibly Ephesus' main attraction. It turns out that Sting, the former lead singer of the rock music group The Police, gave a concert here which packed the theater with 30,000 people. Sting and his band literally made the walls shake and Turkish archaeological authorities locked the gates to the theater a few days later.

I looked through the gates at the theater and then continued down the marble street. There was some indication of megalithic construction in the walls, and the famous Library had an interesting display on ancient construction techniques, including the use of cranes, block-and-tackle pulleys and key-stone cuts for lifting and fastening blocks.

Ephesus is one of several port cities on Turkey's coast that is now more than a mile from the ocean. Once a major port in the ancient world, now one cannot even see the ocean from a high point in the city.

Other nearby ports that are miles away from the ocean are the ancient ports of Priene and Miletus. Priene was an important city until about 300 B.C. because it was where the League of Ionian Cities held their annual congress.

Miletus is 22 km farther south and was once the largest Ionian town, with a population of about 80,000. Unfortunately little remains of it today. Miletus contains the ruins of an earlier "Mycenaean" city, which, as we will see in later chapters, was distinctly related to the Hittites. In fact, it is probably more correct to call this Mycenaean portion the remains of an early Hittite port.

Like other cities in the area, Miletus was invaded by the Ionians during the invasion of the Sea Peoples in the 12th century B.C. According to Herodotus, Ionians killed all the men in the city and married the women, who refused to speak to their new husbands. The town prospered within a few hundred years, though it was constantly being plundered by Persians, Ptolemaic Greeks, Seleucids and eventually Romans.

Today Miletus is an alarming distance from the sea, far enough to wonder if mere "silting" of the harbor would have caused this port city to be many miles from the coast. Indeed, while officially Ephesus, Priene and Miletus are said to have lost their harbors through silting, it seems clear that earth changes and a rising of this area of Turkey have contributed to creating these landlocked ports. Other ancient port cities that are now miles from the ocean include Lothal in Gujerat, India, and Ur in Iraq.

Similarly, when looking for the ancient megalithic port cities or citadels of the Hittites or the earlier Osirian world, we often need look no farther than many of the Roman and Greek cities. The sites for habitation have been settled and destroyed over thousands of years, having been inhabited by Romans, Greeks, "Sea Peoples", Mycenaeans, Hittites and even earlier cultures.

The Knights of St. John and Halicarnassus

I left the next day for the modern Turkish yacht port of Bodrum, which was the ancient city of Halicarnassus. As I sat in the bus station a young boy, a mere eight or nine years old, came through the café tables with his shoeshine kit. Dressed in greasy pants and old shoes, he was looking for shoes to shine.

He paused at my table where I sipped a tea, waiting for my bus. "Shoe shine?" he asked me in Turkish, pointing to my shoes.

I looked down at my shoes. I wore brushed suede walking shoes that simply couldn't be shined. "Sorry," I said and shook my head "no."

He looked at me dejectedly and moved on to a group of Turkish men at another table. They shooed him away. With a sorrowful expression he looked around the station for a possible customer.

My heart ached for this poor boy. He should be in school, not walking the streets in rags trying to make a few pennies. I motioned him over and then reached into my pocket and pulled out some money. I gave him 20,000 Turkish lira, about fifty cents. His eyes brightened at the money, a huge sum to a shoe-shine boy, since it was about ten times what a typical shoe shine would cost.

He settled down on his wooden box and pulled out some brushes with which he vigorously shined my shoes. His expression was now cheery, and I fought off tears of joy and sorrow for this street waif. It was a crazy world with tremendous injustice and often it was children who suffered the most.

I had made a friend for life with that shoeshine boy. He waved goodbye to me as I boarded my bus. I gave him a respectful nod and smile from the door. Building a better world for children was a goal that humanity could appreciate.

It was late in the afternoon when I reached Bodrum, a picturesque port on a peninsula in the Aegean. Bodrum was Halicarnassus in antiquity, a major seaport and the site of the Mausoleum of King Mausolus, one of the Seven Wonders of the World.

After securing a hotel room, I was out on the street walking along the port. Bodrum has kept much of its old city charm and the town center has been remarkably preserved, with small cafés, shops and street vendors. The Castle of the Knights of St. John is situated on a small peninsula overlooking the harbor and dominates the eastern skyline. The boat harbor dominates the western view.

In the summertime the Halicarnassus Disco on the edge of town pounds away until the early morning hours, and Bodrum has a reputation as a place of swinging nightlife. Turkish gigolos in cowboy boots prowl the discos and cafés and sunburned tourists sip drinks along the harbor.

But it was only early spring, the tourists had yet to show up and the town was busy whitewashing its shops in preparation for the coming tourist blitz. I had several restful days in Bodrum, visiting the site of the Mausoleum and the famous Museum of Underwater Archaeology.

After a leisurely breakfast one morning I hiked through the winding city streets to the site of the Mausoleum. It is gone now but was one of the Seven Wonders of the Ancient World. After the invasion of the Sea Peoples, this area of the coast was called Caria and the inhabitants known as Dorians.

After the Persian invasion of the 4th century B.C., Caria was ruled by a satrap named Mausolus. After his death in 353 B.C. the satrap's wife, Artemisia, undertook the construction of an enormous tomb for her husband. According to the historian Pliny the Elder the marble building was 55 meters high with a 15-meter tall pedestal-like lower building upon which were columns. These held a roof that took on the form of a stepped pyramid crowned with statues of Mausolus and Artemisia with a team of four horses.

The Mausoleum stood for 1900 years and was famous as the Mediterranean's most elaborate tomb. And even though the tomb is destroyed, the name of King Mausolus lives on as the term for an elaborate monument to the dead.

The crusader order Knights of St. John captured Bodrum in 1522 and discovered the Mausoleum. The Knights of St. John are not to be confused with the Knights Templar, a different order, often said to be at odds with the Knights of St. John. The Knights of St. John were originally called the Knights Hospitaller. Later they acquired the names Knights of St. John, Knights of Rhodes, and finally, the Knights of Malta. The order still exists today as the Knights of Malta, though they are no longer based in Malta.

According to the various tales concerning the period, the Knights uncovered the Mausoleum over a few days, admired the tomb for a bit and then retired back to their castle. During the night pirates broke into the tomb and stole the treasures of Mausolus, which had been safe as long as the tomb had remained buried. The treasure was now gone and the Knights returned the next day and dismantled the tomb to repair their castle in anticipation for the attack from Suleiman the Great.

I walked around the pit where the Mausoleum once stood. There was little to see, a few pre-Mausoleum stairways and tomb chambers, the Mausoleum's drainage system and the entrance to the underground tomb.

The Castle of St. Peter is more interesting, built by the Knights of St. John in 1402. When the heretical Christian King Tamerlane invaded Anatolia in that year, throwing the Ottoman empire off balance for a time, the Knights Hospitaller or Knights of St. John of Jerusalem based on Rhodes took the opportunity to capture Bodrum. They built the Castle of St. Peter and it defended Bodrum (not always successfully) until the end of World War I.

The castle houses Bodrum's world famous Museum of Underwater Archaeology, the result of pioneer underwater archaeologist George Bass, formerly of the University of Pennsylvania and Texas A&M.

In 1960, Bass, a young University of Pennsylvania graduate student, scraped together a small team of divers to explore a reported wreck off the coast of Turkey near Bodrum. By the end of an exhausting summer, Bass and his associates realized they had uncovered the remains of a Bronze Age merchant ship that had been smashed on the steep rocks of a narrow strait 3,200 years ago.

This is one of the oldest shipwrecks ever discovered, and it now sits in a special glass hall in the castle where its cargo of glass fragments and other objects are on display.

I was familiar with Bass and his work. Bass wrote *Archaeology Under Water*,[82] one of the early books on the subject, plus other later books such as *Archaeology Beneath the Sea*.[85] I wandered through the castle, interested in the displays on ancient ships and seafaring. The numerous amphoras recovered from around Bodrum lined an entire wall of the interior of the castle.

Bass, his books and the museum are entirely confined to the archaeology of shipwrecks. Personally, I have always been more interested in sunken cities.

It is estimated that there are over 200 known sunken cities in the Mediterranean. Since we can logically guess that these cities were not originally built beneath the sea, we are forced to assume that geological changes have put these cities underwater.

A few days later I was at the docks of Marmaris, another Turkish coastal port, opposite the island of Rhodes. The next day a ferry would be leaving for Rhodes. I looked down at the ticket in my hand. Behind me were the mountains of Anatolia and the remains of the megalithic Hittite cities. In front of me were the rolling waves of the Mediterranean. How many more Hittite megalithic cities lay beneath Homer's wine-dark sea?

The reliefs of Yazilikaya at Hattusas drawn in 1834. While the meaning of the reliefs are unclear, it is believed that they depict Hittite kings meeting with gods. Note the curled shoes, pointed hats and the double-headed eagle on the right.

The huge Lion Gate at the Hittite city of Hattusas. The lions faced outward and a huge double door, probably placed on stone balls, opened outward.

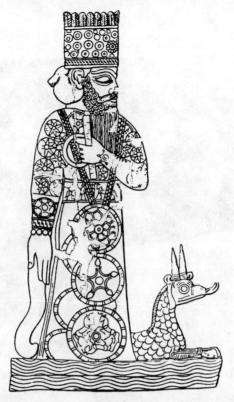

The god Marduk

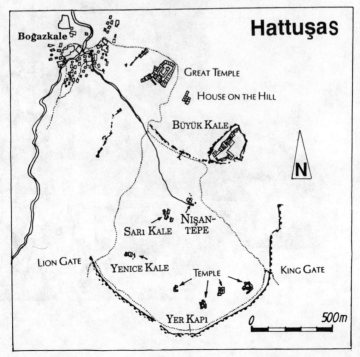

The massive Sphinx Gate at the Hittite city of Alaja Huyuk, near Hattusas.

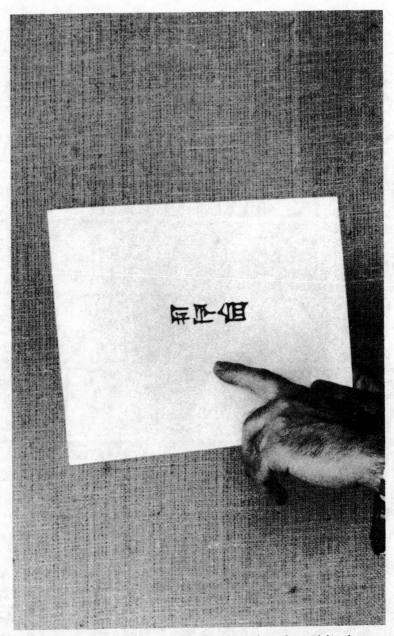

Linguist George Michanowsky maintains that this three-part cuneiform word refers to Atlantis. Michanowsky believes that the word, NI-DUK-KI, a lost land destroyed in the Flood, is the first written mention of the Atlantis concept.

An Hittite hieroglyphic inscription which is read in the boustrophedon manner, or "as the ox plows."

1947 Remains - Newberry Stone

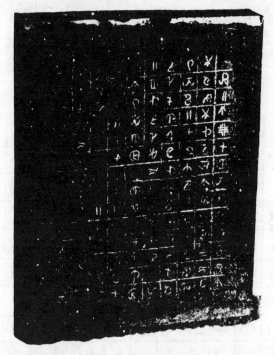

A photo of the Newberry Stone that was taken in 1898. The photo was lost and rediscovered in the archives of an upper Michigan newspaper in 1988. Thanks to Betty Sodders and her book, *Michigan Prehistory Mysteries*.

	1	2	3	4	5	6	7	8	9	10	
11	Pu	nu	si	wa	ko	se	lu	ya	ti	u	12
13	zi	ki	wa	lu	ta	li	ma	la	ta	wa	14
13	le	na	ko	li	li	pu	ri	se	ya	se	
15	sa	le	na	ko	ze	no	po	li	nu	u	16
15	mu	so	no	ze	si	to	mi	ll	lu	wa	
17	sa	mi	sa	le	i	me	sa	zo	se	po	18
17	nu	pu	le	iya	le	mo	ki	li	mi	si	
19	mo	ki	se	ze	we	(ma) (sa)	la	la	ta	pa	20
19	lo	le	o	wa	me	lu	lo	lo	po	nu	
21	no	ze	lo	sa	li	lu	ta	le	ke	re	22
21	pu	iya	li	pa	se	mu	sa	mi	o	so	
23	zi	se	le	li	ri	sa	sa	ki	na	ta	24
23	mu	sa	ki	li	lu	pu	na	sa	lo	sa	
24	(sa)	na	sa	le	zo	pa	ze	se	si	ko	

Professor Barry Fell's decipherment of the Newberry Stone. He concluded that it was written in ancient Hittite and was to be read in a boustrophedon manner. This ancient tablet seems to be irrefutable proof that the ancient Hittites were voyaging to the America.

Chapter 3

CRETE & THE AEGEAN:
The Sunken Cities
of Osiris

*At the usual period the stream from the heavens descends like
a pestilence and leaves only those of you who are destitute of
letters and education; and thus you have to begin all over again
as children; and know nothing of what happened in ancient times
either among us or among yourselves... In the first place you
remember one deluge only, whereas there were many of them...*
—Plato, *Critias*

I stepped off the ferry from Turkey onto the dock at Rhodes. The
sun was shining brightly on that spring morning as I finished the
immigration formalities and stood looking at the walls of the old
city.

"Looking for a hotel?" asked a tanned man who had been on the
ferry. He was an American named Mike.

"Sure," I said. "Do you know a nice, small hotel here in Rhodes?"

"Follow me," he replied. "I was staying here before I went to
Turkey. I'll take you to not only the best guesthouse on Rhodes, but
the cheapest as well!"

That sounded too good to be true, but I decided to follow him
anyway. So, with a couple of Japanese backpackers who were also
on the ferry, we trudged off through the winding narrow back streets
of Rhodes in search of a guesthouse.

I was a bit worried when our guide, Mike, disappeared down alleys
every once in a while, searching out the correct way to our hotel. But
eventually he did manage to find the guesthouse he was searching
for, the Hotel Apollon. The Apollon was more of a family guesthouse
than a hotel, but it was clean and cheap, just as Mike had promised.

I dropped my pack on the bed and then headed out into the city to
see the old town. Within moments I was lost in the narrow, twisting
streets that wound through the whitewashed two-story stone

91

buildings that lined the streets.

The old city of Rhodes is the largest inhabited medieval city in Europe, and its mighty fortifications are the finest examples of defensive architecture of the period. Even though Rhodes is the number one package tour destination in Greece, the city retains its medieval flair and Old World charm.

According to Greek mythology, the island of Rhodes rose out of the sea. Atlas was said to have had seven daughters by Pleionë, one of the daughters of Okeanos. These daughters were known as the Atlantides, or daughters of Atlas. The word Atlantis means "daughter of Atlas." The seven daughters were Alkyonë, Meropë, Kelaino, Elektra, Steropë, Taÿgetë, and Maia. These seven daughters of Atlas eventually became the stars of the Pleiades.

That other god of the sea, Poseidon, fell in love with Kelaino and she bore him a son named Lykos, who lived on the Isles of the Blest in the western ocean. Plato makes Poseidon the father of Atlas by Kleito, and as such, Poseidon was Atlas' father and son-in-law at the same time.

The Greek gods were a lusty bunch, and Poseidon fell in love with Halia, the sister of the Telchines, and "begat six male children and one daughter, called Rhodos, after whom the island was named."

The poet Pindar in the 5th century B.C. wrote:

> Forth from the watery deep
> blossomed the island of Rhodos,
> child of the love goddess
> Aphrodite, to be bride
> of the Sun.

The Colossus of Rhodes

Rhodes is also famous for one of the Seven Wonders of the World, the Colossus of Rhodes. Early on, Rhodes became part of the Dorian Empire at the time of the Sea Peoples' invasion of 1200 B.C. They were originally part of the Athenian League but broke away in 407 B.C.

Rhodes had to continually struggle to retain its independence. First King Mausolus of Lydia conquered Rhodes, and then in 340 B.C. Alexander the Great followed suit. After Alexander's death, Rhodes became independent again and kept its strong trading links with the new Ptolemy dynasty at Alexandria in Egypt.

As the generals of Alexander's empire fought for control of the various areas, Ptolemy I of Alexandria waged war on King Antigonus of Macedonia. Rhodes became allied with Alexandria and even won a naval battle against Antigonus.

Antigonus sent his son Demetrius to ask the Rhodians to ally themselves with him in war against Alexandria. When the island refused, an army of 40,000 soldiers with catapults attacked the island.

But Rhodes was victorious and retained its independence. It made a treaty with Antigonus and retained its trade links to Egypt. To celebrate the victory and independent island status, they built the Colossus, which represented the sun god Helios, the patron god of the three districts of Rhodes, Lindos, Ialysos, and Kemeiros.

The statue was 110 feet high (33 meters) and was said to span the harbor. It took 12 years to build the Colossus, which was made out of gigantic bolted pieces of bronze on a marble platform. The sculptor Chares of Lindos cast sections individually and then bolted them together. There were diagonal iron struts inside the statue for reinforcement.

However, the Greek geographer Strabo tells us that the Colossus was destroyed in a great earthquake that occurred in 226 B.C., only 65 years after it was built. One ancient writer maintains that houses were crushed by the massive structure when it toppled onto the city.

Strabo tells us that because an oracle had said that it would be bad luck to rebuild the statue, the people left it lying fallen in the midst of their city as a reminder to Rhodes of its days of glory. It lay abandoned until 653 A.D. when it was chopped up by the Saracens, who sold it to a merchant in Edessa. The story goes that after being shipped to Syria, it took almost 1,000 camels to convey it to its final destination.

To show the sophisticated technology in use in the ancient world we should look at another of the Seven Wonders of the World, the Pharos Lighthouse, built on the island overlooking the harbor at Alexandria. It was designed by an Asiatic Greek named Sostratus and probably dedicated in 279 B.C. It stood in a colonnaded court and had four stories. The square bottom story was pierced with many windows and contained rooms, estimated at 300, where the mechanics and attendants were housed. There was a spiral ascent—probably a double spiral—and in the center there was hydraulic machinery for raising fuel to the top.[152]

The second story was octagonal and entirely filled by the spiral ascent. Above that was the circular third story, and above that the lantern. There was a mysterious mirror at the top that was apparently a gigantic telescope lens which could be used to view ships from a distance and as a magnifying glass to direct intensified sunlight that could actually light ships on fire.

There is a legend that the Byzantine emperor wanted to attack Alexandria after the Arab conquest in 641 A.D., but was afraid because of the "magic mirror" that would detect and burn his ships. Therefore, he sent an agent who gained the Caliph's confidence and told him that beneath the lighthouse lay the treasure of Alexander the Great. The Caliph commenced demolition, and before the inhabitants of Alexandria, who knew better, could intervene, the two upper stories, including the magic mirror, had fallen into the sea.

Secret Societies and Rhodes

Rhodes was a major center for unusual activities: sciences and technical schools flourished here in the Dark Ages and in classical times. The famous Antikythera device, to be discussed shortly, was made on Rhodes. Rhodes was also the center for so-called "heretical" religious orders that challenged the power of the Vatican.

One religious order, the Knights of St. John, was founded at Amalfi, Italy, in the 11th century. They went to Jerusalem to protect and minister to the Christian pilgrims but soon extended their mission to tending to the sick and poor all over the Holy Land.

As the years went by the Knights of St. John became increasingly militant and soon joined forces with the more mystical Knights Templar and the Germanic order of the Teutonic Knights of St. Mary.

With the fall of Jerusalem in 1309, the Knights of St. John retreated first to Cyprus and then to Rhodes. Through some wheeling and dealing with the ruling Genoese admiral, Viguolo de Viguoli, the Knights became the possessors of the island of Rhodes.

As the main base for the crusaders in their struggle against the Ottoman Empire, Rhodes was a fortress, a prison, and a supply base for the ships and armies on their way to Palestine and Asia Minor. As the easternmost point of the Christian West, Rhodes was the focus for Ottoman offenses.

One interesting story concerning the Knights and their struggle against the Ottoman Empire is that of Çem, the brother of the Ottoman Sultan Beyazit, one of the sons of Mehmet Fatih, the conqueror of Istanbul.

When the Ottoman Sultan Mehmet Fatih failed to clarify the succession question of the newly powerful Ottoman Empire, in 1481, a battle between the two brothers at Bursa resulted and Çem was defeated by his brother Beyazit. Çem fled to Egypt but was denied asylum by the Mamelukes who controlled that country for the Ottomans.

Çem took the irreversible step of fleeing to Rhodes where he availed himself to the archenemies of the Ottomans, the Knights Hospitallers, or Knights of St. John. With his brother now in the hands of the crusader army, Beyazit knew he was in trouble and the Ottoman Empire had to respond quickly.

Beyazit shrewdly contacted the Knights and negotiated a contract to pay 45,000 ducats of gold annually—a huge sum at the time—in return for the imprisonment of his brother on Rhodes and later in the English Tower at the castle in Bodrum, on the Turkish mainland.

The Knights eventually handed their valuable prisoner over to the Vatican, where Çem was made an interesting offer: to lead a crusader army to recapture Istanbul (Constantinople).

To stop this final threat from his wayward brother Beyazit spared no expense, paying to the Vatican 120,000 gold ducats and a number of sacred relics from Jerusalem including the famous "Spear of Destiny." The "Spear of Destiny" was reportedly the spearhead of the Roman centurion Longinus that was used to pierce the side of Jesus while on the cross. Another artifact offered was the "sponge of the last refreshment." This was the sponge used to wet Jesus' lips while on the cross.

Legend has it that the possessor of the Spear of Destiny has the power to rule the world. Adolf Hitler believed in this and removed the spear from the Vienna museum when the Nazis took over Austria.

With this hefty payment, the Pope abandoned Çem and the plans for him to lead an army against Istanbul. Çem died alone at the Terracina prison in 1495. Rumor had it that he was eventually poisoned. Today Çem is but a footnote in history, a victim of the diplomatic maneuvers that brought the Spear of Destiny to the West.

The Knights stayed on Rhodes for 213 years, transforming the city into a mighty fortress with 12-meter thick walls. They withstood two Muslim offenses in 1444 and 1480, but in 1522 the Sultan Suleiman the Magnificent staged a massive attack with 200,000 troops.

A mere 600 Knights with 1,000 mercenaries and 6,000 Rhodians eventually surrendered after a long siege.

I walked up the cobblestoned Avenue of the Knights to the Grand Master's Palace and then to the Archaeological Museum, a former hospital of the Knights now housing Rhodes' rather meager collection.

My evenings in Rhodes were spent at Popeye's Bar, nursing an Amstel beer and discussing the life of travel with several British fellows who preferred the easygoing life of Rhodes to the factory life of Manchester or Liverpool.

To my surprise one night, Harry, an old friend from Arizona, suddenly showed up at the bar, still with his long black hair and curly beard.

"David!" he cried, seeing me at a table against the far side of the room.

"Harry, what are you doing here?" I asked. I had not seen Harry for over a year.

"I'm living here on Rhodes for a while," he said, pulling up a chair and setting down his glass of ouzo. "You know I like the warm weather. This is about as far south in Europe as one can go, so I've been spending the winter and spring here in Rhodes. What are you doing here?"

"Oh, the usual stuff, you know, searching for Atlantis, lost cities, ancient mysteries and whatnot."

"Atlantis?" Harry laughed, taking a slug of his drink. "Ha, ha. Well, you've come to the right place. Atlantis is all around us. This is Atlantis."

"How so?" I asked him.

"Well, when the island of Thera blew up around 1450 B.C. it destroyed Atlantis. That's what Greeks usually think."

"Oh, that story," I said. "Sure, I've heard that one before. But have you heard about the Osirian civilization?"

Harry looked past his thick black beard down at his cloudy glass of ouzo. "You mean Osiris and Isis?"

"Yes," I said, and I told him the story of the Osirian civilization beneath the Mediterranean.

"Well, I can believe that," said Harry. "In fact, I live in a house with a huge collection of books on archaeology and sunken cities in the Mediterranean. Let's go check it out."

We were off through the moonlit backstreets of Rhodes to a house near the back wall of the city. Once there Harry introduced me to his neighbor Spiros, a Canadian Greek now living on Rhodes.

His house was like an antiquarian bookstore. Harry immediately pulled a volume off the shelf and said, "I told David that you had a good collection of underwater archaeology books."

"Ah," said Spiros, pulling another book from the shelf, "have you read *4000 Years Under the Sea* by Diolé?"

We poured over books for the rest of the evening and I took notes. *4000 Years Under the Sea*[87] was first published in France in 1952 and in 1954 in English. The French archaeologist Philipe Diolé gives a lively account of dives to underwater cities of Greece, Algeria, Tunisia and France. The title refers to the early Phoenician port of Cherchel underwater off the coast of Algeria.

Spiros had a copy of George Bass's classic book *Archaeology Under Water*.[82] Published in 1966, the book is a well-illustrated treatise on methodology in underwater excavation.

"Ah, this is one of the best, *Under The Mediterranean*[84] by Honoré Frost," said Spiros, handing me another book. Honoré Frost was a British-Cypriot adventuress and diver who travelled to Tyre and Byblos in Lebanon and throughout the Mediterranean.

Like many of the authors on sunken cities of the Mediterranean,

Frost begins with the megalithic ports of Tyre and Byblos on the Lebanese coast. Both ports are submerged today. Byblos was the ancient Ugarit of the Hittite Empire period circa 4,000 B.C.

Cities In the Sea by Nicholas Flemming[86] (1971) also explores Tyre and Sidon, and Iasos. His most important discovery is the gigantic rock-cut street with rooms that run down to the sea at Phycus. Flemming's book has some particularly interesting photos of a submerged Mycenaean city known as Elaphonisos off the southern edge of the Pelaponnesse.

Secrets of the Bible Seas[90] (1985) is by Alexander Flinder, another British archaeologist with an enthusiasm for sunken cities in the Middle East. Flinder spent time at Eilat looking for King Solomon's famous port for his ships that sailed to Ophir. The journey to Ophir, somewhere to the east, was a three-year journey on a fabulous trading expedition for gold.

Flinder looks at submerged ruins at Caesarea and Akko along the present coast of Israel. He also details the submerged cities of Tyre and the Phoenician double harbor at Athlit.

Spiros' collection boasted yet another classic, *Marine Archaeology*,[89] published in 1966. With a foreword by Jacques Cousteau, this Anglo-French compilation on underwater archaeology covers the fascinating subject of "Ports, Harbours, and Other Submerged Sites" in chapter 5. The book features photos and diagrams of the amazing rock-carved city of Apollonia at Phycus in Lebanon.

"Perhaps the best of them all," said Spiros, "is this one by Hans-Wolf Rackl. *Diving Into the Past*[83] was published in 1964 and has a chapter entitled "Sunken Cities." Rackl begins with a discussion of Tyre, Apollonia, and Syracuse and then reports on lesser-known sites like Epidauros in the Adriatic and Baia on the west coast of Italy near Naples.

"Rackl closes his chapter on sunken cities with a discussion of Pastor Spanuth's theories of Atlantis and the sunken cities of the Helgoland in the North Sea."

"You've got a great collection of books," I said to Spiros, toasting him with a glass of ouzo.

Back at the Apollon Hotel I looked up at the ceiling from my bed. Sometimes the search for Atlantis led one to a room full of books. It was a pleasant thought.

Reading made Don Quixote a gentleman.
Believing what he read made him mad.
—George Bernard Shaw

The next few days were spent cruising along the Dodecanese Islands, heading for the Cyclades Islands. My first stop was at the island of Kos, north of Rhodes.

I stopped briefly, interested in the neolithic sites discovered on the island. By Mycenaean times so many people inhabited the island that they managed to muster 30 ships for the Trojan War.

Kos was a powerful ally of Rhodes in the 7th and 6th centuries B.C. but was destroyed in an earthquake in 477 B.C. Kos recovered, joined the Delian League and became the birthplace of Hippocrates, the father of modern medicine (460-377 B.C.).

Another famous son of Kos was Ptolemy II of Egypt who secured the protection of Kos by Egypt after the dissolution of Alexander the Great's empire.

Just farther north of Kos is the island of Patmos, a small island where in 95 A.D. St. John the Divine was banished from Ephesus by the pagan Roman emperor Domitian. While residing in a cave in the interior of the island, St. John wrote the Book of Revelations.

As he looked out over the Aegean, St. John had the visions of the Four Horsemen of the Apocalypse and the ensuing plagues, earthquakes and wars of Armageddon of the so-called Endtimes. In his apocalpytic visions he saw a final battle of the warring factions of the Middle East and the Mediterranean, a terrible war that was centered upon Israel, and called it the final battle of Meggido fortress, or *Armageddon.*

In 1088 the Blessed Christodoulos, an abbot who came from Asia Minor to Patmos, obtained permission from the Byzantine Emperor Alexis I Commenus to build a monastery to commemorate St. John. Because of pirate raids the monastery looks more like a fortified castle.

I continued my Aegean odyssey by arriving at Mykonos in the Cyclades. Mykonos is one of the most sophisticated and expensive islands in Greece, famous for its nightlife and as the gay capital of Greece.

I was stopping on my way to Delos, the legendary center of the Cyclades Islands and birthplace of the god Apollo. After Athens had defeated the Persians in 477 B.C., they established the Delian League. Delos became a sacred precinct where the treasury was located, and it was decreed that no one could be born or could die on the island. It also became a major religious pilgrimage center.

With the bright spring Aegean sun shining down on me, I hopped by ship from island to island, landing on the island of Ios early one morning. I trudged up the steep steps to Ios Village and plopped my backpack down on a whitewashed wall next to a small grocery store.

Two Australian women, Penny and Shelly, were sitting on the wall drinking beer with two German guys. They were clearly drunk.

"You're up early," I said, taking a seat on the wall. The sun was just coming up over the sea.

"Up early?" laughed Penny, a tall, thin blonde in a blue jean jacket. "We're up late! We've been up all night!"

One of the Germans reached in a bag and offered me a beer. I took a drink of water from my canteen instead.

Shops started to open as did the tourist office opposite us on the main square. Soon I procured a room in a family guesthouse and headed for the beaches of Ios.

I found out later that Ios was the notorious party island where young people danced and drank all night at parties on the beach or at the various discos and bars in the village which spread up the steep mountainside and narrow streets of the town.

I ran into Penny and Shelly again at a restaurant in the village that night and was invited to join them and some friends.

Shelly poured me a glass of wine and said, "Are you over 26? You know, no one over 26 is supposed to come to this island."

"Really?" I said in mock shock. "Is that the law?"

"Orders of the Tourist Police," laughed Shelly. "You are over 26, right?"

"Well, I guess I am," I admitted. "But I'm still youthful in spirit. I think I'm allowed to come to Ios... at least for a while."

"Ha, ha," said Penny, "we'll see what you are made of. Ios is not for old farts who lack energy. This island is for the young and energetic!"

I finished my glass of wine. "Well, I'll agree to test myself, with your permission," I said.

"Very well," said Shelly, looking at her watch. "It's after midnight, that means we can go to the Flame Bar and dance. Let's go!"

The rest of the night was something of a blur. I remember dancing at the Flame Bar—a tall can of Amstel beer in my hand, the room packed wall-to-wall with sweaty bodies jumping up and down to the latest dance music. A beer can was glued to every fist. Once one got into a comfortable spot on the dance floor it was exceedingly difficult to get across the room to either the bar, the toilet or the door.

At one point I gave up on trying to make it to the toilet so I made a desperate attempt to reach the door. Once outside, I headed for my room and not back to the bar. Late the next morning I woke up with my head pounding. "What hit me?" I muttered to myself.

I washed my face and sat on the edge of my bed. One night in Ios was all I could take. I packed my backpack and left the hotel. There was a boat leaving for the island of Thera at 1:00 in the afternoon. My search for Atlantis would continue on a different island.

Thera and the Lost Continent of Atlantis

It was late afternoon when the ferry landed at the base of the steep cliffs that make up the inner shore of Thera, the southernmost of the Cyclades Islands. Also known by its Italian name of Santorini, Thera is now the focal point of many theories on Atlantis.

Hotel owners were there to meet the ferry and I struck a deal with one for a room with a view, and the owner suddenly whisked a Finnish couple and me into a minivan and up the winding road to the top of the cliffs.

By sunset I was sitting on the terrace of the Atlantis Hotel sipping a glass of Atlantis-brand wine, watching the sun set over the crater of the ancient volcano that had exploded around 1450 B.C.

The sun was a great ball of orange fire in the sky as I took another sip and mused over the commercialization of Atlantis on this small volcanic island. Indeed, Atlantis was big business here. The major hotel was the Atlantis Hotel, and wines were named after Atlantis, along with gift shops, tour agencies and snack bars.

A multimillion-dollar tourist industry was based on the lost continent, but was this really Atlantis?

Theories have abounded for nearly a hundred years now that the massive volcanic explosion in the 15th century B.C. that destroyed this island is somehow connected to the Atlantis question. In 1939 the director of the Greek Archaeological Service, Spyridon Marinatos, surmised that this eruption caused the downfall of Minoan Crete by drowning the people of the coastal cities with a tsunami and smothering the inland farms under ash.

In the 1960s, Angelos Galanopoulos, a Greek seismologist, postulated a connection between the eruption of Thera and Plato's Atlantis. Galanopoulos theorized that Thera was Atlantis and that discrepancies between the time and dimensions of Atlantis and the small island of Thera could be explained by assuming that the numbers had been miscalculated by a factor of ten.

By this theory (a popular one in many Atlantis arguments) Atlantis would then have been ten times smaller and ten times more recent than Plato had stated. With the size and age of Atlantis shrunk considerably, Atlantis could be forced to fit into the Minoan-Thera mold, much like a square peg in a round hole.

Professor Galanopoulos actually believed that the small island of Thera was Atlantis, and superimposed a map of the concentric canals as described by Plato on the center of the island. In this belief, the royal city of Atlantis had an active volcano in its center, an unlikely building concept for any city. Later authors were to combine Thera with Minoan Crete into a more holistic concept of the Atlantis-in-the-Aegean theory.

In 1969 the Irish classicist J.V. Luce brought out *The End of Atlantis*,[78] which details the argument for the Thera-and-Crete-as-Atlantis theory. Luce begins his book with a discussion of Plato and Atlantis, and like many classical scholars, decides against an Atlantic island-continent as described by Plato from Egyptian sources. Luce then builds on the Minoan hypothesis and the new evidence for the Thera explosion coupled with the latest carbon dating techniques that date the explosion at about 1450 or 1470 B.C.

Luce makes the argument that Plato did base his Atlantis on a real catastrophe, that of the Thera explosion, and that Plato did indeed get his information from garbled Egyptian sources who were really talking about the Minoan empire of Crete all along. Plato places the island in the Atlantic because it would make the story more exciting, he reasoned.

Luce credits a certain K.T. Frost as the first archaeologist to make the connection between Crete and Atlantis. Frost was on the staff of Queen's University in Belfast when he published his theory, anonymously, in an article entitled "The Lost Continent" in *The Times* of London on February 19, 1909. According to Luce he later argued his case in greater detail in an article, "The Critias and Minoan Crete," published in the *Journal of Hellenic Studies*. In this article Frost admitted to authoring the earlier *Times* article.[78]

However, Frost may not have been the first to suggest that Crete was actually Atlantis. The Egyptologist James Baikie proposed that Crete was Atlantis in 1900. In that same year the explorer E. S. Balch also suggested Crete as the source for the legend.[1]

Frost proposed Crete in 1909 and another classical scholar, Walter Leaf, seconded this in 1915. In 1929 the archaeologist R.V.D. Magoffin also jumped on the Crete bandwagon. In the last 30 years the concept has gained even more popularity.

Frost's article came on the heels of the discovery of Knossos and historians were just beginning to realize how important Crete had been. Said Frost in his original article, "...Crete was the center of a great empire whose trade and influence extended from the North Adriatic to Tel el Amarna and from Sicily to Syria. The whole seaborne trade between Europe, Asia, and Africa was in Cretan hands, and the legends of Theseus seem to show that the Minoans dominated the Greek islands and the coasts of Attica... The Minoan civilization was essentially Mediterranean, and is most sharply distinguished from any that arose in Egypt or the East. ...The Minoan realm, therefore, was a vast and ancient power which was united by the same sea which divided it from other nations, so that it seemed to be a separate continent with a genius of its own.

"As a political and commercial force, therefore, Knossos and its allied cities were swept away just when they seemed strongest and safest. It was as if the whole kingdom had sunk in the sea, as if the tale of Atlantis were true."[78]

It is interesting to note that historians, archaeologists and geologists were so conservative in the early 1900s that Frost was afraid to claim authorship of his first paper, apparently fearing ridicule from his academy colleagues. By the 1950s when *Lost Continents* was written, things had not changed much.

In the late '60s Atlantis in the Aegean surfaced, if you'll pardon the expression, again in the book *Voyage To Atlantis*[34] by James Mavor Jr., first published in 1969. Mavor, an American oceanographic engineer from Woods Hole Oceanographic Institution, gives the same evidence of the volcanic eruption (circa 1650 B.C., according to him) that not only destroyed the Minoan civilization on Thera but affected civilizations all over the eastern Mediterranean.

Mavor, like Galanopoulos, theorizes that Thera was Atlantis, whereas others like Frost had suggested Crete as the location of Atlantis. Certainly one could say that Crete was by far the more powerful island, capable of waging war on the Greek mainland, unlike Thera. Much of the book is spent looking at the Minoan ruins of Akrotiri and analyzing the explosion of the volcano.

In an interesting epilogue, Mavor gives a long list of myths and folktales that may recall the eruption of Thera. Some of these are:

The Biblical books of Genesis, Exodus, Kings, Jeremiah, Ezekiel, Zephaniah, Amos, and Revelations
Jason and the Argonauts
Deucalion's flood
Hippolytus of Euripedes
Phaedra of Seneca
The Hurrian Song of Ullikummi
Hesiod's war between Zeus and the Titans
Zeus' war with Typhon
The Babylonian Utnapishtim
Phaethon
Flooding of the Thracian plain by Poseidon
Flooding of the Argive plain by Poseidon
Plutarch's report of flooding of the Lycean plain
Strabo's reports of flooding around Troy
Diodorus' report of a great flood at Rhodes
Diodorus' report of a flood at Samothrace
Floating island of Greek legend: Asterie-Delos
Phaecians of Homer's Odyssey[34]

Despite the many classical texts concerning floods and disasters, it seems unlikely that all of them are connected with the explosion of Thera. Mavor's concept of geological changes is that of the typical uniformitarian geologist: earth changes are rare, happening slowly over millions of years with the occasional volcanic explosion such as Thera or Krakatoa happening every few thousand years to create legends of localized disasters.

The fact that the Mediterranean is continually wracked by powerful earthquakes and tidal waves every few hundred years (witness the over 200 known sunken cities) seems to escape him.

Luce in *The End of Atlantis* sums up the argument that Thera and Crete are Atlantis, destroyed by the explosion of Thera, by saying that Egypt was vague about geography and other countries: "On the whole, the Egyptians of the Bronze Age knew little and cared less about foreign countries. They were not great travellers or seafarers, and their geographical horizons were quite restricted. Their world was bounded by Nubia and Punt (Eritrea?) to the south, by the Euphrates on the east, and by the Libyan desert tribes on the west. They knew something of Cyprus, the south coast of Turkey, and Crete from long established trading connections."[78]

This is the isolationist historical view that is typical of the old reasoning. Though Solon, quoting Egyptian texts, clearly says that Atlantis is outside the Mediterranean, historians discount this because, in their view, Egyptians simply couldn't have even known that the Atlantic Ocean existed, nor even cared.

We are talking of a society virtually one step removed from that of a caveman—one that barely knew what lay over the horizon. Though this is the Egypt many Egyptologists seem to believe in, it is not in accord with actual history.

The Egyptians had a large navy, one that apparently travelled all over the world. This navy was often a hired one, however. The Egyptians were well known for hiring Libyan (North African) and Phoenician seamen to go on long trading voyages.

The Phoenicians were masters of the sea, knew the routes well, and lived among the cedars of Lebanon, the finest boat-building wood to be found in the Mediterranean. The Egyptians built reed boats originally, much like the Sumerians and the Lake Titicaca Indians of Bolivia.

Phoenician and Libyan trading vessels, complete with a miniature army, could be hired for a price, and an Egyptian merchant or diplomat would be the special passenger. He would be a scribe, an educated man, and would probably be accompanied by part of his family and servants.

King Solomon made a similar deal with the Phoenicians in his effort to gather gold and exotic goods on the three-year voyage to Ophir and back.

Egypt also had an important geographical feature that other countries in the Mediterranean did not—access to a port on the Red Sea for travels eastward as well as ports on the Mediterranean for travel westward.

Only King Solomon's Israel had the same advantage of ports on two oceans. Both Egypt and Israel could send trading vessels direct to Spain, Crete, Arabia or India.

In fact, it would seem that Punt, the land of gold, is much farther away than Arabia or Somalia as often guessed at by historians. Punt must be at least as far away as Southern Africa, Indonesia or Australia. Historians have cited evidence of the Egyptians making voyages across the Pacific to South America and Hawaii (see my book *Lost Cities of Ancient Lemuria & the Pacific*[59]).

〰〰〰〰〰𓂀〰〰〰〰〰

Thera Is Not Atlantis

The theory that the cataclysm that befell the Aegean island of Thera is the inspiration for the tale of the lost continent of Atlantis does not give full credit to Egyptian and Greek knowledge. The Egyptians knew where Crete was and where the Atlantic was. They knew how to keep accurate calendars and did so for thousands of years. They kept huge libraries of books and maps and educated people from foreign countries often came to study in their universities.

When the Egyptian priests of Saïs told Solon that the Greeks are like young children who do not know their ancient past, they meant it. Even though faced with the overwhelming evidence of sophisticated, far-ranging civilizations in the past, many archaeologists still promote the idea that Egypt knew little of what was beyond its borders.

The prolific science writer Isaac Asimov summed up this attitude in the introduction to the book *Atlantis Illustrated.*[157] Says Asimov, "For over a thousand years the tale of that immense catastrophe lived on in the minds of the people of the eastern Mediterranean. When, about 380 B.C., the Greek philosopher Plato wished to tell a story of how a great civilization came to be destroyed, he told the tale of Thera.

"However, the tale was expanded. The Aegean Sea seemed too small an arena for such a cataclysm in a day when the horizons of geography had expanded far beyond ancient Cretan times. Plato therefore imagined the exploding island to have been far larger, far more powerful, and far more magnificent than Thera had been. And he placed the Pillars of Hercules in the vague mists of the unknown Atlantic Ocean, where magnificence has room to spread itself."[157]

Asimov is essentially saying that Plato was ignorant, as were all Mediterraneans of their day, of the world outside of the Mediterranean, and therefore elaborated on a nearby catastrophe that was lost to the history of the time.

So here we see a popular science-fiction writer who can imagine himself and his protagonists traversing the far reaches of the universe and exploring its secrets, yet assuming that such great philosophers and thinkers as Plato or his contemporaries (not to mention those before him) could not imagine beyond the near shores of their small country.

Even though Plato was painfully specific about where his lost civilization was, how large it was, and the various accomplishments it had achieved, Asimov simply cannot believe that ancient man could ever have known of a transatlantic world—whether destroyed or not.

~~~~~~~~~~👁~~~~~~~~~~

I spent several days in Thera, drinking Atlantis wine among the whitewashed buildings and watching the spectacular views over the volcanic crater and cliffs of the island. Greek Easter was happening the weekend that I was on the island, and at midnight the Easter Mass was celebrated with a procession of candles through the town while children shot fireworks in the air.

I rented a motorbike and rode around the island, up to the northern village of Oia, suspended on a cliff above the sea. I motored back to the main town of Fira to see the sunset and then the next day went to the other side of the island where I was fortunate to visit the archaeological site of Akrotiri. The digs were supposed to be closed over the Greek Easter weekend, but I was lucky to find an American tour group that had come on a cruise ship. The site had been opened for them, and I was allowed to visit with the group.

Ancient Akrotiri was a Minoan outpost dated to the 16th century B.C. It was covered with volcanic ash when the volcano blew up. Curiously, no skeletons or treasures were ever discovered at the site, indicating that the inhabitants apparently had sufficient warning to take their belongings and leave the island before the cataclysmic explosion.

The Greek archaeologist Spyridon Marinatos began excavations at Akrotiri in 1967 but was unfortunately killed in an accident at the site in 1974 when he fell from one of the walls. His excavations uncovered an ancient city with Minoan-type frescoes that was remarkably well preserved beneath the volcanic ash—the best preserved prehistoric settlement in the Aegean.

Today the excavation is covered with a large sheet-metal roof and the entire tour takes less than an hour. I walked with the American group that followed obediently as the tour guide took them through the streets of the partly excavated town.

One lady in a straw hat asked in a Georgia accent, "Are you on our tour?"

"No, ma'am," I replied. "I'm an archaeologist and a writer. I just happen to be here today, and I'm glad to be able to join your group. The site is supposed to be closed, so I'm just sneaking along for the ride."

As we finished the tour a man who had been standing nearby suddenly asked me, "If you're an archaeologist, can I ask you a question?"

"Sure," I said, "go ahead."

"Is this place really Atlantis, like they say it is? Everywhere I look everything on this island is named Atlantis. Is this the city of Atlantis?" He waved his arm in a sweeping motion at the walls and streets around us.

I thought for a moment, not sure what to say. "Well, I don't know what your tour guide told you," I told him, "but I don't think that the ancient city of Akrotiri was Atlantis. It is a popular belief around the island, I admit, but Plato clearly said that Atlantis was in the Atlantic, where you'd expect."

He looked at me and nodded. "Thank you," he said and then turned to the lady in the straw hat. "You see, Marge," he said to her, "I told you this wasn't Atlantis."

The lady in the straw hat cast me a quick look. "Well, that's what the tour conductor told us," she said. "They wouldn't lie to us. I'm telling you, Herb, this is Atlantis."

As I stood at the exit gate of the city and looked back into the ruins I could hear the couple still arguing about whether the site was Atlantis or not. Atlantis has caused controversy everywhere, it seems.

Elephants and an Atlantean "Jurassic Park"

A day later I was taking a hydrofoil from Thera to the port of Iraklion in Crete. It was a three-hour trip to Crete and I took out of my bag a book I had bought at Thera. It was *Unearthing Atlantis*[55] by Charles Pellegrino. Pellegrino's book was published in 1991 with a foreword by Arthur C. Clarke. It is largely a rehash of J.V. Luce's 1969 book, *Lost Atlantis*.

Pellegrino, with the aid of several nice maps, reiterates the standard arguments for Crete and Thera being the models for Atlantis, and Plato's text an imaginative fiction based on erroneous memories of the volcanic explosion and the sudden loss of Cretan power. Pellegrino places the date at 1650 B.C.

The book takes us on a tour through Akrotiri and has some interesting maps showing the tsunami funnels of Greece and Turkey that would have been devastated by the shock wave of the volcanic explosion. A tsunami is a huge tidal wave created by the shock wave of an earthquake. A tsunami funnel is where several coastal peninsulas focus the tidal wave into a narrow bay or river valley. The resulting tidal wave is then higher and more devastating than usual.

The Greek tsunami funnel is in the Peloponnese leading to the Argolid plain which was destroyed in a tidal wave. The Turkish tsunami funnel would have devastated an area of the west coast of Turkey near ancient Halicarnassus.

But otherwise, Pellegrino paints the same tired picture of a Minoan empire on Thera and Crete around 2000 B.C. that had some limited contact with Egypt and other ports in the eastern Mediterranean. Thera in the year 6202 B.C., says Pellegrino, in the sort of time-capsule literary style that he uses in much of the book, was uninhabited and most people "lived and died in the same mudwalled hut, never venturing farther afield than seven miles."[55]

There is no room for a sophisticated empire of Atlantis in 9000 B.C. in Pellegrino's history of "Atlantis." Without even discussing such mysteries as Malta, sunken cities, or Atlantic seafaring, Pellegrino assures us that mankind was just beginning to step out of the Stone Age and make pottery in 6000 B.C.

In one interesting section, Pellegrino admits that Plato also described Atlantis as being an island with a lot of elephants though the Minoans did not have elephants. That Atlantis was an island with many elephants is a bit of Atlantis criteria that has confounded many searchers for the lost civilization, as we shall see.

In the *Critias* Plato tells us about the strange metal *orichalc* or orichalcum (literally "mountain bronze") and elephants: "For because of the greatness of their empire many things were brought to them from foreign countries, and the island itself provided much of what was required by them for the uses of life. In the first place, they dug out of the earth whatever was to be found there, mineral as well as metal, and that which is only a name and was then something more than a name, orichalc, was dug out of the earth in many parts of the island, and except gold was then the most precious of metals. There was an abundance of wood for carpenter's work and sufficient maintenance for tame and wild animals.

"Moreover there were a great number of elephants in the island, and there was provision for animals of every kind, both for those that live in lakes and marshes and rivers and also for those that live in mountains and on plains, and therefore for the animal that is the largest and most voracious of them all. Also whatever fragrant things there are in the earth, whether roots, or herbage, or woods, or distilling drops of flowers and fruits, grew and thrived in that land; and again, the cultivated fruit of the earth, both the dry edible fruit and other species of food that we call by the general names of vegetables."

Plato makes a remark that has so far been missed even by the most far-out Atlantis scholars. In the paragraph above Plato says that Atlantis kept what would apparently be parks and nature preserves on the island for every animal no matter how large, in an apparent attempt to create a sort of super-nature park "for the animal that is the largest and most voracious of them all."

Elephants are already mentioned in the text, so we can assume that it is something else that is being referred to. What is this animal that is the largest and most voracious of them all? Could it be the same animal as the dragon at the Ishtar Gate in Babylon? If that were the case, we would have a literal "Jurassic Park"-type nature preserve in Atlantis. In this coastal valley, cut off from the rest of the island, there may have been an antediluvian zoo with real dinosaurs.

These dinosaurs may have been cloned or otherwise raised from eggs. On the other hand, dinosaurs may have still existed in remote parts of the world circa 15,000 B.C. and a few choice specimens, like the dragon of the Ishtar Gate, may have been kept in Atlantis.

The famous "sleeping prophet," Edgar Cayce, mentioned in eight of his thousands of readings that there was a world council during the time of Atlantis that was held to cope with the problem of wild animals, including dinosaurs.[120]

Said one of the curious readings, "...[they] gathered to rid the earth of enormous animals which overran the earth, but ice, nature, God, changed the poles and the animals were destroyed, though man attempted it at the time." (5249-1; June 12, 1944)

Another said, "—when Poseidian land [Atlantis] was greater in power, there was the meeting called for those of many lands to determine means and manners in which there would be control of the animals that were destructive to many lands. [This person] guided the ships that sailed both in the air and under the water, also maker of that which produced the elevators and connecting tubes that were used by compressed air and steam and the metals in their emanations—especially as to things controlled by the facet for the radiation activity of the sun on metals and control of such and airships." (2157-1; March 27, 1940)

Cayce's readings, for what they are worth, tell us that mankind had a worldwide meeting to discuss ways of removing giant lizards, snakes and other predators, possibly even dinosaurs, which were still in abundance 15,000 years ago. Atlantis also had, according to Edgar Cayce, zeppelin-type anti-gravity aircraft that drew power from Nikola Tesla-type power stations. Did Cayce's Atlanteans plan to use death-rays to wipe out pesky dinosaurs? A fascinating thought! But instead of having to hunt dinosaurs into extinction, a cataclysmic pole shift does the job for them and most of the problem animals are killed, becoming essentially extinct.

The whole scenario is worthy of a 1940s action serial, with their buzzing airships, ray guns and dinosaurs to battle. This wasn't everyone's vision of Atlantis, but it was an exciting version, nonetheless!

The time will come when diligent research over long periods will bring to light things which now lie hidden... Many discoveries are reserved for ages still to come, when memories of us will have been effaced. Our universe is a sorry little affair unless it has something for every age to investigate. Nature does not reveal her mysteries once and for all.
—Seneca, *Natural Questions*, Book 7, 1st century A.D.

Crete and the Bull From the Sea

Stepping off of the hydrofoil onto the dock at the port of Iraklion, I stood with my pack on my back looking around at the fishing boats and fishmongers. A fisherman in his black, narrow-brimmed hat took a live octopus in one hand and turned it inside out, instantly killing it. It would end up on someone's plate at a nearby restaurant.

"Are you going to the youth hostel?" asked a tall, dark-haired young man with a wispy beard. "That's where I'm heading. I'll show you the way if you want."

I thanked him and followed him through the streets to the youth hostel. I had been by myself on Thera for several days, and I thought that it might be nice to meet some other travellers.

My new friend was a Dutch college student named Killy. He had been going to school in Athens, and this was his second time to Crete. At the youth hostel we were both given a bed in a room with six bunk beds. There were no pillows or sheets, and the toilets, as in many of the cheap Greek hostels, were small, dirty and in various stages of disrepair.

Killy and I went out to the main square of Iraklion where sidewalk pizzerias served their fare to tourists and Greeks.

It was late when we returned to the hostel and I quickly fell asleep in my bunk. I awoke in the middle of the night to someone vomiting in the toilet next door. I tossed and turned in my bunk, promising myself that I would get a hotel room the next day.

At dawn, still tired from the night before, I packed my bag, checked out of the hostel and headed up to the square where I got a room at a pension for 12 dollars a night. I met Killy for breakfast and then the two of us took a local bus to the famous palace of Knossos.

The sprawling "palace" of Knossos is Crete's number one tourist attraction and, for archaeologists, contains important evidence that Crete was once a highly developed civilization in antiquity.

For over 100 years, the workers in the fields around the hill of Ephala, some 5 km. south of Iraklion, had uncovered various objects as they tilled the soil. Many of the objects were small seal stones with curious designs which the local people made into necklaces.

Then in 1878 a local merchant, Minos Kalokairinos, began to excavate the site and the traces of an ancient city came to light. The German archaeologist Heinrich Schliemann, who had discovered Troy on the basis of Homer's description in the *Iliad*, was the first archaeologist to attempt to uncover Knossos.

However, Schliemann wanted to buy the area around Knossos in 1886 but could not agree on a price with Kalokairinos. Then the British archaeologist Arthur Evans arrived in 1894 and eventually acquired the site in 1900.

When the first excavations began, Knossos was buried under 10 meters of soil. The buildings which were uncovered had suffered the effects of countless earthquakes over the centuries, and were a mass of collapsed stonework. Once uncovered, the soft gypsum stone which had been used in many parts of the palace needed protection against the elements, otherwise it would have quickly deteriorated.

Evans restored the palace, replacing the wooden columns with concrete ones, and continued to work on the restoration for 40 years. Estimates of the number of people who lived at Knossos run from 30,000 to 82,000, and the fact that Knossos is not a fortified structure is said to be evidence of the peace and tranquility that the Minoans enjoyed on their island home. The Minoans are said to have needed no weapons of war, nor did they glorify heroic deeds on distant battlefields.

That the palace of Knossos was an undefended, unfortified citadel is just one of the many mysteries surrounding this ancient city. The archaeological writer Victor J. Kean sums these up in his small book, *Crete: New Light On Old Mysteries*.[137] "These and many other aspects of Minoan life were so divorced from the European cultures, that scholars still struggle to find acceptable explanations for some of the objects that have been found. Bronze double-axes of many different sizes with thin fragile blades. Large areas for ceremonial washing with no supply of water or drainage facilities. Small statuettes depicting half-clothed females, their arms entwined with snakes. Scenes of dangerous rituals combining athletic prowess in the company of fearsome looking bulls."

As in many Atlantis themes, the bull is important in Cretan mythology. The myth goes that Zeus, looking down from the highest mountain of Crete, sees the beautiful Phoenician princess Europa on a distant shore. She is picking flowers and suddenly sees a huge bull in front of her.

The bull comes up to her in a friendly way and she strokes it. The bull suddenly jumps up, with Europa now clutching his back, and runs for the sea. Terrified, Europa holds on as the bull plunges into the sea and swims to Crete. It comes ashore at the sandy bay of Matala on Crete, where the bull suddenly becomes Zeus.

Europa is shocked initially but then retires to the nearby Messara Plain where she and Zeus spend the night together. From their union Europa gives birth to three sons: Sarpedon, Radamanthis and Minos.

Zeus goes on to other things and Europa marries the king of Crete, Astarios, who adopts her three children. As a youth, Minos would go to the mountain cave where Zeus' legendary birth took place. Zeus then comes to his son Minos and for nine years Zeus gives him instruction in kingship and finally gives him a number of tablets of laws. The similarity between this tale and the story of Moses is another example of the many comparisons between the Bible and ancient mythology.

Thus equipped with the tablets and special education from Zeus, Minos came down from the mountains, quickly drove out his two brothers and became king of Crete. With the help of a mighty fleet, he established sovereignty over the whole of the Mediterranean, making Crete master of the seas.

To discourage any other Cretan pretenders to the throne, Minos begs for a miracle from his uncle, Poseidon. This miracle is to be a white bull that will rise up from the ocean waves. To show his gratitude, he would then sacrifice the bull. However, the bull that comes ashore is so incredibly beautiful and strong that Minos causes him to disappear among his own herd under cover of darkness and sacrifices another more delicate bull. Of course, Poseidon notices this substitution and takes revenge by causing Pasiphae, the lustful wife of Minos, to fall in love with the white bull.

Pasiphae turns to the inventor Daedalus, who is from Athens, but living in Crete, to help her in her lust for the bull. Daedalus builds her a wooden frame over which he stretches the hide of a cow.

Pasiphae is inside the frame when the bull mounts the artificial cow and thus conceives the monster who is half man and half bull—the Minotaur.

King Minos is outraged but spares the child and has Daedalus build the famed labyrinth with angled false entrances, countless rooms, and dark corners. The mutant Minotaur must live in this underground labyrinth, and because Minos has won a war with Athens, Athens must send seven young men and seven young women as sacrifice tribute to Crete every nine years.

Then, Theseus, the young son of King Aegeus, decides to kill the Minotaur and put an end to the tribute from Athens. While on Crete Theseus falls in love with Ariadne, the daughter of Minos, who is betrothed to the god Dionysus. On Daedalus' advice Ariadne gives Theseus a ball of string to take into the labyrinth so that he can find his way out again.

Theseus defeats the Minotaur inside the labyrinth and emerges with the head of the monster in his hands. With Ariadne, he escapes to the port where he destroys the keels of all the Minoan ships and then sets sail back to Athens. He loses Ariadne along the way, probably to her betrothed, Dionysus, and forgets to hoist a white sail to show his father that he is still alive.

His father, Aegeus, sees a black sail, and fearing his son dead, hurls himself into the sea to drown. Since this time the sea has been known as the Aegean.

Back on Crete, King Minos orders Daedalus and his son Icarus thrown into the labyrinth. In a labor that lasts for years, Daedalus makes wings out of wax and feathers. Then one day Daedalus and Icarus launch themselves out of the labyrinth and fly over the city. According to legend, they decide to fly to Sicily, but Icarus flies too close to the sun and the wax in his wings melts and he falls from the sky to his death.

Daedalus reaches Sicily and is taken into the court of King Kokalos of Kamikos. King Minos learns that Daedalus is on Sicily and marches his army against Kokalos. King Minos is killed in the battle and the great power of Crete comes to an end.

Historians believe that this legend of Minos, Theseus, and the Minotaur gives us a glimpse of actual events in the dim history of the Mediterranean. A typical reconstruction of the events is that after a war with Crete, Athens (or mainland Greece) had to submit to its Cretan overlords (human sacrifices to the Minotaur). The Mycenaean Greeks (Theseus) were able to break out of the subjugation (defeating the Minotaur). Perhaps refugees from Crete went to Sicily.

It is curious that Daedalus should fly to Sicily in a mechanical invention (no matter how crude) of his own making. Did this refer to a real event when a flight was made from Crete to Sicily? And why to Sicily? Did ancient Crete and Sicily have ancestors in common? Or were they common enemies? Tales of ancient flights are always interesting.

Elaborate displays of bullfighting and acrobatics were part of the Cretan world. The worship of the bull, bullfights, and other festivities concerning the bull are said by Solon, quoted by Plato, to be of Atlantean origin. The cult of the bull is one that is found in many different countries, Spain, Portugal and Mexico being three modern examples of where this cult continues today.

And what of a bull from the sea? Does the symbology of a bull rising up out of the sea have something to do with the sunken land of Atlantis? Perhaps it signifies that the origin of bull worship came from the sea, to Crete, at least.

≈≈≈≈≈≈☥≈≈≈≈≈≈

Knossos, City of the Dead

Back at the palace of Knossos, I sat on a wall and wondered about the labyrinth. A sign pointed into a portion of an underground section. Was this the labyrinth? Some historians claim that Knossos was a confusing, twisting mass of streets and buildings, a vast palace that was easy to get lost in. Others say that "labyrinth" was the name they probably gave to the palace because of the countless double axes (labrys) which had been engraved on the walls and posts there.

Knossos may not even have been a palace of the living as we are generally taught but a grand monument to the deceased—a City of the Dead. This theory was propounded by the German archaeologist Hans Georg Wunderlich in his book *The Secret of Crete*,[144] published in Germany in 1972.

Asks Wunderlich, "Completely unfortified walls, without battlements or watch tower; can this be the residence of a mighty king? Angular, narrow entrances to the palace, living quarters located in a cellar position; can these be the staterooms of the ruler of all Crete? Nearly all the stairs are made of gypsum, an extremely soft material. Were they really intended for use? Bathtubs without drainage, huge clay vessels in what are supposed to have been living rooms, and not a kitchen in the entire complex?"[144]

Wunderlich doubts that natural disasters could have completely destroyed Minoan civilization or that Crete was an island isolated from the rest of Greece. He points out that Minoan records were kept in the standard Greek dialect. The light wells of the palace, he feels, served to ventilate rooms filled with the smell of the putrefying dead and the complicated drainage system was used during the

113

embalming of the dead, while the statues of bare-breasted women with snakes on their arms represented the mourners, who bared their breasts in mourning.

Arguments against Wunderlich are that a kitchen has indeed been found at Knossos and the discovery of the large cemetery at Fourni, near the Minoan city of Archanes, which has the typical vaulted grave crypts that are presumed to have been used during Minoan times.

Another theory, by the French archaeologist Paul Faure, is that the Minoan palaces are in reality large shrines in which the huge priesthood, not the "priest-king," resided as a religio-economic community.

Faure's main argument is that extremely spacious building complexes have been found in the immediate vicinity of all four of the great Cretan palaces and these have mostly been given names such as "the Little Palace" or "the Royal Villa." But would Minos have built a second palace 300 yards from his main residence as at Knossos and other palaces? It is more likely, says Faure, that the smaller building is the palace and the larger one is the "temple"; the gods always lived better than men in antiquity. Minos would have come over from the little palace for great religious ceremonies several times in the year, but worldly political power was not wielded there. Faure gives as an example King Solomon and how he built the great temple near his own palace.[132]

That the ancient Minoans ruled the Mediterranean for a period, and even roamed the world, affecting civilizations in Central and South America, is argued in the book *In Quest of the White God*[76] by the French-German archaeologist Pierre Honoré. Honoré's book first appeared in German in 1961 and is a strange classic in the literature of ancient seafaring.

Honoré expounds upon the American Indian traditions of white gods who "brought a system of science and engineering, gave them their legal codes, and helped them achieve a high level of civilization." Honoré maintains in his book that the "white gods" were from Crete and other countries in the eastern Mediterranean.

Honoré points out such interesting comparisons as the use of feather plume headdresses in both Crete and the royalties of the Americas. He even uses an illustration of a fresco from Knossos of a prince wearing a colorful feathered plume. The Mayans, he points out, often wore plumed headdresses as well. Indeed, the wearing of feathered headdresses, at least in the Mediterranean world, originated with ancient Crete, or so he believes.

The cyclopean construction of walls at Mycenae and Peru is used as evidence of unusual and identical construction. Also used by both cultures is the trapezoidal doorway that tapers toward the top.

Honoré makes an interesting comparison of solid megalithic doorframes at Tiahuanaco in Bolivia and Persepolis in Asia Minor.

Honoré points out the "Atlanteans" of Tula in northern Mexico. These were the huge columns of warriors or gods that stood 80 feet high to hold up some gigantic temple. He compares these columns and other column buildings at Mitla and Chichen Itza with the columns of Knossos and Karnak.

In Quest of the White God[76] is a classic in the field of diffusionist arguments for ancient sea trading. The use of the earlier Hittite-Linear B alphabet by Crete also gives a clue to certain unusual documents and writing systems, apparently derived from ancient Hittite.

One thing is clear: historians are not in agreement as to the history or uses of the palace of Knossos. Was Knossos a city for the living or for the dead? A temple of priests of the Light or a labyrinth of human sacrifice? An island super-base for transatlantic voyages of the Atlantean League to the Americas? Maybe all of the above.

≋≋≋≋≋≋⌾≋≋≋≋≋≋

Then YHWH answered and said,
"write the vision down,
inscribe it on tablets to be easily read."
—Habakkuk 2:2

The Code of Gortyn and the Phaistos Disc

A clue to Atlantis can be found in one of the most important rock inscriptions in the world, which is the Code of Gortyn. The Code of Gortyn is a stone tablet written in the archaic alphabet of Doric Greek upon the facade of a long concave wall. This wall is incorporated in the back of the Roman Odeum at Gortyn, in south-central Crete.

The rock inscription is a fifth-century B.C. law code (the first in Europe, allegedly) that has a number of early codes from Minoan times incorporated into it.[167]

The "Queen of Inscriptions," as it is sometimes called, is inscribed in the boustrophedon system, that unusual technique where a line is read from left to right but the next inversely from right to left. This is the unusual "as the ox plows" writing method used by the Hittites, the ancient Greeks and the people who created the Rongo Rongo tablets of Easter Island.

In the normal world of linguistics and epigraphy, any language written in a boustrophedon system would seem to be related. This would then mean that Hittite, Doric Greek and Rongo Rongo writing are all related.

Similarly, oddball languages such as Basque, Finnish, Hungarian and others, may have been originally written in a boustrophedon pattern. Was the original writing of Atlantis also done in this alternating pattern?

Back in Iraklion I made an afternoon trip to the Archaeology Museum, famous for the enigmatic Phaistos Disc. As I walked past the exhibits the first thing to impress me were the hundreds of stone seals for wax or clay tablets. These bore a startling similarity to the ancient seals of Mohenjo Daro and Harappa in Pakistan, as well as those used by the Hittites. Some of the seals had text on them that looked similar to ancient Chinese ideograms.

The use of seals can be found in such diverse cultures as China, Mexico, ancient India and Crete. One might suggest that the use came from a common source—possibly Atlantis?

Looking at some of them, they seemed to portray a type of oval head with angular features that was similar to the South Sea type of tiki head from Tahiti and other areas of Polynesia. Other seals and pottery decorations depicted a gorgon face with curly hair and pronounced teeth sticking up and down from the mouth. This was a very common motif in Indonesia and the Pacific.

There were many Egyptian and Egyptian-style artifacts, such as statues, scarabs and sarcophagi. There was also the use of ancient sun symbols, used in ancient India as the symbol of the Buddhist religious movement circa 200 B.C.

In order for Crete to have traded with India or the Persian Gulf, it would either have had to sail around Africa (unlikely) or have had access to ports on the Red Sea or Persian Gulf. Considering that the Minoans were strongly allied with the Hittites of Asia Minor and Cyprus in antiquity (circa 2000 B.C.), the Minoans may well have traded with the Far East via the early Hittite port on the Red Sea that was to later become Ezion-Geber of King Solomon's time.

The most important item in the Museum, for me, is the famous Phaistos Disc discovered at the Minoan palace of Phaistos which stands some five kilometers inland from the coast of southern Crete. It was unearthed in 1908 by Dr. L. Pernier, a member of the Italian archaeological mission excavating the site at the time.

The disc is a round terra-cotta plate approximately 2cm thick and 16cm in diameter. The disc is dated as having been produced before 1600 B.C. by the undisputed age of the Linear A tablets that were found in the earth around it. The disc is imprinted with 45 different symbols in a spiral pattern on both sides. The symbols were pressed into the soft clay with individual dies between 6mm and 16mm high. It has been hardened by fire.[179]

The disc's origin has been attributed to Crete and also to lands along the trade routes such as Cyprus, Libya, Anatolia, Palestine and other areas.

It remains undeciphered, although opinions on what it says range widely. Arthur Evans, the British excavator of Knossos, concluded that it was a hymn to the earth goddess. Other opinions were that it was "a hymn to the Rain God in Basque," a "hymn to Rhea in Greek," and a "list of thirteen soldiers' names," among others.[179]

Victor Kean believes that it is of the middle Minoan period (2100-1900 B.C.) and that it is the story of one man's adventures, or part of a story, at least. Comparisons to the hieroglyphic script of the Hittites can also be made.

The disc uses several interesting character-hieroglyphs. One is of a man wearing a feathered headdress, reminding me of Honoré's theory of the "White Gods" and the feathered headdresses used in North and South America.

Another glyph is of a man with a shaved head except for a central ridge of bristling hair, the famous "Mohawk" haircut of American Indian fame. Perhaps this unusual hairstyle has a Minoan origin.

For the "Gods from Outer Space" school of prehistoric thought, there is the unusual symbol in the third spiral row on the front side of the disc that looks a great deal like a flying saucer. It is a disc-shaped object with a small dome on the top of it. While it does indeed look like a small flying saucer, archaeologists claim, probably correctly, that it is a jar lid or dish with a cover. It may also be a personal seal for wax or clay, with the small dome the handle.

Back on the street, I looked up in the sky to see if any flying saucers were hovering over the museum, hoping for a clue as to the origin of the Phaistos Disc. But no such sign appeared, so I continued back to the main square and my hotel.

I left the next morning, taking a bus to Rethymno, a major port to the west of Iraklion along the north coast of Crete, and the third largest city on the island. When I arrived at the bus station, a large, older woman approached me.

"Hello, mister," she said. "You want a room? Come with me, mister, and see it." I followed her through the city and to her house, a small pension with no sign except "Rent Rooms" on the second story. She showed me a clean bedroom with a bathroom next door, and after a brief bit of obligatory bargaining, I took it.

The next few days were spent shopping in the narrow streets and watching the sunset from cafés along the beach. I continued west along the coast to Hania, Crete's second largest city.

I secured a room in a hotel near the port and began exploring the old Venetian port and fortified walls.

Hania was an ancient city in Minoan times when it was called Kydonia. Excavations on ancient Hania began in 1960. Hania was a flourishing city-state in Hellenistic times and continued to prosper under the Romans. The city became Venetian at the end of the 13th century. The Venetians called the city La Canea and built a fortress to keep out marauding pirates and invading Turks. However, the Turks took the city in 1645 after a siege of two months.

The museum was small but interesting. I was particularly impressed by the Minoan double pots that are highly similar to those found in Peru. These pots, two round pots linked with a channel, are sometimes "whistling" pots that make a musical noise when one blows into them. One of the double pots even seemed to depict a South American llama with its long neck and ears.

The entire museum begged comparison with ancient American artifacts: the large pots called "pithoi" are identical to the huge burial pots found on the island of Majaro at the mouth of the Amazon River.

There were also small clay wheeled toys, similar to those found in Mexico, and clay spindle whorls as used in Peru for spinning wool.

Other curious exhibits were of horses suspended in a harness in a ship for a transoceanic voyage and of Minoan statues with Egyptian-type headdresses. There were beautiful carved quartz crystal seals with animals and the Linear A and B scripts on them. One had a lovely depiction of the winged horse Pegasus carved into a ring seal.

Ancient Technology and the Antikythera Device

I left one afternoon for the far western port of Kastelli where I would be able to get a ferry to the Peloponnese on the mainland of Greece. The bus left me off at the main square of Kastelli, a small fishing village with a modern harbor outside of town.

After sitting in town for a few hours I was informed that there was no bus to the ferry harbor and I would have to walk the two miles to the port. I shouldered my backpack and walked past the fishing boats to the modern harbor.

The ferry would not leave until midnight, so I spent my time in the small restaurant having a meal of fish and reading some books about Crete that I had bought.

Shipwrecks around the Mediterranean give us an idea of the science that the ancient Greeks, Romans and other Mediterranean maritime cultures had. As with most of history, modern historians and archaeologists have not given ancient man enough credit for his science and ingenuity and are therefore surprised when technical wonders are discovered that seem to belong in the modern world, not the ancient past.

When one looks at frescoes in Pompeii, one sees blonde women in bikini bathing suits, no doubt by the latest and most expensive designer. The July 27, 1959, issue of *Chemical Engineering* had an article about an 80-pound valve that had been salvaged from one of Emperor Caligula's yachts. The valve was made of a zinc-free, lead-rich, anticorrosion, antifriction bronze.

Said the article, "The Caligula valve was found submerged at the bottom of Lake Lemi in Rome. Although 19 centuries old, it still exhibits highly polished surfaces and retains its plug tightly." While modern fashion and sexual trends may simply mimic those of ancient times, scientific types are always surprised at the high level of technical and scientific knowledge of ancient man.

Becoming familiar with ancient science is a good start for the layman, and two good books that are easily obtainable are *Technology In The Ancient World*[54] by Henry Hodges and *Engineering In the Ancient World* by J. Landels.[116] With these books, the science of classical times can be seen to be very similar to our own.

What is amazing about the modern world versus the ancient one is that in the modern world the average citizen has access to advanced technology such as electricity, a personal vehicle, telephone, fax, and computer technology while in the ancient world high technology was largely denied the masses.

Indeed, according to many authors, the high technology of electric lighting was used in temples to gain power over people by controlling their belief system.

In 1900, an amazing discovery took place on the small island of Antikythera, 25 miles northwest of Crete. A sunken Greek galley had been discovered just offshore from the tiny island and some fishermen and sponge divers managed to salvage its cargo of marble, pottery and other objects near the shore.

Among the items was an encrusted bronze object of undetermined use. It languished in the reserve section of a museum until 1955 when a curious scientist decided to clean it. He found that it was a complex instrument with cogwheels fitting one into another. Finely graduated circles and inscriptions marked on it in ancient Greek were obviously concerned with its function. The object seems to have been a sort of astronomical clock without a pendulum.

The cargo has enabled the shipwreck to be dated to around the 1st century B.C. No Greek or Roman writer has ever described the workings of such an ancient computer, though other marvels of antiquity are mentioned that seem incomprehensible to us.

Like Finding a Jet Plane in the Tomb of King Tut

In 1958 a British scientist named Derek de Solla Price was researching the history of scientific instruments when he came across the Antikythera device in the Athens Museum. He was astonished at the complexity of the device and later wrote, "Nothing like this instrument is preserved elsewhere. Nothing comparable to it is known from any ancient scientific text or literary allusion. On the contrary, from all that we know of science and technology in the Hellenistic Age we should have felt that such a device could not exist."[131]

Price was later quoted as saying, "Finding a thing like this is like finding a jet plane in the tomb of King Tut."

Price had previously believed that the first time that such complicated gear work had appeared was in a clock made in 1575. For more than a decade Price studied the fragments of the machine and in 1971 had X-ray photographs taken of it by the Greek Atomic Energy Commission. This finally revealed the astonishing array of intercogged wheels.[131, 133]

Price described the computer in an article that appeared in the March, 1962, issue of *Natural History* (71:8-17) entitled "Unworldly Mechanics." It was entitled "Unworldly Mechanics" because Price and others never imagined that the ancient Greeks, Egyptians or other cultures of 100 B.C. could have had the astronomical or mechanical knowledge to construct such a device, an idea which is just plain wrong, as Price explains: "Some of the plates were marked with barely recognizable inscriptions, written in Greek characters of the first century B.C., and just enough could be made of the sense to tell that the subject matter was undoubtedly astronomical.

"Little by little, the pieces fitted together until there resulted a fair idea of the nature and purpose of the machine and of the main character of the inscriptions with which it was covered. The original Antikythera mechanism must have borne a remarkable resemblance to a good modern mechanical clock. It consisted of a wooden frame that supported metal plates, front and back, each plate having quite complicated dials with pointers moving around them. The whole device was about as large as a thick folio encyclopedia volume. Inside the box formed by frame and plates was a mechanism of gear wheels, some twenty of them at least, arranged in a non-obvious way and including differential gears and a crown wheel, the whole lot being mounted on an internal bronze plate. A shaft ran into the box from the side and, when this was turned, all the pointers moved over their dials at various speeds. The dial plates were protected by bronze doors hinged to them, and dials and doors carried the long inscriptions that described how to operate the machine.

"It appears that this was, indeed, a computing machine that could work out and exhibit the motions of the sun and moon and probably also the planets. Exactly how it did this is not clear, but the evidence thus far suggests that it was quite different from all other planetary models. It was not like the more familiar planetarium or orrery, which shows the planets moving at their various speeds, but much more like a mechanization of the purely arithmetical Babylonian methods. One just read the dials in accordance with the instructions, and legends on the dials indicated which phenomena would occur at any given time."[17]

The British-Greek historian Victor J. Kean maintains in his book *The Ancient Greek Computer From Rhodes*[133] that the Antikythera device was made on the island of Rhodes around 71 B.C. Kean theorizes that the machine was made at the ancient metallurgical science city known as Kamiros and was destined for Rome when the transport ship sank off the small island of Antikythera.

What the Antikythera device has shown historians is that the ancient world did in fact have a higher science than we had previously given it credit for. As in tales of the Rama empire, Osiris and Atlantis, the ancient past was a world in which isolated areas had complex machinery, electricity, and metallurgical sciences. History has been destroyed, just as Solon the Greek told Plato.

Another article in the mainstream media about amazing ancient technology appeared in the April 1957 issue of *Science Digest* entitled "Electric Batteries of 2,000 Years Ago." (Harry M. Schwalb, *Science Digest*, 41:17-19). Says the article, "...in Cleopatra's day, up-and-coming Baghdad silversmiths were goldplating jewelry—using electric batteries. It's no myth; young scientist Willard F. M. Gray, of General Electric's High Voltage Laboratory in Pittsfield, Mass., has proved it. He made an exact replica of one of the 2,000-year-old wet cells and connected it to a galvanometer. When he closed the switch—current flowed!

"These B.C.-vintage batteries (made by the Parthians, who dominated the Baghdad region between 250 B.C. and 224 A.D.) are quite simple. Thin sheet-copper was soldered into a cylinder less than 4 inches long and about an inch in diameter—roughly the size of two flashlight batteries end to end. The solder was a 60/40 tin-lead alloy—'one of the best in use today,' Gray points out.

"The bottom of the cylinder was a crimped-in copper disc insulated with a layer of asphaltum (the "bitumen" that the Bible tells us Noah used to caulk the Ark). The top was closed with an asphalt stopper, through which projected the end of an iron rod. To stand upright, it was cemented into a small vase.

"What electrolyte the Parthian jewelers used is a mystery, but Gray's model works well with copper sulfate. Acetic or citric acid, which the ancient chemists had in plenty, should be even better.

"This evidence of man's first industrial use of electricity was discovered 20 years ago by a German archaeologist, Wilhelm Konig, at the Iraq Museum. A small hill with the resounding name of Khujut Rabu'a, on the outskirts of Baghdad, was being dug away and the remains of a Parthian town were revealed. The Museum at once began scientific excavations, and in the digging turned up a peculiar object that—to Konig—looked very much like a present-day dry-cell."[17]

Yet, it is not an accurate scientific statement to say that this is the "first industrial use of electricity" as we simply just do not know whether this was the first or not. Probably not, in fact, and certainly the believer in Atlantis would say that electricity was known in Atlantis, if not before then.

The popular British scientist and author Arthur C. Clarke made these comments about the Antikythera device: "Looking at this extraordinary relic is a most disturbing experience. Few activities are more futile than the 'what if...' type of speculation, yet the Antikythera mechanism positively compels such thinking. Though it is over 2,000 years old, it represents a level which our technology did not reach until the eighteenth century... I have often wondered what other treasures of advanced technology may lie hidden in the sea."[131]

Indeed, what ancient artifacts of high technology might be found in the more than 200 known sunken cities of the Mediterranean? I had brought my scuba diving certification card with me to Greece only to find out that because of the many sunken wrecks and cities, and the archaeological treasures that they held, diving was off-limits in Greece.

In fact, it is illegal to go scuba diving in Greece near any underwater archaeological site. The problem with that is that there are so many submerged harbors and wrecks that much of the coastline of Crete and the rest of Greece must be excluded from recreational diving.

I looked at my guidebook on Crete and read the following under "Diving": "Snorkelling is permitted almost everywhere, as is scuba diving, except in the immediate vicinity of an archaeological site. Such underwater sites are particularly common on Crete, since the west coastline of Crete has risen by a few metres in historical times, whereas the east coast has sunk. For those who like exploring the ancient sunken harbors such as *Olous* (near Elounda), *Limin Chersonisou, Itanos, Mochlos* etc. are of interest. It is only possible to dive with a snorkle and flippers at these places. There are severe penalties for the removal of archaeological material."[132]

When one looks at a modern map of ancient Crete, often only one or two cities such as Knossos or Archanes are mentioned. Yet, Crete was supposedly a powerful empire with a huge fleet and port cities to support it.

The reason that most ancient Minoan ports are not on maps is that they are generally under water! Crete has lost a great deal of coast just in the last 3,000 years. Other ports in western Crete have been raised up from sea level.

Crete is a good example of the kind of earth changes that have been going on in the Mediterranean for thousands of years. My guidebook even had a whole subsection in the introduction on "Sunken Cities." Says the author, "Even in historical times—that is, in the first few centuries A.D.—the land level in the west of Crete rose by around 26 feet, while the coastline sank below sea level in the east. The evidence for this is to be seen in the ancient harbor towns, which according to tradition were situated by the sea. Thus, for example, there is Phalassarna in the extreme west, the ruins of which are situated about 153 yards inland and above sea level; and then there are the walls of ancient *Olous* near Elounda in eastern Crete, which are visible several feet under the sea."[132]

Of the now high and dry port city of Phalassarna, it exists on the extreme western end of Crete which is mainly cliffs. Says my guide to Crete, "Only a little can be seen of the former ancient harbor city of *Phalassarna*—today, its supposed remains lie 20 feet above sea level, on the cliffs!"

This is likely to have been a megalithic city as well. Just near to Phalassarna are the megalithic Mycenaean ruins of Polirrinia. These ruins include the remains of a cyclopean wall, the walls of a temple, burial chambers and even the walls of a later Venetian castle. The earlier Mycenaean cyclopean wall might have been built even before the port city of Phalassarna.[132]

Was Phalassarna one of the ancient cities of sunken Osiris? At the eastern end of Crete is the famous Palm Beach of Vai, with a unique variety of palm tree apparently from North Africa. This unique area is possibly a remnant of Crete when it was part of Osiris.

The sign at the beach says, "The beautiful forest of Vai is a unique habitat, created through the indigenous species of palm known as Phoenix theophrastii. This is the northernmost occurrence of the species and therefore a place of international interest."

Botanists do not know how this date palm came to Crete, and suppositions have been made that it was left behind by invading Arabs and Turks. But the date is not edible! Nor do dates float across a sea. Another explanation is that the dates were once part of a forest that is now beneath the Mediterranean.

This sunken forest was once part of the lost land of Osiris, I believe.

As the large ferryboat pulled into the harbor at midnight, green and yellow lights flashed up and down the wharf, giving the port a glow like St. Elmo's fire. The waves of the Mediterranean washed up against the docks. Were the ancient cities that we view today built on the mountaintops of ancient Osiris? In many ways, the lost world of Atlantis is all around us.

A modern depiction of the Colossus of Rhodes.

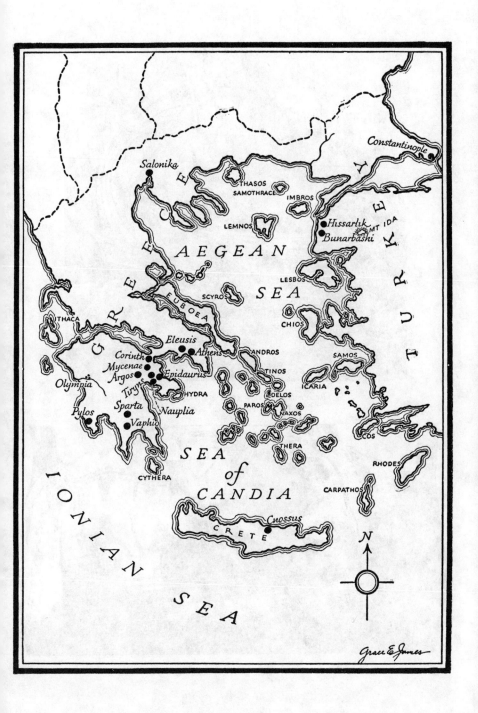

Reconstruction of a relief showing the stern of
a Rhodian galley, ca. 200 B.C.

Two-banked warship, probably a triaconter, late 6th B.C.

The Thera volcano erupting in 1925–6.

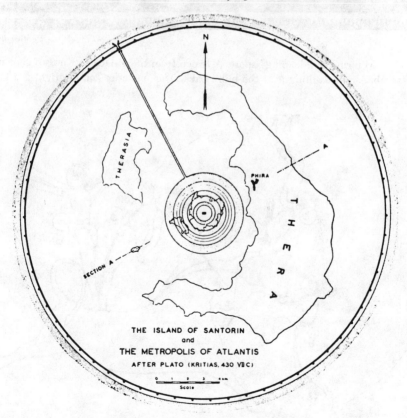

THE ISLAND OF SANTORIN
and
THE METROPOLIS OF ATLANTIS
AFTER PLATO (KRITIAS, 430 VIBC)

0 1 2 3 4 km
Scale

Professor Galanopoulos' superimposition of Atlantis onto Thera,
demonstrating how closely they correlate.

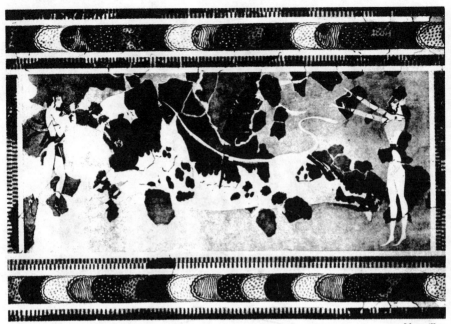

The Minoan "bull-leaping" sport. A fresco from the Palace of Knossos showing the acrobat somersaulting over the bull's back. The "matador" on the right is a girl.

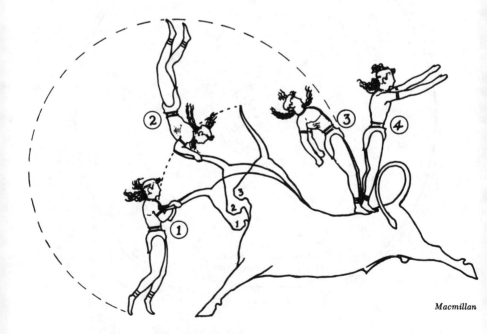

How the acrobats performed the feat (see above).

The two sides of the Phaistos disc

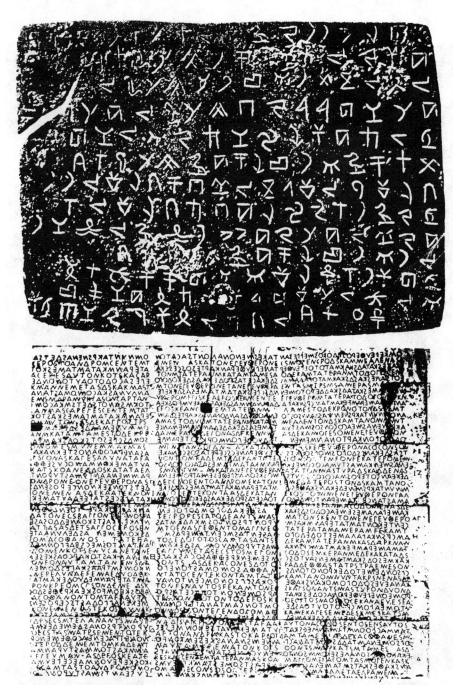

Top: A Hittite inscription on a bronze plaque found at the Hittite port of Byblos. It is read in the boustrophedon manner and dates to about 2000 B.C. and is similar to the Newberry Stone. Bottom: A section of the Code of Gortyn, a Doric Greek inscription on Crete. It is also read in the boustrophedon manner.

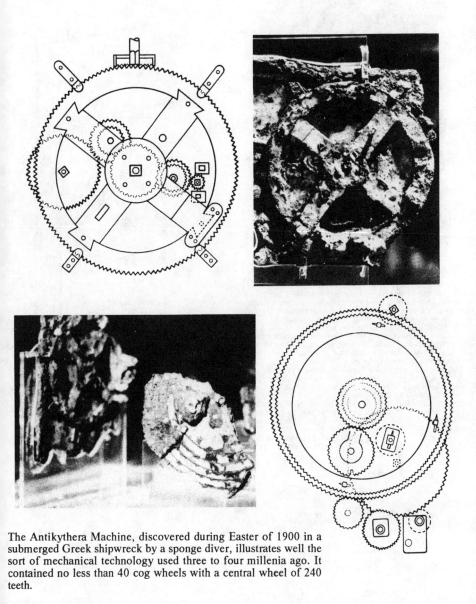

The Antikythera Machine, discovered during Easter of 1900 in a submerged Greek shipwreck by a sponge diver, illustrates well the sort of mechanical technology used three to four millenia ago. It contained no less than 40 cog wheels with a central wheel of 240 teeth.

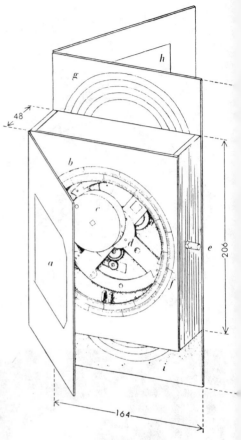

The parts of the mechanism of the 'computer' or astronomical clock were in a sorry state when discovered (*above*), but through the careful work of the museum technicians, and with the help of George Stamires who deciphered the inscriptions, Mr. Price was able to reconstruct the position of the pieces.

The labelled parts in the reconstruction are: *a*: front door inscription; *b*: front dial; *c*: eccentric drum; *d*: front mechanism; *e*: input shaft; *f*: fiducial mark; *g*: four slip rings of upper back dial; *h*: back door inscription; *i*: three slip rings of lower back dial. The dimensions are given in millimetres.

Left. Segment of the lower back dial. At right is a fixed scale; within it were three slip rings and within them a subsidiary dial.

Right. Segment of front dial. The upper scale pertains to the months, the lower to the zodiac. The inscribed area is a para-pegma (astronomical calendar) plate. The various dials show the annual motion of the sun in the zodiac and also the main risings and settings of bright stars and constellations throughout the year.

Photograph *Derek Price*
Diagram *Scientific American*

ANTIKYTHERA

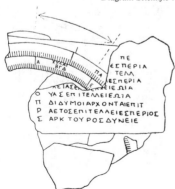

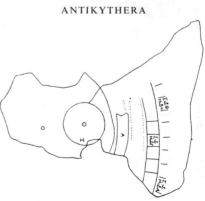

The 'computer'

Chapter 4

GREECE:

The Cyclopean Walls of Olympus

Not to know what happened before we were born is to remain perpetually a child. For what is the worth of a human life unless it is woven into the life of our ancestors by the records of history.
            —Cicero (106-43 B.C.)

I awoke at dawn the next morning, still on my journey by ferry from western Crete. Outside were the high, sheer cliffs of the southern Peloponnese. After cruising along the rugged coast for an hour, the ferry pulled into the port of Kalamata.

As I stumbled off the largely empty ferry, I met a young British couple who were teaching English in Tripoli. "Want to share a taxi to the bus station?" asked the dark-haired man.

"Thanks," I smiled and slung my pack into the waiting trunk of the taxi.

From the central station, I was off by bus through the dry rugged mountains of southern Greece to Nafplion.

Nafplion was the first capital of modern Greece, but the capital was moved to Athens in 1834. Today, Nafplion is a pleasant city that sits along a wide, sweeping bay with cafés where one can watch the fishing boats in the harbor. Tourists walk down esplanades by the sea where black-vested waiters serve beer and retsina wine from round trays.

As I stepped off the bus near a park in the center of town, I spotted three people sitting at a sidewalk café speaking English, so I asked them if they could recommend a cheap hotel.

As often happens on the road, I ended up sitting at the table with these other travellers, a British couple and a Canadian woman. The British couple were dressed in black leather biker gear with obligatory tattoos and chains. They introduced themselves as Mark and Sylvia. The Canadian woman was Lynn, a fire department dispatcher from Alberta who was waiting for her friend Margaret to come back from Athens where she had gone to change money.

"Here, have a beer and a shot of ouzo," said Mark.

I declined the shot of ouzo, but ordered a beer and some french fries. Mark had been in the British Hell's Angels and had ridden his bike all over Europe. He and Sylvia were on an extended biker holiday through Greece and points beyond.

They had clearly been sitting in the café all day drinking since all three of them were pretty drunk. Lynn got up at one point and went to the train station, later bringing back her friend Margaret.

I was somewhat intrigued by these four fun-loving travellers, so I willingly resigned myself to spending the rest of the afternoon and evening with them at the café, but I wanted to get rid of my pack at a hotel.

I convinced Lynn and Margaret to show me a nearby hotel, a few blocks away, and felt a bit more secure once I had checked in and safely stored my luggage. I returned to the café where I found a fresh bottle of ouzo on the table and the four of them hunched over plates of gyros.

"So you're a writer," said Mark, a tall wiry fellow with black hair. "What do you write about?"

"Oh, lost cities, Atlantis, mysteries of the past. Stuff like that," I answered.

"Oh, Atlantis, I love that stuff," said Sylvia, playing with one of the zippers on her black leather jacket. She had long black hair and wore aviator sunglasses most of the time. She licked the ouzo off her full lips as she repeated, "Atlantis. I love that."

"I read a book on Atlantis once," said Mark. "*Atlantis, the Antediluvian World*.[5] Did you ever read that book?"

"Sure," I said. "That's one of the original classics in Atlantis literature."

We talked about the author, Ignatius Donnelly, the former governor of Minnesota, who contended that the Atlanteans were so intellectually superior to the Greeks and the rest of the Mediterranean world, that they were viewed as gods.

Said Donnelly, "The history of Atlantis is the key of Greek mythology. There can be no question that these gods of Greece were human beings. The tendency to attach divine attributes to great earthly rulers is one deeply implanted in human nature."[5]

Essentially, Donnelly was saying that the Egyptian Osiris was the personification of a world-travelling civilization-builder and in the same way the Greek gods were the personification of the famous statesmen, heroes and heroines of Atlantis. Instead of solar worship or nature worship, they worshiped the ancient deities who ate, got drunk, made love, got jealous, and even died. These all too human gods lived on Olympus which in reality, according to Donnelly, was Atlantis.

Donnelly summarized his theories on Atlantis in seven main points:

1. The gods were not the makers, but rather the rulers of the world.

2. They were human in their attributes; they loved, sinned, and fought battles, the very sites of which are given; they founded cities, and civilized the people of the Mediterranean.

3. They dwelt upon an island in the Atlantic, "in the remote west... where the sun shines after it has ceased to shine on Greece."

4. Their land was destroyed in a deluge.

5. They were ruled over by Poseidon [god of the sea] and Atlas [who bears the world upon his shoulders].

6. Their empire extended to Egypt and Italy and the shores of Africa, precisely as stated by Plato.

7. They existed during the Bronze Age and at the beginning of the Iron Age.

Donnelly went on to say that Atlantis was the true antediluvian world in all mythologies, including the Garden of Eden with its four rivers, the Garden of the Hesperides, the Elysian Fields, the Garden of Alcinous, and the Olympus and Asgard abodes of the Greek and Norse gods.

Donnelly believed that the gods and goddesses of the ancient Greeks, Phoenicians, Egyptians, Hindus and Scandinavians were the simple kings and queens of Atlantis with their legend the confused recollection of real historical events. The Incan and Egyptian sun-worshiping religions were relics of the true Atlantean religion.

Yet, in my opinion, while the ancient world may have been dominated by the culture of Atlantis, much of the world was just as civilized. Areas like the flooded Mediterranean, the Turfan Basin between Tibet and Mongolia, and the Pacific coastal areas, would have been the inspiration for local mythology, not Atlantis. If anything, immediately after the wars and cataclysms associated with the destruction of Atlantis, anti-Atlantean feeling must have run pretty strong among the survivors.

Brad Steiger states in his book *Atlantis Rising*[73] that the Mediterranean peoples spoke of the Atlanteans as being possessed of great physical strength "so that the earth shook sometimes under their tread." Steiger and Donnelly suggest that this refers to the Atlanteans' use of explosives to make roads and tunnels.

The primitive Mediterraneans were also in awe of the Atlanteans' ability to move "through space without the loss of a moment of time," says Steiger, quoting Donnelly. This could be a reference to air travel in mechanical vehicles or even some sort of high-tech teleportation device.

Curiously, in his book *The Cosmic Conspiracy*[139] author Stan Deyo reports that he witnessed the late William P. Lear, inventor of the Lear jet and the eight-track car stereo (and father of C.I.A. pilot John Lear of UFO fame) on a nationwide television talk program about 1969 or 1970. William Lear told the television audience that within the next few years a person would be able to walk into a New York "travel booth"—somewhat similar to a telephone booth in shape—deposit his fare; push a button; and walk out the other side of the booth in San Francisco—having been "teleported" across America in seconds!

"That is fascinating," said Mark, through a mouthful of gyros, "to think that we may already have this technology and that, like everything else—because there is nothing new under the sun—it is a reinvention of earlier Atlantean devices.

"You know," he laughed, "even the modern media has popularized your Atlantean invention. On British telly we have the transporter technology of Star Trek and the Tardus of Dr. Who—a telephone booth-time machine-spaceship that looks exactly like a red phone box."

"Ha," I grinned, "and Superman, curiously, likes to change clothes in a phone booth."

Mark gulped some ouzo. "Is there a pattern here?"

I hoped not, I thought as I finished off my third beer. I glanced around the café; it was starting to close down.

"Let's go play pool at a bar back by your hotel," suggested Mark.

"I'm ready to go," said dark-haired Sylvia. The Canadian women were going back to their room.

"Well, I'll have a game of pool with you," I said.

We staggered down the street to a chrome and glass style ladies bar with pool tables. Three gorgeous young ladies in revealing dresses were serving drinks. Several young Greek soldiers in uniform sat at one table drinking beer. One waitress sat at their table most of the night, apparently being paid to sit there.

"The waitresses here are pretty friendly," said Mark, racking up a pool table. "That young one over there was all over me last night."

"Really," I said, ordering a beer. "But weren't you with Sylvia?"

"I think she wanted a threesome," said Sylvia, unzipping her black leather jacket and winking at me. I raised an eyebrow and reached for a pool cue.

In the corner some young sailors watched a waitress in a tight minidress walk past them to another table. Mark and I played pool.

A young waitress played with the zippers on Mark's leather jacket. My head was spinning. It was late and I knew it was a good time to leave.

"Look, I think I'm going to go," I said. "Where are you two staying tonight?"

"Oh, probably in an empty building down the street that we spotted yesterday," said Mark.

"We've already stashed our bedrolls there," said Sylvia.

Back at my hotel I fell on my bed; at least I wasn't sleeping in an abandoned building tonight.

The War Between Greece and Atlantis

The next morning I took a bus to the nearby megalithic citadel of Mycenae. I read Plato's account of the war between Atlantis and Greece as the bus rolled through pastures and granite hills.

The Egyptian priests tell Solon in the *Timaeus* that the goddess Athena founded Athens 9,000 years ago and that "Many great and wonderful deeds are recorded of your state in our histories. But one of them exceeds all the rest in greatness and valor. For these historians tell of a mighty power which was aggressing wantonly against the whole of Europe and Asia, and to which your city put an end. This power came forth out of the Atlantic Sea, for in those days the sea was navigable; and there was an island situated in front of the straits which you call the Pillars of Herakles; the island was larger than Libya and Asia together, and was the way to other islands, and from the islands you might pass to the whole of the opposite continent which surrounds the true ocean; for this within the straits is only a harbor, having a narrow entrance, but that other is the real sea, and the surrounding land may be most truly called a continent.

"Now in the island of Atlantis there was a great and wonderful empire which had rule over the whole island and several others, as well as over parts of the continent, and besides these they subjected parts of Libya within the Straits as far as Egypt, and of Europe as far as Tyrrhenia. This vast power, thus gathered into one, tried to subdue at one blow our country and yours and the whole of the land which was within the Straits; and then, Solon, your country shone forth, in the excellence of her virtue and strength among all mankind, for she was the first in courage and military skill and was the leader of the Hellenes. And when the rest fell from her, being compelled to stand alone after having undergone the very extremity of danger, she defeated and triumphed over the invaders, and preserved from slavery those who were not yet subjected, and liberated all the others who dwell within the limits of Herakles. But afterwards there occurred violent earthquakes and floods, and in a single day and night of rain all your warlike men in a body sank into the earth, and the island of Atlantis in the like manner disappeared, and was sunk beneath the sea. Wherefore the sea in those parts is impassable and impenetrable, because there is so much shallow mud in the way, caused by the subsidence of the island."

The Egyptian priests have made it clear in Plato's record that outside of the Mediterranean was once a large island. From this large island, one could continue to move across the ocean to an even greater continent beyond. This continent beyond Atlantis was undoubtedly North America. Plato's knowledge of geography, derived from the Egyptians, would seem to be quite good.

It was just before noon when the bus arrived at Mycenae, the ancient megalithic fortress that may shed some light on the Greece of 9000 B.C. that fought with Atlantis.

The excavation of Mycenae by the German archaeologist Heinrich Schliemann in 1874 was a great boon to Atlantists. Schliemann had a particular interest in the great Greek epic poems of Homer, the *Iliad* and the *Odyssey*, and undertook to prove to the scientific world that Troy really had existed. Having succeeded in this he then went on to do extensive excavation work at Mycenae, again searching for evidence of Homer's heroes.

Schliemann discovered a large quantity of gold treasure in the grave circle of Mycenae and scholars were instantly convinced that this unknown, pre-Greek civilization did indeed exist. Mycenae may in fact be the ruins of the ancient Greek civilization said to have fought with Atlantis.

One thing that struck Schliemann and other archaeologists was the awesome building technique used at Mycenae and other similar sites. The use of huge polygonal blocks of stone that are perfectly cut and fitted together was termed "cyclopean" by Schliemann in reference to the giant Cyclops of the *Odyssey* fame.

This unusual form of construction is not only megalithic on a grand scale, it is also a method that is as earthquake-proof as any stone construction gets. Because the stones are fitted in a jigsaw manner without mortar, the wall may move and jiggle when the shock of an earthquake hits the wall, but because the stones interlock, the wall generally does not collapse, and settles back into place after the shock.

Regular masonry with squared blocks, or worse, bricks, will sheer with the shock of an earthquake and the wall will collapse. Therefore, construction with large polygonal blocks that are interlocked is the finest and yet most difficult type of construction man has ever devised.

Structures built out of this polygonal cyclopean construction are found on mainland Greece (but not on any of the islands, as far as I know), as well as Egypt, Turkey, Morocco, Malta, Peru, Bolivia, Ecuador, Mexico, Spain and underwater off the Bahama island of Bimini. The famous walls at Sacsayhuaman, Cuzco, Ollantaytambo and Machu Picchu in Peru are all built in the amazing cyclopean manner that was first identified at Mycenae.

Yet even this form of construction is not earthquake-proof. Ruins at Tiahuanaco and Ollantaytambo in Peru are cyclopean but were destroyed by major earthquakes. Underwater ruins off the coasts of Morocco, Spain and Egypt are built in this same manner but have been destroyed and sunk by earthquakes.

Another area of Greece with cyclopean construction is the state of Epiros in northwestern Greece. In the vicinity of the capital city of Ioannina are a number of ancient ruins with polygonal construction like that found in Peru or Mycenae.

The question that archaeologists ask themselves is why would primitive ancient man have gone to such terrific effort to construct gigantic walls of huge boulders when it would have been so much easier to construct walls out of smaller stones or bricks? Did ancient man know something that we don't about cataclysmic earth changes and earthquakes that regularly shake the earth and destroy cities? Many of these walls are built out of huge stones which are so perfectly cut and fitted that a modern construction company would have great difficulty in duplicating the feat.

As I walked from the bus parking area up to the citadel, I was transfixed by the massive stones that made up the walls. Huge, 50-ton boulders were well cut, each one fitted to the stone next to it. Directly ahead was the famous Lion's Gate of Mycenae. This huge trilithon doorway has a gigantic carving of two lions facing a pillar. Massive blocks of interlocked stones made up the walls on either side.

Walls over 40 feet high made of cyclopean blocks rose above me as I walked toward the Lion's Gate. It was as impressive as the Lion's Gate at Hattusas, I thought as I walked beneath it. Were the Hittites and the Achaeans of Mycenae descended from the same Osirian warriors of that last war with Atlantis as described by Plato?

They used similar cyclopean architecture and used the same motifs of the lion and the sphinx. I climbed up on the walls around the city to the very back where an ancient tunnel went deep into the earth beneath the fortress. I looked in my day pack for my small travel flashlight but, damn, I had left it back at the hotel. I found a lighter and walked into the tunnel down the megalithic staircase that descended beneath the fortress.

As I crept down into the Stygian darkness, stepping carefully on the slippery, narrow steps, I could hear some voices beneath me.

"Do you have a flashlight?" I shouted below as the lighter became too hot to hold any longer.

"Yes," came a call from the depths as a brief ray of light shone up from below.

I lit my lighter again and carefully negotiated the ancient stairway. Water dripped on me and a bat suddenly flew over my head. I wondered what horror might be around the next corner when—eeek!—it was only a Dutch man with his two young children standing in front of me. Around them was the bottom of the dry cistern.

The stairs had been cut in solid rock down this steep tunnel so thousands of gallons of water could be stored in case of siege. It was an impressive, and spooky, place to be.

I looked around and then followed the Dutch family back up the stairs, the small flashlight shining on the steep steps. My lighter cast eerie shadows on the walls, but soon we saw the light of the entrance. Suddenly the bright sun struck me full force on my face and I had to shade my eyes.

Mycenae has several finely carved megalithic gates and the back fortifications are of nicely fitted cyclopean stone. After circling the ruins and retracing my steps back to the famous Lion's Gate, I walked down to the Treasury of Atreus. The Treasury of Atreus is a gigantic underground dome exemplifying the finest megalithic architecture ever seen anywhere.

The Treasury is a massive beehive room built out of perfectly cut and fitted rectangular blocks creating a one-room structure with a small room adjacent to it. The gigantic lintel over a door 20 feet high is one of the most famous masonry stones in the world. The entire room is of large red granite blocks and the lintel above the door is the largest of all the stones.

The Treasury of Atreus is an amazing structure and one that is essentially a total mystery. We do not know who built it, when, or for what purpose.

Farther down the road is a small village where I was pleased to discover that Heinrich Schliemann's house had been turned into a restaurant.

I couldn't resist having lunch in Schliemann's home and sat at one of the terrace tables. Mycenae, like Hattusas, was one of the great cities of the remote ancient world and since no armies were attacking the city this year, it was a good time to enjoy a leisurely lunch.

Sipping a glass of wine, I looked over one of the most recent books on Atlantis, *Flood From Heaven*[48] by Eberhard Zangger. In his book,

Zangger relates Plato's Atlantis to a garbled Egyptian account of the Trojan War between Mycenae and Troy.

Says the dustjacket of the book, "Now Dr. Eberhard Zangger, a well-known geoarchaeologist, with many years of fieldwork experience in the Mediterranean, has discovered the true nature of Plato's story and the real location of Atlantis in his ground-breaking book, *The Flood From Heaven*, which draws on modern science, legends, and ancient poetry to solve one of the world's most mysterious puzzles.

"The story of Atlantis is in actuality an ancient Egyptian account of the Trojan War. Under the auspices of Stanford University and the German Archaeological Institute, Eberhard Zangger conducted a geoarchaeological research program in Greece between 1984 and 1988, where drill cores taken near Bronze Age citadels led to this conclusion. Just like Homer, Plato was relating the story of a war involving bronze weapons, chariots, and twelve hundred ships. Both Homer and Plato discuss the fact that the Greeks, despite desertion by allies and deadly perils, were able to lead the forces of a united army to a magnificent victory in a land, like Troy, characterized by its position at narrow straits of difficult navigability, a pair of hot and cold springs, strong northern winds, and a number of artificial canals."[48]

Indeed, ancient Troy had a number of sophisticated canals for its port, but it was not a concentric circle pattern as described by Plato. As we will see in a later chapter, the circular pattern of Carthage was similar to that described by Plato, and far more likely to have been the citadel of Atlantis than Troy.

Like others before him, Zangger struggles to explain why Atlantis is in the Aegean, rather than the Atlantic. The size, shape, date, whereabouts and ultimate fate of Atlantis are all wrong in Plato's account according to Zangger. But known history can be twisted and turned in order to fit with Plato's Atlantis.

Zangger's theory is the latest from the school of Atlantis scholars which also holds that Plato made some pretty serious mistakes of geography and time period. Actually, the Greeks of Plato's time had a pretty good idea of their own history of a thousand years earlier—witness the *Iliad* and *Odyssey*, or the adventures of ancient travellers like Jason and the Argonauts.

Those historians who prefer to believe that Plato made up the whole story of Atlantis often quote Aristotle, one of Plato's pupils. Aristotle (384-322 B.C.) is quoted as saying "He who invented Atlantis also destroyed it." However, Aristotle was a well-known skeptic on many things and in the same quote also doubts the reality of the Trojan War in Homer's *Iliad*.[1, 44, 191]

Many modern historians echoed Aristotle's beliefs about both

Atlantis and Troy, but then Schliemann went out and proved them wrong—about Troy at least.

Aristotle's quote about Atlantis is itself from a lost work, but is quoted in other Greek texts. Curiously, however, Aristotle himself wrote about a large island in the Atlantic that the Carthaginians knew as Antilla.[191]

Another student of Plato, Krantor (4th century B.C.), reported that he too had seen the columns on which was preserved the story of Atlantis as reported by Plato. The Roman historian Plutarch (46-120 A.D.) told of a transatlantic continent called Saturnia and of an island called Ogygia about five days' sail west of Britain. According to Homer, Ogygia was the home of the nymph Calypso, who was visited by Odysseus.[191]

From Mycenae I visited the other megalithic ruins in the vicinity, the Mycenaean fortress of Tyrns. The local bus driver dropped me off at Tyrns on the outskirts of Nafplion, and I walked up the road to the entrance kiosk.

A bored-looking young man took a few drachmas from me to visit the ruins. Tyrns does not get the large amount of visitors that Mycenae gets since the fort is smaller and was largely ransacked for stone building material. All that really remains are the colossal base stones and a tunnel-archway made of gigantic boulders.

Still, the cyclopean walls were impressive and well worth a visit. I got a bus back into Nafplion and rested in the hotel. After a shower, I headed down to the waterfront to watch the sunset.

As I sipped a beer at a sidewalk café I thought about the ancient Greek epics. The scholar Henriette Mertz, a Chicago patent lawyer who had a penchant for ancient history, wrote several books about how some of the ancient Greek epics and legends told of the great transatlantic voyages made by the Greeks.

In *The Wine Dark Sea*[185] Mertz takes a scholarly look at the voyage of Odysseus (Ulysses to the Romans) from Homer's epic and tracks the voyage of the legendary sailor through the North Atlantic.

According to Mertz's detailed itinerary, Odysseus sails through the Straits of Gibraltar and into the North Atlantic, eventually arriving at the dangerous Bay of Fundy in Nova Scotia, the area she identifies as the "monsters" of Scylla and Charybdis. Homer has Odysseus attacked by Charybdis; being "sucked down into the salty sea—we could see within the swirling cataclysm of the great vortex and at the bottom the earth appeared black with sand while round about the rock roared terribly..." He is in reality (according to Mertz) caught in the deadly tidal bore of the Bay of Fundy.[185]

Similarly, Mertz gives a detailed account of how the story of Jason and the Argonauts is actually a story of a trip across the Atlantic, down the east coast of South America, past the mouth of the Amazon and Rio de Janeiro to the Rio Plata of Argentina. Jason and the Argonauts then go up this river to the altiplano of Bolivia and to Tiahuanaco, the location of the Golden Fleece.

Traditionally myopic scholars often place Jason's voyage in the Black Sea, a nearby location that every local sailor would have visited, and hardly the stuff of heroic epic voyages to the ends of the earth. Once again we are back to the idea that ancient sailors never journeyed beyond the sight of land. Where are the brave Greek heroes of yesterday—were they not as good seamen as the crew of Columbus? Indeed they were!

Mertz actually proposed in her book *Atlantis: Dwelling Place of the Gods*[184] that the eastern section of the United States, from the Mississippi and Ohio rivers east, was the Atlantis of Greek myth. It is a fascinating and well-thought-out book, but Mertz relies too heavily on the 1436 A.D. Andrea Bianco map which includes the Atlantic island of Antilla as proof.

She demonstrates a similarity between the map of Antilla, "Atlantis" as far as she is concerned, and the eastern portion of North America, using the Mississippi as the western shore of this "island." It is a theory that is fun to consider, but it is easily rejected because of Plato's dates, his statement that Atlantis actually sank beneath the ocean, and the fact that the 1436 Andrea Bianco map depicting Antilla most likely shows Cuba or Hispaniola.[184]

〰〰〰〰 ☥ 〰〰〰〰

Gigantic Construction Schemes of Ancient Greece

On the bus to Athens from Nafplion, I paged through a *Lonely Planet* guidebook and looked out the window. I read with interest that the island of Aegina has one of the best preserved ancient temples in all of Greece, the Temple of Aphaia. Aegina is also known for its sparkling white chapel dedicated to Saint Nicholas, of Santa Claus and Saint Nick fame.

Saint Nicholas is the patron saint of both Greek children and Greek sailors. In reality he was a 4th century A.D. bishop who was exiled during the Nestorian Heresy. The Dutch celebrate his feast day on December 6, which is a children's holiday. From this Dutch custom, New Yorkers began our current Santa Claus tradition.

Everyone in the bus watched as we passed over the Corinth Canal, a deep gash cut into the Greek mainland to link the Aegean Sea with the Ionian Sea across the narrow Corinth Isthmus.

The Corinth Canal idea was first proposed by Periander, the

"tyrant king," who founded ancient Corinth. The enormity of the task defeated him, so instead he built a paved slipway across which sailors dragged small ships on rollers, a method which was used until the 13th century.

Over the centuries many leaders including Alexander the Great and Caligula revived the idea of a canal to link the Ionian and Aegean. The digging actually started in 67 A.D. with Nero, who began the first digging by ceremoniously striking the earth with a golden pickax. He then set 6,000 Jewish prisoners to work digging out the six-kilometer-long canal. The work then had to be stopped because of the Gaulish invasion shortly afterward.

Appropriately, it was a French engineering company that finally completed the canal in 1893. Today the canal, cut through solid rock, is 23 meters wide with vertical sides rising 90 feet above the water. It is an impressive sight, and it shows the large scale of building that both modern and ancient man have undertaken.

Other gigantic construction projects exist in Greece. An 1884 article in *Knowledge* magazine discussed an ancient tunnel carved in solid rock. "The Governor of Samos, Abyssides Pasha, has at last succeeded, after years of work, in uncovering the entrances to a tunnel of which Herodotus speaks with admiration as the work of Eupalines and Megaira, and which, according to the same authority, was built during the tenth century B.C. The tunnel, about 5,000 feet long, was intended to secure a supply of fresh water to the old seaport town of Samos, and consists of three parts. They are the tunnel proper, 5 1/2 feet high and 6 feet wide; a canal about 5 feet deep and nearly 3 feet wide, which runs in the middle or on the side of the base of the tunnel; and the aqueduct running in this canal. The aqueduct consists of earthen pipes, each 2 1/2 feet long, 32 to 33 inches in circumference, the sides averaging about 1 1/2 inch in thickness.

"Every other joint has a hole, for what purpose has not yet been fully explained. Mr. Stamatiades, a Greek archaeologist, believes that they were intended to facilitate the cleaning of the pipes, and to make the flow of water easier. The canal is arched over, but twenty-eight manholes were provided to admit the workmen who were charged with cleaning and repairing the aqueduct. The tunnel is not quite straight, forming an elbow about 1,300 ft. from one of the entrances. This elbow, according to Mr. Stamatiades, was caused by a mistake in the calculations of the engineers, who had none of the instruments used in tunnel-building nowadays.

"The tunnel starts near a small water-course, which may have been quite a stream in olden times, pierces the mountain Kastri, which was formerly crowned by the fort Samos, and ends a few hundred yards from the old town of Samos, about 10 ft. below the surface. From the mountain slope to the city, this subter-ranean aqueduct is protected by a massive stone structure, ending within the walls of the present convent of St. John. The preservation of this work—which is truly wonderful, considering the imperfect mechanical resources at the disposal of the builders—for nearly three thousand years is probably due to the care taken by Eupalinos, who, in all cases where the rock did not seem of sufficient firmness, lined the tunnel with several layers of brick, running on the top into a peaked arch."[17]

Another article on early tunnels in Greece was written by the British archaeologist John Denison Champlin in 1895 for the magazine *Popular Science Monthly*. Said Champlin, "To guard against the recurrence of a similar catastrophe [flooding around Lake Copais in Greece], the ancient engineers planned several cuttings and tunnels through the hills, which, if they had been carried to completion, would have rounded out the original design and accomplished what the Greek government is today trying to effect—the thorough reclamation of the basin and its protection from any contingency of flood. On the southeast shore of the lake are vestiges of an immense cutting, thirty metres deep, through the Hill of Carditza toward Lake Hylicus, and beyond that traces of works to connect Hylicus with Paralimni, and the latter with the sea. Across the Hill of Carditza, too, are a series of excavated shafts marking the line of a tunnel through the hill constructed with an object similar to that of the cutting—to convey the waters to the sea through the smaller lakes; but the shafts are now filled up and there are no indications that the work was ever completed.

"This route is the one adopted by the modern engineers, who, by a tunnel through the Hill of Carditza, not far from the line of the ancient tunnel, seek to carry the waters into Lake Hylicus, thence into Paralimni, and finally through another tunnel into the sea. There is also a plan to deflect a portion of the waters for use in irrigating the plain of Thebes.

"A still more ambitious undertaking of the ancient engineers was an attempt to penetrate the Hill of Kephalari in the northeast end of the lake by a tunnel more than a mile and a quarter long."[17]

The creators of these tunnels are a mystery to archaeologists who wonder, "Who were the authors of these great works concerning which history is silent and which are themselves their only witnesses? Perhaps this question will never be satisfactorily answered. Leake and others attribute all the wells of Kephalari, as well as the canals, to the Minyans, while some believe that Crates of Chalcis was responsible for the parts exhibiting the most engineering skill, and others ascribe them to some of the earlier Roman emperors."[17]

~~~~~~~~~~☞~~~~~~~~~~

Ancient Athens and Sunken Greece

That night I stayed in a hotel in the Plaka district of the old city of Athens where I could see the Acropolis lit up by floodlights on the stone mountain above the city.

In Plato's *Critias* the Egyptian priests describe ancient Greece and Athens this way, "Now the country was inhabited in those days by various classes of citizens: artisans, tillers of the soil, and a warrior class originally set apart by divine men; these dwelt by themselves, and had all things suitable for nurture and education; neither had any of them anything of their own, but they regarded all things as common property; nor did they require to receive of the other citizens anything more than their necessary food. ...The land was the best in the world, and for this reason was able in those days to support a vast army, raised from the surrounding people...

"Now this country is only a promontory extending far into the sea away from the rest of the continent, and the surrounding basin of the sea is everywhere deep in the neighborhood of the shore. Many great deluges have taken place during the 9,000 years, for that is the number of years that have elapsed since the time of which I am speaking...

"Hence, in comparison of what then was, there are remaining in small islets only the bones of the wasted body, as they may be called; all the richer and softer parts of the soil having fallen away, and the mere skeleton of the country being left. But in former days, and in the primitive state of the country, what are now mountains were regarded only as hills; and the plains, as they are now termed, of Phelleus were full of rich earth, and there was an abundance of wood in the mountains."

What is clearly being said in the *Critias* is that the many small islands of Greece were once the mountaintops of a large, fertile country that was well wooded and with a larger population than Greece had in Plato's time.

The *Critias* goes on to describe ancient Athens: "Such was the natural state of the country, which was cultivated, as we may well believe, by true farmers, and had a soil the best in the world, and abundance of water, and in the heaven above an excellently tempered climate. Now the city in those days was arranged thus: in the first place the Acropolis was not as now. For the fact is that a single night of excessive rain washed away the earth and laid bare the rock; at the same time there were earthquakes, and then occurred the third extraordinary inundation, which immediately preceded the great deluge of Deukalion..."

~~~~~~~~~~~🜨~~~~~~~~~~~

During my days in Athens I wandered through the city and visited the National Museum.

The museum showed how Egyptian influence was strong in Greece with many sphinx-type motifs. Some of the early Greek figurines looked to me very much like the South Sea Island statues called tikis.

There were many wax seals of the Cretan, Indus Valley and Chinese type, all found in Greece. Many had ancient Hindu designs such as monkeys, peacocks and Buddhist crosses. In the metallurgy room I was able to view the famous Antikythera device, discussed in the previous chapter.

I spent evenings having dinner in the Plaka below the Acropolis. While the current Parthenon was only built in 438 B.C., the megalithic foundations of the Acropolis go back many thousands of years.

If Plato, Solon and the Egyptian priests are correct, then ancient Athens was a high valley fort when the Aegean valley was also dry. Megalithic ruins such as those at Ba'albek and Jerusalem are the basis for other ancient megalithic cultures that began again after the cataclysm that destroyed Atlantis.

During the war between Greece and Atlantis, as described by Plato, Athens was but a satellite city. The capital city, at least of this region, would now be underwater beneath the Aegean.

Catastrophic earthquakes and floods were familiar to classical Greek writers. Thucydides in *The Peloponnesian War* (written in 411 B.C.) says, "In the ensuing summer the Peloponnesians and their allies ...intended to invade Attica, but were deterred from proceeding by numerous earthquakes, and no invasion took place in this year. About the time when these earthquakes prevailed, the sea at Orobiai in Euboia, retiring from what was then the line of the coast and rising in a great wave, overflowed a part of the city; and although it subsided in some places, yet in others the inundation was permanent, and that which was formerly land is now sea. All the people who could not escape to high ground perished. A similar inundation occurred in the neighborhood of Atalantë, an island on the coast of the Opuntian Locri, which carried away a part of an Athenian fort, and dashed in pieces one of two ships which were drawn up on the beach. At Perarethos,also the sea retired, but no inundation followed; an earthquake, however, overthrew a part of the wall, the Prytaneus, and a few houses."

Though earthquakes and tidal waves can cause devastating loss of life and property, such a relatively small quake is not the same as the cataclysmic earth changes that sank Atlantis and flooded the Mediterranean. This disaster, which Plato, Solon, the Egyptian priests and the Bible speak of, was in the far distant past, thousands of years before.

My time in Greece was coming to an end. I browsed the many bookstores in Athens, and after a few days I was on my way north. I was headed for the mystical oracle of Delphi. My ultimate destination was the island of Corfu and then on to Italy.

Super-Quarries Around the World

In a number of diverse locations around the world a distinct type of super-quarry has been discovered. These are located in Peru, opposite Ollantaytambo, in Greece at Pieria, at Ba'albek in the Middle East and other places.

Megalithic quarries around the world are important in our understanding of Atlantis. Other megalithic quarries are those at Mitla in Mexico, Uaxactun in Guatemala, the Bolivian altiplano 20 miles from Tiahuanaco, and the quarries in Wales and Ireland.

The amazing megalithic quarry at Pieria is located about 20 kilometers north of Mount Olympus in the mountainous forests of Macedonia. On the mountain of Pieria, in one of the last vestiges of the ancient forest that covered much of ancient Greece, can be found a strange marble quarry from which thousands of tons of gigantic marble blocks were removed in remote times.

The quarry still has the remains of some of the blocks and odd parallel grooves can be found in the sheer walls of cliffs where the blocks have been cut. Huge blocks, waiting for transportation to their final destination, lie stacked and scattered about the quarry area. Each has the strange parallel grooves on one or two sides. The quarry appears to have been abandoned in great haste, much like the megalithic quarries at Ba'albek and Ollantaytambo in Peru.

Some years ago I climbed with my Peruvian guide to the granite mountain above the Urubamba River that runs beside the megalithic fortress of Ollantaytambo. The three-hour climb eventually brought us to the quarry site where gigantic blocks of stone, the size of railway cars, were squared off and waiting to be moved down the mountain and across the river to the fortress site.

As at Pieria, many of the blocks lie at the quarry, never having made the journey. What had stopped the construction and movement of these stones at Ba'albek, Pieria and Peru? Why are stones that had taken a great deal of effort to quarry just left at the quarry site? Had a sudden cataclysm and corresponding collapse of civilization (and therefore megalith building) suddenly ended the effort of quarrying and moving the blocks? Apparently so.

It is assumed that the parallel grooves in these blocks are the lines drilled in the stone to separate the blocks from the quarry cliffs. Yet, it has not been explained how this was accomplished. In his book *Mysteries In the Human World and Mind*[161] the Greek writer Konstantinos Zissis discusses the megalithic quarry and its mysteries.

Says Zissis, "One observes a definite pattern of parallel grooves in the rock walls, which obviously means that extremely advanced, sophisticated 'machines' have been used to loosen enormous blocks of up to 10 to 15 meters in length, all of this done with great precision. Thousands of blocks have been transported to unknown places, while many others still lie where they were left, spread out in front of the rock. This could very possibly indicate that the quarry, for reasons unknown, was suddenly abandoned."[161]

Continues Zissis, "What kind of machines do we have at our disposal today that would enable us to extricate such massive stone blocks in such a complicated way as was done at Pieria? The technological resources of our age would not be able to achieve anything of the kind. Minute examination of the grooves will confirm this. Something else that renders the parallel grooves even more inexplicable, is that they appear at the rounded corners formed in the rock when the blocks were loosened. The surfaces of fracture show that some kind of boring process was used. If we proceed from the assumption that the grooves were created by drilling, they hardly become less puzzling—just the opposite! Then it becomes all the more exciting to find out just how they were created, since it is impossible for us to drill in this way today. A method vastly superior to our own was used at the quarry at Pieria."

Zissis then gives evidence that a melting of the stones has occurred: "...the parallel grooves mentioned earlier ...have been partially melted away ...small, crater-like holes, similar to pores, can be clearly seen over the entire surface. Such holes appear on all surfaces of fracture on the rock walls, even on the surfaces of the blocks. The size of the holes varies: in some places they are quite deep, in others hardly discernible. But here, in the depressions of the grooves, they are highly visible. This kind of cavity is one of many signs indicating that the surfaces had been exposed to some kind of melting process. (On most cement walls similar cavities can be seen, the result of drying of the wet cement.) The fact that the entire surface had been melted down renders the quarrying method all the more inexplicable and complicated."

Zissis says that the grooves show a wavelike form, rather than being perfectly straight. "On some surfaces of fracture the grooves wholly or partially disappeared. In these places the marble has reached its melting point and turned liquid, resulting in the melting away of the grooves. The question is really how the marble could have gone through a melting process at all! Was the rock exposed to intense heat which caused the melting process? In that case, how could the exceedingly high temperatures necessary to melt stone be produced? With lasers? Perhaps chemical liquids, unknown to us today, were used in prehistoric times to soften and melt stone?"[161]

And what does Zissis attribute the quarry to? Well, Atlantis, of course! And it is not a bad theory; at least it would explain some of the mysteries. Where have the thousands of megalithic blocks gone? Why, to the megalithic cities that are now beneath the Aegean, as the Egyptian priests told Solon at Säis. We might presume that the event which suddenly caused the abandonment of the quarry is the same cataclysmic event that sank Atlantis and flooded the Mediterranean.

Zissis finds it interesting that his "Quarry of the Gods" is near Mount Olympus, the legendary abode of the Greek gods. Near to Olympus is the ancient and mysterious site of Dion. Only recently discovered, Dion is an extensive, well-watered site at the foot of Mt. Olympus. According to my guidebook, Dion was the sacred city of the Acedons, who gathered there to worship the Olympian gods. Alexander made sacrifices to the Olympian gods at Dion before setting out to conquer the world.

Says my *Lonely Planet Guide to Greece,* "Dion's origins are unknown but there is evidence that an earth goddess of fertility was first worshiped here. Later, other gods were worshiped, including Asklepios, the god of medicine. The most interesting discovery so far is the evocative Sanctuary to Isis, the Egyptian goddess, in a lush low-lying part of the site. Its votive statues were found virtually intact with traces of color remaining."

Why an Isis temple at Mount Olympus? A leftover from the days of Osiris and Isis? A reminder of the Egyptian-Osirian origin of civilization in the eastern Mediterranean? Perhaps Osiris and Isis still reign as gods from lofty Mount Olympus.

Said Homer of Mount Olympus, "...the goddess, flashing-eyed Athena, departed to Olympus where, they say, is the abode of the gods that stands fast forever. Neither is it shaken by winds nor ever wet with rain, nor does snow fall upon it, but the air is outspread clear and cloudless, and over it hovers a radiant whiteness. Therein the blessed gods are glad all their days and thither went the flashing-eyed one, when she had spoken all her word to the maiden."(*Odyssey* VI, 41-47)

The Nekromanteion and the River Styx

I checked into a hotel at Delphi and began to read about the fascinating but little-known ruins of northern Greece.

The ruins of Nekromanteion, Cassopé and Pandosia are megalithic sites near Amoudia on the western coast, clustered around Lake Acherousia, an ancient lake, now drained. The impressive walls are made of finely cut angular and polygonal blocks as fine as any in Peru. Many of the ruins are so old that the cyclopean walls are incorporated in other ancient ruins of a more classical period.

The Nekromanteion of Aphyra is one of the oldest and most unusual structures in all of Greece. The Nekromanteion is found along the River Acheron where the ruins can be reached by foot. According to Greek mythology, the River Acheron was the ancient River Styx across which the old boatman, Charon, rowed the dead. Until the departed had taken this journey they could not enter Hades, the world of the dead, and so were kept in a state of limbo.

The Nekromanteion was believed to be the spot where the Gates of Hades lay, and so the labyrinthine ruins became an oracle of the dead and a sanctuary dedicated to Hades and Persephone. Pilgrims came to the site with votive offerings in the hope that the souls of the departed would communicate with them through the oracle.

In the lore of Atlantis, when the Mediterranean was a valley, it was the River Styx that ran through Egypt, past Greece and Malta and then out into the Atlantic past the Pillars of Hercules.

As it happened, on my last day at the Nekromanteion, I rented a motorbike and went touring around the countryside. On my way back to the city, coming down a mountain road, I rounded a corner—a large truck blocked my path! I hit the brakes, desperate to avoid it, but the motorcycle swerved and I lost control.

Over the handlebars I went. Luckily, I missed the truck and fell sprawling on the pavement. I lay there stunned. My head was OK, though I had not been wearing a helmet, but my right leg, which had been caught in the handlebars, was broken just below the knee.

I lay in agony on the road for a while until several truck drivers stopped to help me. From a nearby small town they called an ambulance, which came in about half an hour. I managed to crawl onto a stretcher and was placed in the back of the ambulance.

On the way, I blacked out. I awoke in the emergency room of the local hospital. There they forcibly straightened out my leg while pain shot up my side. Later in a hospital bed I was told of my torn knee and broken leg. It was a difficult operation, the doctor said, but they could do it.

"Your leg is badly broken," the surgeon informed me. "Can you feel your toes and move them?"

In pain I looked down at my broken leg and wiggled my toes

together. "Yes," I said.

"Good, then it is not an emergency, your nerves have not been severed. We will operate tomorrow."

I had surgery about noon the next day and woke up in the evening in a bare room, my leg bandaged in a splint. Directly in front of my bed was a poster of Donald Duck in his classic blue sailor suit. To the right of him were three postcards of Greek saints and the Archangel Michael. Otherwise the walls were pale blue and bare. I wondered if size had any relationship to the importance of these characters.

For the next week I lay in the hospital practically delirious with an I.V., painkiller shots, anticoagulation shots and occasional doctor visits. Every few days someone would wander into the room selling religious artifacts and icons of Greek saints to the sick. One day I succumbed to the salesman and bought a small scene of St. George defeating a dragon and had it hung on my wall next to Donald.

My first roommate was a retired Greek gigolo who had married a Swedish tourist and lived in Stockholm. He was back in Greece on holiday and had begun drinking retsina wine late one afternoon. His drinking session had ended at four in the morning when he crashed through the plate glass window of a storefront and broke his left leg and cut his right arm quite badly.

He spoke English well, but I quickly decided that he was quite mad—he would yell at the nurses late at night, complain about the food constantly, and channel surf on his rented television all day and night.

"Have you ever been in love?" he asked me one day. "You haven't because when you're in love, you learn to hate. You start by being in love, but then you become jealous and you hate that person. You learn to hate. That is love."

I tried to roll over, but I couldn't. He yelled at the nurses a bit. Donald and the other saints looked down compassionately at us.

The nurses took good care of me. I was the American archaeologist who did not speak Greek but studied the classical texts. One was the beautiful young nurse Helen, whose face might easily have launched a thousand ships. Sometimes when I looked up from the delirium of my bed she would be standing there smiling sweetly at me, a syringe in one hand to inject my stomach with anticoagulants.

"Can I help you get comfortable?" she would ask in English, offering to shift my leg on the pillow it rested on.

"Helen..." was all I could manage to say before falling back into my hospital stupor.

While in the hospital I thought of the devastating wars that had been fought over and over again since the time of Atlantis. Lying in bed I saw armies marching across the Middle East leaving a wake of destruction behind them while they murdered and looted. The survivors were now slaves, the soldiers showed no mercy and delighted in their sport of warfare.

How long must the earth suffer this violence and depravity? What had mankind sown and what must he ultimately reap? The savage wars of Atlantis and its aftermath continued today, with the reincarnated combatants still fighting for nationalism and religious ideology. Only Armageddon, it seemed, could put a stop to mankind's slaughter of his fellow man. Technology was advanced to serve the men of war as more and more sophisticated forms of dealing death are being invented.

"Are you all right?" asked Helen, suddenly standing at my bedside. I realized I had been crying. Tears ran down my cheeks.

"I heard you crying," said Helen. "Do you need anything? Should I call a doctor?"

"No," I said, wiping my eyes. "No, I'm fine. Thank you."

"Are you comfortable?" she asked. Her smile was reassuring as she gently lifted my bound leg and fluffed the pillow underneath it.

A few days later an ambulance took me to the airport where I would fly back to the United States. I thanked the gods of Olympus that I was still alive. I thought of the many close calls I had had around the world—nearly killed in an avalanche in the Himalayas, almost knifed by a soldier in Uganda, held at gunpoint on a bus in the Ecuadorian Andes, and other close calls—had I used up all nine lives?

I hoped I still had a few left...

The Lion Gate at Mycenae as it looked in 1874 when Schliemann first began to excavate.

Top: The Lion Gate at Mycenae with the cyclopean walls that surrounded the city.
Below: The nearby cyclopean fortress of Tiryns, also excavated by Schliemann.

The gigantic entrance door to the Mycenaean beehive structure
known as the "Treasury of Atreus."

An underwater photo of the edge of the main street in the submerged
Mycenaean city of Elaphonisos off the southern Peloponesse coast.

Top: Megaliithic blocks lie scattered and abandoned at the quarry of Piera. Bottom: Huge blocks are stacked and waiting to be transported. Apparently the megalithic construction projects came to a sudden halt, possibly because of some catastrophe.

The Super-Quarry of Piera, near Mount Olympus.

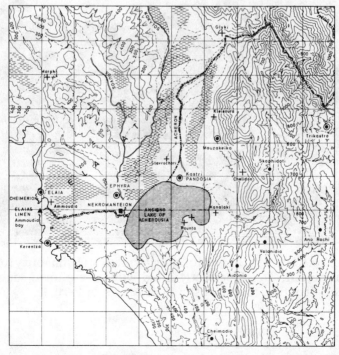

Map of ancient Lake Acyherousia and the megalithic city of Nekromanteion.

Top and bottom: The beautiful polygonal stone masonry of the Nekromanteion. These perfectly fitted walls are almost identical to the construction found in the high Andes of Peru.

Linear A writing found on Cretan tablets.
Note the frequent sun-wheels.

THE MOTHER GODDESS

In the Cyclades

In Crete

In Malta

Chapter 5
ITALY & SICILY:
Etruscans &
the Legacy of Rome

The years will come, in the eld of the world
When Ocean will loosen his grip on things,
When the land will extend itself afar,
And Tethys new continents will disclose
Nor will Thulë then be the end of the earth.
—Seneca, *Medea*

After my motorcycle accident in Greece, it took several months of physical therapy before I could walk again, but soon I was back on my feet—literally. While laid up, I studied books on Atlantis and planned my next trip to Europe and the Mediterranean so I could complete my research on Atlantis. Finally, my doctors told me that I could travel again, and though I used a cane for a few weeks, I could soon walk without a limp.

It was late summer when I arrived at the airport in Rome. Within moments I was in a taxi and was swept into the magnificent old city.

Several days of seeing the old city of Rome, including the city-state of the Vatican, impressed me with the majesty of Roman civilization. I was amazed to learn, for instance, that the Romans had engineered the Colosseum to be flooded through a system of hydraulic locks so as to be able to stage mock naval battles.

The Romans built great aqueducts, bridges and roads all over Europe, the Middle East and North Africa. The Romans are not without their mystery, but the world of ancient Italy goes back many thousands of years. One of the most mysterious peoples who ever existed lived in an area just north of Rome. They were called the Tyrrhenians or Etruscans.

The Etruscans and the Atlantean League

The area just north of Rome is the center of a cultural mystery that may well go back to the civilization of Atlantis. In the Po River region a sophisticated people lived and vanished. History cannot decide who these people were.

The Etruscans are barely known to historians, but we do know that by the seventh century B.C., the Etruscans had founded a confederation of twelve city-states in Italy, united more by religious solidarity than by political union, probably at Veio, Caere, Tarquinii, Vulci, Rusellae, Vetulonia, Volsinii, Clusium, Perugia, Cortona, Arretium and Volateera. They extended their domain by a series of conquests, subjugating other Italian tribes including the Latins. An Etruscan dynasty, the Tarquins, ruled Rome from 616 to 509 B.C. Uniting their naval strength with that of the Carthaginians, the Etruscans held in check the Greek colonists of southern Italy, defeating the Greeks at the battle of Alatia in 535 B.C. That was the apogee of Etruscan power. Then slow decline set in. The Etruscan fleet was defeated by the Greeks at Cumae in the Bay of Naples in 474 B.C. The republican Romans destroyed Veio in 396, Volsinii in 265. The first Italian civilization had been vanquished and the Romans now ruled the peninsula.[236]

Many theories have been advanced to explain the Etruscans' decline and fall. They may have failed to weld themselves into a nation. They suffered from social stagnation, from over-rigid class distinctions. All power was held by the ruling families. They guarded their ancestral habits too jealously. Says historian Rupert Furneaux, "They were too conservative, fearing change. They suffered from slavish obedience to their soothsayers, the 'haruspices,' or priestly caste who divined the will of the gods from the clap of thunder, the flight of a bird, the scrutiny of livers. They gave the Etruscans false hopes of greatness, too strong a certainty of their destiny."

Furneaux goes on to say that according to the Roman historian Livy, the Etruscans were more addicted to religious practices than any other nation. They passed on their practice of liver-reading to the Romans. "It suggests an oriental influence on Etruscan life, derived from Canaanite beliefs, or the Assyrian Magi. A bronze model of a liver found at Piacenza is divided into forty-five areas, each inscribed with the name of the presiding divinity. The Etruscans were equally concerned with the afterlife. Therein lies the paradox of their culture. Gay, pleasure-loving, self-indulgent, they were obsessed with death. Nearly all knowledge of the Etruscans is derived from their mausolea. They revealed their activities in their art, the shape of their temples, the plans of their houses, the streets of their cities, their banquets and games, their hope of resurrection. They created an image of the present as a stubborn challenge to the future. No other ancient people equaled the Etruscans in self-esteem."[236]

Did this self-esteem come from their knowledge that they were descended of a powerful and civilized nation and were therefore more sophisticated than other Mediterraneans?

Following their absorption by the Romans, the Etruscan cities and tombs were submerged and lost to view. Several of their statues and tombs were found during the period of the Renaissance. Some art historians have detected Etruscan motifs in fifteenth-century Italian sculptures. The rediscovery of two great bronzes, the famous Capitoline wolf and the statue of the orator, excited interest and led to the search for the subterranean dwellings of the Etruscan dead.

The first modern rediscoveries of the Etruscans were made in 1728 when the first of the underground tombs was discovered. The chance discovery ten years later of a tomb at Palestrina revealed the Ficoroni coffer, depicting various episodes of the voyages of the Argonauts, one of the ancient masterpieces of engraving in bronze. By mid eighteenth century the excavators had penetrated the frescoed tombs of Corneto (present-day Tarquinia). Archaeologists, mostly amateurs, scoured the Etruscan countryside searching for more ancient treasures. In 1828 a team of oxen fell into a tomb at Vulci. In 1834 a beautiful sarcophagus was found in a tomb at Tuscania. During the next hundred years, subterranean tombs were discovered at Cerveten, Vulci, Tarquinia, Veio, Orvieto and many other places. An amazing, forgotten world had been revealed.[236]

In *The Buried People*[232] by German archaeologist Sibylle von Cles-Reden, the author shows how the Etruscans were sophisticated seafarers and travellers. Says she, "Mysterious as the appearance of the Etruscans in Italy must remain, we know even less—almost nothing, indeed—of their history and their very way of life. Nothing survives of the kingdom of Rasenna, except hundreds and thousands of tombs. Yet, from the eighth to the fifth century B.C. they were a great power in occupation of the whole coastline of the Tyrrhenian Sea. The Greek city of Cumae was the sole independent enclave in the whole extent of the empire from Paestum in the south, including probably the whole valley of the Po to the Adriatic, and to the foot of the Alps in the north. It included the island of Elba with its valuable deposits of ferrous metals, as well as the eastern part of Corsica."[232]

The Romans inherited the Etruscans' ambitious dream of a Mediterranean empire and the uniting of the entire Italian peninsula into a single power. The Etruscans were defeated by the Romans, who waged war on their former lords and masters. Says von Cles-

Reden, the Romans were "inexorably drawn into conflict with the people to whom they owed their civilization. They had no alternative but to subject the dying race under their own protectorate, to destroy its very consciousness of its own individuality and independence, before they could feel themselves entirely free in the cultural sphere as well as in the political."[232]

By 200 B.C. or so the Tyrrhenian people were disappearing from the map of history. The art, religion and customs of the Etruscans were absorbed into those of Rome. As Roman religion is very similar to that of the ancient Greeks, we may assume that the Etruscan religion was also similar, as the bronze depiction of Jason and the Argonauts suggests.

Sadly, as libraries and ancient knowledge have been destroyed throughout history, such is also the case with the Etruscan language. The Roman Emperor Claudius wrote an eight-volume work on the Etruscans, but these books are lost.

Says von Cles-Reden, "Not a single bilingual inscription or document has been discovered to make possible a definitive solution to the riddle of the Etruscan language. We can read the texts, and we know how the words were pronounced; but despite the recent efforts of Etruscology based on the comparative method, it is impossible to determine the sense of more than about 100 words, which is far too few to provide a basis for the serious study of the language.

The short funerary inscriptions, a great number of which have survived, almost invariably use exactly the same words. The longer scrolls were written rolls of cloth which have not withstood the passage of time—with one exception. This exception is a roll that was cut into strips and used to wrap round a mummy, and found at Agram. Philologists have devoted years to trying to decipher the 1,500 words of its text, but they have produced strikingly different results. On one point at least, however, they are unanimous: the language of the Etruscans, which was written in an archaic version of the Greek alphabet, belongs neither to the Indo-European nor to the Semitic group of languages. It is believed to have been a purely Mediterranean language, antedating the period of expansion of the Indo-European group (2000 B.C.?), and surviving from an archaic linguistic era which probably embraced Greece and Crete as well. This language was already in process of disappearing at the beginning of the historical period. Traces of it remain in the pre-Indo-European names of families and places in Greece and Asia Minor, as well as in one surviving language of our own day, namely, Basque. But nothing is to be gained by turning to Basque to elucidate the meaning of Etruscan words."[232]

We see how the only language related to Etruscan was found to be Basque and this language has been related to Atlantis. The strange

Basque language is more fully discussed in the chapter on Spain, but let us say that Basque is a strange and unique language whose origin is a complete mystery.

Like the Basques, the Etruscans were apparent survivors of the catastrophe that destroyed Atlantis and caused the deluge in the Mediterranean. Later, survivors from Central Asia and Iran (the land of the Aryan) invaded Europe and the eastern Mediterranean. They eventually left isolated pockets of the original Atlantean tongue, such as the Etruscans, Basques and Berbers. The Egyptians may have already had a separate language from the Atlantean tongue, but we will probably never know exactly the correct pronunciation of ancient Egyptian words.

The Etruscans probably were part of the Sea Peoples' invasion of 1200 B.C. and may well have been allied with the powerful naval empires of northern Europe that are still a mystery to historians today. The Etruscans used an axe that is very similar to the double-headed axe (called "labrys") used on Crete. This same type of axe is engraved onto one of the megalithic slabs at Stonehenge.

Agnes Carr Vaughan in her book *Those Mysterious Etruscans*[231] writes that the Etruscans were steeped in magical spells and superstitious rites. She also mentions that the first Etruscan archaeologist, Fustel de Coulanges, a professor of history at Strasbourg, noted the similarity of the Etruscans and their obsession with religion to the Hindus of India. According to Vaughan, de Coulanges believed the early Greeks, Etruscans and Hindus sprang from the same source.[231]

Here we see how the Etruscan world can be compared to the ancient world of India. In the ancient Indian epic of the Mahabharata, several advanced civilizations on earth fight a horrific war, similar to Plato's Egyptian account of Atlantis. Were the Etruscans one of the enemies of Rama and his empire of central India?

Curiously, Etruscan statuary often shows the Hindu "tika" or third-eye mark on the forehead between the eyes. The Etruscans also made masks and statuary of Gorgons, those mythological monsters with the face of a man and large fangs going both up and down. Gorgon images are common in Hindu mythology and commonly seen as far east as Bali in Indonesia.

The Etruscans generally depicted Gorgons as having the "tika" third-eye mark between the eyes. In Atlantis lore it is said that the Atlanteans believed in reincarnation and astral projection just as modern and ancient Hindus do. The ancient Greeks and apparently the Etruscans believed in reincarnation and the eternal life of the soul.

However, like the Egyptians and other cultures, a priestly cult of the dead took control of the people and fostered an expensive funerary custom, one of entombing the dead in fabulously carved and furnished tombs. Mummification or embalming of the dead also occurred in ancient Italy, much as the Egyptians practiced it.

Diodorus of Sicily (circa 25 B.C.), who wrote his *University History* during the reign of the Roman Emperor Augustus, when the Etruscans were only a memory, provides a humorous view in this cleverly satirical description:

"The Etruscans, who formerly were distinguished for their energy, conquered a vast territory and there founded many important towns. They also disposed of powerful naval forces and for a long time enjoyed mastery of the seas, so much so that the one which washed the western shores of Italy was called by them the Tyrrhenian. They perfected the equipment of their land forces by inventing what is called the trumpet, which is of the greatest utility in war and was named by them Tyrrhenian; they also devised marks of honor for the generals who led them, assigning to them lictors (attendants), an ivory throne and a toga bordered with purple. And in their houses they invented the peristyle (an open space or courtyard surrounded by a colonnade) which is a great convenience in that it deadens the uproar caused by their great crowds of servants. The majority of these discoveries were imitated by the Romans, who incorporated them into their civilization.

"They encouraged the progress of letters, science, nature and theology and developed to a higher degree than any other people the interpretation of thunder. This is why today they still inspire those who are masters of nearly all the world (the Romans) with such deep admiration, and why they are employed today as interpreters of the celestial signs. As they inhabit a land fertile in fruits of all kinds and cultivate it assiduously, they enjoy an abundance of agricultural produce which not only is sufficient for themselves but by its excess leads them to unbridled luxury and indolence. For twice a day they have tables sumptuously dressed and laid with everything that can contribute towards delicate living; they have coverings embroidered with flowers and are served wine in quantities of silver bowls, and they have at their call a considerable number of slaves. Some of the latter are of a rare beauty; others dress themselves in clothes more magnificent than befits their station of servitude, and the domestic staff have all kinds of private dwellings: as have indeed most of the freed men.

"In general they have abandoned the valiant steadfastness that they prized so much in former days, and by their indulgencies in banquets and effeminate delights they have lost the reputation which their ancestors won in war, which does not surprise us. But what served more than anything to turn them to soft and idle living was the quality of their land, for, living in a country that produces everything and is of inexhaustible fecundity, they are able to store up large quantities of fruit of every kind. Etruria is indeed very fertile, extending for the most part over plains separated by hills with arable slopes and it is moderately well-watered, not only in the winter season, but also during the summer."[236]

Diodorus' satirical view of the Etruscans is a clever criticism of Rome, with its many servants, constant warfare and obsession with divining the future from various omens. The Etruscans were clever as well, but who were these sophisticated but mysterious people? Were the Etruscans from Atlantis or some colony of Atlantis? No one knows where they came from. Furneaux says that when Herodotus wrote his history in the fifth century B.C. he related that they had migrated from Asia Minor in about 1000 B.C., as refugees fleeing from the great famine which had struck the kingdom of Lydia (western Turkey). Writing five centuries later, Dionysius of Halicarnassus was fully convinced that they were a very ancient indigenous people who "do not resemble any other in its language and its customs."[236]

Says Rupert Furneaux, "...excavation alone is unlikely to solve the problem of Etruscan origins. The craniological study of Etruscan skulls has failed to elucidate the mystery. The blood grouping of their descendants, those who have been little ethnologically disturbed, has proved equally inconclusive. The slightly higher proportion of blood groups A and B than amongst their neighbors seems to connect them with certain oriental peoples. The Etruscan language is considered not to belong to the Indo-European group of languages, the speech of their Greek and Roman contemporaries. The French linguist Zacharie Maigani believes they originated in Albania. The German scholar, Barthold Georg Niebuhr, asserts that they came from beyond the Alps."[236]

The suggestion that the Etruscans had come over the Alps is an interesting thought. They may have been coming from the newly submerged areas around the North Sea as suggested in Jurgen Spanuth's *Atlantis of the North*. [237]

It seems unlikely that the Etruscans had come from the Middle East as Herodotus says, so I will have to agree with Dionysius of Halicarnassus. The Etruscans may have been part of the Sea Peoples' invasion of the eastern Mediterranean circa 1200 B.C. The Etruscans were more probably from the west, like the Basques. What ancient library of Etruscan history have we lost to the destroyers of history? What tales of lost cities and ancient catastrophes might they have told?

As I went by train up north to Milan and then across to Venice, I thought about the Etruscans and the lost cities of Italy. Many Etruscan cities are literally under water while others have been submerged and later reemerged.

The Etruscan city of Spina in the Adriatic was mentioned by Pliny the Elder and by Strabo, according to Andrew Tomas in his book *Atlantis: From Legend to Discovery*.[24] This once thriving city is presently submerged.

Tomas mentions other sunken cities in the Adriatic and Black Sea: "Dioscuria, the city in the Black Sea of Sukhumi visited by the legendary Argonauts, is at present under water. Phanagoria, an ancient Greek port of considerable size—also in the Black Sea—has sunk into the waters of Taman Bay."[24]

In *Mysteries From Forgotten Worlds*[9] Charles Berlitz says, "A large part of the bottom of the Mediterranean seems to consist of cliffs, crags, and valleys, as if it were not sea bottom but land covered by the sea. Many of the cities and ports of the Mediterranean now under water have been engulfed or sunk within historic times, sometimes even going down and then coming up again, as can be seen in the case of ancient temple columns in Pozzuoli, Italy, now above water, which show distinct marks of underwater borers from the temple's last prolonged immersion in the sea. However there are other earlier sunken cities in the Mediterranean and the Aegean located at much greater depths, to which they may have fallen as the result of the many earthquakes endemic to the region."[9]

Hugh Auchincloss Brown, the well-known author of *Cataclysms of the Earth*,[35] also used the Temple of Serapis at Pozzuoli on the Adriatic Sea's Gulf of Venice as evidence for the cataclysms that he claimed affected the earth every 10,000 years or so.

According to Brown, the temple must have been first erected above sea level (Brown estimates between 12,000 and 19,000 years ago, though this period of submergence, as this book attempts to prove, may have happened much closer to classical history), then submerged and finally reemerged from the sea. Brown cites the evidence that the temple must have been at least 20 feet under water for a period of time because of the holes left by boring clams 15 to 20 feet above the present sea level.

Brown, like Charles Hapgood, was an early proponent of so-called "pole shifts" during which the earth's crust allegedly shifts several degrees. Says Brown, "The present location of Pozzuoli is approximately 46° N. latitude, but at the time the Temple was erected, its latitude was 40°. The earth did a roll-around which was caused by the eccentric rotating mass of ice at the North Pole, and Pozzuoli moved to approximately 65° N. latitude at which time the temple was submerged."35,73

Tomas mentions another temple of Serapis that is submerged on the west coast of Italy, the Jupiter-Serapis temple in the Bay of Naples. Built by the Romans (possibly on Etruscan ruins) in 105 B.C., it gradually sank into the Mediterranean, but in 1742 the temple rose again from the sea bottom. Currently the temple is once again sinking into the bay.24

Tomas also mentions the fortress of Caravan-Sarai, an oasis fortress on the desert shores of the Caspian Sea erected in 1135. "In the course of time it slowly disappeared underwater. From then on all references to this fort in ancient records became so puzzling that Caravan-Sarai turned into a fable. In 1723 the islet rose above the sea and is still clearly visible."24

Indeed, the fabled city of Caravan-Sarai even came into the languages of Arabic, English and all European languages as caravanserai, which is the term for a fortified or guarded oasis along the ancient trade routes of Asia, especially the Silk Road through Central Asia.

≈≈≈≈≈≈≈≈ ❧ ≈≈≈≈≈≈≈

Out-of-Place Roman Artifacts

When Rome vanquished the Etruscans and Carthaginians it inherited their maritime routes and expertise and began to travel far beyond the Mediterranean. Roman influence spread as far north as England, and Roman coins have been found in Iceland, Mexico, Illinois, South America and various other places around the world.

These out-of-place artifacts are called Ooparts by Ivan T. Sanderson and his scientific investigative team at INFO (now defunct; Sanderson died in 1973). Ooparts of a Roman kind appear all over the world. A simple Roman coin in a farmer's field in Iowa is considered an Oopart today for the simple reason that the reigning academic school of history claims that the Romans were never in Iowa, or anywhere outside of Europe and the Mediterranean region of Asia and Africa.

Says William Corliss in his scholarly collection of oddball scientific items, *Ancient Man,*17 "Almost from the time of the first American settlers, people have been discovering old coins in unlikely places. Roman coins, especially, have turned up in farmers' fields, on beaches, and elsewhere across the country. It seems that the Romans and other pre-Columbian peoples either strayed far beyond the Gates of Hercules or a lot of numismatists had holes in their pockets."

Corliss repeats an entire article from *Antiquity* (No. 23, pages 161-163, 1949) entitled "Roman Coins Found In Iceland." Says the 1949 article: "The State Antiquary of Iceland, Kristjan Eldjarn, M.A., published in January this year a fine volume containing a report of his recent excavations of pagan graves, and other contributions to early Icelandic history, under the title of *Gengidh a Reika* (1948). It is very important that we have got here reliable accounts of systematically explored Viking burials, with diagrams and photographs, all very well done, as Iceland had produced, till now, very little of similar publications. But really exciting is undeniably the news of the discovery of three Roman coins in Iceland.

"...The three coins date from the time of the emperors Aurelian (270-5), Probus (276-82) and Diocletian (284-305)—a period some 600 years before the Norse colonization of Iceland towards the end of the 9th century, and thus is raised a most interesting problem concerning the early navigation of the north Atlantic Ocean."[17]

More importantly, Roman artifacts have been found in Latin America. A large hoard of Roman jewelry was found in graves near Mexico City by Dr. Garcia Payón of the University of Jalapa in 1961. Roman *fibula* (a clip used to hold together a toga) as well as Roman coins have frequently been found. In fact, a ceramic jar containing several hundred Roman coins, bearing dates ranging from the reign of Augustus down to 350 A.D. and every intervening period, was found on a beach in Venezuela. This cache is now in the Smithsonian Institution. Experts there have stated that the coins are not a misplaced collection belonging to an ancient numismatist, but probably a Roman sailor's ready cash, either concealed in the sand or washed ashore from a shipwreck.[238, 57]

Evidence for Roman trips to the Americas is overwhelming. In 1976, a Brazilian diver named Jose Roberto Teixeira was spearfishing around a rock off Ilha de Gobernador in the Baia de Guanan-bara near Rio de Janeiro, when he found three intact Roman *amphorae* (clay vessels used to hold wine) in an area with several shipwrecks from various dates. He reported that the area of his find is littered with pottery shards and large pieces of other amphorae.

The Brazilian Institute of Archaeology was extremely interested in these amphorae and sent photos to the Smithsonian Institution, which identified them as Roman. Later, Dr. Elizabeth Lyding Will of the Department of Classics at the University of Massachusetts, Amherst, identified the amphorae as second to first century B.C., "...apparently manufactured at Kouass, the ancient port of Zilis (Dchar Jedid) on the Atlantic coast of Morocco, southwest of Tangiers." Dr. Michel Ponsich, the archaeologist who had conducted excavations at Kouass, agrees with Dr. Will on the place of manufacture, and gives the amphorae a date of second century B.C.[189, 57]

An American archaeologist who specializes in underwater digs, Robert Marx, investigating the site near Río de Janeiro where the amphorae were found, located a wooden structure in the muddy bottom of the bay. Using sonar, Marx discovered that there were actually two wrecks at the site, one a sixteenth-century ship, and another which was apparently a more ancient ship, the source of the amphorae.[189, 57]

The Romans traveled the world, just as we do today. In many ways we are really the tail end of the Roman empire. In certain ways, we can see in Western culture the final days of Rome, with its gladiator sports and Latin-based science system. We use a Latin-based alphabet and the Vatican still retains influence over much of the world.

The most amazing find was discovered in southern Arizona. On September 13, 1924, Charles Manier found an array of ancient Roman artifacts, mostly made of lead. The trove, discovered in a lime smelter, numbered more than 30 objects, including a 62-pound cross, spear, daggers, batons and swords. The objects were encrusted in caliche—a sheet of hard, crusty material that "grows" due to a reaction of chemicals and water in desert soils over many years. This encrustation was proof to the excavators that the objects were quite old.[109]

In 1925, University of Tucson archaeologists working in the lime smelter discovered by Manier unearthed a short, heavy broadsword of apparent Roman manufacture. Other artifacts found at the site bore both Hebrew lettering and a form of Latin used between A.D. 560 and 900. As with many discoveries, even though many of the Tucson artifacts were unearthed by professionals, controversy rages over their authenticity.

Dr. Cyclone Covey, a history professor at Wake Forest University in North Carolina, writes that various Jews had sailed from the Portuguese port of Porto Cale and founded a city in Florida, naming it Cale. This city is now modern day Ocala in north-central Florida. Further, Covey believes that other Jews escaped Rome and also left Porto Cale, Portugal, for the New World. The Latin form of Porto Cale was Calalus, which became a Jewish-Roman outpost in 775 A.D. The city, situated where modern Tucson lies today, was then named Rhoda, according to the Latin inscriptions found there. One of the leaders, or captain of one of the ships, Covey believes, was born on the island of Rhodes.[109]

Covey's fascinating thesis is that the Toltec Empire existed in northern Arizona about 700-900 A.D. Covey believes that 100 years after the Toltecs had finally defeated the Jews at Calalus and Rhoda, they migrated to Mexico to found the late Toltec capital of Tula. They brought Jewish captives with them on their journey to Mexico, and continued south, defeating the Maya and capturing Chichén Itza. There they built the so-called Temple of Warriors. Covey claims that their king, like many Toltecs, wore a beard.

This scenario, quite possible considering the various evidence, can also be viewed as a continuation of the various wars in Europe, Asia and Mesoamerica. The Toltecs, by one theory, are descendants of the Phoenician Empire after the Punic Wars, when all Carthaginians and Phoenicians were either killed or had to flee across the Atlantic. Later, further wars would occur in the Americas, including new invasions of now Toltec-Phoenician areas such as Arizona, northern Mexico and areas near the Rio Grande. The hated Romans, plus Jews and other Roman subjects, arrived to explore and colonize the new lands.

One of the most startling of the Roman discoveries was a short, heavy broadsword with the clear depiction of a brontosaurus carved into it! Common sense tells us that someone wanting to create a hoax of a Roman-Jewish outpost in Arizona and wanting to be taken seriously, would not have inscribed a brontosaurus on a sword.[109,23]

~~~~~~~~~~~~~~~~~~~~~~~~~~

Strange Italy

I was sitting in a café in Venice on a sunny afternoon watching the boats go by with a pair of Australian ladies who were travelling around Europe for a year.

"Italy with its castles and estates reminds me of the medieval days of damsels in distress, brave knights and the dragons that they had to slay," said Joan, a dark-haired woman from Melbourne.

"Those days of dragons may not be as far away as we think," I replied, taking a sip of red wine. I told them about the Roman sword in Tucson with the brontosaurus. I then pulled out a well-worn copy of author and Fortean investigator John Keel's book, *Strange Creatures from Time and Space*.[122]

"It says here that a London *Sunday Express* article for July 26, 1970, reported a dinosaur on the loose in Italy." I quoted as follows:

"'Troops and police are hunting a multi-legged monster which is reported to be roaming the woods near Forli in Central Italy. The monster—some call it a dinosaur—was first seen last Tuesday by Antonio Samorani, a 48-year-old peasant. He reported that he had been chased by a 'huge scaly thing at least 15 feet long. It walked on thick legs and its breath was searing hot. I ran for my life and it followed me for a couple of hundred yards.'"

I continued reading the article while we drank wine. "'Police were skeptical at first but changed their minds when they saw large footprints in a glade near where Samorani says he saw the monster.

Police Chief Dr. Pedoni said: "We are convinced some sort of creature of colossal size is hiding in the woods. Three other people have seen it. We are combing the area with armed police and soldiers with nets. If possible we want to catch it alive. Over a thousand guns will be out looking for this animal when the hunting season opens on August 1. If the local hunters reach it first we will be powerless to stop them.'"[122, 123]

"But wait," said Tiffany from Adelaide, "scientists tell us that dinosaurs became extinct 65 million years ago in some cosmic catastrophe."

"But maybe the dragons of old were dinosaurs or other monsters that are still alive in rivers, lakes and swamps. Like Saint George and the dragon," said Joan.

I put my cup of wine down on the table. "The searing hot breath sure sounded like a typical dragon. I suppose now it's gone underground or to the bottom of some creek."

With reports of dinosaurs in lakes, oceans and swamps around the world, one can't help but wonder if large saurians weren't actually battled by various adventurers or unlucky travellers. If large saurians of a komodo dragon-type nature or larger still survive around the world, what sort of critters were around during Atlantean times?

Edgar Cayce, the famous sleeping medium, made many statements about Atlantis (which he also called Poseid) which included several comments about the problem of large animals in the distant past, particularly those "dinosaurs" and large lizards and snakes that had survived the various earth changes up to that time.

Cayce essentially says that the gigantic architecture of earlier times was partially to keep large animals from entering a city and partially for earthquake stability. Cayce says that at one point during the many thousands of years of Atlantean history a convention of nations was called in which to discuss the problem of "dinosaurs." Indeed, such oddball ceramic collections as the Acambaro collection of Mexico show mankind interacting with dinosaurs. Dated by thermoluminescence methods as being from circa 3,000 B.C., this would place such human-dinosaur interaction as taking place well into modern times. See my book *Lost Cities of North & Central America*[23] for more information on the Acambaro mystery.

Italy's Ten-Million-Year-Old Man

On a train heading south to Sicily, I thought about Italy and its unusual places and unusual artifacts. Three miles west of

Ventimiglia are the Grimaldi Caves, inhabited by early man at least as far back as 35,000 years.

These caves were the subject of extensive excavation at the beginning of this century. They served as a shelter during prehistory and contained a considerable number of archaeological layers, each corresponding to a different period of occupation. The earliest period so far excavated is the Aurignacian, which dates back to about 35,000 B.C. Skeletons uncovered from the Aurignacian period were of members of the Cro-Magnon race of hominids, to which the first true men known to have lived in Europe belong.

The Grimaldi skeletons had been buried carefully, and their bones had traces of red ochre which had been ritually sprinkled over them at their funeral ceremonies. They were still wearing ornaments in the form of necklaces and bracelets of shells and animal teeth. In a ditch were found the skeletons of a man, a woman and an adolescent, buried together.[38]

The most surprising find at Grimaldi was that of two fossilized skeletons, one of an old woman and the other of a boy. They had been buried together with their heads protected by a horizontal slab placed on two vertical stones. The shape of their skulls, the structure of their facial bones and the length of their forearms tend to suggest that they belonged to a Negroid race.

This latest discovery is a surprise to archaeologists who don't believe that Negroids ever lived in Europe. They prefer holding on to their "Blacks are from Africa" theories then to look at the evidence that Negroes, and all races, have been all over the world.[38]

Blacks were said to live on Atlantis, according to various books on the subject. Depictions of Blacks are extremely common in Olmec and Mayan statuary. The gigantic heads at Cambodia's mysterious Angor Wat have Negroid features and the ancient Egyptian Sphinx is said to depict a Negroid man or woman.

There are strange fossils that apparently go even farther back than the division of mankind's races. According to Martin Ebon in his book *Atlantis: The New Evidence*,[119] "Dr. Johannes Heurezeler of Basel University, Switzerland, found a complete skeleton hundreds of feet deep in an Italian coal mine. He concluded that it was definitely a humanoid, classified as a 10-million-year-old man. Modern animals and plants in remarkably well-preserved condition were near the fossil, and all were found to be of the same age (10 million years old). Such animals and plants were not known to exist in that time—yet there they were."[119]

Considering that the current uniformitarian dating used in geology may be in error, the man found in the coal mine may be of a far more recent period, perhaps 50,000 years old, or 100,000 or 1,000,000. Needless to say, the man seems to have been an antediluvian dweller, caught in the cataclysmic earth changes of some forgotten era.

The mysterious rock carvings at Val Camonica (62 miles northeast of Milan) are said to go back only 6,000 years, but they show a sophisticated culture. It has been calculated that there are as many as 15,000 very old carvings on the rocks in this valley. They show the houses, religious practices, farming methods and a variety of scenes from the daily lives of the people who carved them.

When the stones were first studied, it was noted that a large number of them were on rocks which had become buried. The early carvings are similar to those at Mount Bego in France, so perhaps it is possible that the people who did them had settled there after being driven from Mount Bego by invaders. Their art has been compared with the much older art of the Iberian peninsula. Why these thousands of engravings are so high in the mountains is a mystery. One theory is that the engravings are the work of pilgrims who came to this high valley for religious reasons.[38]

Perhaps the land that is described in the engravings is a lost land, a land now beneath the Mediterranean.

The Mysterious Megaliths of Sicily and Sardinia

Stepping off the ferry at Messina, I was reminded that Sicily had not always been an island and is mentioned in Greek sources as having have split from the mainland. An ancient earthquake made Sicily the largest island in the Mediterranean.

Early sailors could see the smoking volcanic cone of Mount Etna from far out at sea. This awe-inspiring peak was believed to be the furnace where Hephaestus and his Cyclopean minions forged the thunderbolts that Zeus hurled about during storms.

Sicily has been occupied for thousands of years, yet its early inhabitants are a mystery. Just prior to Roman contact, both the Greeks and Carthaginians had powerful colonies on Sicily. The Greek theater at Syracuse is arguably Sicily's most popular tourist attraction, and Syracuse became such a major power that Athens began to consider its own colony a threat and launched an attack on the city.

In one of the great maritime battles in history, Syracuse managed to defeat the Athenian fleet in 413 B.C. Western Sicily was a Carthaginian colony at the time. With the expansion of Rome, conflict with the powerful naval empire of Carthage was inevitable, yet the Romans were not great sailors. The Greek historian Polybius claimed that Romans had no idea even of how to construct a large warship until a Carthaginian vessel was grounded and taken by the

Romans, who then constructed a replica of the huge battleship. Roman occupation of Sicily took place in 210 B.C. at the end of the second Punic War.

Unfortunately there is a lack of ancient megalithic ruins on Sicily, though many are found on the nearby island of Sardinia. Perhaps the major ancient sites are now submerged as the Mediterranean changed shape and gradually flooded. The mountainous center of Sicily is also dominated by the volcanic activity of Mount Etna and many ancient sites are likely buried under volcanic ash.

There seems little doubt that Sicily was broken off from the Italian mainland within the last few thousand years. Says the philosopher Philo Judaeus (died circa 50 A.D.) who wrote about ancient cataclysms in his treatise *On the Incorruptibility of the World*, "Consider how many districts on the mainland, not only such as were near the coast, but even such as were completely inland, have been swallowed by the waters; and consider how great a proportion of land has become sea and is now sailed over by innumerable ships. Who is ignorant of that most sacred Sicilian strait, which in old times joined Sicily to the continent of Italy? And where vast seas on each side being exited by violent storms met together, coming from opposite directions, and land between them was overwhelmed and broken away; ...in consequence of which Sicily, which had previously formed a part of the mainland, was now compelled to be an island.

"And it is said that many other cities also have disappeared, having been swallowed up by the sea which overwhelmed them..."[1]

Indeed, geologists believe that Sicily, along with Malta, was part of a lost world of large lakes that was connected to Africa and populated with pygmy elephants and hippopotami, along with Ice Age hunters to stalk them. The naturalist Buffon in 1746 suggested that Atlantis had existed near Sicily when the Mediterranean was largely dry land. Atlantis and Sicily were then destroyed when the waters of the Atlantic flooded into the Mediterranean.[1]

Princeton professor Kenneth J. Hsü was the chief geologist on the 1970 *Glomar Challenger* deep-drilling expedition to the Mediterranean. In 1983, Princeton University Press published his book *The Mediterranean Was A Desert*.[30] Hsü concluded that the Mediterranean had indeed been dry and that at some point it had flooded from the Atlantic.

The Glomar Challenger, a sophisticated oceanographic vessel, made a number of ocean core samples in various places around the Mediterranean. By studying core samples that showed gypsum, salt and evaporite deposits, Hsü concluded that the Mediterranean was a salt sea that had somehow dried up and was below sea level, like Death Valley in eastern California.

Chapters in Hsü's book are more interesting than your average

178

geology text, and Hsü entertains us with his "Atlantis Core" samples and chapters with headings such as "Lost Secrets of the Mediterranean," "The Deluge" and "A Mediterranean Seabed Tucked under an Island." After discussing a dry salt pan near Sicily that was suddenly flooded, Hsü says, "Perhaps the whole Mediterranean was drowned when the floodgate at Gibraltar was crushed. The evidence was tantalizing..."[30]

Hsü places the dry Mediterranean possibly as old as five and a half million years. Yet, no carbon dating is involved here, just guesswork at how long it takes layers of strata to build up on the surface of the earth. Uniformitarian geologists maintain that it takes millions of years for strata to accumulate. In the cataclysmic point of view, the cataclysms themselves create several feet of strata in a matter of days. Who is correct?

Hsü's dry Mediterranean may have been only 10,000 years ago, or possibly the Mediterranean may be alternatively dry and wet as tectonic plates rise and fall.

Sardinia may have been connected to mainland Europe until about 6,000 B.C. In Sardinia there are almost 7,000 "nuraghi," drystone structures usually said to date from the beginning of the Bronze Age, circa 2,500 B.C., but they may be thousands of years older. The oldest are round towers, with the inside reached through a narrow corridor. Others are corbel-roofed, that is, the roof is built up from overlapping slabs of stone. Still others make up complexes comprising several towers linked by corridors.

At one time it was thought that they were temples, but it has now been proved that they were fortresses in which people from surrounding villages took refuge in times of danger. Each nuraghi was visible from a neighboring nuraghi, so that the defenders could communicate by means of smoke signals. Such a system of defense would seem likely to have been established to protect the island from foreign raids.[38]

Says *Reader's Digest*, "The puzzling fact is that the nuraghi are less numerous on the coast, from which danger was most likely to come, than in the interior. After the Carthaginians landed, they settled in the largest nuraghi, from which they were later driven by the Romans."[38]

Can it be that the nuraghi-towers were actually built at a time when there wasn't the present coastline of today? These finely built megalithic round towers may come from the same period that saw the construction of Mycenae and Hattusas.

As I looked out over the Mediterranean from the southern coast of Sicily, with Mount Etna smoking behind me, I wondered where the large cities of these people could be? Perhaps beneath the Mediterranean, covered with ash from Mount Etna.

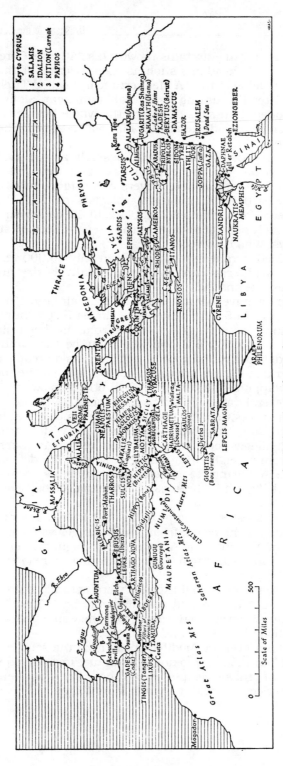

Ancient ports in the Mediterranean.

The marble columns at the Temple of Serapis at Pozzuoli. The thick band of holes in the lower half of each column were bored by marine organisms, showing that the land had sunk into the Mediterranean for some time and then reemerged from the sea.

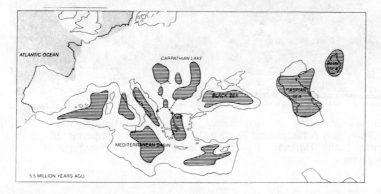

A conjectural map of the various seas that existed in the Mediterranean at various times in prehistory.

Top left: Apollo riding his sun chariot, discovered by Schliemann at Hisarlik (Troy). Top right: A bikini-clad Roman "bather" from the Imperial villa at Piazza Armerina, Sicily. Bottom: A Roman relief from Ostia showing Roman ships and elephants.

Spina, the long-sought Etrusco-Greek city in the Po Valley. The grid of canals and city blocks was neatly sketched in lighter and darker shades of marsh grass. Note the wide black strip top left, which represents the principal port canal. Superimposed white parallels belong to modern drainage system.
Courtesy Fotoaerea Valvassori, Ravenna

Courtesy, Dr. C. M. Lerici

An aerial view of an Etruscan necropolis. The hidden tombs show as patches of light.
Both as an instrument of large-scale reconnaissance of extensive and difficult terrain
and as a means of spotting buried ruins, graves, walls, streets, and canals, aerial
photography has become a vital aid to archaeology.

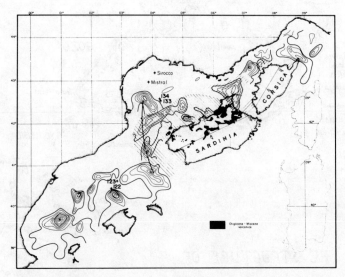

Map illustrating the counterclockwise rotation of Sardinia and Corsica. The contours show the intensity of magnetic anomalies of submarine volcanoes buried under soft sediments.

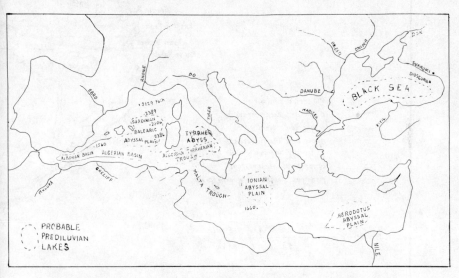

Joseph Ellul's map of the dry Mediterranean valley that he says is Atlantis.

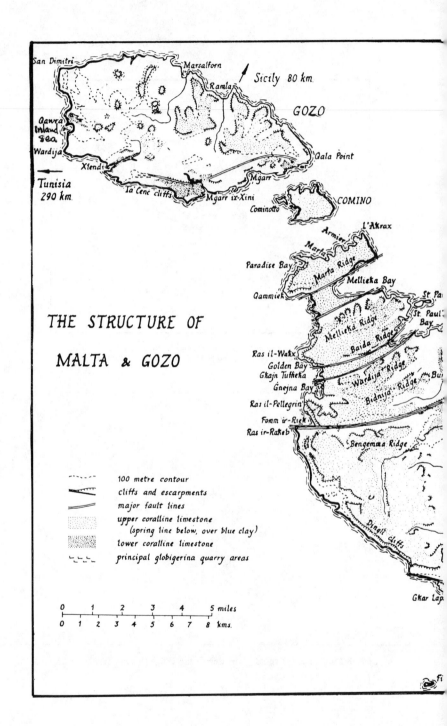

San Dimitri
Marsalforn
Ramla
Sicily 80 km.
GOZO
Qawra Inland Sea
Wardija
Gala Point
Xlendi
Tunisia 290 km.
Ta'Cenc cliffs
Mgarr ix-Xini
Mgarr
COMINO
Cominotto
L'Akrax
Armier
Marfa
Marfa Ridge
Paradise Bay
Mellieħa Bay
Qammieħ
St. Pa
St. Paul's Bay
THE STRUCTURE OF
MALTA & GOZO
Mellieħa Ridge
Baida Ridge
Ras il-Waħx
Golden Bay
Għajn Tuffieħa
Gnejna Bay
Wardija Ridge
Bidnija Ridge
Bu
Ras il-Pellegrin
Fomm ir-Riħ
Ras ir-Raħeb
Benġemma Ridge
Dingli cliffs
100 metre contour
cliffs and escarpments
major fault lines
upper coralline limestone
(spring line below, over blue clay)
lower coralline limestone
principal globigerina quarry areas
Għar Lap

0   1   2   3   4   5 miles
0   1   2   3   4   5   6   7   8 kms.

fi

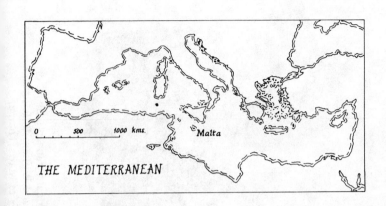

0   500   1000 kms.

Malta

THE MEDITERRANEAN

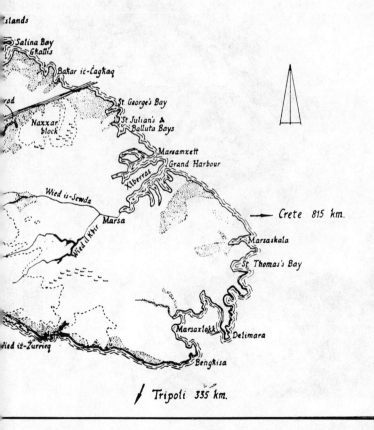

Islands
Salina Bay
Gkallis
Bakar iċ-Ċagħaq
rad
St. George's Bay
Naxxar block
St. Julian's & Balluta Bays
Marsamxett
Grand Harbour
Xiberras
Wied is-Sewda
Marsa
Wied il-Kbir
Crete 815 km.
Marsaskala
St. Thomas's Bay
Marsaxlokk
Delimara
Wied iż-Żurrieq
Bengħisa
Tripoli 335 km.

Schematic diagram showing the submarine topography of the Mediterranean seabed; prepared from bathymetry studies by Bruce Heezen, Marie Tharpe, and William B. F. Ryan of the Lamont-Doherty Geological Observatory. Photograph courtesy of Marie Tharpe.

Chapter 6

MALTA:

Ancient Gods of Osiris

For nothing is secret,
that shall not be made manifest;
neither any thing hid,
that shall not be known and come abroad.
—*The Gospel of Luke* 8:17

It was late afternoon when I cleared Maltese customs and walked into the lobby of the clean, new airport. The tourist office stood right in front of me and I asked officials there for any maps or brochures they might have as well as the easiest way into the capital city of Valetta.

I had expected to be assailed by taxi drivers when I first arrived, but the airport was virtually empty. The tourist office recommended some guesthouses in the old city of Valetta for me and said that there was an island bus that stopped just outside the airport every 20 minutes.

This was my first trip on the colorfully painted, old-style buses of Malta. I sat near the driver as we drove downhill along the dry wheat fields and apartment buildings of the small island. The bus stopped at the gates of the old city of Valetta, where no traffic was allowed to enter.

Shouldering my pack, I strode through the gates and into the shadows of the tall buildings and narrow gates. It was late on Sunday afternoon and most of the shops were closed, but a few people still walked along the steep, stone streets.

I wandered down narrow steps and dark streets in search of several guesthouses. I finally found a small hotel called the Asti Guesthouse, an old building that had been converted into a guesthouse. A sink was in each room, with a bathroom down the hall.

The proprietor, France Galea, was an amiable, helpful older gentleman who was trying to turn his ancestral home into a museum and guesthouse. He gave me a good room with double windows over the street.

"It lets in the morning sun," said France. "Yes, be sure to open the windows in the morning. We serve breakfast until 9:00. Do you prefer coffee or tea?"

I thanked France and rested on the bed. Malta! Because of the ancient megalithic ruins, Malta excited me. Coming to Malta was like returning to Atlantis.

The next morning I took one of the colorful local buses to Zurrieq, the town nearest to the ruins of Hagar Qim. Soon, I was walking through the impressive megaliths of this famous ancient temple. The ruins of Hagar Qim, Mnajdra and Ggantija Temples are often said to be the world's oldest (yes, all three of the above words are spelled correctly, and the Maltese use a curious double-G sound).

The large complex is made of semicircular structures and huge walls with upright stones often 20 feet in height. These massive blocks are finely cut and fitted together. All of the blocks used in the various megalithic buildings on Malta are made of limestone. Unfortunately limestone is soft stone and does not wear as well as granite or other igneous stones.

Indeed, the whole complex is severely weathered and worn. I walked down a special sidewalk to the nearby sea cliffs and the equally impressive megalithic Temple of Mnajdra. Mnajdra was also built of huge blocks of limestone and reminded me of the construction in Peru such as that of Sacsayhuaman, except that the Mnajdra was much more eroded.

I walked along the road and through a few rock-strewn fields to the Blue Grotto, famous for its cliffs, grottoes and turquoise-blue waters. Restaurants clustered against the cliffs and I had a leisurely lunch of spaghetti bolognaise at one of the cafés.

After taking a bus back to Valetta, I spied a small pub built into the huge walls of the fortified citadel. It was a local hangout for the taxi and bus drivers who parked at the entrance to the city.

I got a beer from the counter and stood near one of the tables. A tourist couple from Manchester was sitting at a table talking with a local Maltese fellow. I was clearly a tourist as well, and the woman, in her early 40s with thick spectacles, said a few words to me.

"I'm Bridget," she said. "My husband and I are from Manchester."

The husband set down his beer and said, "I'm John."

The Maltese fellow looked at me and said, "I'm Paul."

I looked at them and said, "Well, I guess that makes me Ringo!" We all laughed and I bought a round of Cisk lager beers for everyone.

We chatted for awhile. Bridget and John had flown over on one of those cheap British charter flights from London and were staying on the beach down the coast.

As we sat in this hole-in-the-wall pub laughing and drinking, an unusual-looking woman came in and got a cup of coffee. She was tall with long black hair, a tight black dress and black net stockings. All the men eyed her carefully and she sat with one man and casually chatted with him.

In the small pub, I couldn't help looking at her myself, and I suddenly said to John, "Am I going crazy or is that a man?"

John glanced at the woman again and then nodded. "Yeah, you're right, that is a man. Must be a transvestite prostitute. That's what they have here on Malta."

Another man dressed as a woman came in and they both sat together for awhile and then left. I chalked it all up to the Arab influence in Malta, where females are kept hidden, and prostitutes are either transvestites or teenage boys. Malta, apparently, had an entire class of transvestite prostitutes.

Battleground Malta

Back in my room at the Asti Guesthouse, I lay on my bed and looked up at the full moon and thought about my quest for Atlantis on this small island of Malta.

In 1922 the archaeologist Joseph Bosco proposed Malta as the site of lost Atlantis. After all, it had its mysterious and ancient megaliths and gave evidence of having once been part of a larger, now drowned, land.[1]

L. Sprague de Camp lists another scientist, G.G. de Vasse, who postulated Malta as Plato's Atlantis in the 19th century. Given the ancient monuments at Malta and Gozo, now said to be the oldest ruins in the world, the theme of Atlantis leaps immediately to mind. And so it might. Malta is strong proof for a Mediterranean Valley civilization in prehistory.[1]

Malta was an island with an early Phoenician colony, and the characteristic eyes that are still painted on the prows of Maltese ships reflect a Phoenician-Egyptian practice of using the Eye of Horus as a magic talisman.

Says Ernle Bradford in his epic history book, *Mediterranean, Portrait of a Sea*,[192] speaking of the tiny island of Levanzo on the west coast of Sicily, "The small fishing boats in Levanzo still bear upon their bows the *Oculus,* or Eye of Horus. This too is a Phoenician legacy, for they first brought out of the east this device which they themselves copied from the Egyptians. ...In Malta, once a Phoenician colony, they still paint eyes upon their small fishing boats; but no fisherman can tell you why."[192]

Malta's early history is unknown and mysterious. Dates for the massive temples vary, and get pushed back farther and farther as new discoveries and dating techniques are used. It is agreed that the megalithic remains on Malta and Gozo go back at least five and a half thousand years to 3500 B.C., if not earlier.

Little is known of Malta until the Punic Wars when Carthage made Malta a naval base. Around 60 A.D. the Apostle Paul was being taken to Rome as a prisoner when he was shipwrecked on Malta. He lived in a cave and laid the foundations for the strong Christian faith that still exists on Malta to this day.

In 870 Malta was invaded by the Arabs, who ruled benignly, leaving behind the legacy of the current Maltese language. Generally in the Middle Ages, though, Malta was ruled over by whoever controlled Sicily. Count Roger the Norman took Malta from Sicily in 1091, but it was the acquisition of Malta by the Knights of St. John in 1565 that made Malta an independent island.

The Knights of St. John or Knights Hospitallers had been founded in 1085 as a crusader order to care for and protect Christian pilgrims who were visiting the Holy Land. This quasi-religious order of armed priests took vows of chastity, read the Bible and ancient books and studied the fascinating sciences of the Muslim world. They were also experienced military strategists and combat veterans.

The pilgrims generally landed at one of the port cities in Palestine and then proceeded overland to Jerusalem. When Godfrey de Bouillon, one of the leaders of the first crusade, captured Jerusalem in 1099, the knights suddenly became a powerful military order. The Knights of St. John ruled the eastern Mediterranean for nearly eighty years. In 1113 the order was placed under papal protection but in 1187 Jerusalem fell to the Saracens and the crusaders, including the Knights of St. John, retreated to their fortress-harbor at Acre, an old Phoenician port.

When Sultan Kahil took Acre in 1291 the knights moved their headquarters to Cyprus. In 1310 Rhodes was made the maritime fortress of the Knights of St. John. For the next 200 years the knights challenged, fought and beat the Turkish Ottoman Empire in the eastern Mediterranean.

It was the Knights of St. John who negotiated the acquisition of the Spear of Destiny from the Ottoman Sultan as part of a deal to keep his brother in prison, as told about earlier in this book. The Ottoman navy eventually attacked Rhodes and, in 1522, after a six-month siege, Suleiman the Magnificent allowed the knights to leave Rhodes with their honor intact.

They set about in search of a new home. In 1529 Charles V, grandson of Ferdinand and Isabella of Spain, offered Malta to the Knights of St. John as their permanent base and they began to build fortifications around the Grand Harbor. In 1565 the Ottoman fleet arrived at Malta and immediately attacked the fortifications.

With 181 ships carrying a complement of over 30,000 men, the fleet bombarded the fortress with over 7,000 rounds of ammunition every day for over a month and finally took St. Elmo. But the Turkish marines had suffered many casualties and could not take the other heavily defended forts that were around the bay and inside the island. News of reinforcements coming from Sicily caused the Turks to retreat from the island and the Great Siege was over. The Knights of St. John were ultimately victorious and the Maltese tend to see this moment as their finest hour, the turning point in the great wars between the Christian West and the Muslim East. The knights that Suleiman the Magnificent had spared at Rhodes had lived to ultimately defeat the Sultan at another time and place.

Valetta was then designed and the current fortifications built. What made the crusades important to Western civilization was that they gave men (and women as well in many cases) the opportunity to broaden their horizons and learn new truths.

In the Middle Ages, science and scientific enquiry were largely suppressed by the Roman Catholic church, and the reading of books or the writing of them could mean burning at the stake. Incredibly, it was forbidden (except by the clergy) to learn to read in most countries and even the Bible was not to be read by the masses but rather interpreted by the priestly hierarchy.

When the crusaders returned from their various duties in Palestine, Rhodes or Malta, however, they were well aware that there was more to science, theology and history than the Vatican would acknowledge.

In the Eastern world, which the Knights had encountered, arcane wisdom was taught by special groups and schools who operated in various cities in Asia Minor. Jewish cabalists taught the Zohar; Armenian Christian mystics had their schools, as did the Sufis and Zoroastrians. Nestorian Christians with their Eastern beliefs in reincarnation and karma taught that Jesus had visited India, Tibet and Persia before the important ministry of the New Testament. In later centuries, the Knights of St. John lived in great wealth and luxury. Other knights' orders such as the Knights Templar and the Teutonic Knights were outlawed by Rome, but the Knights of St. John were allowed to continue at Malta. The Knights of Malta were known variously throughout their history as the Knights Hospitallers, Knights of Rhodes and Knights of St. John, but should not be confused with the Knights Templar.

When these informed travellers returned to their native lands of England, France, Germany, Holland and the rest of Europe, they held in them the seeds of intellectual revolution that would change the world forever.

The Knights of St. John were said to be fanatically loyal to the Vatican, and the Pope apparently used them as his personal crusaders and soldiers. Other orders such as the Knights Templar and the Teutonic Knights were far more independent, and if anything, were trying their best to subvert the church that was centered on Rome. In fact it was sometimes said that the Knights Templar and the Knights of St. John (later to be known as the Knights of Malta) sometimes fought in combat against each other. The Knights Templar were sworn to fight the Vatican while the Knights of Malta became the Pope's private army.

It was Napoleon who finally ended the rule of the Knights of St. John over Malta. The French knights had sent money to Louis XVI and when the French "Sun King" was executed, the Knights of St. John on Malta were denied any French revenues by Napoleon.

The knights then turned to the Russian Tsar Paul I who offered to found an Orthodox League of the Knights of St. James. This deal with the Russian Tsar particularly enraged Napoleon.

Napoleon sailed to Malta and made anchor just outside the Grand Harbor in June of 1798. When he was refused entry by the Knights of St. John, he began to bombard the fortress. After two days of shelling the French landed and gave the knights four days to leave, thus ending their 268-year presence on the island.

Napoleon melted down the silver service of the huge hospital to pay his troops in the disastrous Egyptian campaign. Napoleon paid his navy and marines with crusader silver and then visited the Great Pyramid where he spent the night in the King's Chamber. Napoleon did not hold Egypt for long, as he was defeated shortly thereafter by Lord Nelson.

A blockade of Portuguese and British ships prevented Napoleon's navy from returning to Malta and Napoleon eventually capitulated in 1800. The Maltese felt that the British ruled fairly and preferred to stay allied with them. Today Malta is a British Commonwealth member, and many Maltese live and work in Australia or Britain. Perhaps the Maltese, as they sometimes say, are more British than the British themselves.

The Pope restored the office of the Grand Master in 1879 and the Knights of St. John still exist today, and they are known as the Knights of Malta, though they no longer reside in Malta at all, but have offices in various cities in Europe. Even though they have no actual territory, they are still recognized as a separate state by 40 or more countries around the world, similar to the recognition of the Vatican.

Critics of the Knights of St. John/Malta claim that they are a right-wing Catholic organization that worked in Eastern Europe to suppress non-Catholic ethnic groups. The Nazi S.S. chief Rheinhard

Gellen received the highest honor given by the Knights of Malta shortly after World War II for "services rendered." Gellen has been credited with helping to mastermind the notorious Project Paperclip in which many members of the German S.S. were absorbed by the American Office of Strategic Services (O.S.S.) to create the Central Intelligence Agency.

"I like Malta," I thought the next morning as I headed for the bus station to be off to the Tarxien temple and the Hypogeum. At the main square were all of the buses, old, green and roomy. Each was painted with various unique designs and side trim. Saints protected passengers from the dashboard and tassels hung from various parts of the fantastic bus.

One can go anywhere on Malta for 10 Maltese cents, which is about 25 cents American. The tourist brochures tell you that you are never more than 15 minutes from a beach. But that beach may be at the bottom of the ocean beneath one of Malta's many cliffs!

I sat behind the driver of the bus and looked out the window. He took money with one hand and peeled off little tickets with the other. I smiled at the minute cigar stub that lay on the money tray. I was later surprised when he actually put it in his mouth and lit it!

As he puffed away on the stub, I cursed myself for sitting behind a driver who smoked cigars. Fortunately he had trouble keeping it lit, and I savored the rustic flavor of the bus.

Tarxien was near to Valetta and the Grand Harbor. Like Hagar Qim, Tarxien was made of gigantic blocks of stone, and as I paid my entrance fee at the small museum there, I couldn't help looking out at the huge megaliths in anticipation.

Once inside the courtyard of the Tarxien ruins I was instantly impressed by the gigantic slabs that were impressively restored. At the entrance lay a set of huge round stones, "ball-bearings" for the massive doors, now gone, that once swung on these giant stone balls.

Though the site was on a megalithic scale very similar to other megaliths on Malta, it was said by "experts" to be of a different "phase." Parts of Tarxien were once used as a Roman cellar.

The ruins of Tarxien have the distinct spiral pattern that can be seen at Knossos and Newgrange in Ireland. There are also the common bull motifs, similar to those found in Crete, the former Hittite empire, and Spain. Here too is the large, fat figure typically said to be a Mother-Goddess statue.

Many of the spiral stones are also pockmarked, while common motifs are bulls, rams, and pigs. Other designs are of fish, boat and wave motifs. Huge stone bowls, for burning aromatic herbs(?), are found near the entrances to rooms. Stone tools and the remains of a crematorium have also been found at Tarxien.

As I walked through the ancient city, I noticed a narrow staircase going up to a nonexistent second floor. The few roofing slabs that remained were huge, similar to the massive walls around them. Although it is one of the oldest structures in the entire world, Tarxien is also a very sophisticated one.

It is a magnificent sanctuary, built at least 5,000 years ago out of large, perfectly cut blocks of stone. The stones made of limestone are so eroded after 5,000 years or more that they no longer perfectly fit together.

After walking around the ruins for an hour or so, I continued on to the underground chamber of the Hypogeum nearby.

A hypogeum is a particular form of underground tomb cut out of solid rock. It generally consists of a large underground chamber, usually a burial chamber, preceded by a smaller antechamber, reached from the outside by a sloping passage.

According to Jean-Pierre Mohen in his book *The World of Megaliths*,[158] other similar structures can be found in such diverse places as the group of hypogea at Coizard, in the Marne region, and the Arles hypogea in Bouches-du-Rhône of France.

Sardinia has a hypogeum, and in the area around the Tagus estuary in Portugal they form a homogeneous group characterized by a domed chamber. Mohen says that Egypt is also an area of these strange underground burial chambers and that the Valley of Kings should also be included in the term hypogeum.

Mohen is in fact suggesting that the ancient Egyptians were the originators of the hypogeum concept. Yet, Mohen contends in his book that the Hypogeum at Malta was built during the height of the megalithic construction period, which would make it earlier.

The underground chambers have also led to stories of a system of underground tunnels on the island. The August, 1940, issue of *National Geographic* had an interesting article on Malta. The article, "Wanderers Awheel In Malta" by Richard Walters, contains a curious reference to a network of caverns underneath the island. According to the article the entrances to these caverns were sealed by the military after a group of schoolchildren entered them and never returned.

The founder of the Borderland Sciences Research Foundation, Riley H. Crabb, also wrote in his rare book, *The Reality of the Cavern World*, about a strange cavern system beneath Malta. As quoted in the 1940 *National Geographic* article, he mentions a report of "giant men" seen in a closed-off section of the Hal Saflini catacombs deep beneath the island.

Researchers like Crabb, who believe in subterranean cavern systems, inhabited by giants and other beings, have collected a great deal of lore and news clippings on caverns, tunnel systems, underground rivers and the like. My own travels and researches have shown me that there is reality behind the fantastic tales.

Tunnel systems in the earth do indeed exist! Many are natural, but many are undoubtedly artificial. Others are a combination of artificial and natural work. Artificial tunnels and inner-earth mysteries often lead to a discussion of Atlantis and ancient technology, or even extraterrestrial astronauts. At the very least, we can attribute much of the manmade tunnel systems to ancient mining.

〜〜〜〜〜〜🜚〜〜〜〜〜〜

Back in Valetta, I sat in one of the sidewalk cafés and thought about the ruins I had seen so far. Early on it was recognized by archaeologists that the megalithic temples on Malta must be very ancient.

An article published in *Antiquity* entitled "The Prehistoric Remains of the Maltese Islands" by T. Zammit (4:55-79, 1930) says: "Besides noticing the minor neolithic remains of these islands, it is well to give a cursory glance at the megalithic buildings methodically arranged for a definite purpose such as dwellings or sanctuaries. It is astonishing how numerous these buildings must have been in the Maltese islands. Some of them in the course of ages have partly or completely disappeared; but those that still remain are sure evidence of the activity of a race already formed into a large, organic and peaceful society.

"The number of buildings is more bewildering than their magnificence. If the islands had only one or two complete megalithic structures one would feel that the neolithic population had raised a monument to the Power they believed in, or in honor of a hero or for the hero's use, but when these complete dwellings, towers or temples, whatever they may be thought to be, are met with all over the island the explanation of their presence is certainly perplexing.

"Standing on the shores of the Grand Harbor the importance of this splendid haven is shown by the number of megalithic monuments surrounding it. We can only mention what remains on the southern shores, for those that were probably raised on the northern side were completely demolished when Valetta was built on Mount Sceberras in 1568."

Says Zammit of the Tarxien group, "Not far from the Corradino ruins, another group of megalithic buildings can now be seen to the southeast before reaching Tarxien.

"The monument was completely buried under field soil until 1914, and nothing on the surface pointed to its existence. The farmer who rented the fields near Tal-Erwich cemetery volunteered the information that a certain depth below the surface his tools struck blocks of stone; this led the Curator of the museum to investigate the site, which was completely excavated in about six years.

"This magnificent megalithic monument consists of three groups of buildings which the excavator believes to be temples, of three different periods, but all of them in the Stone Age, or at least before the diffusion of the Bronze Age culture (2500 B.C.). The temples are freely connected with each other, and at present they have a common approach from a large semicircular forecourt.

"...The main corridor extends further north to a semicircular shrine on a high platform, of which the front is decorated with a delightful pattern of spirals. An apse to the left of this platform is connected with an archaic shrine, and, to the right, the eastern apse, symmetrical to the one to the west, was modified to afford an entrance to the second temple.

"During the excavation of this site it was found that the floor of these temples was covered with about three feet of silt, a sandy dust that had spread over the site in the long length of time during which the monument was a heap of ruins. After this accumulation of soil a Bronze Age people made their appearance in Malta; they disposed of their dead by incineration, and utilized the open space under which the Stone Age remains were buried for the deposition of their funerary urns."

Zammit is saying that the ruins at Malta predate such civilizations as ancient Egypt, Mesopotamia, or the Hittites. This unknown culture was destroyed by a cataclysm that deposited three feet of silt into the ruins. Afterwards, Malta was reinhabited by a different culture.

What archaeologists all admit is that Malta has the oldest stone ruins in the world. By the current evidence, the great master builders went on to build Mycenae, Hattusas, and the great Egyptian temples. But why should tiny Malta be the origin of megalithic building?

The Mysterious Cart Tracks of Malta

The next morning I awoke early to seek the mystery of the cart ruts that can be found at various places around both Malta and its sister island Gozo. I took a bus into the interior of the island to find Clapham Junction, the most famous intersection of cart tracks.

I got off the bus at the village of Dingli and began walking toward the Dingli Cliffs, which crash hundreds of feet down directly into the ocean on the west side of the island. A Maltese man in a dump truck suddenly stopped and gave me a ride to where the cart ruts could be found.

I walked up a dirt road where a signpost pointed the way to Clapham Junction. I arrived at a grassy rock field where over 30 ruts come together and radiate away in various directions. I wandered around looking at the various weird ruts carved into the rock. They were perfectly parallel, of a certain gauge curiously equal to the British railway gauge, and go over cliffs and into the water.

Scientists have studied the cart ruts since the turn of the century. M. A. Murray, in a 1928 article entitled "The Cart-Ruts of Malta" in the British scientific journal *Man*, formulates the problems facing archaeologists concerning the cart tracks:

"The ancient wheel-tracks which are found in many parts of Malta have long been of interest to archaeologists. As they are being rapidly destroyed—owing to road-making, increase in the area of cultivation, and other causes—it seems worthwhile to record at least a few of them. Professor Zammit and Commodore Clark Hall hope to make a complete map, from air-photographs, of all the known tracks on the island. This paper must, therefore, be considered only as a preliminary introduction to the study of the subject.

"The first point to be considered is whether the ruts are natural or artificial. It is, of course, well known that parallel fissures often occur in limestone, and, if these ruts were only straight lines of varying gauges, there might be considerable doubt as to their origin. But they often curve, and when they do so the distance between the two parallel lines remains the same; in other words, a pair of tracks are always equidistant throughout their length, whether straight or curving. The gauge is also fairly constant, being rather wider than a modern Maltese cart.

"The archaeological evidence for the human origin of the tracks is fairly strong. In ancient Greece such ruts were cut in the rocky slopes of hills for the passage of wheeled traffic, which could not otherwise surmount the uneven surface. Caillemer, in his description of ancient Greek roads, speaks of these tracks as probably cut quite shallow and were deepened by wear. ...Caillemer gives instances of such artificial cart-tracks in Italy and in the south of France.

"There seems to have been a network of these roads over the whole island. The best examples now remaining are on the rocky slope near the Nashar (Naxxar) Gap, close to San Paul at Targia, down which the new Military Road has been constructed. Another group is at Ta Frattita on the west side of the Bin Gemma hills. Short lengths of such roads are often found in connection with megalithic monuments, apparently leading directly to the monument, as at Santa Sofia and Santa Maria tal Bakkari. In each of these cases the remainder of the road has been obliterated by modern alterations, such as the making of fields, construction of metaled roads, building of houses, and so on."

Murray then mentions that Malta must have been different when the cart tracks were made: "The age of these ancient roads seems to be indicated not only by their connection with the megaliths, but by the fact that they were made when the configuration of the island was different from its present condition. At St. George's Bay near Birzebuggia a cart-track crosses a little spit of land which juts out into the Bay. Before the houses and Marina were built, this track could be traced on each side of the Bay. It is evident that at one time the sea had not advanced so far as it has now and that there was a road across the valley. Tracks are also found leading to the edge of the cliffs, where they end abruptly owing to a fall of rock into the sea. On the south side the island is continually losing by the breaking down of the rocks and cliffs. The temple of Shrobb-in-Ghagin is rapidly disappearing in this way; only a small part of it still remains.

"...A map of the tracks will give the centres of population in early, possibly neolithic, times; and will throw light on many of the archaeological problems connected with Malta.

"There remains a tradition in the island that the tracks were made for 'a boat which went on wheels,' a kind of *via sacra*. The tradition is perhaps the origin of Father Magri's theory that the motive power for the ancient vehicles was sails. But, as Caillemer has noted in the Greek examples, there would be no difficulty for an animal to draw a cart along these artificial ruts when the surface on which the animal walked was made more or less even."

These ancient cart tracks are remarkable in many ways. They go over cliffs, they are of consistent gauge, and they criss-cross both Malta and Gozo. The more archaeologists looked into the cart tracks, the more mysterious and puzzling they became.

~~~~~~~~~ ☥ ~~~~~~~~~

Cart Tracks Lead Underwater

The British archaeologist H. S. Gracie wrote an article on the mysterious ruts that appeared in a 1954 issue of *Antiquity* magazine (28:91-98). Entitled "The Ancient Cart-Tracks of Malta," The article begins by mentioning that the barren hilltops of Malta are scored in many places by ancient ruts cut deeply into the rock. "They can be seen also on the slopes and on the lower plains, but less frequently because these areas are normally under agricultural soil. They always occur in pairs from 52 to 58 inches apart and were quite clearly used by vehicles. They have been discussed in print for 300 years but no agreement has been reached on how, when or why they were made or what vehicles used them. In fact, there are as many theories as there are authors."

Continues Gracie, "The depths of the ruts range from a mere smoothing of the surface to more than 2 feet. The greatest depth noted was 27 inches and there were several measurements between 22 and 24 inches. These are the mean depths of a pair of ruts taken from the highest point of the intervening rock. A wheel to negotiate such ruts would need to be 5 feet in diameter, allowing only 6 inches for the hub.

"There are a number of instances of sharp turns in the tracks ...In no case was there any widening or flattening of the bottoms of the ruts such as would necessarily have been formed by a sledge runner. Sledges, therefore, could not have been used. Fenton excluded sledges on account of the undulatory nature of the bottoms of the ruts.

"Frequently a track will bifurcate, the two parts coming together again after a short distance. Sometimes the two will separate widely enough to enable two vehicles to pass, but more often the separation is only a few inches and may even show only as a widening of the ruts. These last are said to be duplicated. Triplicated tracks occur and... an example of quadruplication can be seen. Zammit concluded that the wider of these bifurcations were deliberately made shunts and shows an air photograph of Tal Minsia as an example."

Gracie goes on to say, "The date of this road system is more difficult to arrive at. Tracks pass over Punic graves in at least four places. At Imtarfa, the lip of the rut is a sharp right angle, indicating that the rut is older than the grave, which has cut through and truncated the rut. Professor Zammit claimed that the grave goods dated from 600 B.C., but Dr. Baldacchino, Director of the Valletta Museum, considers that they may be up to a few hundred years later than this. We have seen above that the tracks are older than the bulk of the terracing but the date of this work is not known. Zammit found traces of its going on in Roman times at Tarxien. Finally the land at St. George's Bay has sunk at least three feet since the tracks were made. Unfortunately one cannot say how long this might have taken. Local movements in this area can be quite rapid, but one would expect such a subsidence to have been noticed had it taken place in historical times. It seems reasonable to put the date before the advent of the Romans in 217 B.C.

"To sum up, it appears that a simple system of natural tracks joining settlements with each other and with springs and the sea was formed about the beginning of the first millennium B.C. but possibly earlier. The land was soil-covered and only one track of a group was visible at any one time. The tracks were worn down by friction and not deliberately cut. The vehicle in use was some form of slide-car, which became larger and more strongly made as time went on."

Furthermore, cart tracks have been found on Filfla Islet, a tiny ocean rock across from the cliffs of Hagar Qim. This tiny, uninhabited rocky islet would seem an unlikely spot for a cart rut of any use unless it was once connected to the main island. In other areas of Malta and Gozo cart tracks can be seen going over the edge of cliffs. Once such place is at Ras-Ir-Pilgrim near Manikata on the northwest side of Malta.

Cart tracks go into the ocean at Marsaxlokk Bay, near to the Ghar Dalam cave with the miniature mammoths. The evidence would seem to show that the cart ruts were part of an extensive network of tracks that went over a much wider area than can be found today. Some of the former areas with cart ruts are now currently under water.

One of the mysteries of the cartruts is that while grooves for the tracks are clearly worn, there are no worn tracks between the ruts for a draft animal. It has been suggested that sidecars were used in moving quarried blocks or other cargo, yet there are still no tracks or depressions for an animal or man to push or pull the cart.

Were the carts self-powered? Did a primitive form of steam engine move them along their rock-cut tracks? Probably not, I mused as I regarded a chameleon that had unexpectedly crawled onto my daypack.

As I walked toward the Dingle Cliffs and the road, I wondered why so many cart ruts converged at Clapham Junction. The cart ruts seemed to be near quarry sites, both ancient and modern. Is it possible that the ruts were for wagons that were used in moving quarried stone?

As I reached the road a young dark-haired Maltese man came along in a pickup truck and offered me a ride back down to the valleys of central Malta.

I accepted gratefully and found that he was an engineer at the nearby quarries.

"Really," I said. "I've just come to visit the cart ruts."

"Oh, yes, I know about them," he said.

"And quarries," I asked. "Are there many ancient quarries on the island?"

"Oh, yes, many," he said. "There are so many ancient quarries on Malta that I don't think anyone has ever taken a count. That would be a good survey."

Just then we passed an ancient quarry. Huge blocks of stone had apparently been removed from the solid rock. I asked him if this was indeed an ancient quarry. He said that it was and that he had no knowledge of its having been used in modern times.

"However, many ancient quarries are being used again," he pointed out.

He dropped me off at Mdina, "the silent city," a tightly clustered walled city built on a hill in the center of Malta. It had narrow streets and had turned the Mdina Dungeons into a "Dark-Walk" attraction, a gruesome tour of the actual dungeons showing Malta's unsavory past during medieval times with the tortures and imprisonment suffered during the Inquisition, as well as earlier Roman and Arab periods.

A great view of the countryside could be had from the walls of Mdina, particularly of the church dome in the town of Mosta. I stopped by the church and was impressed by the huge size of the dome. It is the third largest in the world, according to the tourist literature, and what the hell, they are probably right.

As I walked out of town, one of Malta's grand buses suddenly came by and I was able to flag it down. I jumped on board and asked the driver where he was going.

Golden Bay, was the answer, a popular beach spot on the west side of the island. I rode up front with the driver to the beach. It was spring, and the tourists that would pack this beach had not come yet.

I had a good look at the megalithic ruins in the town of Mgarr. The massive temple of Ta Magrar was down an alley and was largely neglected. There was an iron grate fence around the site and a gate that had been locked for years.

I looked around for some official who might suddenly yell at me if I climbed over the gate. But no one seemed to even live in this little village, much less care about these ancient doors and walls.

Using a corner concrete pillar, I climbed up over the 10-foot iron fence and jumped down into the grass and scattered stones of Ta Magrar. There was a large trilithon that was the gate to the inner sanctuary, but it was largely eroded away. Still, I was impressed by the site; obviously a gigantic structure had once stood here at Mgarr, but after over 5,000 years, it was largely gone.

I walked on up the road to a similar megalithic structure called the Temple of Skorba. Like Ta Magrar, it had massive stones, though it did not have a trilithon.

At sunset, I was sitting next to the driver on one of Malta's decorated green buses, heading back into Valetta. My head was full of Malta's wonders. Here on a tiny island in the Mediterranean were so many things: mysteries of the past and the modern

Mediterranean world trying to keep up with the 21st century.

~~~~~~~~~~~☞~~~~~~~~~~~

The Prehistory of Malta

On my next day in Malta, I paid a visit to Joseph Ellul, one of the many writers on the mysteries of Malta. A friendly, retired businessman, Joseph met me at the bus station in Zurrieq and took me to his home. He had written the book *Malta's Prediluvian Culture*[171] and I felt that he was one of the premier advocates of the view that Malta was a lost civilization such as Atlantis. In his book, Ellul theorizes that the Mediterranean was a dry valley when the megalithic structures were built.

Indeed, all geologists agree that Malta was once attached to the mainland. In this dry valley of the Mediterranean were several huge lakes, say even conservative scholars such as Ernle Bradford. Bradford says in his book *Mediterranean, Portrait of a Sea*,[192] "The western Mediterranean, the area from Gibraltar to Malta and Sicily, is separated from the eastern by a submerged ridge on which the Maltese islands stand. This now hidden land once joined Europe to North Africa, and on either side of it—long after the Tethys had receded—there probably lay two great lakes. The skeletons of miniature elephants found in Ghar Dalam (Cave of Darkness) in Malta certainly suggest that the two continents were once united."

One of the chief studies of the island, *Malta* by J.D. Evans, says this about the dwarf mammoths found on the island: "Three species of elephants have been distinguished according to size, the smallest being only 3 feet high. ...Similar, though not identical, dwarf elephants have been found in deposits in other islands of the Mediterranean, such as Sicily, Sardinia, Crete and Cyprus. In some stratified sites it can be demonstrated that the smaller ones are later than the larger ones, because they are found higher up in the deposits. A plausible explanation of this is that a number of beasts of normal size were trapped on the newly formed islands and that their descendants decreased in size owing to a scarcity of fodder and worsening conditions generally. This hypothesis also has the merit of explaining why species of dwarf animals found on different islands are not identical, since they would have developed in isolation from each other though along parallel lines."[198]

Bradford describes how the Mediterranean was flooded: "At some unknown point in time (but one which has persisted in man's memory), the land bridge which connected Africa with Spain at the Straits of Gibraltar was broken through and the ocean roared in, flooding first the western lake, then overrunning the land between Sicily and North Africa (marooning small islands like Levanzo,

Malta, and Gozo), and finally uniting the western with the eastern to form what is now the Mediterranean Sea. This event, so momentous to the human race, is remembered in the Greek legend of Deucalion and possibly in the story of Noah in the Bible."[192]

As the Bible says in *Genesis,* "All the fountains of the great deep were broken up, and the windows of heaven were opened." With this sudden rush of water into the Mediterranean Valley-Basin, hundreds of cities were drowned and a huge wave washed up over Asia Minor and flooded the ancient cities of Sumerian and Hebrew legend.

In the living room of his home, Joseph poured me a cup of tea and we talked about the lost world of Malta and the dry Mediterranean.

"In this prediluvian era," he said, "a large part of the land was submerged under the waters of the Mediterranean. Thus, the continents of Asia, Europe and Africa formed, in those days, one vast land mass. This continent was covered with vast forests and large herds of elephants, mastodons, and other wild animals roamed."

Ellul then asserted, like others before him, that the gigantic walls were built to keep wild animals out. As he says in his book, "Because of these animals which naturally abounded in the low grounds, the human beings of that era had to make their dwellings on the high grounds and ridges away from the lakes and marshes. Moreover, to keep these animals away, those men even constructed a kind of bastion made of big blocks of stone to form a perimeter for their dwellings and temples.

"The ruins at Hagar Qim were protected by such a wall, a big part of which may still be seen today on the Northwest, North and East sides of the main ruins."

Indeed it is a fascinating vision of ancient man, himself a giant at seven or eight feet tall, having to keep 14-foot cave bears from wandering into his living room at night. And there is evidence that the dragons of old were something of a problem 10,000 years ago.

Things were even worse, actually, with tales of continual warfare and the use of trained war elephants to wreck havoc wherever they went. It's one thing to have a herd of woolly mammoths come through town, but much worse is a siege army with war elephants.

Sitting with me in his living room, Ellul maintained that the temples were built on the crests of hills overlooking the huge valley and its lakes. "What we today call the Maltese Islands, were in those far-off days the peaks of mountains or high ground, and so it is no wonder that these islands are dotted with no less than 9 prehistoric remains." According to Ellul, an article on the geological destruction by Ernest G. Geoghegan appeared in *The Malta Chronicle* of 29th April, 1933. The article described the effects of the water on land, but he attributes the water to a different source than the Gibraltar wave.

Geoghegan says that "sections measuring thousands of cubic miles of water hit the earth on the land between Pantelleria and Gibraltar, while other great sections hit between Malta and Palestine, and small sections of merely hundreds of cubic miles hit the Upper Rhone. The effect of that blow was to scoop out the two Mediterraneans, for the water had a terrific motion from west to east which would have swamped every ship on the ocean and would have swamped Noah but that his ship had been built some thousands of feet above sea level."[171]

Says Ellul, "All this destruction caused by a colossal wave rushing from west to east can be witnessed in the stone age megalithic ruins of Hagar Qim. When one examines these ruins closely, one will easily see that the wall facing directly Westwards has been completely destroyed. This wall which had to bear the brunt of this gigantic wave followed by the rush of the water in its wake could not withstand the onslaught, no matter how massive it had been. According to the other remaining outer walls it must have been very massive. Huge blocks of stone from the western wall have been blown off from their original position and piled up in a heap some ten metres away towards the East as if they had been so many wooden boxes and not blocks of stone almost a metre square and about 3 metres long.

"...These blocks are a witness to another very important fact. They have a lot of mortar petrified to them and some of it actually joins the stones themselves to each other. This solidified mortar proves without any doubt that mortar was used in those days and also proves that when the stones of the building fell, they were for a time under water so that the mortar could soften and harden again in a different position. If the stones fell under dry conditions the mortar would have crumbled and fallen to dust and never stuck again."[171]

"So you believe that the Malta temples were destroyed by a giant wave coming from the Atlantic?" I asked.

"Certainly no earth tremor or strong wind could throw such heavy stones to such distances and all in the same direction," he writes. "Only a gigantic wave of water from the West could reasonably explain these movements. Several other instances could be observed where huge blocks of stone have been moved from their proper place. But the motion will be found to be always towards the East. The high southern wall was not thrown down because it is directly in line with the rush of the wave, in an exactly East-West direction.

"Even the highest stone of the ruins at the North-West corner, although it is propped up by huge slabs in the wall on its leeward (eastern) side, was quite obviously dislodged from its original position. The wave gave it such a push at the top, knocking it against its eastern supports, that it was dislodged from its close-fitting position with its neighboring western block and in the process kicked the shoring block at its foot some 3 feet away. This shoring block has been put back during works in the 1950s."[171]

Was Malta Atlantis?

I asked Joseph Ellul about the three feet of silt that had been deposited at the Tarxien and Hagar Qim temples.

"How could this sediment, which has all the appearance of being deposited by water," said Joseph, "come inside Tarxien and Hagar Qim when these stand on a hill and are in no way in the path of running water? The solution is that this sediment came during the time when Malta was under the waters of the Great Flood which covered the land for more than three hundred days.

"During that time the sand particles carried by the water settled down to a thickness of three feet on the floor of the ruined temple where it remained unmolested till its excavation in 1914. This water-deposited sediment was not found only in Malta, but it was also discovered in Iraq near the town of Ur. The archaeologist Sir Leonard Wooley discovered this kind of virgin silt to a depth of nine feet. Under this layer were found the remains of another civilization. This layer of virgin silt was also discovered in the south of France to a depth of six feet.

"During excavations in Mesopotamia," he went on, "in a place called Xari Suste, a whole town was found buried under a layer of sand. Skeletons were found, some in a praying, others in a crouched sleeping position. Pottery was found in perfect condition laid out in position ready for meals. The comments of the archaeologists were that 'a civilization of 5000 years ago was terminated abruptly for some unknown reason'."

Concluded Joseph as he finished his cup of tea, "I cannot understand why they still pretend that the reason is unknown when there has been so much evidence of a worldwide flooding. This destruction was caused by the instantaneous onrush of a monstrous sea wave from the Atlantic coming through the Straits of Gibraltar."

It was getting late, but I asked him a few more questions. "Does Atlantis fit into your theories about Malta?"

He then mentioned that in 1984 it was reported that oceanographers had found structures reminiscent of a human settlement at the bottom of the Mediterranean Sea near Gibraltar. "Those scientists speculated this was Atlantis, an island which Greek mythology says was inundated by water after an earthquake."

He went on to mention that in the 1950s Soviet archaeologists discovered the stonework and statues of the legendary town of Dioscuria which had disappeared from ancient maps. "It was found at the bottom of the Black Sea off Sukhumi. All this proves that the level of the Mediterranean and Black Seas was not always at this high level."

"And Atlantis...?" I asked.

Ellul's answer essentially recapitulated the opinion expressed in his book: "Atlantis was nothing less than the now submerged land under the Mediterranean and Black Seas. ...Why is it that the big lakes in central Eurasia, known as the Caspian Sea and the Sea of Aral, contain salty water? And why is it that Lake Balkash and Lake Baikal contain fresh water? It is just because the Atlantic wave reached only up to the Caspian and the Aral but did not reach to Lake Balkash."[171]

Well, I was convinced, at least in my host's sincerity. As I left, I thanked him and mentioned that his book is probably the best one currently available on prehistoric Malta.

On the bus ride back to Valetta I thought about what he had said, and I realized that I disagreed with him when he stated that the drowned Mediterranean and the Black Sea are the Atlantis of ancient legend. I believe this sunken area was the pre-Greek state that warred with Atlantis—the Osirians and Athenians of 10,000 B.C.

Atlantis was beyond the Pillars of Hercules and was an island in the Atlantic between Europe and the farther continent. In fact, it seems likely that the cataclysm that sank Atlantis played a large part in the cataclysm that sank Osiris.

The next day I grabbed a decorated green bus from the plaza and headed north across the island to the port of Marfa where I would be able to get a ferry to Gozo, Malta's sister isle.

The crossing was quicker than I had expected. I hardly had time for a cup of tea when the ferry was docking at the port of Mgarr. I stepped off the ferry in the bright morning air and discovered that everyone was heading for the bus to Victoria, the "capital" of tiny Gozo.

No place on Gozo, I learned, is more than 4 km from the ocean. In Victoria I explored the town a bit, looking for postcards and books on Gozo. I stumbled onto a derelict shop where an old man in a crumpled coat sold postcards and magazines.

"Do you have any books about the island?" I asked him as he shuffled some postcards towards me.

He suddenly gathered energy and produced an amazing old book that was covered with dust.

He wiped the worn copy against his sleeve. "It's only 80 cents," he said, "because it's so old." Gozo apparently didn't get many tourists.

I glanced at it, noticed a few interesting old photographs, and gladly paid him a full Maltese pound. I bought a good selection of postcards as well. He was pleased with his sudden sale and I looked at my book eagerly. Gozo had much for inquisitive researchers to see.

〰〰〰〰〰𓂀〰〰〰〰〰

The Megaliths of Gozo

I took a local bus to the town of Zagra where Ggantija, Gozo's most famous ruins, could be found. A small ticket booth controlled the entrance and after paying I strolled through the massive walls that are said to be Europe's oldest.

I walked around the high walls made of cyclopean stones. In some places they were 20 feet high and made of perfectly fitting stones, though the blocks were very eroded. I noticed some large round stones near the southern temple complex, probably for moving the large blocks. The doorways had holes at the base as sockets for the huge doors that once stood. There were the familiar spiral designs on some of the blocks plus a snake motif, which according to the tourist brochure that I bought at the ticket office had something to do with reincarnation.

Boundary stones were as long as 15 feet and weighed up to 50 tons or more. According to the tourist brochure, a quantity of clay models were found with deformed body parts, indicating, the archaeologists thought, that this was some sort of healing sanctuary.

An early mention of the ruins can be found in James Fergusson's book *Rude Stone Monuments in All Countries* (London, 1872). He included a description of Ggantija: "The best known monuments of the Maltese groups are situated near the centre of the Isle of Gozo, in the commune of Barbato. When Houel wrote in 1787, only the outside wall with the apse of one of the inner chambers and the entrance of another were known. He mistook the right-hand apse of the second pair of chambers for part of a circle, and so represented it with a dolmen in the centre, led to this apparently by the existence of a real circle which then was found at a distance of 350 yards from the main group. This circle was 140 feet in diameter, composed of stones ranged close together and alternately broad and tall..."[7]

Fergusson is talking about the Von Brockdorf Circle, a partially underground site which is closed off to the public. As I walked around the ruins, I was told by a guide about the Von Brockdorf Circle. Apparently, a German university had been doing some digging at the site and made some startling claims!

According to the guide that I met on Gozo, the German university had discovered some 100 or so skeletons buried among the megaliths, and each one had been decapitated; moreover, the skulls were completely missing. Furthermore, they were unable to carbon-date the skeletons as no carbon-14 was left in the bones.

Analysts claim that carbon-14 dating can go back as far as about 30,000 years before the carbon-14 is so negligible that the material can't be dated any longer.

If this were the case, then the skeletons of Ggantija would be over 30,000 years old. This seems unlikely, but who knows? Carbon-14 dating has been proven to have some serious inaccuracies, and many bones may be older or younger than carbon-dating shows. Carbon-14 dating also assumes a constant figure in the amount of carbon-14 in the atmosphere 20,000 years ago, which may not be correct.

On the other hand, the ruins at Gozo must be very old, built perhaps 15,000 or more years ago. It would be likely that all the megalithic ruins on Malta are of a similar age, as well. If the ruins on Gozo are tens of thousands of years old, the ruins of Hagar Qim and Tarxien are probably close to the same age.

The amazing antiquity of Ggantija was on my mind as I walked back into the town of Xagra. After a pleasant lunch of ravioli and homemade bread with Gozo goat cheese at Gesther's Home Cooking Café, I asked Gesther when the bus back to Victoria, the main town, would arrive.

"Not until 2:30," she said. "Two and a half hours from now."

"Really," I said. I didn't want to wait two and a half hours for the bus. "I guess I'll have to hitchhike," I said to myself.

I began walking downhill along the road out of town. Xagra was on the top of a hill and I had a great view of the brown rolling hills of Gozo. Suddenly a tiny Morris Mini came toward me. I stuck out my thumb and motioned down the road, indicating I wanted a lift.

The faded blue car stopped and I jumped in the passenger's seat. The owner was an older man with a thick gray mustache. "Are you going to Victoria?" I asked him.

He didn't appear to speak much English. "Just to the farm," he said, pointing downhill. He ground the car into gear and we began rolling downhill. He was barefoot, and I looked around at the torn-out interior of this ancient car.

"Wow, this is a great car," I told him and pulled out my camera. "Can I take a photo of you?" I asked, and he nodded.

Just as I got the camera ready and leaned against the door we went around a sharp curve on the mountain road. Suddenly the door flew open and I was flying out the door!

"Whoa!" I screamed. Fortunately I had my elbow through the open window and it kept me from flying out of the car completely.

I scrambled to get back inside the car and the old man continued to barrel on down the hill in his old Morris Mini. Once I was back inside the car I laughed, and he laughed too.

He let me off at a roundabout and from the safety of the ground I took a photo of my driver. I got another quick lift into Victoria and then took a bus to Dwerja Bay on the other side of the island. This was once an inland sea that is now connected to the outer ocean by a tunnel through the cliffs.

I explored the cliffs above Dwerja Bay looking for cart tracks that were said to be in the area. It took a while, but I finally found several sets of cart ruts running across the barren rock. Around me were high cliffs that had rounded caves washed out by wave action. This indicated to me that the ocean had at one time been hundreds of feet higher.

The cart ruts were well worn into the rocks at some places and at others they disappeared entirely. Some went over the cliffs into the ocean. Others seemed to curve around toward the inland sea.

As I walked back toward the main road, I passed a modern quarry, quite possibly the site of an ancient quarry as well. I hitchhiked back across the island to the cliffs of Ta Cenc to look for more cart ruts along the sheer cliffs. In the late afternoon wind I searched carefully along a sheer drop of hundreds of feet into the ocean directly below.

Then, near a rock wall, I found several sets of tracks that ran along near the cliff face and then disappeared. It was getting late and I would have to get the ferry back to Malta. At the ferry terminal I thought about the strange ruins of Ggantija and the mysterious skeletons... the cart tracks that ran off the edge of cliffs... This was a small, but mysterious island indeed.

My last few days in Malta I spent relaxing, visiting the Dhar Galam cave where the pygmy elephants and hippopotamus had been found along with the bones of deer, bear, fox and other animals no longer found on Malta.

Nearby were the leftover ruins of Borg-n-Nadur, a Bronze Age cyclopean wall. The site was difficult to find and largely neglected by the government, it appeared.

One night I met some students at a pub along Malta's Saliema beach area. They told me how that same day the local bird hunters had defaced Hagar Qim with cans of orange spray-paint to protest Malta's entrance into the Common Market. With Malta in the European Community the hunters will have to go by strict EEC hunting rules.

"If you are an archaeologist you should cry," said one of the students. "These are the oldest ruins in the world according to carbon-dating!"

"It is a terrible thing," I agreed. I had just visited Hagar Qim before the temples were defaced. I pointed out that the dating of the temples was not known exactly and that the temples themselves couldn't be carbon-dated.

"But they have carbon-dated the temples. They know how old they are. That's science, man," said the student.

I pointed out that rock cannot be carbon-dated, only organic matter: a bone or piece of wood found in the temples.

Then, a young man in his 30s with a beer in his hand broke in. "Excuse me, but I am a professional geologist," he said. "And you can carbon-date those temples. The rocks are made of limestone and limestone has carbon in it and that is how they have dated the temples."

I was amazed at this lack of understanding by a "professional geologist," but it is typical. I then explained to them how even that stone couldn't be carbon-dated because carbon-14 won't date anything over about 30,000 years old; and anyway, you would be dating the formation of the rock itself, not the quarrying of the stone and the building of the temple.

We discussed the matter for a while over a friendly glass of beer and eventually the geologist started to get the idea.

"Well," he said, "no matter what, those stones are old. Probably the oldest in the world!"

"I'll drink to that," I said.

We all held up our glasses and said in unison, "Hear, hear! To the oldest stones in the world."

Spiral drawings, similar to those at Newgrange, Ireland, on the megalithic walls of Tarxien.

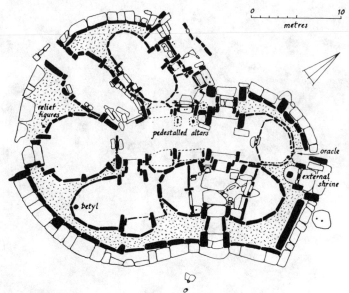

Ħaġar Qim, the main temple block

Ħaġar Qim, the façade

The Holy of Holies in the Hypogeum of Hal Saflieni

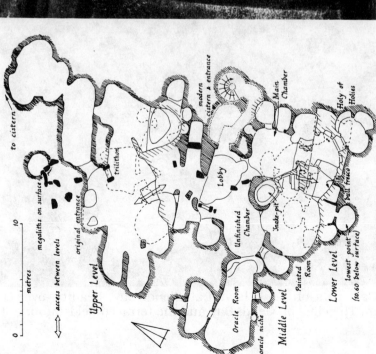

The Hypogeum of Hal Saflieni

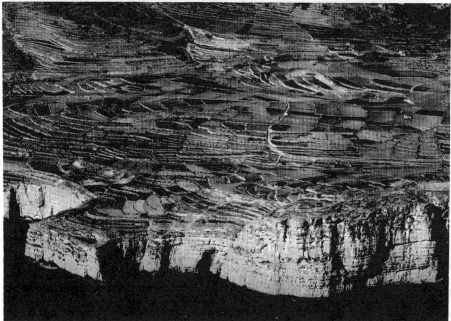

Top: Cart ruts on Gozo Island at Xlendi Bay, heading over a cliff.
Bottom: The cliffs of Xlendi Bay and the terraced fields around it.

Various intersecting ruts on the plateau of Ta'Cenc, Gozo.

Top: A 1926 aerial photo of the many ruts near Nadur Tower on
Malta. Center: One of the many deep ruts at Naxxar Gap, Malta.
Note the variations in depth and the relative smoothness. Bottom:
Clapham Junction, Malta, where about 30 sets of tracks are visible.

Above: One corner of the massive walls of Ggantija on Gozo. Below: The threshold and central passage of the South Temple of Ggantija.

Tanger.

Puerta de la Alcazaba

Chapter 7

TUNISIA & MOROCCO:

Carthage & the
Lost Cities of Atlas

*Don't let your minds be cluttered up
with the prevailing doctrine.*
—Alexander Fleming (1881-1955)

I looked down from my seat at the blue Mediterranean below me. I was on an Air Malta flight to Tunis, and would be landing shortly. By mid-afternoon I was walking through customs at Tunis airport and out onto the sundrenched sidewalk. A taxi driver in blue jeans and a white shirt offered to take me into town and I accepted.

I was coming through Tunisia on my way to Morocco. I planned to visit Carthage, the greatest of the Phoenician cities that once ruled the oceans. There is more written about Carthage than about all the other cities of the Phoenicians put together.

And where the Phoenicians were, stories of Atlantis were nearby. During the 1800s North Africa became a popular site of speculation for Atlantis theories. Atlantis writer L. Sprague de Camp comments specifically on this, saying that D. A. Godron, a French botanist, started the Atlantis-in-Africa school in 1868 by placing Atlantis in the Sahara. Following Godron, Felix Berlioux in 1874 claimed to have located the capital of Atlantis on the west coast of Morocco between Casablanca and Agadir, where the Atlas mountain chain slopes down to the sea. Here, said Berlioux, and not on any island, lay Plato's city of Atlantis, otherwise Kernë, the capital of the Atlantioi in the account of Diodorus the Sicilian.[1]

Atlantis was not to be found beneath the Atlantic Ocean, this new school of Atlantis scholars believed, but rather in the sands of the Sahara Desert and coastal Morocco, Algeria and Tunisia.

Sir Francis Bacon suggested North Africa and the coast of Morocco as Atlantis circa 1600. The traveler Domingo Badia y Leblich, known as Ali Bey, proposed North Africa as well in 1814. Other writers such as Albert Hermann in 1925 suggested that Tunisia was the site of legendary Atlantis.

In 1920 a novel about Atlantis in the Sahara, called *L'Atlantide,* was published in France. Written by Pierre Benoit, it was immediately popular and was translated into English as *The Queen of Atlantis* (1922, London, Hutchinson). *L'Atlantide* was the fictional story of a pair of French Army officers who find Atlantis in the Ahaggar Mountains of southern Algeria.

In the mysterious world of mountains, caverns and sand, the tall veiled men of the Tuareg worship their queen Antinéa, historically the name of the Tuareg queen Tin Hinan, hereditary matriarch of the lost world of the Ahaggar.

Antinéa is like a character from an H. Rider Haggard novel: she seduces all the men, some of whom kill themselves when she switches to a new lover, and sits at the throne of Atlantis with a pet leopard named Hiram at her side.

The author, Benoit, apparently knew the Ahaggar well and his book was full of realistic detail. The book spawned at least two movies and was said to have inspired the archaeologist-adventurer Count Byron Khun de Prorok to hunt for Atlantis in the Sahara.

Count de Prorok was a wealthy and credible amateur archaeologist along the same lines as Lord Carnarvon. De Prorok was one of the early excavators of Carthage and was a believer in Atlantis. In 1925 de Prorok penetrated into the Ahaggar Massif in search of Atlantis, five years after *L'Atlantide* was published.

De Prorok's book *In Quest of Lost Worlds*[212] was a popular travel adventure book in its time. Byron de Prorok also believed he had discovered Atlantis and the first chapter of *In Quest of Lost Worlds* was about an expedition into the Ahaggar that described adventures and legends that were remarkably parallel to those in *L'Atlantide.* Travelling in specially equipped Citroen cars, they found that the Tuaregs had poisoned an important water hole. This was in the region of Moudir, "where great precipices form a wall of rock, believed by the Tuaregs to be the fortress of the 'Amazons,' ruled by a white goddess: the fable of old Atlantis." They then discover an underground lake: "We threaded our way down a narrow corridor, which speedily darkened, so that we had to use our torches, and were surprised to come upon a clear, transparent pool, with a fine sandy beach. The walls around were covered with inscriptions and rock drawings of elephants, buffaloes, antelopes, and ostriches. Not one or two; but scores of drawings were there, and we knew that we were definitely on the trail of the old caravan routes to the gold and ivory lands of the ancients."[212]

De Prorok and his company then continue through the *Bled es Khouf*, the land of fear. It is here that the rocks could explode from the sudden heating and cooling. One of de Prorok's men begins shooting wildly, thinking that they are being attacked by Tuaregs. Afterwards they come to the Valley of Giants, giant rock formations, thought to be natural(?), that look like hippopotami, elephants, and dinosaurs. When they finally meet some Tuaregs, de Prorok describes them as seven feet tall, with their faces always veiled by their blue or purple robes, much the way the ancient Phoenicians dressed.

All in all, de Prorok's book gives a good look at the mysteries of a lost world in the Sahara. Indeed, ancient writers wrote of a navigable sea within the Sahara and mysterious people called the Atarantes.

The Ancient Triton Sea

Herodotus (died c. 425 B.C.) speaks of an ancient sea called Triton that has since dried up. He says in *The Histories* (IV, 184.): "At the distance of ten days' journey from the Garamantians there is again another salt-hill and spring of water; around which dwell a people, called the Atarantes, who alone of all known nations are destitute of names. The title of Atarantes is borne by the whole race in common, but the men have no particular names of their own. The Atarantes, when the sun rises high in the heavens, curse him, and load him with reproaches, because (they say) he burns and wastes both their country and themselves.

"Once more at the distance of ten days' journey there is a salt-hill, a spring, and an inhabited tract. Near the salt-hill is a mountain called Atlas, very tapered and round; so lofty, moreover, that the top (it is said) cannot be seen, the clouds never quitting it either summer or winter. The natives call this mountain the Pillar of Heaven, and they themselves take their name from it, being called Atlantes. They are reported not to eat any living thing, and never to have any dreams."

In Herodotus (IV, 188) we also learn of Lake Tritonis: "The inhabitants of the parts about Lake Tritonis worship in addition Triton, Poseidon, and Athena, the last especially."

According to the geologist and Atlantis writer L. Taylor Hansen in her book *The Ancient Atlantic*,[27] Lake Tritonis was part of a huge inland sea in the Sahara east of the Atlas Mountains. Lake Chad would be the last remnants of this ancient sea.

Sitting in my hotel, I mused over L. Taylor Hansen's fascinating book, *The Ancient Atlantic*.[27] She discusses the ancient Triton Sea and the antediluvian kingdom of the Tuaregs in the Ahaggar Mountains.

According to Hansen, the Triton Sea was held by the curve of the Atlas Mountains like the rim of a cup, and the water thus held covered the land from the Gulf of Gabes where it entered the Mediterranean to the mountains south of Lake Chad. Only after the sudden sinking of the southern arm of the Atlas did the Niger River break through these southern mountains and tear its way out to the Atlantic. Lake Chad and the underground lakes of the Sahara were all that was left of the Triton Sea, except for the massive port cities that existed in the Sahara![27]

Do such megalithic ports really exist in the sands of the Sahara? Hansen assures us that they do. According to her, the Ahaggar Mountains in central Algeria were an island during the time of the Triton Sea, which would be contemporaneous with the civilizations of Osiris and Atlantis.

The area of the Ahaggar is not easy to gather knowledge about, both because of its remote location and because the fierce Tuaregs, the Veiled People, jealously guard their secrets and heritage. The Arabs are very much afraid of these people, as one Arab told Hansen in her book. Her conversation with an unnamed Arab is quite fascinating. He relates that "Near In-Salah there are three high peaks of the Haggar. No Arab will go there if he can help it. These peaks touch the sky with claw-like fingers. Once a friend of mine got lost and saw the ruins of one of their cities on the Atlas. It was built of giant stones—each one the size of an Arabian tent. In the front is a great circular wall. But in the desert they live underground. I have heard that under Ahaggar are many galleries deep in the earth around an underground lake. These galleries are filled with paintings of the long age."[27]

The Arab qualified his statements by saying that he had travelled to areas of the Tuareg people as a messenger. "On one of these times I took a message from my sheik to Tamen-Ra-Set (note the Egyptian name here)—that is the Tuareg capital city. That is where Amen-Okhal, their king, lives." Hansen comments that these are names of Egyptian gods that were ancient at the dawn of history.

The Arab went on to describe how the original inhabitants of the Sahara were the Tibesti people who were Dravidians from India. The Tuareg tribes invaded from the ocean (Hansen believes from Atlantis) into the Triton Sea and settled in the Ahaggar area and the Atlas. The Tibesti tribe was then driven into the Tibesti Mountains of northern Chad and southern Libya. James Churchward in his book *The Children of Mu*[42] gives information corresponding to this, that the Ethiopians are also of Dravidian stock, coming from Mu to Burma and India many thousands of years ago, and then on to Ethiopia by crossing the Indian Ocean. According to the Arab, they also settled the fertile areas of the Sahara during the period of the Triton Sea.

Hansen asks the Arab how he knows this, and he replies that the Tuaregs told him. Therefore Hansen surmises that "...the underlying blood of the Mediterranean is Dravidian and the Tuaregs are invaders... That must have been what the priest of Vulcan in early Egypt meant when he told Solon that the Greeks and Egyptians were really brothers in the days when the Mediterranean was a valley filled with cities!"[27]

The Arab goes on, "The land I speak of is beyond the Mya River—one of the great dead rivers of the Sahara. The terraces rise from its ancient bed in colors of red and white. Once it emptied into the Triton Sea and carried ships up to the great cities of the Tuaregs on top of the Atlas and the Ahaggar mountains. I believe the Mya emptied where the dry lakes of the Chotts are today. As the sea level of the Triton sank in long dry spells, another lake was where Lake Chad is now with a waterway in between. That land was green then. Ostriches, buffalo, deer, tigers roamed the woodlands and crocodiles slept in the rivers... This place is called the land of the monsters because the cliffs are shaped like monster animals—such as you have never seen. There are enormous shaggy elephants and a giant lizard that sends your hair arising when you first see it. In the heat of the Sahara, they seem to come to life and move... The Tuaregs say that when they first came to the land, the living monsters really gathered here to fight over their feeding grounds, but of course, that was untold ages before my people appeared."

The Arab told Hansen of galleries and tunnels in the mountains, and how a friend climbed one of the peaks and discovered a shaft that was covered by a metal grate. And also of another friend with whom, when they were younger, he went to the Ahaggar Mountains one night out of curiosity. Crouching in the moonlight, they saw a ceremonial war take place between two mounted Tuareg groups who clashed until some of their members were killed. Then, while the young Arab boys watched from their hiding place, one group of Tuaregs rode into a cliff wall and disappeared!

The Arab ended his incredible tale to Hansen with the legend that, "Down in the miles and miles of underground galleries, where it is said that they wander about a beautiful artificial lake, and then pass along torchlighted passageways looking at pictures painted of their cities so many thousands of years ago—are their libraries. There are kept the books which are the oldest libraries of the earth. There are the histories which go way beyond the great deluge, to the times when the Tuaregs ruled the seas. How do I know? They told me, that is, the emperor did. But save your next question. I could not get to read them. Neither could you, or anyone else—no one will ever read them except the people of the veil."[27]

Hansen continues her chapter on the Triton Sea by relating a conversation she had with a wealthy retired American couple named Johnson in Palm Springs back in the 1960s. Mrs. Johnson talked about an old Arab whom they paid to tell them the ancient history. "The old man told me that above a mighty gorge in the very heights of the Atlas are the ruins of the city of Khamissa. It has towers of marble which have been deserted for untold thousands of years. Yet at certain times, when the weather is just right and the atmospheric conditions are perfect, it becomes a kaleidoscope of galleys, triremes and ghost ships from long forgotten nations. And the beauty of the rounded towers are reflected in the sea like those from a never-never land."[27]

The old Arab's tale becomes reminiscent of Hansen's earlier informant on the Triton Sea and the Tuaregs when he says, "In the galleries which are not lakes, or places for the storage of water, the unimagined splendor of the Tuaregs in the full pride of their power is still pictured in endless gallery paintings."

The old Arab mentions another lost city near the Air Range of southern Algeria and the curious city of Heracles: "Between the ranges of the Air and the Ahaggar, is once proud Tafassaset, and southeast of the Ahaggar range is Essouk, the imperial capital of Heracles, once the most important city on Earth."[27]

L. Taylor Hansen mentions that a ship was once found in the desert: "During the Middle Ages a ship was found not too far from the Draa Depression [the present border of Morocco and Algeria, just east of the Atlas Mountains] in which skeletons of the rowers were lying with the chains still around their bones. The Arabs, I understand, charge a very high fee to take you there. It still must be in existence."[27]

The French archaeologist Henri Lhote discovered many strange drawings in the Tassili Mountain range, south of the Ahagger. Lhote even calls one of the drawings "the Martian God." One of the chapters in his book, *The Search of the Tassili Frescoes*,[211] was entitled, "Did We Discover Atlantis?" It seems evident that there was some sort of lost world in the Sahara. Scholars just argue how advanced the civilization was. I guess when they see men running around with bows and arrows, as on the paintings, it plays into their natural bias that mankind was primitive many thousands of years ago.

Lhote's book is full of bizarre people with feathered headdresses and masks, bird women with long beaks, elephants and huge herds of long-horned cattle. It is without question that this lost world of the Sahara is a strange place. But is it Atlantis?

~~~~~~~~~~𝕾𝕿~~~~~~~~~~

Atlantis In Tunisia

As I walked around Tunis, visiting the museum and sitting in cafés, I read various books on Tunis, Carthage and Atlantis. A theory similar to the Atlantis-in-the-Ahaggar idea was put forward by the famous German explorer Leo Frobenius and the English Captain Elgee, who believed that Atlantis was in Nigeria. The two formulated their theory between 1908 and 1926 because Frobenius had discovered things in Yorubaland that convinced him that West Africa had been Atlantis.

Nigeria bordered on the Atlantic and had the requisite elephants, copper mines, luxuriant vegetation and blue-clad people. Nigeria had been a powerful maritime nation in the past, Frobenius and Elgee agreed. Frobenius equated the Nigerian god Okolon with Poseidon, and maintained that Yoruba culture contained many non-African elements such as number magic, the short bow and the king's sacred umbrella.

Frobenius, interestingly, believed that civilization had begun on a lost continent in the Pacific Ocean, where it had spread to Asia and then westward, stimulating the rise of such cultures as the Egyptian and the Atlanto-Nigerian. Tartessos in Spain was an outpost of this African Atlantis. To Frobenius, the Uphaz mentioned in the Bible as a source of gold and trade goods was Yorubaland itself, whose capital was at modern Ilife.

The search for Atlantis in North Africa didn't have to go as far into the Sahara as the Ahaggar Mountains or Nigeria. Some Atlantis writers felt they had found it near Tunis. In 1926 archaeologist Paul Borchardt of Munich undertook to find Atlantis in the salt marshes that stretch westward from the Gulf of Gabes which the ancients called Little Syrtis.

Borchardt believed that the Shott el Jerid, the largest of the swamps near Tunis, was once a huge body of water and the original Atlantic Sea. The outer ocean, he claimed, was Tethys, the all-encompassing sea. Furthermore, Borchardt identified the Ahaggar Mountains as the real Atlas Mountains rather than those in Morocco. He tried to correlate the names of Poseidon's ten sons as given by Plato with the names of modern Berber tribes, and thought that the Pillars of Hercules were actual pillars in a temple, rather than tall mountains flanking the Straits of Gibraltar.

227

Borchardt thought that the ancient mines in the Shott country were confirmation of his theory and suggested that Atlantis with its brass and orichalc, the bronze palace of Alkinoös in the *Odyssey*, and the City of Brass in the *Arabian Nights* were all one and the same. In the end, Borchardt found the remains of a fortress which he took to be the fabled city of Atlantis itself. Sadly, it turned out to be of Roman origin.

Then in 1925 the archaeologist Albert Herrmann went hunting Atlantis in southern Tunisia. Says L. Sprague de Camp in *Lost Continents*, "He thought he had found it in the village of Rhelissia, where he discovered traces of irrigation works pointing to a higher culture than that of the present Rhelissians. He reasoned that Plato had been wrong on three counts. First, he took Herodotus' meaning for Atlantic instead of the older meaning referring to Lake Tritonis. Second, Atlantis fell in the 14th or 13th century B.C., instead of the 96th century B.C."[1]

Lastly, Herrmann also believed that the measurements of the plain of Atlantis were incorrect and everything was 30 times too large. With these corrections, Herrmann could fit Plato's Atlantis into the region of Tunisia.

Herrmann, de Camp tells us, went on to derive all civilization from Friesland, the sunken area of Holland and northern Germany. He maintained that Atlantis (in Tunisia) was but a colony from the days of Frisian glory.

Actually, a more interesting theory was that of the French writer F. Butavand who claimed that Atlantis was at the bottom of the Gulf of Gabes, in the Mediterranean off the Tunisian coast. Butavand published *La Véritable Histoire de l'Atlantide* (Paris) in 1925 and said that the gulf was once dry land, out to about the present 100-fathom line, until an earthquake lowered this land beneath the waters of the Mediterranean and at the same time raised the bottom of the Triton Sea in the Sahara, causing it to drain off and dry up, leaving only marshes. The straits of Gibraltar had opened up at this time as well.[1]

Another similar theory proposing that Atlantis was in Tunisia was published by the German historian Otto Silbermann in his book *Un Continent Perdu: L'Atlantide* (Paris, 1930). Silbermann pointed out that in view of the known chronology of Egyptian civilization and the difficulty of handing down a story accurately by word of mouth alone for more than a few centuries, Plato's dating of the rise and fall of Atlantis 9000 years before Solon's time could be dismissed right away; if such a civilization had existed, it would have been entirely forgotten long before the rise of Egypt.[1]

Therefore Silbermann thought that the Atlantis story was originally a Phoenician account of a war with Libyans of the Shott region of Tunisia that took place around 2540 B.C. About the eleventh or tenth century, he thought, some Egyptian of Saïs made this story into a romance, placing the events "in the time of Horus," which date Plato interpreted much later as about 9600 B.C.

Silbermann maintained that this episode of history was forgotten but then revived again about 600 B.C. when Niku II rebuilt the Egyptian navy and there was a search for books about Libya. The story was also translated into Greek for the benefit of the Hellenes of Saïs, and one Greek version formed the basis for Solon's account while another was preserved as the story of the *Atlantioi* related by Diordorus of Sicily.

And so Silbermann sought to justify his theories of Tunisia as Atlantis. Yet, it is wrong to think that the Egyptians were not capable of keeping ancient books in storage at their universities and libraries. Important stories were not handed down orally but written on papyrus and even chiseled into granite. Unfortunately in many cases these repositories of knowledge have been destroyed.

Besides, the Egyptians had explored all of North Africa and certainly knew where Tunisia was. Like Crete, Tunisia is the site of a lost civilization, but it is too close to Greece and Egypt to be Atlantis.

~~~~~~~~~~⚓~~~~~~~~~~

The Punic Wars

One morning I took a bus to the ruins of Carthage. Located a few miles outside of Tunis, Carthage was founded about 850 B.C. by a Phoenician princess from Tyre named Elissa (sometimes called "Dido"), a daughter of King Mutton I. Legend says that she was fleeing the tyranny of her brother Pygmalion and founded the city. Other Phoenician ports existed in North Africa, but Carthage grew quickly and after Tyre fell to Nebuchadnezzar in 573 B.C., Carthage became the main Phoenician naval port.

To secure control of the western trade routes, especially with the tin region of southwestern Britain, Carthaginian warships stopped non-Carthaginian trading vessels and threw their crews overboard. This ironclad monopoly, not broken until the Punic Wars, also helps explain why the Greeks were a bit hazy about Atlantic sea routes.

The Carthaginians colonized Sicily, as did the Greeks, and both tried hard to throw the other out. The Carthaginian general Malchus almost conquered the whole island in 550 B.C., and wars continued, with time out for recovery and local revolutions, for three centuries. The Carthaginian general Hamilcar almost conquered the entire island in 480 B.C. but the forces of Syracuse and Agrigentum beat him at Himera in an important battle.

Carthage sent her ships on transatlantic voyages that took them to ports in Mexico, North and South America. Part of the military power of the Carthaginians was their use of war elephants in their campaigns. These war elephants were a species of the now-extinct Moroccan elephant that was similar to the Indian elephant used from Ceylon to China.

One of the greatest military generals of all time was the Carthaginian general Hannibal Barca, son of Hamilcar Barca, of the famous Barca family. Hannibal, whose name means "grace of Ba'al" in the Punic language of the Phoenicians, was born in 247 B.C.

Hannibal came from an influential trading family of Carthage who had traditionally held important positions in the military, and Hannibal succeeded his brother-in-law, Hasdrubal, as commander in the Punic province of Spain.

Hannibal was born just before the Punic Wars between Rome and Carthage. This struggle for maritime power in the Mediterranean—and beyond—was to have a lasting effect on Europe, North Africa and the Americas.

With a small force of hand-picked troops he set out to invade Italy, and crossed the Alps with a full baggage train which included war elephants. Hannibal's troops and cavalry invaded northwest Italy, overrunning the Po Valley and occupying it for several years.

This was in the years of the early Republic era of Rome, and its armies were regional, locally controlled and unorganized. Hannibal had a major victory over a Roman force in 217 B.C. and then set out for Rome. After defeating the Romans again at Lake Trasimeno, he went to south Italy and gained many allies among these separatist provinces.

At Cannae in 216 B.C. he won one of the most brilliant victories of history, it is often said, by his use of the now proverbial "fifth column," the local populace, who were the descendants of the Etruscans, and unhappy with Rome.

But Hannibal failed to get the support of Carthage in his campaign against the capital of Rome. In 207 B.C. Hannibal's brother-in-law, the general Hasdrubal, was defeated on the Metaurus River and Hannibal had to withdraw from central Italy.

Meanwhile, the Romans realized that they must defeat powerful Carthage by striking at its North African capital in a daring naval raid. So successful was this battle at the heart of the Carthaginian empire that Hannibal was recalled from his amazing Italian campaign in 203 B.C.

The brilliant Roman Admiral Scipio Africano was laying siege to Carthage and the tide was turning in the second Punic War. The Battle of Zama in 202 B.C. brought the second Punic War, which had lasted seventeen years, to an end, with the defeat of Hannibal and the total collapse of Carthaginian power.

Scipio Africano, from whom we get the modern Latin name for the continent, took control of Carthage. Prior to Africa being named after the Roman admiral, regions were called by various names such as Ethiopia, Libya, Kush, etc.

Peace was declared in 201 B.C. and Hannibal was allowed to be governor of Carthage. Rome remembered the bitter fighting, however, and demanded that Hannibal be returned to Rome as a prisoner to stand judgment. Hannibal fled Carthage into the desert to live in exile and sadly, this great man poisoned himself to avoid being captured by the Romans.[145]

A Carthaginian Colony in North America

The Phoenicians, and by extension, Carthaginians, were the masters of the Atlantic and traded with the transatlantic world of the Americas. In one fascinating theory, it is postulated that the Carthaginians and their remaining navy left North Africa and immigrated to North America.

It is said that the Carthaginians invaded their trading colonies in the Yucatan and Gulf of Mexico. The Carthaginians became the Toltecs of Mexican history. The Toltecs looked very much like warriors from the Middle East. They had long, thick beards, helmets, spears and shields. Cities such as Chichén Itzá and Uxmal in the Yucatan are famous for their occupation by the Toltecs. Chichén Itzá was originally a Mayan city until it was conquered by the bearded Toltecs.

North of Tenochtitlan (Mexico City) was the Toltec capital of Tula. In the Carthaginian-Toltec theory, the battle-hardened Toltecs ranged as far north as the deserts of the American Southwest.

Many ancient Phoenician inscriptions have been found all over the Americas. In my book *Lost Cities & Ancient Mysteries of South America* I discuss the well-known Paraiba inscription found in Brazil in the 1800s. The respected scholar Cyrus Gordon identified it as a Phoenician inscription documenting a sea voyage.[143]

Gordon also identified as Phoenician a stone that was discovered by the Smithsonian Institution at Bat Creek, Tennessee. The now famous Bat Creek inscription is a small slab of stone covered with ciphers, nine letters and one partial letter, and was found in 1885 by Smithsonian Institution archaeologists. The stone was discovered inside an undisturbed burial mound 28 feet in diameter and five feet high.

If the Carthaginians were the founders of the Toltec empire, were other earlier civilizations such as the Hittites and early Egyptians in evidence in North America? In 1909 the front page of the Phoenix *Gazette* reported that the Smithsonian Institution was excavating a huge Egyptian vault-tomb in the Grand Canyon.

The article, published by the *Gazette* on April 5, 1909, mentions that a Smithsonian archaeologist named S. A. Jordan was carrying out excavations in a rock-cut cave somewhere on the north rim of the Grand Canyon. This cavern-crypt system had been discovered some time earlier by a prospector-explorer named G. E. Kinkaid.

When Kinkaid first saw the cave entrance on the cliffs, he thought it was an old mine. The cave was apparently full of mummified bodies, hieroglyphic tablets, and copper artifacts. The *Gazette* article quoted the Smithsonian Institution as saying the caves were "of oriental origin, possibly from Egypt, tracing back to Ramses."

The fascinating story of the Egyptian discoveries in the Grand Canyon is fully explored in my book *Lost Cities of North & Central America*.[23] Suffice it to say that if the Carthaginians were in northern Mexico several thousand years ago, they may have been inheriting megalithic cities that went back to the time of ancient Egypt, or Atlantis.

We have already mentioned how the gods distributed the whole earth between them in larger or smaller shares and then established shrines and sacrifices for themselves. Poseidon's share was the island of Atlantis and he settled the children borne to him by a mortal woman in a particular district of it... He begot five pairs of male twins, brought them up, and divided the island of Atlantis into ten parts which he distributed between them. He allotted the elder of the eldest pair of twins his mother's home district and the land surrounding it, the biggest and best allocation, and made him King over the others; the others he made governors, each of a populous and large territory. He gave them all names. The eldest, the King, he gave a name from which the whole island and surrounding ocean took their designation of 'Atlantic', deriving it from Atlas the first king.
—Plato, *Critias*

The Lost Cities of Atlas

I rushed to the Tunis airport one morning to catch a flight to Tangiers in Morocco. I was forced to leave hurriedly, because Algeria was now closed and all foreigners who remained after December 31 would be marked for death by the fanatical Islamic terrorists who combat the current liberal government. Algeria had essentially closed its borders to foreigners and my dream of visiting the Ahaggar or crossing Algeria was not to be. Now the Atlas Mountains of Morocco shimmered at a distance in the hot sun.

It was mid-afternoon when I stepped out of the airport and got a taxi into the old city of Tangiers. I slipped past the many tourist touts that hang like vultures near the port, and was soon in a small hotel in the *petite souk* area. The next morning I had breakfast in the Casbah and watched the merchants set up shop. I sipped a cup of coffee and thought of Morocco—the land of Atlas.

The mountains of Atlas were well known to the Greeks. The blind poet Homer wrote in the *Odyssey*:

I, ll. 44-54: "And the goddess, bright-eyed Athena, answered: 'Our father, son of Kronos, most exalted of rulers... my heart is torn for wise Odysseus, wretched man, who so long parted from his friends suffers on a seagirt isle at the very navel of the sea. On this forested isle dwells a goddess, daughter of crafty Atlas who knows the depth of every sea and keeps the tall pillars that sunder earth and heaven.'"

XI, ll. 13-19: "And then [Odysseus's ship] reached the boundary of the world, deep-flowing Okeanos. There lie the land and city of the Kimmerioi, veiled in fog and cloud. Never does the sun shine upon them with his rays, either in his climb into the starry heavens or in his return to earth, but deadly night covers these miserable men."

Kronos, it has been said by various authors, such as Nicholas Roerich, was a former king of Atlantis. The Kimmerioi may be the amazing empire of Tiahuanaco in the misty cloud and fog of the Andes.

Okeanos, according to these theorists, is the Gulf Stream, a powerful ocean-river that moves clockwise around the north Atlantic. This was the ancient "ocean-stream" that the sailors followed across the Atlantic. In the time of Odysseus the islands of Atlantis and Antilla had already sunk, therefore their trips were to North and Central America and the islands around them.

In the *Odyssey*, Odysseus has gone far beyond Morocco, across the ocean to the very "boundary of the world." Odysseus journeyed beyond Morocco, but could it be that Morocco was Atlantis? Atlas seems like the root word for Atlantis. Much of Morocco was beyond the Pillars of Hercules. Were there lost civilizations in Morocco?

As early as 1874 the French geographer E. F. Berlioux suggested that Morocco and the Atlas Mountains were Atlantis. A. F. R. Knötel, 1893, and Gustave Lagneau, 1876, maintained that Morocco was Atlantis. The explorer E. L. Gentil proposed Morocco again in 1921. The geologist A. L. Rutot suggested Morocco as Atlantis in 1920, as did the Spanish writer Mario Vivarez in 1925. In 1930 Otto Silbermann's book *Un Continent Perdu: L'Atlantide*[198] was published in which he claimed that Atlantis was Morocco and the Sahara, including the Ahaggar range.

When Europeans began colonizing North Africa, they were

astonished at the ancient ruins, the antiquity of the civilizations and the apparent climatic change that occurred in the region many thousands of years ago. As a result, many historians, searching for answers to Morocco's past, came to believe that Morocco was Atlantis. And indeed there are many mysteries and lost cities in Morocco.

The ancient Phoenicians, Greeks and Romans fought over Tangiers for thousands of years and the area around Tangiers in particular has changed hands many times throughout the centuries. It was occupied by the Romans (1st to 5th century A.D.), Vandals (5th century), Byzantines (6th), Arabs (8th), Berbers (8th), Fatimids (10th), Almoravids (11th), Almohads (12th), Merenids (13th), Portuguese (15th and 16th), Spanish (16th), British (17th) and French (19th).

As I looked at a donkey cart full of vegetables coming through the market, I wondered what Morocco had been like before the Mediterranean filled up with water following the sinking of Atlantis. What megalithic cities lay in the high Atlas? What sunken cities lay off the coast?

I visited the museum later that day and was impressed by the various exhibits of ancient relics. Maps showed the ancient cities and megalithic sites. I was particularly interested in the displays showing how elephants, now extinct, were used in Morocco until relatively recent times. Hannibal had used trained war elephants from Morocco in his first campaign against Rome in 218 B.C. Even in historical times, elephants were living in their natural environment near Tangiers.

At the Tangiers museum is also the famous Celtic stele (circa 300 B.C.) which depicts a helmeted Celtic warrior with two friends. The two friends are wearing decorated tights and one of the tights has Celtic ogam writing up one leg. Ogam writing was a system of long and short bars marked along a line. It was extensively used in Ireland where most of the knowledge of mysterious ogam writing currently comes from.

With the Celtic warrior and the ogam writing in the Tangiers museum, a link between North Africa and Ireland is most certainly indicated and clues to Atlantis can be found in these associations.

The next morning I left by bus for Tetouan, a town along the northern slopes of the Atlas range. At the bus station at Tetouan I bought a ticket for a bus to Chechaouen and went to have an egg sandwich. While I waited for my bus, I had a strange conversation with one of the touts.

A young man in a blue windbreaker was standing by the wall of the exit to the station. "Why do you want to go to Chechaouen?" he asked me when he learned where I was going. "It is dangerous for

234

you," he said, sitting down on the wall by the exit. "There are no towns and the people will steal from you."

I paid no attention to the young man, yet was forced to be his captive listener while I waited for my bus.

"You are being followed!" he announced. "You want to know who is following you?"

Suddenly the driver of the bus interrupted the bizarre conversation by announcing that the bus was leaving. Was someone following me like he said?

Next to me on the bus was a Basque traveller, a young man with a backpack who spoke English and said that he had been to Chechaouen before.

I couldn't pronounce his last name, but he volunteered to take me to his hotel in Chechaouen, which he highly recommended. On the way into the mountains he told me he was from San Sebastian and had been to Morocco twice before.

A few kilometers from Chechaouen several touts got on the bus and began to insist that they escort us to a certain hotel that they worked for. As we headed out of the bus several more touts latched on to us, but the Basque kept moving past them. One made vicious remarks and threw a wad of paper in my face.

"We are for Saddam Hussein," he declared, and then said to the Basque, "Bastard Spanish. We hate the Spanish." He spat on the ground.

We trudged on up the hill to the Pension Castellano, where the Basque had stayed before. The folks who ran the hotel were easygoing and friendly.

"Here, have a seat," said the manager. "Would you like a cup of tea?"

Now, at least, without the constant attacks by "tourist guides," I could relax for a while.

I was ready for the magical world of Morocco, a land of mountain peaks, minarets, snake charmers and ancient cities. Little is really known about Morocco in prehistory, and known history starts at the end of the Punic Wars when Rome assumed control of all Carthaginian ports, including those in Morocco.

Rome ruled Morocco until 429 A.D. when the Germanic Vandals invaded from the north. By the following year the Vandals had taken Carthage in Tunisia. The Arabs invaded Morocco in the middle of the 7th century and by 711 A.D. had spread to the Atlantic coast despite some stubborn Berber resistance. One of the most famous instances was the defiant stand of the princess Kahina who, according to tradition, made her last stand with her personal guard at the amphitheater at El Jem in Tunisia.

With a shift of the caliphate from the Omayyads in Damascus to the Abbasids in Baghdad, the Muslim west split from the east and after a period of unrest three major Islamic kingdoms emerged: the Idrissids in Fés, the Rustamids in Tahart and the Aghlabids in Kairouan, Tunisia.

The most important of these caliphs was Idriss who was a *sherif,* or a direct descendant of the Prophet. Idriss had fled persecution from the Abbasids and come to Morocco. Here he received support from the Berbers and established the Idrissid kingdom. He and his son, Idriss II, founded the Islamic city of Fés.

A Shia uprising in the northern Algerian region of Kabylie brought forth Obeid Allah, a Berber who declared himself the *Mahdi* (Chosen One, Prophet of Allah). Obeid created the Fatimid caliphate and set his sights on conquering Cairo and all of Islam. After several unsuccessful attempts a new Fatimid leader, Emir al-Mu'izz, defeated the Egyptians and founded Cairo in 972.

When Berber tribes back in Morocco reverted back to Sunni Islam (the sect which disavows the Mahdi), the Cairo caliphate ordered the Beni Hilal and Beni Sulaim tribes of upper Egypt to invade the Mahgreb, which means *west* in Arabic and is taken to mean Tunisia, Algeria and Morocco. Cities were devastated throughout North Africa and the invading tribes were the first major influx of Arabs into the Mahgreb. Until then the area had been populated by a vast majority of people of Berber ancestry. Today Morocco, Tunisia and Algeria are mostly of an Arab-descended population, though many Berbers still live in the area.

~~~~~~~~~~🜨~~~~~~~~~~

The Mysterious Berbers

The Berbers are a mysterious people and according to current theory are thought to be the descendants of light-skinned invaders from the Middle East circa 10,000 B.C. Archaeologists named these people Capsian Man after the archaeological discoveries at the ancient site of Capsa at present Gafsa in Tunisia. The artifacts discovered at Capsa consist mainly of well-made and unusually large stone axes. It is from these people that the Berbers are typically said to be descended.

Other writers, such as René-Maurice Gattefossé, had other ideas about the origins of the Berbers. René-Maurice Gattefossé wrote *La Vérité sur l'Atlantide*[203] in 1923 and proposed among other things that the Berbers were descendants of the matriarchal Atlanteans.

Gattefossé believed that civilization had begun on the lost northern continent of Hyperborea and later spread to the mid-Atlantic continent of Atlantis. The people of Hyperborea spread south through the Shetlands, Britain, Brittany and Spain to the island of Atlantis, he said. Along the way they erected various megalithic monuments such as Stonehenge and Carnac.

Gattefossé also believed that the Cro-Magnon people of paleolithic Europe were pure Hyperboreans. Later the Atlanteans developed the so-called cyclopean style of architecture, involving the use of large irregular blocks without mortar.

According to Gattefossé, the "War of the Titans" from Greek myth is a recollection of periodic changes in the earth's axis, causing worldwide alterations in climates and coastlines. Zeus, Poseidon, Atlas, and Hesperus were all Atlantean kings. Under Poseidon the Atlanteans learned to domesticate animals, and fought the Gorgons and Amazons who had a matriarchal government of which traces are still found among their descendants, the Berbers.[1, 203]

Lewis Spence in his book *The Problem of Atlantis*[6] proposes that Cro-Magnon man remains, which are mainly found in Spain and France, are linked to Atlantis and the Berbers. Cro-Magnon man had a high forehead, a strong chin and averaged over six feet in height. Spence says that many Cro-Magnon men were seven or eight feet tall, according to early skeletal finds.

Instead of the current theory of man slowly spreading around the globe from East Africa, Spence sees a negroid people in the Riviera and a mongoloid people in Central Europe. Spence theorized that there had been several waves of Atlantean invasion: the Aurignacian, the Magdalenian, and the Azilian. He mentions that the Guanches of the Canary Islands spoke Berber when the Spanish annexed them in the 15th century.

Spence felt that the Basques and the Berbers were direct descendants of the Cro-Magnon-Atlanteans and that the languages that they spoke were the closest to the actual Atlantean language.

Spence theorizes that the Azilians arrived about 10,000 years ago, about the time of Plato's Atlantis. Significantly, he said, they were buried facing west. They probably founded the civilizations of Egypt, Crete and later Iberia, now Spain. The type of town planning they developed in Atlantis was reflected in the later plans of Carthage and Knossos, thought Spence. He believed that the druids were descended from the early Osirian religion, and that Celtic legends pointed to unattainable islands and submerged cities.

That the Berbers were a matriarchal, or at least matrilinear, culture is evident by what is known of them today, although this part of their culture is now largely gone. Today, the patriarchal codes of Islam govern Morocco, and the king is also a *sherif*, or descendant of the Prophet. The king, like others in Morocco, awaits the return of the Mahdi.

The Secret of Chechaouen

While in the mountain town of Chechaouen, my Basque friend, a New Zealand traveller, and myself, walked with our Moroccan guide over a trail in the mountains to a village that could not be reached by car.

In a small restaurant at the village we drank mint tea and watched the old men play the Indian game of Parcheesi. As we sat there a young man in his 30s who spoke perfect English came and sat down with us.

"Do you know the secret of Chechaouen?" he asked us. We all said no.

"Chechaouen has healing waters," he asserted. "It is one of two special holy sites in Morocco. There are caves about 10 kilometers from Chechaouen. So far they have been explored as far as 68 kilometers back into the mountains, but the end has never been discovered. There are rivers and underground lakes. The caves have been blocked off by the government because people have gotten lost in them."

"But what is the secret?" I asked, taking a sip of tea.

"People have died because of the secret," he warned. "The water of Chechaouen comes out of caves near the city and it is connected to another larger system of caves. The secret is that the caves are filled with gold! They have a tremendous amount of placer gold in them and the water is filtered through all this gold sand in the caves. The people of Chechaouen are drinking gold water."

"Is that why the water is said to have healing properties?" asked Kevin. The man nodded.

"These mountains are full of tunnels and underground rivers?" I asked. "Are they all natural?"

"Some are natural and others are man-made. The 14th-century Portuguese fort has an escape tunnel beneath it that goes for several kilometers before exiting at a secret place above the city."

We had some bread and scrambled eggs for lunch and then walked back toward Chechaouen via a higher trail in the mountains. A flock of children followed us through the village and we all stopped to take some photographs of the smiling boys and girls who watched us with wide and wondering eyes.

On the way back we came to a curious bend in the trail with many huge granite blocks on either side. Most were pretty much square and gave the appearance of being hewn for a cyclopean wall. The trail went right through this unusual pile of rocks. We stopped to look at them more closely. Were they the scattered ruins of some

Atlantean city?

While some of the blocks were 15-foot-high squared blocks of granite, others were rocks of no particular shape. Around us were scattered pebbles and small stones. There were no small blocks suitable for easy lifting; probably they had all been taken away by villagers, leaving only the largest and heaviest blocks.

"What is this," asked Kevin, "the stones of Atlantis?"

"Maybe," I answered as we headed along the trail back to Chechaouen. "Maybe."

After a few more days in Chechaouen drinking the healing gold water, I left by bus for the former capital of Meknes, farther south and deeper in the Atlas. As I stepped out of the bus station I saw the Hotel Maroc just down the street and quickly got a single room. It was typical of Moroccan hotels; the room had a bed, chair and a table. It also boasted a sink and a toilet that was a porcelain hole in the floor with footpads on either side.

I had come to Meknes to visit the ancient city of Volubulis, a Roman city built on the ruins of an early Phoenician city. I took a bus to the holiest town in Morocco, Moulay Idriss, with its tomb for Idriss, grandson of the Prophet and founder of the Idrissid caliphate, the first Arab dynasty in Morocco, of which the current king is a descendant.

Just past Moulay Idriss is Volubilis, the best preserved ancient city in Morocco. I was impressed walking through the ruins, which mostly date from the 2nd and 3rd century A.D. At that time, Volubilis was the capital of the Roman province of Mauritania and was one of the empire's most remote outposts.

Volubilis had been a Phoenician city before the Romans came, part of the far-flung trading empire that was centered around the massive port cities and their fleets. Like the Hittites before them, they sought precious metals which were to be found near mountain cities like Volubilis.

Volubilis' main attraction is the beautiful Roman frescoes in situ, including one of the labors of Hercules, at the north end of the city. Still, I was just as pleased to find Phoenician keystone cuts in some of the foundation blocks. There were megalithic blocks that were finely articulated and cut, but had been reused in the building of other walls and were out of place.

There were double doorjambs similar to those found in Inca cities in Peru. In fact, the articulation of the blocks reminded me of Puma Punku and Tiahuanaco at Lake Titicaca. The Phoenician heyday in Volubilis had been circa 1000 B.C. and the city was apparently continuously inhabited until 1755 when a massive earthquake hit the entire Atlantic seaboard from Portugal down through Mauritania. This famous earthquake destroyed not only Lisbon, but many cities in Morocco as well, including Meknes and Volubilis. Meknes was rebuilt but Volubilis, after existing 3,000 years, was abandoned.

My next stop was Fés, the famous walled city that tradition says battled with Marrakesh for domination over Morocco. I checked into a small hotel next to the gates of the old city, Fés el-Bali, and then set off to explore the covered bazaar.

It was late afternoon as I walked past the many carpet shops, tea stalls and brassware vendors. Soon, I had one of the ever-present Moroccan touts walking next to me, wanting to be my guide. He looked tougher than most of them and his nose had been badly broken, but he spoke excellent English.

I tried to get rid of him but he insisted on walking with me. "Here, come and have a tea in this carpet shop," he insisted. I made the mistake of joining him and the carpet shop owner for a cup of tea in the shop.

I politely told them that I wasn't interested in buying a carpet and sat patiently for 20 minutes while the shop owner explained the finer points of Berber carpets to me. Afterwards I thanked him and we left.

Outside the carpet shop the tout suddenly became very angry with me. "Why didn't you buy a carpet?" he demanded. "You owe me 100 dirhams so I can get my tourist guide card back from the shop owner. Give it to me now!" He snarled at me and tried to grab my hand as we walked along the backstreets.

"The police beat me in jail one time for being a tour guide. I won't go back there! Pay me," he snarled.

It was starting to get dark and I decided to head for the hotel. I knew he was lying to me about the tourist card, and 100 dirhams was quite a bit of money, about 40 dollars. He was the tourist guide from Hell, and he was becoming a serious problem.

"You know," he said menacingly, "in Fés bad people can be cut with a knife! Give me the 100 dirhams you owe me!" He seemed to be clutching a knife in his hand.

"What is that in your hand?" I asked him as we walked along.

"Nothing." he said. "Give me the money!" I noticed that he was leading me to a dark section of the street beneath an arch in the city wall. He was a vicious criminal and fully intended to get money out of me. What was I to do?

I suddenly began running in another direction. This surprised him and he began running after me. I ran through the side streets until I got to the main bazaar street with its many shops. Still, he was pursuing me.

I dodged vendors with plastic buckets on their heads and donkey carts coming down the narrow street. It was a mad dash for safety, away from the psychopathic tour guide who wanted to slash my throat. I dodged past a group of old ladies and then jumped between a mule and a cart of straw.

I glanced behind me and could see him no more. I stopped running and walked for a distance up the street, catching my breath.

Soon he came up to me on the street. "Hey, listen..." he began to say. I started running again, dodging people, carts and animals. Chickens fluttered and squawked from their cages. Finally I came to the city gate where my hotel was. I ran to the hotel door where several young men were standing. I was safe back at the hotel, but I realized that I would have to be more cautious while I was in Morocco.

Things went better after that, and I enjoyed Fés while I was there. I was told that the problem of the incredibly rude touts in Morocco had reached such proportions, that King Hassan had addressed the entire nation about it and made it illegal for anyone but state-authorized tour guides to interact with tourists on the street.

Those who were caught bothering tourists in Marrakesh, Fés, Casablanca or other cities were arrested by the police and beaten up. Typically their noses were broken to help identify them when they were back on the streets.

I avoided young men with broken noses after that, and after a bus trip through the High Atlas arrived at the legendary city of Marrakesh.

Soon I had a hotel in the main square of the city and was sitting in a café watching snake charmers and fire-eaters entertain the many people who passed by. Marrakesh seemed a little more laid-back than Fés, perhaps because there are so many police patrolling the city.

Nightly I would walk down to the Jama El Fna square from my room to have a bowl of pea soup and bread. Musicians drifted through the square playing eerie eastern music and turbaned snake charmers coaxed cobras out of their baskets. Marrakesh had all the exotic charms of the orient and its beautiful mosques and buildings were famous throughout the world.

In the late afternoon and evening the Jama El Fna square fills up with row after row of open-air food stalls with their delectable aromas that waft down the narrow streets. Jugglers, storytellers, magicians, acrobats and benign lunatics quickly take over the rest of the space, each of them surrounded by a laughing crowd while assistants hustle the crowd for contributions.

In between the groups are hustlers, knickknack sellers, bewildered tourists and a motley crew of thieves, henchmen and beggars.

Marrakesh became a mecca for travellers in the 1960s and it has continued to be to this day. Today Marrakesh is overrun by tourists, yet beyond the snow-covered Atlas are forbidden cities that no tourist may enter.

Smara: the Forbidden City

A curious travel book was published simultaneously in France and New York in 1932. It was entitled *Smara: The Forbidden City*[11] and it was the travel diary of Frenchman Michel Vieuchange. Vieuchange was a young man who had vacationed in Greece and was fascinated by lost cities and forbidden territory. When he did his military service in Morocco he learned that the ancient city of Smara beyond the Atlas had never been visited by Europeans and was forbidden to them.

Michel Vieuchange and his brother Jean concocted a scheme to penetrate the southern desert to the forbidden city of Smara. Thus in 1930, 26-year-old Vieuchange disguised himself as a Berber woman and started out on a journey to realize a dream: to witness the ruins of Smara, a great walled city built and abandoned centuries before. Never seen by a European, even its location uncertain, Smara was known only as a stopping place for the ferocious Moorish nomads.

Michel Vieuchange's story is a sad one. After travelling for weeks through the desert, first on bleeding feet and later hidden in a camel's pack basket, he could risk only three short hours in the place that had become his obsession. He took some photographs of the brick-walled streets and mosque. Abandoned because of poor water supply several hundred years before, it was now a forbidden city. Sadly, on the return trip Michel succumbed to terrible dysentery and died upon reaching Agadir.[211]

Vieuchange's book is an obsessive quest to a forbidden city that lay in ruins. Vieuchange paid the ultimate price for his quest, a few hours to savor in the dusty ruins of a lost city. Who has not visualized that nomad walking through the windblown streets of time? The searcher of lost cities crosses the dried-up seas of yore and stands in the dust of his ancestors.

Things have not changed much for Smara, the Forbidden City. It is still forbidden and lies in the Spanish Sahara area of Morocco, an area that is not entirely secured by government troops. Out in the vast desert beyond the Atlas Mountains, the sands of time still spin around the mysterious cities of the Sahara.

The Ancient Port of Lixus

One morning I suddenly decided to check out of my hotel in Marrakesh and took a taxi to the train station. "What time is the Marrakesh Express?" I asked the ticket seller.

"The Marrakesh Express to Casablanca and Rabat leaves in 48 minutes. Would you like a ticket?"

I bought a ticket and soon was speeding along in a train compartment with the wheat fields of Morocco moving past in a yellow blur. I stopped in Casablanca to have a drink at Rick's Cafe and then headed further south to Rabat, the colorful capital of Morocco. After a day or so I continued on to Larache, near the ancient city of Lixus.

Lixus was a major Atlantic port for the Phoenicians. It is mentioned in the Carthaginian Admiral Hanno's (circa 7th century B.C.) text *Periplous*: "In the neighborhood of the mountains lived the Troglodytes, men of various appearances, whom the Lixitae described as swifter in running than horses. Having procured interpreters from them, we coasted along a desert country, toward the south, for two days.

"Thence we proceeded towards the east in the course of a day. Here we found in a recess of a certain bay a small island, five stadia around, where we settled a colony, and called it Kernë. We judged from our voyage that this place lay in a direct line with Carthage, for the length of our voyage from Carthage to the Pillars equaled that from the Pillars to Kernë."[1]

This is Lixus, probably the most impressive of the megalithic port cities on Morocco's Atlantic coast. I walked from town to the ancient ruins, approaching from the west side. What appeared to be massive walls like those at Sacsayhuaman in Peru were in front of me, but then I saw that the walls were a natural geological formation, ingeniously used by the Phoenicians. I looked for the port near the river but only found a few large, worn stones.

A megalithic dolmen guard-post overlooked the area. I climbed up to the dolmen and then past a huge squared and split stone to a large wall of perfectly cut stone blocks. The sun was just setting and I looked out over the river and bay in the distance.

I walked through the amphitheater and followed a wall to the road. I was surprised to find an auto junkyard at the end of one Roman wall. As I stepped onto the road, I decided to hitchhike into town and held out my thumb for 15 minutes. Finally a truck stopped and, as I clambered aboard, I looked back at Lixus, a ghostly citadel on a hill overlooking the bay.

Morocco's Underwater Megaliths

At a café in Larache that night I thought about what the great linguist Charles Berlitz said about the roots of the word "Atlantis." "We may never know what Atlantis was really called, although legends and memories from races on both sides of the Atlantic and the Mediterranean ascribe names to a lost land or people that have a convincing similarity even in their disparity. It is interesting to note that the initial sound of the word Atlantis, *atl*, common to so many traditions, also means water in the language of ancient Mexico and among the Berbers of North Africa. Even the word we use for this part of the world ocean may be said to constitute a further reminder of a dimly remembered but persistent past."[97]

Berlitz shows how Mediterranean words for the western sea and far-off lands are similar to those used in the Americas for the eastern sea and lands to the east: Atlantis or Antilha to the Phoenicians and Iberians, Atlaintika to the Basque, Atalaya to the Guanche of Iberia, and Atlala, Atarantes or Atlantioi to the Berbers and other North Africans.

In the Americas there are the Mayan names of Atlán and Atitlán, the Toltec names Tollan and Tlapallan, and the Aztec names Atl and Aztlán. All just a coincidence? Linguist Berlitz doesn't think so. Isolationist scholars and Atlantis skeptics have never really addressed the linguistic evidence, possibly because they are ignorant of it.

Charles Berlitz has had a lifelong interest in Atlantis and lost cities. He says in *Mysteries From Forgotten Worlds*[9] that massive underwater ruins have been discovered off the coast of Morocco. "Enormous walls composed of blocks 8 meters long and 6 meters high, at a minimum depth of about 14 meters were found on the bottom in Moroccan waters on the Mediterranean side of Gibraltar by Marc Valentin in 1958, while free-diving in pursuit of fish, and were eventually traced for a distance of several miles. The general construction of these walls, surrounded by smaller stones, bears a striking resemblance to prehistoric cyclopean stonework on the coasts of the Atlantic and on the Mediterranean islands that are still above water. Further deep sinkings of prehistoric buildings and towns have been noted near Thera and especially near Melos where another free diver, Jim Thorne, in a series of dives connected with the possible retrieval of the arms of the Venus de Milo, inadvertently found a prehistoric sunken citadel at several hundred feet, from which other roads and pathways proceeded downward to even greater depths."[9]

〜〜〜〜〜〜𝔖〜〜〜〜〜〜

When I got back to Tangiers, I called up Fatima, whom I had met on the bus to Lixus, and asked her to meet me at the museum. We looked at displays of Moroccan elephants and Phoenician relics. One display was a large transparency of the Cromlech of M'Soura, located just near Asilah and Tangiers. "Where is this?" I asked Fatima. She explained that it was on a plateau not far from Tangiers and we decided to visit the site.

She arranged for her brother to borrow the family car and take the two of us to the cromlech. I came to the apartment the next morning and was introduced to her mother and brother. Her father was working in Saudi Arabia. Her mother seemed pleased to meet me, and apparently approved of me for a date with her daughter with the brother as our chaperone.

We drove north out of town to the small village of M'Soura, where we asked directions to the megalithic site. Driving down a two-rut dirt track eventually got us to the huge stone circle.

We parked the car and I walked around the ancient standing stones. It was an impressive 50-foot-wide circle with some menhirs 30 feet tall. It seemed to be an astronomical observatory with large lichen-covered standing stones in a circle, marking key directions such as west and east. There appeared to have been buildings in the center of the circle that were now mere mounds.

Fatima told me that the word for circle of standing stones in Berber was "ou-tet." I gathered that there were others known in the region. No carbon date that I know of has been assigned to the Cromlech of M'Soura, but Moroccan archaeologists date it as over 5,000 B.C., which would place it in an age category similar to Malta's and other megalithic sites. I looked at the large lichen patches on the stones. There seemed to be writing on the stones, but they were so weathered it was impossible to tell. The sun was starting to set and Fatima's brother suddenly showed up with the car and we drove back to Tangiers.

They dropped me at my hotel where I packed my bags for the ferry trip to Spain in the morning. Later I sat in the courtyard of the hotel next to a 45-foot-tall banana plant and talked to the sons of the hotel owner, two young men in their 20s. We discussed the many problems in the Middle East and the Islamic world.

"Ultimately," said one, "we are on the side of Saddam Hussein. He is our hero. We hate America and Israel. We hate the western Europeans, too. One day we will show the West."

I had talked to him before. He was friendly to me and knew I was an American. "Will you overthrow the king?" I asked.

They both nodded. "We will overthrow the king and then all the Islamic world will unite against Israel, Saudi Arabia, America and Europe. We will kill all of the Israelis, all of the Americans, and all of the foreigners in our country."

I raised an eyebrow and moved back in my chair a little.

"Don't worry," he assured me, "you are OK. It is just that when this time comes, all the foreigners will be killed. That time hasn't come yet."

For that I was thankful. Back in my room, I looked out over the rooftops of Tangiers and to the Atlantic beyond. In the distance a new moon was rising over the Atlas Mountains. The search for Atlantis would have to continue past the megaliths of Morocco.

A street in old Carthage.

SCIPIONE AFRICANO

SCIPIO

In Christallo.

Nel Tesoro di S. Alt. il Duca Odescalchi

PSBI

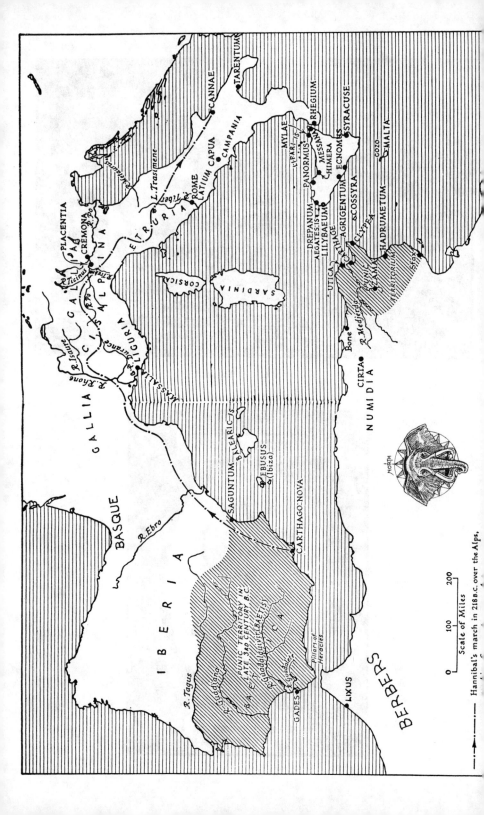

PLACENTIA
CREMONA
R.Ticinus
R.Po
R.Trebia
GALLIA CISALPINA
LIGURIA
R.Rhone
R.Isaure
R.Durance
MASSILIA
GALLIA
BASQUE

ETRURIA
L.Trasimene
R.Tiber
ROME
LATIUM CAPUA
CAMPANIA
CANNAE
TARENTUM

CORSICA
SARDINIA

BALEARIC IS.
SAGUNTUM
EBUSUS (Ibiza)
CARTHAGO-NOVA

IBERIA
R.Ebro
R.Tagus
R.Guadiana
R.Guadalquivir (BAETIS)
PUNIC TERRITORY IN LATE 3rd CENTURY B.C.
BAETICA
Pillars of Heracles
GADES

LIXUS
BERBERS

RHEGIUM
MESSANA
MYLAE
(LIPARI IS.)
PANORMUS
HIMERA
SYRACUSE
ECNOMUS
DREPANUM
AEGATES IS.
LILYBAEUM
AGRIGENTUM
COSSYRA
GOZO
MALTA

UTICA
CARTHAGE
CLYPEA
PUNIC ZAMA
HADRUMETUM
TERRITORIUM
Bone
R.Mejerda
CIRTA
NUMIDIA

NORTH

Scale of Miles
0   100   200

------- Hannibal's march in 218 B.C. over the Alps,

Twenty different stelae of hard, fine-grained limestone found in the vicinity of Carthage. Note such motifs as the ankh, bull, winged disc, moon, elephant and other symbols.

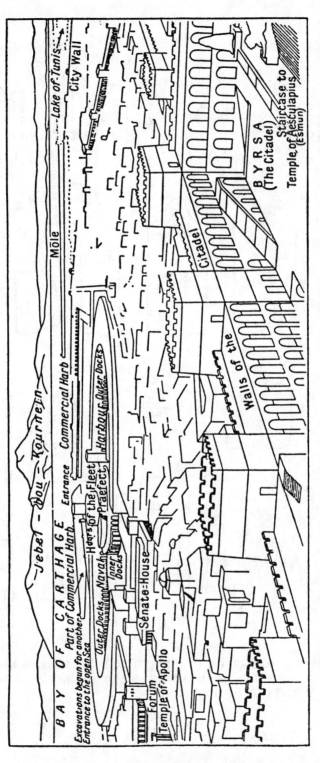

A restoration of Carthage showing the circular harbor, Sea-Wall or Mole, and the main citadel. Carthage, like the citadel of Atlantis, had a circular harbor.

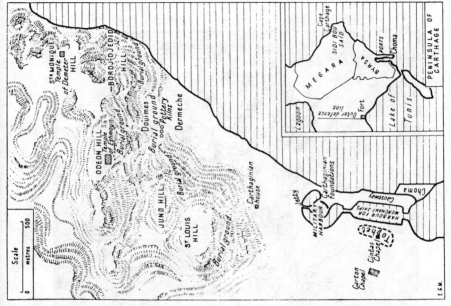
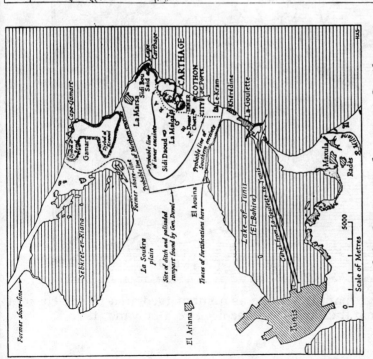

Two maps of the location of ancient Carthage in comparison of modern Tunis and Lake Tunis.

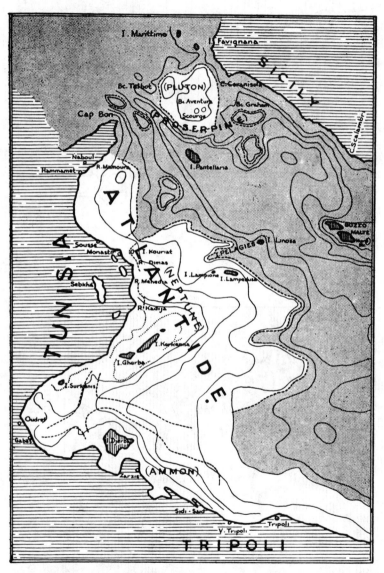

A conjectural map of Atlantis as a submerged area off the coast of Tunisia. From the French archaeologist F. Butavand, 1925.

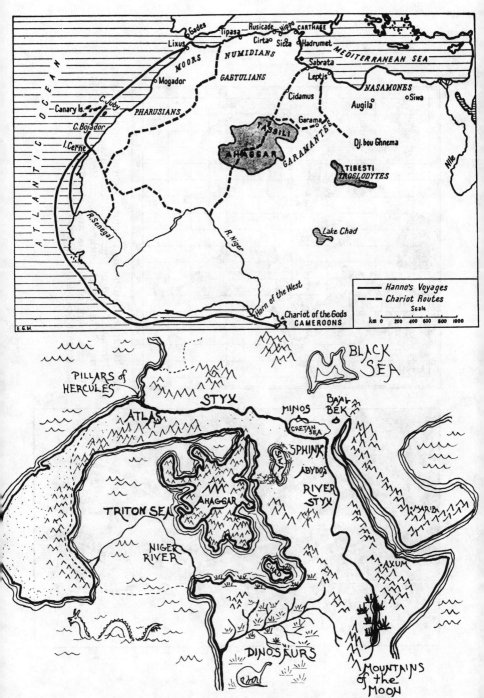

Top: Ancient routes across the Sahara. Bottom: A conjectural map of the Triton Sea.

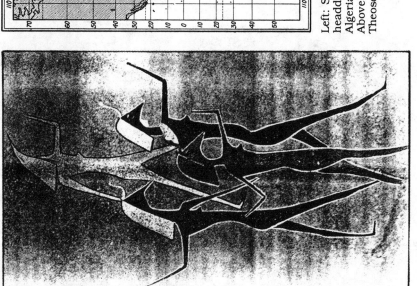

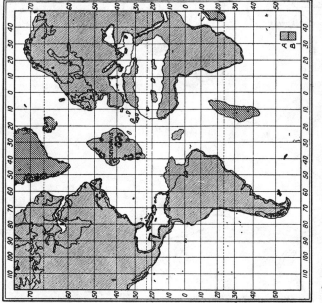

Left: Strange bird-headed women wearing Egyptian-type headdresses found at the Tassili mountains of southern Algeria by the French anthropologist Henry Lhote (1959). Above: A map of Atlantis and the Triton Sea by the Theosophist Scott-Elliot in 1896.

Top and bottom: Archaeological diver Bruno Rizatto's photos of megalithic ruins off the coast of Morocco. They are at a depth of 50 to 60 feet and extend for several miles.

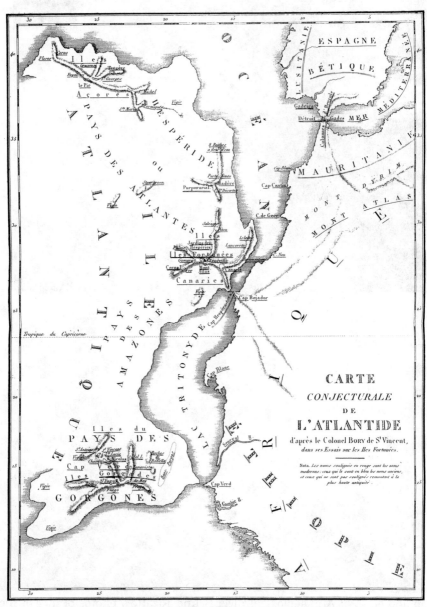

A conjectural map of Atlantis made in 1803 by the French Col. Bory de St.Vincent.

Chapter 8

SPAIN & PORTUGAL:

The Lost Cities
of Hercules

Aristotle in his book *On Marvellous Things* reports a story
that some Carthaginian merchants sailed over the Ocean Sea
to a very fertile island... this island some Portuguese showed
me on their charts under the name of Antilia...
—Christopher Columbus, 1484

I left Morocco by ferry the next morning, before the Jihad could
start, and all foreigners would be killed. The Spanish ferry moved
quickly across the Straits of Hercules (Melqart to the Phoenicians)
and our modern-day Straits of Gibraltar. In the distance was the
huge Rock of Gibraltar, Britain's last vestige of its once powerful rule
of the Mediterranean.

I was glad to arrive at Spanish customs at noon. They waved me
through and I found myself on the street looking for the train
station. At the station I was informed that a train left for Granada in
20 minutes. Moments later, ticket in hand, I was tucked into a seat
next to a wide window. And a few hours later, I was walking up a
street in the old city of Granada with the Alhambra Palace on the
hilltop in front of me.

The Alhambra is a spectacular example of Moorish architecture
located on a hill overlooking Granada. It is comprised of a citadel, a
palace and quarters for nobles and officials. Halls and chambers,
with intricate geometric ornaments and honeycomb vaulting,
surround a series of open courts with fountains and gardens. The
Alhambra was built between 1238 and 1354 but was partially
mutilated in 1492 when the Moors were expelled from Spain. It was
restored after 1828.

As I walked through the pleasant gardens, I thought   how
beautiful and exotic it must have been during the Moorish period. It

257

is interesting to note that the year 1492 was an extremely important year in Spanish and world history.

It was in 1492 that Spain completely eliminated all Moorish control of the Iberian peninsula. In January of 1492 the last Moorish king left the Alhambra and a few months later Cristobal Colon, known to us as Christopher Columbus, met with Queen Isabella to decide on his voyage west across the Atlantic.

Columbus left from Cadiz on the very day, August 3, 1492, that all Jews were to either convert to Christianity or leave the Iberian Peninsula.

My next stop was Cadiz, the ancient Phoenician port on an Atlantic harbor ideally suited for transatlantic voyages. Once comfortably settled in a small hotel near the Plaza de San Francisco, I headed out to explore the city.

Cadiz was the ancient Phoenician port of Gades, probably built on even older ruins. During Phoenician times the city was divided into different sections. In the west part (Punta del Nao) was the Temple of Astarte. To the east, along the San Sebastian causeway, sat the Temple of Ba'al, while the Phoenician city itself lay inland, where modern-day Cadiz is located. To the far eastern end of the Cadiz peninsula was the Temple of Melgart, the Phoenician name for Hercules.

Today, both the Temple of Ba'al and the Temple of Astarte are submerged megalithic ruins. The Temple of Astarte (the goddess called Venus by the Greeks), is submerged in the bay off the Santa Catalina area near Punta del Nao.

The massive ruins of the Temple of Ba'al can be viewed in the water as one walks out to the lighthouse on the San Sebastian causeway. I gazed in wonder at the giant blocks of stone weighing 40 to 80 tons lying in about eight feet of water along the causeway. They were square with slots and grooves in them to be fitted with other stones. They were terribly worn and clearly many thousands of years old. It is believed these were the ancient temple foundations.

Apparently, the huge trading ships would dock at the Temple of Ba'al first and possibly observe some religious custom such as giving thanks to Ba'al for a safe trip. Standing on the causeway I looked west out over the Atlantic. Beyond were the great empires of the Mississippi valley, the Toltecs, Mayans, and Chimu. Were these transatlantic kingdoms the inspiration for Atlantis? Many Atlantis researchers have suggested this.

One of the first historians to suggest America as Atlantis was Sir Francis Bacon in the early 1600s. Bacon went on to write *The New Atlantis*. This was Bacon's unfinished utopian romance which was further elaborated on by Bacon's friend John Swan in his *Speculum Mundi* (1644) who said, "...this I think may be supposed, that America was sometimes part of that great land which Plato calleth the Atlantick island, and the Kings of that island had some intercourse between the people of Europe and Africa."[1]

L. Sprague de Camp mentions other historians who accepted the Atlantis-in-America theory: the historian Albinus in 1598, Jens Bircherod in 1683, the naturalist G.L. Buffon in 1749, Alexander von Humboldt in 1807, the German philosopher Jakob Kruger in the 19th century, and the geographer J.R. MacCulloch who believed that Central America was Atlantis.

Quite a few of the early geographers believed that North America was Atlantis. Among others there were the 16th-century carto-grapher Gerardus Mercator, the cartographer Guillaume Sanson in 1689, the 16th-century cartographer Abraham Ortelius and the French cartographer Robert de Vangoudy in 1769.[1]

In his book, *Legendary Islands of the Ocean Sea*,[147] Robert Fuson theorizes that all lands in the Ocean Sea were considered to be islands by the ancients. Therefore, upon reaching areas like Florida, the Yucatan or Brazil, Phoenicians or other early travellers may have believed each area to be a separate island. As America became more familiar to Europeans, it lost its attraction as the location of Atlantis. In 1922 the German archaeologist Adolf Schulten proposed Spain, instead, as Atlantis.

〰〰〰〰〰🜚〰〰〰〰〰

Tartessos and Atlantis

It was once thought that Cadiz was the fabled lost city of Tartessos. Tartessos was a legendary city of gold and silver to the west. It was a port city for large ships and is called Tarshish in the Bible. It was the destination of Jonah when he was thrown overboard and supposedly swallowed by a whale.

Phoenician ships are sometimes called "ships of Tarshish" in the Bible. One of the first references to Tartessos comes from Isaiah in the Old Testament, where the prophet is sermonizing about the end of the Phoenician city of Tyre: "Howl, ye ships of Tarshish; for it is laid waste..."

In this curious reference to the eastern Mediterranean port of Tyre, it would seem as if Tarshish, the Spanish city, were its mother port. Though the ships are in the eastern Mediterranean port of Tyre, they are still called "ships of Tarshish."

Indeed, it has been pointed out that the Phoenician founding of Carthage was "retro-colonization" in that the Phoenicians already had ports on the Moroccan Atlantic coast before the founding of Carthage. Similarly it may be possible that the original founding of Tyre and the other Phoenician cities in the eastern Mediterranean may have been originally founded by "ships of Tarshish."

The Greeks also wrote about Tartessos. Herodotus in *The Histories* says, "Now the Phokaians were the first of the Greeks to perform long voyages, and it was they who made the Greeks acquainted with the Adriatic and Tyrrhenia, with Iberia, and the city of Tartessos. The vessel they used in their voyages was not the round-built merchant-ship, but the long fifty-oared galley. On their arrival at Tartessos, the king of the country, named Arganthonios, took a liking to them. This monarch reigned over the Tartessians for eighty years, and lived to be 120 years old. He regarded the Phokaians, with so much favor as, at first, to beg them to quit Ionia and settle in whatever part of his country they liked."[1]

Tartessos was famous in the Old World as a wealthy silver mining area and was linked to the legendary exploits of Hercules/Melgart who was typically associated with the far western Mediterranean.

In legend, Hercules comes to Tartessos on his way to fetch the Apples of the Hesperides and to capture the infernal watchdog of Hades, Kerberos. While at Tartessos Hercules erected two pillars, which are associated with both the Rock of Gibraltar and Ceuta and as two stone pillars in the Temple of Melgart at Gades.

It has also been suggested that two underwater seamounts that are on the edge of the continental shelf just beyond the Straits of Gibraltar are the real Pillars of Hercules. They rose out of the ocean when the sea level was considerably lower or before the sinking of Atlantis and the flooding of the Mediterranean Valley.

So where was Tartessos? Was it a sunken city, or was it Cadiz or some other place? The gigantic ruins, now partly submerged, in Cadiz prove that this city is ancient and might well have been Tartessos. However, it is thought that Cadiz was a separate city called Gades by the Phoenicians, possibly a satellite city of Tartessos.

In 1922, just south of Cadiz, the German archaeologist Adolf Schulten announced that he had found the ruins of Tartessos at the mouth of the Baetis or Tartessis River, now the Guadalquivir. This is a flat, sandy region bordered by a sea of strong surf and dangerous tides. Schulten said that the region is populated today by a dark people taller and broader-headed than most Spaniards. This suggests a strong connection with Morocco and Africa, Schulten believed.

Schulten maintained that in ancient times the river had ended in a great bay which once reached as far inland as Seville. At circa 2000 B.C. Seville was an ancient sun-worshipping center known as Hispalis.

Tartessos stood on a large island that closed the mouth of the bay; therefore, the Guadalquivir had two mouths. Earthquakes, wars and the silting up of the harbors ended Tartessos. The city lies today half sunken in a malarial marsh, Las Marismas, and the river has dried up and changed course, according to Schulten.

Schulten was only able to discover one archaeological relic from the site, a ring with curious characters inscribed on the inside and outside. The characters are as yet undeciphered but Schulten believed that they were related to Etruscan.

Tartessos may well have been a Hittite-Cypro-Minoan port as early as 5,000 B.C. Hittite ships would have left Tartessos on the voyage across the Atlantic. They would then trade up the Mississippi to the copper islands of Lake Superior, as evidenced in the Newberry Tablet. These ships may have stopped at the Azores and Caribbean Islands. Further south they would have met with Proto-Mayan/Olmec ports at La Venta and the Yucatan. Even farther south, on the Pacific coast of Peru were the early Chavin and Tiahuanaco cultures.

To say that Cadiz and Tartessos were megalithic seaports over 7,000 years old is contrary to accepted history now taught in Europe, but it is quite likely the case. Megalithic ruins in Spain and Portugal may go as far back as the Atlantis described by Plato.

According to the museum at Cadiz, the huge megalithic standing stones and dolmens with capstones that can be found all over Iberia are 10 to 12 thousand years old. This would make them virtually pre-flood artifacts from the period of Atlantis.

I suggest that the Mediterranean flooded circa 9,000 B.C. and it wasn't until circa 6,000 B.C. that the great sailors of the Atlantean League began to explore the world again. These would be analogous to the ancient Sea Kings of Charles Hapgood's classic book, *Maps of the Ancient Sea Kings*.[36]

These ancient Sea Kings, sometimes called the Atlantean League, were a mixture of sailors from the Hittite empire, Mittani, Sumeria, Egypt, Cyprus and Crete. The giant temples at Tartessos and Gades may have been built in this period of 4,000 to 6,000 B.C.

Later, the Babylonians, Phoenicians, Minoans and Egyptians began to take over the old trade routes. By 200 B.C. earthquakes had changed the coastline enough that Tartessos and its harbor were silted up and portions of Gades were under water.

The Basque language may be related to the language of Tartessos, as well as to Etruscan and Catalonian. (More on the fascinating language of the Basques later in this chapter.)

One possible origin of the name Gades (Cadiz) is thought to come from the Phoenician word Ha-gadir, "the hedge" or "the stockade." The modern city of Agadir in Morocco may have the same roots.[1]

However, the name is also connected to Atlantis because Gadeiros was one of the sons of Poseidon in Plato's story. If Gades (Cadiz) is named after Gadeiros, then it is named after one of the children of Poseidon, just as Atlantis was named after Atlantida.

Gades appears to have been founded before the rise of the

Carthaginians and was at one point subjected by them. Says L. Sprague de Camp in *Lost Continents,* "Tartessos and Gades coexisted until the rise of the Carthaginian Empire. Between 533 and 500 B.C. the Carthaginians were active around the Pillars; they sent Hanno down the African coast, reduced Gades to subjection, and in 509 extorted a treaty from Rome confirming their western monopoly."[1]

The Carthaginians sent out another general to explore the outer coasts of Europe where his later written report said that he had visited "the Tin Islands" which were probably Cornwall and the Scilly Isles of England.

The Carthaginians went to great extremes not to talk about their profitable sea routes, and when they did talk about the routes, they purposely exaggerated the dangers and difficulties so that the sailors of other nations would be too frightened to attempt the dangerous voyage. Says Himilco about the dangers of the Atlantic:

> *There no breeze exists to propel the ship forward;*
> *Deadening is this sluggish sea's vapor.*
> *Many seaweeds grow in the troughs of the billows,*
> *Slowing the ship like bushes, he says, thus showing*
> *Here to no great depth the sea descends, and*
> *Here the water barely covers the bottom.*
> *Here the beasts of the sea move slowly wandering,*
> *And among the sluggishly creeping vessels*
> *Languidly swim the great monsters.*[1]

Here the Carthaginian admiral seems to be describing the Sargasso Sea, that morass of kelp, flotsam and jetsam of the western Atlantic. The kelp floats with the help of its gas bladders and drifts for years until it sinks. Babcock in his book *Legendary Islands of the Atlantic*[195] surmises that some Phoenician crew had once penetrated the Sargasso Sea and, assuming that the floating weed was growing from the bottom as seaweed usually does, deduced that they were over a bank or shoal.

No one knows what happened to Tartessos. It virtually disappeared from history after the Punic Wars. Later geographers confused Tartessos and Gades/Cadiz. Eventually Schulten showed that there were at least two cities, one from circa 3,000 B.C. and one from circa 1500 B.C. Excavations at both cities are nearly impossible since both are mostly submerged.

Yet, Tartessos (and Cadiz) may be much older than even Schulten thought. Rene Noorbergen in his book *Secrets of the Lost Races*[92] says that there is evidence that Tartessos may be as much as 10,000 years old.

Noorbergen relates the script on a 12,000-year-old reindeer bone with the writing of Tartessos. Says Noorbergen, "A piece of reindeer bone found in a cave near Rochebertier, France, has markings on it that are more than just decoration. They have every appearance of being the letters of some form of writing. At first glance, one might think that this is conclusive evidence of the existence of a written language during the Paleolithic age, but the implications of the reindeer bone go one step further. The letters resemble or in some cases are identical to the enigmatic script of Tartessos, a city civilization that existed in southern Spain and is believed by some to be the Biblical Tarshish."

Noorbergen goes on to say, "What makes the similarities of the writings truly remarkable is that orthodox prehistorians place the reindeer bone in the Magdalenian period—by their chronology, about 12,000 years old—and the Tartessian civilization recently has been assigned to the period between 2500 and 2000 B.C. There is an obvious discrepancy with this dating, for it is highly unlikely that a script, once developed, would have remained relatively unchanged for ten millennia. What the two scripts do demonstrate is that the cultures in which they were found must have been contemporaneous, rather than separated by a vast span of time. The date of the peak civilization in Tartessos is becoming better established, and if there was a contact between the Paleolithic people and the city of Tartessos, then they must have existed in the same time period."[92]

The script of Tartessos may be the mother of modern phonetic scripts, predating Phoenician, and may well have originated in Atlantis. We see here also how the Phoenicians and other "Sea Peoples" may have originated on the Atlantic coast of Spain and migrated to the eastern Mediterranean as the Philistines and Sea Peoples of ancient history, taking over the Hittite ports of Byblos, Cyprus and Crete. Later the Phoenicians moved westward again, establishing Carthage and other ports in the western Mediterranean.

If we must find an existing city to be the inspiration for Atlantis, Tartessos would seem our most likely subject. Said L. Sprague de Camp, "Atlantis is even more strikingly like Tartessos than it is like Carthage or Crete: Tartessos, like Atlantis, lay in the Far West, beyond the Pillars; it was enormously rich, especially in minerals, and had wide commercial contacts with the Mediterranean; it was associated with shoals; behind it lay a great plain bordered by mountains; and it mysteriously disappeared. While the Tartessians were not known to have performed a bull-ceremony, the region was and still is a cattle country."[1]

Indeed, the worship of the bull, something associated with Atlantis, is still a major preoccupation in Spain, with its bullfights and running of the bulls in various cities. The idea that Spain is intricately associated with Atlantis was propounded in the 1928 book *Atlantis in Andalucia*.[20]

The author, Elena M. Whishaw, was the widow of archaeologist Bernard Whishaw, and she succeeded him as the director of the Anglo-Spanish-American School of Archaeology. The Whishaws made many interesting discoveries in Spain, including cyclopean ruins and rock-cut canals around Niebla, southern Spain, and the remains of an ancient Sun Temple in Seville. They also collected various examples of "Libyan-Tartessian script," as they called it.

Tartessos was reputed to have written records going back 6,000 years. The German archaeologist Schulten found a ring with unidentified characters and Whishaw discovered at Niebla a "solar-cult" stone with 123 signs incised.

Elena Whishaw learned that in the middle of the nineteenth century, "In a neolithic sepulchral cave, known as the Cave of Bats, in the province of Granada, 12 skeletons were discovered sitting in a circle round a central skeleton of a woman dressed in a leather tunic. At the entrance of the cave were three more skeletons, one wearing a crown and dressed in a tunic of finely woven esparto grass. Beside the skeletons were hide bags containing carbonized food, and other bags filled with poppy heads, flowers and amulets; poppy heads were scattered all over the floor of the cave. Among a number of other objects were some little clay discs identified by archaeologists as necklace ornaments connected with the sun-cult, found in the land harbor of Niebla and in a building trench near Seville."[20]

Whishaw theorizes that these people were a royal family with their attendants who committed mass suicide by taking opium. She contends that ancient Spain was a matriarchal society like the Berbers of Morocco. While Schulten believed that Spain was Atlantis, Whishaw believed that Spain was a colony of Atlantis.

At the Cadiz museum the next day, I enjoyed wandering through the many exhibits of ancient cultures that once inhabited the area. There were many Egyptian, Etruscan and Greek statues in the museum, giving proof of the maritime trade that linked these ancient empires.

Especially interesting to me were the two massive marble sarcophagi, 8 feet long, one depicting a man with a curly beard and the other a woman who is clutching a knife. They were impressively large and seemed to be older than everything else in the museum. Curiously, there is no writing on these sarcophagi, and the museum gave no actual date, though it was assumed to be over 3,000 years old.

Also in the museum is a three-sided bronze stele with a ship on the top, yet no writing. There are some Egyptian burial urns and these do indeed have some cartouches and hieroglyphs on them. There are huge bronze anchors on display and the museum shows a 30-minute movie entitled *Phoenicians and Greeks in the Iberia Peninsula.*

The museum did a good job of mounting displays about the megalithic tombs and sarcophagi to be found around southern Spain. There was clearly a strong Phoenician and Egyptian connection to many of the burials.

The museum also had displays on the distribution of dolmens around Portugal, Cadiz and the Laguna de la Janda. North of Cadiz, to the border of Portugal, is a huge wilderness of swamps and lagoons now inhabited mostly by birds and swamp critters. No road goes through this area, nor was there one in Roman times. Yet megaliths are found all over the nearby vicinity and it is possible that more megalithic ruins could be found in the swamps, just as ancient Tartessos has been taken over by a swamp today.

A particularly interesting display was the "early Neolithic" display of rock paintings which depicted ocean-going ships with oars and sails. Early Neolithic is a vague term and these could be ships from 6,000 to 8,000 B.C. Were these depictions of Hittite ships or earlier "Atlantean" vessels? In any event, oceangoing ships this old lend credence to the theory that ancient sailors ventured far beyond their home ports.

At a local fisherman's beach bar, I watched the sun set over the bay which held the sunken Temple of Astarte. While drinking a bottle of Muscatel and eating a cheese and tomato sandwich I looked out the window at the long gray waves on the bay. Despite a bit of rain, some windsurfers were just coming out of the water, dragging their boards behind them. In the corner of the bar was a Phoenician amphora wired to the wall. A few fish trophies completed the simple decoration.

As I sipped the Muscatel, I mused on what I had seen at the causeway and the museum. The ticket lady at the museum had told me the Legend of Cadiz. According to legend, the Pillars of Hercules had split open and the Mediterranean began to flood. At the ancient temples, sacrificial offerings were made to the gods, but it was to no avail. After the cataclysm, Cadiz was founded and new temples were built to Ba'al, Astarte and Melgart (Hercules).

Tartessos and Gades were only part of a larger Iberian empire, one that may have stretched from Morocco to Ireland, and beyond. Tartessos was not Atlantis, it turns out. Yet Atlantis is everywhere, and we can find traces of it in Tartessos and Gades.

Out on the bay the constant washing of the gray waves over the sunken city seemed to say that "time waits for no one."

~~~~~~~~~~ ☥ ~~~~~~~~~~

The Sun Temple of Seville

From Cadiz I journeyed north to Seville and Madrid. Seville once had a megalithic sun temple in its center which was probably used during the time of Tartessos. Whishaw in *Atlantis in Andalucia*[20] devotes a chapter to the megalithic character of ancient Seville. The Whishaws discovered the remains of a "sun temple" 27 feet below the present street level of central Seville. Naturally, this temple was megalithic. Whishaw says that modern Seville is built on top of an ancient city many thousands of years old, much like Rome or Mexico City.

Seville might well be Tartessos, Whishaw theorizes, buried beneath the hustle and bustle of the modern city. I walked down the tree-lined streets and ate a Seville orange.

Whishaw discusses the Rio Tinto copper mines of southern Spain, which are estimated to be 8,000 to 10,000 years old. The hydraulic works at Niebla were also ancient and impressive.

Says Whishaw, "My theory, to sum it up concisely, is that Plato's story is corroborated from first to last by what we find here, even the Atlantean name of his son Gadir who inherited that part of Poseidon's kingdom beyond the Pillars of Hercules and ruled at Gades... The marvelously civilized prehistoric people whose civilization I have put on record sprang from the fusion of the prehistoric Libyans, who in an earlier stage of the history of humanity came to Andalusia from Atlantis to purchase the gold, silver, and copper provided by the neolithic miners of Rio Tinto, and in the course of generations... welded the Iberian and African cultures so closely together that eventually Tartessos and Africa had a race in common, which was the Libyan-Tartessian."

I spent a few sunny days in Seville and continued north to Madrid, the hub of central Iberia. I looked forward to exploring the bookstores, museums and cafés of the city.

At the Madrid museum one can see a mock-up of the famous Alta Mira caves and their spectacular prehistoric paintings of wild bison, woolly rhinos, mastodons and other animals.

According to the mock-up, there was no smoke on the ceiling of the cave, which raises the question of how the artists lit their cave in order to make the paintings?

I was walking with a small group in the museum and we had the official museum guide telling us about the Alta Mira caves in several different languages. I asked her about the lack of smoke on the walls. Didn't they use torches for light?

"This has been a puzzle to archaeologists," she said, "but they now believe that small candles, not torches, were used to light the caves. When you use lots of small candles with a clean wax or oil, very little smoke comes out."

I raised an eyebrow and thought about it. It was possible, I admitted, but it seemed like a lot of fussy effort for some cavemen to go through. At the very least, they apparently had a very well-developed candle industry back in 20,000 B.C.

Also at the museum is the famous statue known as Our Lady of Elche. It is a marble bust of a woman found in 1897 on a local doctor's farm 20 miles south of Alicante in Andalusia. The beautiful statue is about a meter high and appears to have been part of a larger life-size statue.[20,94]

Nothing else was found with the statue which might allow it to be dated. There was no trace of a burial, temple or dwelling. Its jewelry is unlike that which was customary in Greek or Roman times and unlike the Visigoths who came even later. In fact, the woman's hair, which is done up in two circular buns on either side of her head, is most similar to the hairstyle of Hopi Indian maidens of northern Arizona.

Indeed, the Hopi, known for their mysterious origins and various prophecies concerning past and future earth changes, have a tradition in which unmarried women arrange their hair in a wheel design along the sides of the head. (After they marry, they arrange their hair in a different manner.) This is the same design found on the Lady of Elche.

The statue was thought to be Carthaginian, for it was in the Elche region from which Hannibal's father obtained esparto grass to make ropes for his fleet; and the local population certainly maintained relations with Carthage and North Africa. According to some archaeologists the sculpture dates from the 4th century B.C., a time of Carthaginian expansion in Spain. Yet, it may well be much older, possibly from 2,000 B.C. or more. Certainly, there was a sophisticated seafaring nation in Spain circa 2,000 B.C. It may well be connected to Atlantis, as Elena Whishaw contended in her book *Atlantis in Andalucia.*[20]

The Lady of Elche is such a beautiful piece of sculpture that it has captured the imagination of many Atlantis researchers. The Louvre Museum in Paris bought the statue from the doctor on whose farm it was found, but in 1941 the Spanish government, which was very anxious to recover her, managed to exchange her for several valuable paintings, and now the Lady of Elche is at the Prado Museum in Madrid.

In *Atlantis in Andalucia* (republished by Adventures Unlimited Press as *Atlantis in Spain*) the Lady of Elche is depicted with a flowing gown and an Atonist sun symbol on her chest. Here we see a correlation with the Atonists of ancient Egypt, a revival of an even more ancient sun religion, and the fascinating Hopis of the American Southwest.

There has been some recent controversy over the Elche statue in that it is now claimed by some Spanish historians to be a fake. If it was a fake, it would seem likely that it was a reproduction of some authentic piece. Its unusual style and ancient sun symbols make it difficult to fabricate without a model to work from.

Despite its controversial origins, Our Lady of Elche is a remarkable work of art, one that deserves our attention.

I was pleased with my time in Madrid and the National Museum. I decided to move west into Portugal, and take my search for Atlantis out into the Atlantic itself!

The Canary Islands and the Mystery of the Basques

On a bright afternoon I took a bus travelling from Madrid to Lisbon. Up front a movie was being played on the video monitor above the driver. It was some Spanish sex comedy that occasionally caught my interest. Otherwise I looked out the window and wondered about Atlantis.

According to a display at the National Museum in Madrid, there is evidence in the Canary Islands of various different peoples having inhabited the islands from time to time, including Celts, Semites and Negroes. The islands are famous for their ancient ruins and the now vanished Guanche people who apparently spoke a language similar to Berber.

The Canaries have long been thought of as the possible remnants of Atlantis. Incredibly, the original language of the Canaries may have been Basque. The Basques of northwestern Spain and southwestern France reputedly have legends of a cataclysm in which fire and water were at war. Their forebears hid themselves in caves and survived.

The Basques speak a tongue which has no European relatives, yet sounds much like many American Indian languages. Both Basque and Nahuatl of the Aztecs have a higher than usual use of the x-sound and the atl-sound.

Says Tomas, "The Basques believe in the mythical seven-headed serpent 'Erensuge' which links them with the snake worshiping Aztecs on the other side of the Atlantic. The old Basque custom of counting by twenties instead of tens, has a parallel in Central America where a similar arithmetic was practiced. Undoubtedly, the French have inherited their 'quatre-vingts' (four score or 80) from the Basques."[24]

Similarly, the Mayans played a ball game called pok-a-tok that was very similar to the Basque ball game of Jai-alai. Both games are played with a wicker basket tied to the arm.

The Basques are unique as far as European blood groupings go, with a high frequency of group O, a relatively low frequency of group A and the lowest frequency of group B in Europe. With regard to the Rh blood groups, they show the highest frequency of Rh-negative found in any European population and, with the possible exception of some Berber tribes, the highest in the world.

The British Colonel Alexander Braghine in his book *The Shadow Of Atlantis*[25] (London, 1940) makes several interesting points about the Basques. For instance, he says that archaeologists have found on the Canary Islands many remains, including a "settlement of cavern-men, which consists of several tiers of caverns in the rocks, and is called by the natives 'Atalaya': it is interesting to note that near Biarritz, in the country of Basques, there exists a mound with the same name."[25]

Says Braghine, "Some other scientists also derive the Basques from the Atlanteans: certain physical features of this people and distinctive peculiarities of the Basque language indicate their affinity with some Central American tribe, who are supposed to be of Atlantean root, but on the other hand the language of Basques possesses many roots and sometimes entire words similar to Japanese and Georgian (Southern Russia). I was present when a former Russian officer of Georgian origin found himself able to talk with the natives of Vizcaya immediately upon his arrival in Northern Spain: he spoke Georgian, but the Basques understood this language. It is necessary to remind the reader that in antiquity Georgia was called 'Iveria,' a name almost identical to 'Iberia.'"[25]

Braghine goes on to say, "When in Guatemala, I often heard about one Indian tribe, living in the Peten district (Northern Guatemala): this tribe speaks a language resembling Basque, and I have heard of an occasion when a Basque missionary preached in Peten in his own idiom with great success.

"As to the resemblance of the Japanese and Basque languages, I once saw a list of analogous words with the same significance in both tongues and I was stupefied by the quantity of such words. The word *iokohama*, for instance, signifies in Basque 'a seashore city,' and everybody knows the great port of Yokohama in Japan."[25]

L. Sprague de Camp in his book *Lost Continents*[1] looks briefly at Braghine and sadly dismisses him in a few sentences. Says de Camp, "As for the South American rock-carvings in which Braghine, Frot (a French prospector who published on Phoenician writings in Brazil), and others have professed to see Phoenician, Hebrew, and other Old World writing, these are mostly crude pictures of men and animals which the Indians have carved, sometimes for magical reasons and sometimes for amusement. We know this because some of them still carve them."[1]

This is a very weak argument that de Camp is presenting, and one would think that the knowledgeable scholar would claim forgery rather than "crude pictures of men and animals which the Indians have carved..." After all, Phoenician is a matter of reading written signs, and inscriptions such as the Brazilian Paraiba inscription do indeed exist. Authenticity is the question, not whether these "crude pictures" are writing or not.

To quote de Camp's assault on Braghine's book, he states: "...the author starts off appropriately with a frontispiece that is a photograph of a pair of forged antiquities, passed off as Atlantean relics. Then the author, though he repudiates the occult inspirations of the Theosophists, goes on to make a fantastic series of flat and ridiculous misstatements of fact: that all Mayan statues have beards, that the Breton language is unconnected with other European tongues, that the extinct auroch or European wild ox was the same as the American bison, that camels were never native to North America, that the remains of elephants have not been found in America north of Florida, that there were no lions in Classical Greece, that the Otomis speak ancient Japanese, that the biographer of the famous wizard Apollonios of Tyana was 'Theophrastes,' that the pyramids of Gizeh and Teotihuacan were built many thousands of years B.C.... and so on; mistakes of the sort that would be cleared up by a little selected reading and a visit to a couple of good museums. You believe Colonel Braghine at your peril."

It seems to be de Camp who is mistaken here, not Braghine. Nowhere in his book does Braghine say that the Breton language is unconnected with other European languages—it is in fact Basque that Braghine is referring to. The pyramids at Giza and Teotihuacan are indeed many thousands of years old, and their actual date has never been proven to any satisfaction.

Braghine does not say that all Mayan statues have beards, but instead refers to the curious use of false beards, as among the Egyptians. Admittedly, Braghine does say that "A very interesting Indian tribe called the Otomis lives in the neighborhood of Tula in Mexico: these Indians speak the old Japanese idiom, and once when the Japanese ambassador to Mexico visited this tribe he talked with them in this old dialect."[25]

Ultimately, de Camp's criticisms of Braghine are just an attempt to skirt the real evidence. Braghine's book is packed with fascinating detail after detail; one is amazed at his worldly travels, acquaintances and knowledge of ancient cultures.

The Azores: Island Remnants of Atlantis?

Lisbon was a fresh change from Madrid, with its ocean breezes and startlingly different language. Because of my extended travels in Latin America, my Spanish was good, but Portuguese was going to be tricky.

Staying at a small guesthouse in central Lisbon, I walked down by the old port where the caravels would leave for the Spice Islands and the New World. Lisbon has played an important role in the exploration of the world. Henry the Navigator was a Portuguese prince who lived from 1394 to 1460 and founded the School of Navigation. His relative was William St. Clair of the Orkney Islands, discussed in the chapter on Scotland.

After Ceuta had been captured from Morocco in the turning tide of the Moorish Wars, Prince Henry of Portugal retired to Sangres along the coast and collected the most famous astronomers, cartographers and mariners of the day, thus founding his famous school.

Improvements in the astrolabe and the sextant and increased knowledge in their use, enabling calculations to be made far out to sea, led to the prince's introduction of navigation by the stars: mariners who had been used to a chart and compass as guides and had gauged their position from an estimate of the distance travelled, learned to calculate their latitude from the height of the stars above the horizon and chart their positions with greater accuracy.

Improvements in cartography were also made so that Portuguese maps were the most detailed and accurate obtainable. With the introduction of a new kind of ship, that had a stern rudder, shallow draft and a large variety of square and triangular sails, the Portuguese caravels could carry a large crew and sail close to the wind, an important feature when sailing against the wind on the return trips from Africa.

The Portuguese could now make the long and difficult trip to the Spice Islands in search of cloves, cinnamon, cardamom and vanilla. Cloves were so valuable, and only obtainable in the remote Molucca Islands off New Guinea, that an entire industry based on shipbuilding and exploration was developed.

Lisbon was hit by a devastating earthquake on November 1, 1755. Ignatius Donnelly felt that this earthquake was key to proving that serious earth changes take place with some regularity. Describing the 1755 quake he says, " ...In six minutes 60,000 persons perished. A great concourse of people had collected for safety upon a new quay, built entirely out of marble, but suddenly it sunk down with all the people on it, and not one of the dead bodies ever floated to the surface. A great number of small boats and vessels anchored near it, and, full of people, were swallowed up as in a whirlpool.

"No fragments of these wrecks ever rose again to the surface; the water where the quay went down is now 600 feet deep. The area

271

covered by this earthquake was very great. Humboldt says that a portion of the earth's surface, four times as great as the size of Europe, was simultaneously shaken. It extended from the Baltic to the west Indies and from Canada to Algiers. At eight leagues from Morocco the ground opened and swallowed a village of 10,000 inhabitants, and closed again over them.

"It is very possible the center of the convulsion was in the bed of the Atlantic, and that it was a successor of the great earth throes which, thousands of years before, had brought destruction upon that land."[5]

Lisbon has long been an important naval port and its name is said to be derived from Ulysses, Homer's hero of the *Odyssey*. Lisbon is *Ulysses-bon*, meaning *Port of Ulysses*. An even more interesting port was to be found in the ancient city north of Lisbon called Obidos. Obidos, or Abydos, is the ancient Egyptian temple along the Nile in southern Egypt that holds the pre-Egyptian megalithic ruins of the Osirion, the Tomb of Osiris.

Names like Obidos appear at ancient sites and indicate that there is an important connection between Egypt and these other lands. Another place-name like this is Karnak, Egypt's largest temple, which appears in France as Carnac and in India at the Karnak sun chariot temple in Orissa.

But my destination was the Portuguese province of the Azores, a group of nine islands in the middle of the Atlantic. I purchased a ticket on Air Portugal and was soon making the four-hour flight to São Miguel, the largest city in the Azores.

The airline's inflight magazine gave me some idea of what to expect as to the commercialization of the Azores: it was entitled *Atlantis*. Not only that, but I was to discover that the Azores played up the Atlantis tourism angle as much as the Greek island of Thera/Santorini did.

The Azores boast an *Atlantis Rent-a-Car*, *Atlantis Pizza*, several *Atlantis* restaurants, and a number of *Atlantis* guesthouses. There is also the local radio station, the colorful *Radio Atlantida*. *Atlantida* is the Portuguese word for Atlantis. At the airport in São Miguel I picked up some tourist literature at the information booth and stepped outside to the curb where a young taxi driver was waiting in a Peugeot.

"Need a taxi?" he asked me in English.

"How far is it to Ponta Delgada?" I asked.

"Only five minutes," he said, opening the door for me. I threw my rucksack in the backseat and sat up front next to him.

I pulled out my tourist map and read the introductory paragraph, which also mentioned Atlantis: "São Miguel, the 'green' island, is the main island of the Azores. Its variety of landscape and botanic life fascinate both first-time visitor and resident alike. Within the 747 square km area of the island exist plants from all 5 continents. Many of the island's 180,000 inhabitants believe that São Miguel is the remains of the legendary 'Atlantis'."

I looked over at my taxi driver. "Do you believe in Atlantis?" I asked him.

He looked at me and then back at the road again. "Oh, well, yes," he hesitated. "Atlantis, yes, I believe in that."

"Does everyone in the Azores believe in Atlantis?" I asked.

"Well, not everyone," he said. "But many."

As we came into the outskirts of the island's main town, the port of Ponta Delgada, I asked him if he knew of a nice, inexpensive guesthouse in the center.

"I know a good one," he said. "One where they believe in Atlantis." We both laughed.

The Azores are an archipelago of nine volcanic islands situated about 1500 kilometers west of Portugal. With a total population on the islands of less than 250,000, the Azores provide a pleasant year-round climate for an economy based on tourism, fishing and small farms.

The official discovery of the Azores was by the Portuguese navigator Diego de Silves in 1427 but the actual discovery is known to have been long before this. Current archaeologists today debate whether the Phoenicians ever discovered or used the Azores on their voyages.

It is thought by some historians that the island of São Miguel in the Azores can be identified with Homer's Island of Calypso, or the isle of Ogygia in the 'navel of the ocean sea.'

Almost certainly the Phoenicians and Carthaginians, plus other seafarers must have arrived at some time in the Azores, although there is only circumstantial evidence for this. No major archaeological ruins of any kind have so far been discovered on the Azores, but as recently as 1995 famous underwater archaeologist Robert Marx was in the Azores looking for Phoenician, Roman and other shipwrecks.

University of Florida geography professor Robert Fuson says in his book *Legendary Islands of the Ocean Sea*,[147] "There is absolutely no doubt that the islands were known and charted as early as the 14th century. One of the archipelago appears on the Dalorto chart of 1339, and another of the islands may be on that chart. Eight of the nine islands are listed in the Libro de Conoscimiento (circa 1345) and a goodly number of scholars believe that Niccolosos da Recco and Angiolino del Tegghia dei Corbizzi passed that way in 1341."

Fuson goes on to say that the Azores may have been the inspiration for such legendary lands as "the Island of Brazil, the Island of Seven Cities, and the magic island of Antila. Some have thought they posed as the Fortunate Islands of St. Brendan, and even Atlantis finds a mythical remnant here for some."[147]

Charles Berlitz in *The Mystery of Atlantis*[238] mentions that Paul le Cour, founder of the French organization "Friends of Atlantis," visited the Azores and reported in their newsletter that a stone slab bearing an engraving of a building was discovered in a cavern on São Miguel. Paul le Cour enthusiastically classified the engraving as a representation of an Atlantean temple. This would seem unlikely; if it's an authentic relic, it might rather depict some Carthaginian or other building.

Le Cour and his friends of Atlantis also pointed out the quaint use of sledges in the Azores to move objects over the round pebbles of the shore. This, thought le Cour, was a survival of Stone Age transportation methods such as the Egyptians were known to use to transport large statues.

Carthaginian coins have been discovered on the Azore island of Corvo, a small island on the northwest corner of the archipelago. Braghine in *The Shadow of Atlantis*[25] reports that a statue of a man on horseback was also found on the western coast of Corvo. The statue was made of stone and had an undecipherable inscription at the base. Unfortunately, the king of Portugal ordered it removed in the 16th century and it was inadvertently broken by the workers sent to remove it. The statue and inscription are now lost.

Braghine reports that when Portuguese explorers, in search of new lands, reached the Azores and saw the statue, the man on horseback was reportedly pointing westward to the Americas. The inhabitants of Corvo were reported to have called the statue *Catés*, which has no meaning in either Portuguese or Spanish but curiously resembles the Inca-Quechua word *cati* which means "go that way" or "follow."[25]

With the volcanic nature of the Azores, it is probable that serious tectonic disturbances occurred over the last several thousand years. Phoenician port cities may have existed in the Azores that are now hundreds of feet underwater or covered in volcanic lava or both. Even today the tallest mountain in the Azores is the towering Mount Pico, a smoking volcano 2,351 meters high. In fact, Pico is the highest mountain in all of Portugal.

Any day, I thought as I rode on a bus early one morning heading for the Seven Cities lake district, all of the Azores could be shoved up or down on the Atlantic tectonic plate and the whole archipelago could be drowned. If the area around the Azores was submerged by 100 meters or so, most of the major towns would be under water.

Equally likely, the Azores might be thrust upward, with the volcano Pico spreading large lava fields. The Azores could become a unified mini-continent with a tectonic plate thrust of only 1,000 meters. Atlantis could rise out of the ocean and be located right where Plato and the Egyptian priests had said it was.

Was this really Atlantis? I wondered as the bus rose up along a narrow paved road into the green hills of São Miguel. There were small towns along the road and carts of hay being pulled by horses. The driver stopped at the small post offices along the way and dropped off mail. It was a paradisical setting of small farms, luscious green pastures and happy cattle chewing their cuds. Atlantis would have had a nice climate.

The bus let me off at one of the main tourist spots in the Azores, the Lagoa das Sete Cidades or the Lake of the Seven Cities. It was a tremendously beautiful setting of two lakes inside an extinct volcanic crater, with a small picturesque village along the lakeside. It was late morning as I walked through the quiet village down to the shores of the lake. Some women were washing clothes in the shallow water along the edge. Cows grazed lazily on the deep green grass that was everywhere.

Legend says that the two lakes, one green and one blue, are these two colors because a princess and a shepherd wept these two lakes into being with their tears when their love was thwarted. The story of the Seven Cities goes back to the early Portuguese legend of seven cities created by Portuguese seamen fleeing from the Moors. They went westward into the Atlantic and were never seen again, though legends of their "seven cities" persisted in Portugal for centuries. Some writers, like Berlitz, prefer to equate the legend of the Seven Cities to the lost cities of Atlantis—a romantic thought, at least.

I walked along the road that wound through the crater between the two lakes and then shot up the steep slope to the rim of the crater. There did not seem to be anymore buses coming along that morning, so I decided to hitchhike and was fortunate to get a ride with a young man in a pickup truck heading back to Ponta Delgada.

Forests of pine trees and fields of flowers lined the road that wound through the mountains back to the coast. One of the unusual facts about the Azores is that they have a strange tree that has survived since prehistoric times. This tree is the *Criptoméria*, a gigantic tree of the Taxodium species. This huge prehistoric remnant is known to exist only on the Azores and in certain remote regions of Japan![230]

Says Mauricio Abreu in his book *São Miguel, Azores*,[230] referring to the name which means something like *puzzling-tree:* "The *Criptoméria*: hence the tree of the only Azorean myth still told. It was sent by the gods, I believe, to prove that life is eternal and so that Man could believe in his own myths. See how this is ever-present in hamlets, fairs, places of worship or our homes, representing the sweat and tears of the people of the Azores. Resting one's head on its porous trunk, one can hear people both near and far breathing, heavy with longing for their island."[230]

The first chapter of *The Azores: Fairy-Tale Islands of the Atlantic*[231] is entitled "The Nine Peaks of Atlantis." The book then goes on to briefly describe how the Azores may be part of the lost continent of Atlantis where civilization began.

It seemed that everywhere I turned in the Azores there was some sign proclaiming Atlantis this or that. The inhabitants of the Azores believed that they were living on the mountaintops of Atlantis, and that was that.

I flew on a local Air Azores flight to the island of Terceira, part of the central group of the islands. In the distance to the west I could see the towering volcanic cone of Pico, the highest mountain in Portugal. Had this been the great peak that rose above the plain and city of Atlantis?

I looked down at the blue waves of the Atlantic lapping the shores of the islands. Charles Berlitz in *The Mystery of Atlantis*[238] mentions the sightings of underwater structures from the air: "Sightings from aircraft of undersea buildings and entire cities in the vicinity of the Azores were reported as far back as 1942, when air ferry pilots flying from Brazil to Dakar glimpsed what seemed to be a submerged city just breaking the surface on the western slope of mountains in the Mid-atlantic ridge, of which the Azores are the highest peaks. Such random sightings occur when the sun and surface tension attain optimum condition for underwater sightings. Other sightings of submerged architectural remains of what was perhaps the central Atlantean area have been noted off Boa Vista Island in the Cape Verde Islands, off Fayal in the Azores. Nonsubmerged remains of buildings and cities, perhaps dating from Atlantean times, were found by the early Spanish conquerors of the Canary Islands."[238]

Berlitz goes on to mention how the Guanches of the Canaries, when the Spanish arrived, had preserved a legend of a great civilization lost in the sea but were no longer capable of constructing anything more than simple huts. Nor did they have the ability to create oceangoing vessels.

Berlitz, the author of several excellent books on Atlantis, believes that the Azores hold the key to Atlantis and are most probably the mountaintops of the sunken land. Says Berlitz, "Volcanic activity is constantly occurring in the Azores area, where there are still five active volcanoes. In 1808 a volcano rose in San Jorge to a height of several thousand feet, and in 1811 a volcanic island rose up from the sea, creating a large island which was called Sambrina during its short above-water existence before it sank again beneath the sea. The islands of Corvo and Flores in the Azores, which have been mapped since 1351, have constantly changed their shape, with large parts of Corvo having disappeared into the sea."[238]

William Corliss in his *Science Frontiers*[280] reports that a news article appeared in the Baltimore *Sun* on April 5, 1981, under the headline "Undersea Discovery May Be Atlantis." The story concerned a Soviet oceanographic expedition that was taking underwater photos of the Ampere Seamount, 450 miles west of Gibraltar, southwest of the Azores.

The article said that when the photographs were developed they showed underwater ruins that might be associated with Atlantis. According to the article, "they discovered what seem to be walls, stairways, and other artificial stone work."[280]

Charles Berlitz reported on the same expedition, which published several photographs taken by the USSR research ship Academician Petrovsky at the Ampere and Josephine Seamounts. Both seamounts rise from a depth of 10,000 feet or more to a flat summit only a few hundred feet beneath the surface.

Professor Aksyonov described steps on the Ampere Seamount that were partially covered with lava. "In my opinion these structures once stood on the surface," he said. The Soviet Academy of Sciences announced that it had found evidence for Atlantis and photographs were released to the news media.

Perhaps one day Jules Verne's scene of two divers beholding the ruins of the great city of Atlantis may be a reality.

~~~~~~~~~ 𓂀 ~~~~~~~~~

Bullfighting Returns to Atlantis

On the island of Terceira I took a taxi to the main town of Angra do Heroismo and checked into a small hotel appropriately named Residential Atlantida. I read a bit about the island and then headed to the port and the center of town. Sitting in a café on the main plaza I met a couple of local Azorean fellows who had a dune buggy parked next to us, half on the sidewalk, half in the street.

"That's my dune buggy," said a friendly fellow in a t-shirt that read "Pittsburgh Steelers."

"That's a cool dune buggy," I admitted. "Where do you go in it?"

"Oh, we go to the beach or other places. Today we are going to a small village in the mountains where we will run with bulls."

"Really?" I asked, fascinated by sports that concern the legendary bull of Atlantis. "They run with the bulls here, like in Pamplona, Spain?"

"Not quite like in Pamplona. Here they tie a rope to the bull and let one of six bulls out into the street at a time. It is less dangerous that way. We are leaving right now. Do you want to come with us?"

Always ready for an adventure, I accepted their invitation and climbed into the back of the dune buggy with my three new friends. We drove up the narrow winding roads toward the center of the island to a small village on a steep hill. There we parked along the street and walked up to a central plaza where a beer-drinking crowd stood around the small square.

My friends wandered off and I looked around the plaza and the narrow streets radiating up and down from it. Six bulls were kept in separate cages, each waiting to be released into the square. Families had put boards across their front windows and doors in anticipation of a bull charging down the street.

Would-be matadors were warming up for their tryst with the bulls. I searched down one street for something to eat. Sure enough, small sandwich and beer stalls were to be found along the alleys.

Soon I was walking down the street with a sandwich in one hand and a beer in the other. I stood in a doorway as they let the first bull out of his steel cage, a long, thick rope tied to his neck. Three or more men held the other end of the rope and kept the bull from running too far down one street or another.

The bull snorted and ran across the square. The crowd scattered and ran up the street. I walked back into the square and was looking at the church, when the crowd suddenly began running. I looked across the square and saw the bull come charging against a door. The people screamed and jumped back.

Suddenly I was alone in the square with a snorting bull at the other corner, pawing the pavement. The crowd cheered as the bull took off toward me with a loud snort. In sheer terror I began to run down the alley in search of a doorway or window to dive into. Where should I go? My recently broken leg was slowing me down. How was I to escape this raging bull?

Just then a young man came out from a doorway of the church and waved his coat like a matador's cape in front of the bull. I scrambled up to a stone windowsill where I could jump to an upper balcony. The bull turned toward the coat while the man stepped to the side of the bull.

Abruptly the bull went charging down another street, giving me time to escape. Later they used the rope to get the bull back into its steel cage and prepared another bull to enter the streets.

I was keen to get out of the streets and up to a higher place where I would be safe from bulls crashing up and down the street. I finally found a door to an upper balcony where I could watch the spectacle in relative safety.

My friends had explained to me how someone had been killed the year before by being gored against the wall by a bull. In the summer of 1995 a young man from Illinois was killed in the running of the bulls at Pamplona. Watching the sport firsthand, I could see how dangerous it was.

As I looked down at the young men who thrilled the crowd by dashing about the charging bulls, I wondered about the ancient worship of bulls and their connection to Atlantis. It seemed fitting that the cult of the bull had returned to the Azores from Spain. Whether it is in ancient Catal Huyuk, Minoan Crete or ancient

Spain, the tradition is said to stem from Atlantis. Cattle represented wealth in the ancient world just as it does in many areas of the world today.

I was able to get a ride back to Angra do Heroismo with my friends in their dune buggy.

"How did you like the bullfights?" asked one.

"It was great," I said. "It scared me though, and I had to find a balcony to watch it from."

"Oh, yes," he laughed, "the bulls are exciting. It is an ancient tradition."

"Yes," I nodded with the wind in my face. "I'm sure it is."

~~~~~~~~⚓~~~~~~~~

After a week of exploring the Azores, I flew back to Lisbon, where I relaxed in a café near the port thinking about where to go next. I searched through my guidebook for unusual places in Portugal and it mentioned the boulder-strewn summit of the Serra da Estrela in the upper valley of the Zezere River. This area is a granite mountain range along the Spanish border and has an interesting summit ridge that is strewn with huge boulders.

These boulders, many of them squared blocks of granite, are lying in a helter-skelter fashion along the top of this mountain. Are they just an unusual natural formation, or are these the scattered blocks of a megalithic hilltop fortress?

While lounging in the café I flipped through a Michelin guide to Portugal and noticed an interesting tourist attraction called Almourol castle, near the town of Abrantes. It's a fortress with a tower and walls located on a small rocky island covered in greenery in the center of the river Tagus.

It was constructed by Gualdim Pais, Master of the Order of the Knights Templar, in 1171. The castle is built on the site of an earlier Roman fortress. The Roman fortress in turn may well be built on the foundations of an earlier structure.

The mysterious Knights Templar had an extensive sea network and may have inherited some of the maps and other secrets of the Phoenicians. When the Templars were outlawed and arrested in 1307 by King Philip IV of France, the huge Templar fleet at La Rochelle, France, vanished and many Knights Templar sought refuge in lands outside of France. Portugal was one of the few places where they could find some asylum, and it is likely that the Templar fleet made a stop at Almourol castle before continuing to their final destination.

While in Lisbon I was informed that a publisher in Barcelona wanted to do a Spanish-language edition of my *Lost Cities of Ancient*

Lemuria & the Pacific book which I had written a few years before. I arranged to meet my new publisher and took a night train via Madrid to Barcelona.

I stayed in a small pension for a few days while I visited Barcelona and discussed the publication of my book.

Barcelona was originally a Phoenician port and this area along the border of Spain and France has long thought of itself as Cataluña, a state, people and culture separate from the rest of Spain. The populace speaks their own language, Catalunian, a language that may have originated with ancient Phoenician.

I enjoyed Barcelona for a few days and then made a day trip to the ancient monastery of Montserrat in the mountains outside of the city.

Montserrat has been a site of religious pilgrimage for a long time, probably going back even before the Christian era. It is a mountain rising 4,054 feet above the coastal plain which eventually became the site of a celebrated Benedictine monastery. It was at Montserrat that Saint Ignatius of Loyola vowed to dedicate himself to a religious life.

The monastery can be found about halfway up the steep, barren mountain. Only ruins can be found of the 11th-century Benedictine monastery and the new monastery on the site was built in the 19th century.

According to the *Columbia Viking Desk Encyclopedia* (1968 version), Montserrat was thought in the Middle Ages to have been the site of the castle which contained the Holy Grail. Says the encyclopedia, "The Renaissance church contains a black wooden image of the Virgin, carved, according to tradition, by St. Luke. In the Middle Ages the mountain, also called Monsalvat, was thought to have been the site of the castle of the Holy Grail."

Indeed, there is a certain mystery surrounding Montserrat. The monastery makes an almond liqueur called Aromes del Montserrat which uses the unusual symbol of Montserrat, which is the steep mountain peak with a box and cross at the summit.

Standing in the monastery with a group of tourists, I wondered if the box on top of the mountain was the legendary Ark of the Covenant, a wooden and metal box which held the sacred relics of the Temple in Jerusalem. The mystery of the location of the Ark of the Covenant and the Holy Grail has intrigued Christians for centuries.

Was the Ark of the Covenant and, later, the Holy Grail, taken to a secret cavern complex in the mountains of Montserrat? Legend says that a secret Brotherhood of Essenes moved to Cataluña and Montserrat in the early centuries before Christ. This secret brotherhood built a network of subterranean caverns, castles and monasteries in the Pyrenees Mountains along the border of southern France and Spain.

Was the Holy Grail once kept in these underground tunnels for a time? Perhaps the Ark of the Covenant was kept here as well, and may still be hidden inside the mountain.

Curiously, Barcelona is the city where Columbus landed upon his return to Europe from the New World. Why did Columbus come all the way to Barcelona when he had left from Cadiz, a port that he had to pass on his way to Barcelona? Perhaps Barcelona was a safer port to land at than Cadiz? All Jews had been banished from Spain on the very day that Columbus had sailed for the New World. Some historians have claimed that Columbus was actually a Spanish Jew and not an Italian from Genoa as later historians were to claim. If Columbus was a Jew, perhaps Barcelona and the Cataluña area was a safe haven for him and his crew. (For more information on the mysterious life of Christopher Columbus see my book *Lost Cities of North & Central America.*[23])

Mystery of the Balearic Islands

From Barcelona I took a ferry to the Balearic Islands in the Mediterranean just off the east coast of Spain. Today, islands like Majorca and Ibiza are the playgrounds for Europe's jet-set who come to lay in the sun during the day and party in the discotheques at night. But in ancient times the Balearics were the site of an amazing megalithic culture that continues to cause amazement today.

Throughout the islands are the ruins of remarkable stone structures known as *talayots, navetas,* and *taulas.* While the culture that made these megalithic structures remains a mystery, it is known that they had connections with the eastern Mediterranean because Greek bronzes and a variety of ceramic ware from the first millennium B.C. have been discovered among the ruins, which are apparently many hundreds or thousands of years older.

According to the Barcelona archaeologist L. Pericot Garcia in his book *The Balearic Islands,*[239] the original inhabitants were so adept at the use of the sling, that it is believed by many historians that the sling was invented on these small, remote islands. Considering how widespread the sling is, and its use by David to kill Goliath circa 1000 B.C., this is an amazing statement.

Garcia, trying to make sense of the strange ruins, tells us that the island inhabitants "engaged in seafaring, at least to maintain communications between the individual islands, though no trace of the vessels they used has so far been found."

What is more, the massive monuments throughout the islands present a serious obstacle to the farming of the land, a problem which the inhabitants must deal with. In many cases local farmers would like to remove the megalithic ruins that are scattered about the fields, but it would be impossible to do so without the most modern of heavy equipment.

Says Garcia, "It is difficult to specify exactly when or in what form the techniques of cyclopean or megalithic construction were introduced into the Balearics, presumably by new and immigrant peoples. The surprising profusion and the massiveness of the building which ensued in the islands has put a stamp on the landscape which neither the passage of time nor depredation by later inhabitants has managed to efface.

"The people of the islands have never ceased to be conscious of the grandiose ruins which they encounter at every turn, and which present such obstacles to farming. The most outstanding and considerable of the monuments are those called *talaia*, or *talayot*, the local word for 'watch-tower'. These, with other remains which are impressive for the amount of stone they contain, are also called *clapers*, while *antigors* is also used as a general term for all types of ruins. When, on occasion, these assume particular shapes, they are called by special names, like the boat-shaped *navetas* or the strange megalithic *taulas* of Minorca."[239]

The depth of the mystery of the megalithic remains in the Balearics can be deduced from an early article entitled "Antiquities On the Island of Minorca" by Hernandez Sanz which appeared in the *American Antiquarian* (No. 8, 1886). Said Sanz in the article, "Even today the enormous heaps of stone called *talayots* cause great astonishment; the great stone tables, the artificial caves or cellars, rows of pillars and circles of menhirs, and those strange constructions in the form of a ship, the only ones in the world. It would be a most difficult task to suggest a creditable account of their origin wrapped as they are in the obscurity of history."

In an article on the megaliths entitled "Stone Monuments of Minorca" that appeared in the British scientific journal *Nature* (No. 119, 1927), the anonymous author says: "It has generally been held that the *talayots* of Minorca, great mounds of huge, rough uncemented stones 26 ft.-30 ft. high, were comparable with the better known *nurhags* of Sardinia. This comparison was based on the view that the *talayot* in some, if not all, cases was built hollow with an entrance, resembling in this respect a chambered cairn. Mr. Chamberlin examined 186 *talayots*, some previously unknown. Of these, 107 were in a sufficiently good state of preservation to permit him to say that 32 only, or one out of three, had ever had an entrance of any sort, while three alone had an interior chamber, and only one more than one apartment. It is clear, therefore, that the *talayot* is not comparable to the *nurhag* and, indeed, is a monument without a parallel. Associated with the *talayot*, and usually within a hundred feet of it, is a class of monument known locally as a *taula*—a two-stoned monument 5 ft.-12 ft. high in the shape of a Greek T, the flat top stone being fully 12 ft. long. Ten of these are now known. Each is surrounded by a horse-shoe-shaped wall pierced by a doorway surmounted by a single-stone lintel."

The article goes on to say that "Sir Wallis Budge has expressed the opinion that the *talayots* are pyramids of a funereal nature, and the *taulas* altars for sacrifice or other funereal ceremonies. A third class of monument, called *naus* from its resemblance to a ship, of which sixteen are known, has an elliptical chamber 15 ft. long by 7 ft. high, and appears to have served as a tomb for dwellers in the numerous caves in the neighborhood."

So here we have cave dwellers who come out of their caves to build these exceptionally huge monuments, not to live in (they have their caves) but for sacrifice and funerary services. Yet the monuments are built in such places as to inhibit the farming of the land, and no trace of the ancient seamanship that must have accompanied the builders can be found.

While many of the monuments appear unique, others are similar to the beehive buildings found on the Aran Islands off the west coast of Ireland. In other ways, the rock-cut tombs, circular buildings and cyclopean scale of building is reminiscent of the structures on Malta. But conservative archaeologists have not been able to make a connection between these similar monuments because they assume that ancient man did not travel.

As I walked from massive ruin to cyclopean site on Majorca, I wondered just how old these ruins were. Orthodox archaeology says that they are at least 4,000 years old, and possibly more. If they were about the same age as those on Malta, then they might have been built 10,000 years ago before the Mediterranean was flooded.

In this theory, the megaliths were built, like the megaliths on many other Mediterranean islands, when the area was not a group of small islands but part of the Osirian civilization in the fertile Mediterranean Valley. The towers may have been built on the hilltops of the land as lookouts, or perhaps they were tuning towers for agriculture as the Round Towers of Ireland have been portrayed.

As I returned to Barcelona on the ferry, after a few days of visiting the Balearics, I wondered how many similar megalithic ruins might be found in the waters between Spain and the islands. The Balearics also had their bull figurines, indicating that the age-old cult of the bull had existed on those islands as well.

The shadows of Atlantis cast themselves to even the smallest islands of the Mediterranean.

Top: an old engraving of the devastating earthquake that hit Lisbon, Portugal, i 1755. Bottom: The rock of Gibraltar in the early 19th century.

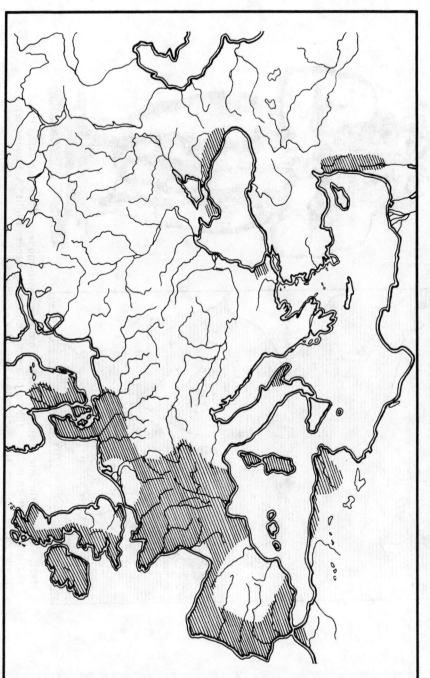

The distribution of megaliths in Europe and the Mediterranean area.

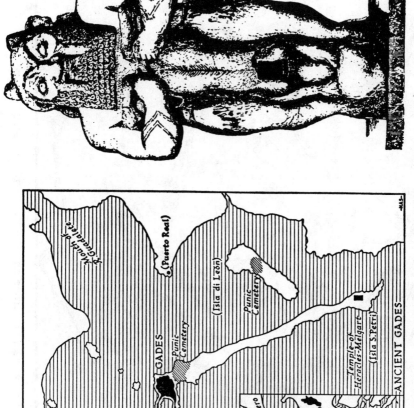
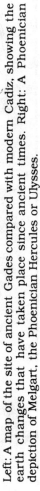

Left: A map of the site of ancient Gades compared with modern Cadiz, showing the earth changes that have taken place since ancient times. Right: A Phoenician depiction of Melgart, the Phoenician Hercules or Ulysses.

A huge Phoenician sarcophagus belonging to Eshmunazar, a king of Sidon (c. 1000 B.C.). A similar Phoenician sarcophagus can be seen in the Cadiz museum.

A View of the Cyclopean Wall at Niebla.

The Cyclopean Wall at Lixus on the River Lucus, near Larache in Spanish Morocco.

Two photos from Wishaw's book *Atlantis In Andalusia.*

The Lady of Elche, reconstructed. She wears her hair in an unusual fashion said by Whishaw to originate in Atlantis. Unmarried Hopi maidens of Arizona still wear their hair in this unusual fashion today. Note the Atonist-type sun symbol at the base of the statue.

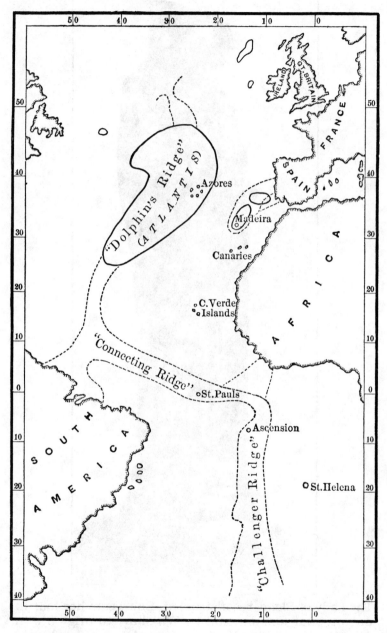

Donnelly's 1882 map of Atlantis in the Azores.

Photograph of part of an apparent wall taken with automatic underwater camera by the *USSR Academician Petrovsky* expedition in the vicinity of the Ampere and Josephine Seamounts southwest of the Azores. These seamounts rise from a depth of 10,000 or more feet to a summit of several hundred feet below the surface. Round object at right is end of plumb line lowered from research ship.

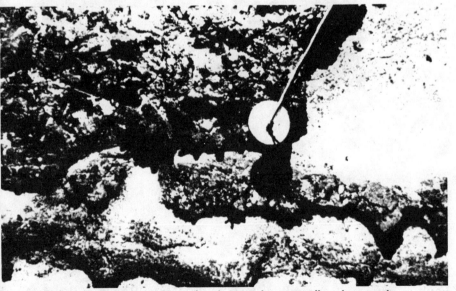

Another *Academician Petrovsky* photograph, reportedly taken on the fairly flat summit of the Ampere Seamount showing apparently artificial steps partially covered by lava. A leading Soviet scientist, Professor Aksyonov, has stated, "In my opinion these structures once stood on the surface."

Thanks to Charles Berlitz.

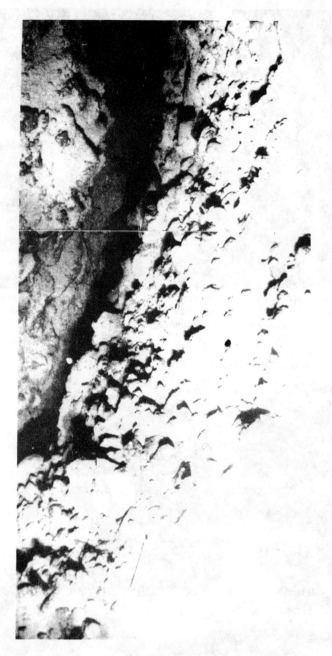

Fault in bottom of ocean floor near Mid-Atlantic Ridge, in the vicinity of the Azores, typical of constant activity between pushing, ascending, and descending tectonic plates. *NOAA*

Thanks to Charles Berlitz.

Top: Two megalithic crosses, or Taulas, on the island of Minorca in the Balearics. They are highly similar to the megalithic cross on Tory Island at the northern tip of Ireland. Bottom: Cyclopean ruins at Sa Canova on the island of Majorca, Balearics. This wall seems similar to the ruins of Ggantija on Gozo, said to be over 7,000 years old!

Two views of Els Tudons "naveta" structure in the Balearics. It is similar to some of the buildings in the Aran Islands of Ireland.

Chapter 9

FRANCE:

Atlantis & the
Priory of Zion

And the first angel sounded the trumpet, and there followed hail
and fire mingled with blood, and it was cast upon the Earth; and
the third part of the Earth was burnt up, and the third part of
the trees was burnt up, and all green grass was burnt up... and
as it were a great mountain was cast into the sea; and the third
part of the sea became blood, and there died the third part of
those creatures that have life in the sea, and the third part of
the ships was destroyed.
                                        —*Revelation* 8:7-9

I entered France on a local train bound for Narbonne. It was early
afternoon when I departed from Barcelona and the sun was still
high in the sky at the frontier. A French police dog entered the train
and ran up and down the aisle presumably looking for drugs and
bombs. I looked out the window; the dry hills of the Pyrenees could
be seen around the border station.

An hour or so later I arrived at Narbonne, and was whisked away
by taxi to Rennes-le-Château, the site of a fascinating controversy. A
large number of books have been written recently which concern, in
one way or another, the mystery of Rennes-le-Château.

The books include *Holy Blood, Holy Grail*,[240] *The Messianic
Legacy*,[240] *GENISIS*,[229] *The Secrets of Rennes-le-Château*,[243] and
many more. The story of Rennes-le-Château is one of secret
societies, lost treasure, and the struggle against the dark power of
the Vatican. This convoluted history is so intriguing that I will
outline it for the reader, but be aware that hundreds of pages have
been written seeking to "prove or disprove" it.

The story goes back to ancient times, and, according to some
authors on the subject, back to Atlantis.

In the year 376 A.D. the Visigoths, fleeing from the Huns, fled into

Roman territory. The Romans sent a punitive force which was completely defeated and ultimately led to the sacking of Rome by the Visigoths in 410 under Alaric I. His successor, King Ataulf, led the Visigoths and took the treasure of Rome into southern France and the Pyrenees.

Centuries later, the Visigoths lost their lands north of the Pyrenees when the Franks defeated Alaric II. However, the dynasty of the Visigoths was to continue by intermarriage with the Franks and the creation of the Merovingian dynasty of kings.

In modern times the story begins in 1885 when a new priest named Berenger Sauniere was assigned to the remote hilltop village of Rennes-le-Château. The tiny village held only about 200 inhabitants, but is located in a historic area of the Pyrenees foothills. Not far away is the famous Cathar fortress of Montségur.

The church of Rennes-le-Château dates back to 1059, and beneath the church are the foundations of a much older Visigoth church which was built in the time of Alaric (circa 411 A.D.) who is alleged to have hidden a great treasure, including relics from his sacking of Rome, in the vicinity of Rennes-le-Château.

In the ancient Visigothic church (the one beneath Rennes-le-Château) the Merovingian King Dragobert II (651-679) married the Visigoth Princess Giselle de Razes in 671. Shortly after this wedding, Dragobert became suddenly very wealthy, apparently from some huge treasure hoard. He used this wealth to regain the throne of the Merovingian kings, but was soon murdered.

In 410 A.D. Alaric, the Visigoth chieftain, had sieged Rome for the third time and broke into the city, sacking it of valuables from the churches and government offices. Many of the writers on Rennes-le-Château believe that a portion of the Treasure of Solomon and other sacred items from the Middle East were taken by Alaric. Was this the treasure buried at Rennes-le-Château that was discovered by Dragobert and later Father Sauniere?

In 1891 Father Sauniere was restoring the church and discovered four parchments inside a hollow column in the church. The parchments were Latin translations of parts of the New Testament and genealogies dating back to 1244. Sauniere discovered a code in the texts which presumably led him to at least part of Dragobert's treasure.

Sauniere, who as a priest made only 30 dollars a year, suddenly became very wealthy. He made trips to Paris and mingled with high social circles, and was often seen with the opera star and occultist Emma Calve. Sauniere also made tremendous improvements on the church, including a new tower; constructed an opulent residence for himself; and built a new road into the village along with a new water conduit.

He collected a huge library and entertained distinguished visitors at his magnificent mansion named Villa Bethania, which included botanical and zoological gardens. It is estimated that between 1896 and 1917 the once-poor priest spent about ten million dollars. By today's prices, this sum would be a staggering 120 million dollars! The Vatican asked him where this wealth was coming from but he refused to tell them or to be relocated to another parish. He was relieved of his duties as a priest but was shortly reinstated, perhaps after Sauniere had made a sizable donation to Rome.

Sauniere died on January 17, 1917, of a massive heart attack, leaving his entire estate to his housekeeper, Marie Denarnaud. She died of a stroke on January 29, 1953, at the age of 86, taking the secret of Rennes-le-Château to the grave with her.

It is believed by some researchers that the literal genes of Jesus are in the blood of some of the royalty in Europe. According to the theory first propounded in *Holy Blood, Holy Grail*,[240] Jesus had voyaged to England as a young man before his ministry began and later, after the crucifixion (which he survived), he came to southern France where he raised a family with Mary Magdalene.

Buechner in *Emerald Cup, Ark of Gold*,[242] theorizes that at the age of 14 Jesus had accompanied his uncle, Joseph of Arimathea, on a trading trip to Europe. Buechner believes that they left the ancient Phoenician port of Byblos (a Hittite port before that) for Cyprus, Crete and ancient Carthage (now a Roman port) and finally landed in Marseille, a former Phoenician port. In Marseille, Jesus supposedly bought a silver cup from a merchant there, which he then used throughout his life as his drinking cup. This cup was to ultimately become the drinking cup at the Last Supper and the legendary Holy Grail.[242]

Buechner then says that the young Jesus and Joseph of Arimathea journeyed on to Barcelona and then to Cornwall and eventually to Glastonbury in England. He alleges that Jesus lived in Glastonbury for many years before returning to Egypt and Palestine.

Other ancient books and traditions have Jesus first going to India and studying in Orissa, south of Calcutta. He journeyed to Nepal and Tibet and then returned to Persia and Greece. He may have visited England at this time as well. Eventually he returned to Zoan, Egypt, near the Nile delta, where he had lived as a child with his cousin John the Baptist. Zoan was an Essene retreat and apparently had strong connections with Marseille and Barcelona.

It is believed by many Coptic, Gnostic and Nestorian Christians that during the six-year ministry of Christ, the Archangel Melchizedek "borrowed" the body of Jesus and was Christ. In this belief, it was the Archangel Melchizedek who was crucified, not Jesus of Nazareth. Therefore, Jesus is distinct from Christ, in this heretical Christian belief. Christ is an Archangel, a literal God on the planet, while Jesus was the son of Essene Adepts Mary and

Joseph.

Jesus had received an uncommonly excellent education for a young man two thousand years ago. He went to boarding school at an ancient college in India, and in his early adult years he wandered through the Himalayas, Persia, and Greece before returning to his mother's home in Zoan. The Koran calls Jesus "the Traveller" because of his famous travels.

Incredibly, the travels of Jesus may not have ended with his crucifixion as one might expect. According to Nestorian, Gnostic and Coptic beliefs, Christ, an Archangel, ascended back into the Archangelic dimensions with a shower of light (some say Jesus dissolved his astral body in shower of light to make a final, lasting impression on the Apostles).

Since the body of Jesus was relatively unharmed, the Essenes regained it and after a few days of quiet rest, Jesus simply walked out of the tomb. And whose tomb was it? The family tomb of Joseph of Arimathea!

It is this incredible time that now concerns us: the years after the famous crucifixion. Jesus is thought by many Moslems to have died in Kashmir about 75 A.D. His tomb supposedly can be found outside of Srinigar under the name of Yuz Asaf.

However, others claim that this is not the tomb of Jesus and that the Master journeyed on to Montserrat, near Barcelona, and then to Glastonbury. At Glastonbury, Jesus supposedly founded the first Christian church in Britain. The popular British church hymn "Jerusalem" by William Blake claims that Jesus did "walk upon England's mountains green." More on mystical Glastonbury and Jesus in the chapter on England.

There are stories that Jesus travelled all over the world, such as the well-known legends of Viracocha in South America and of Quetzalcoatl in Central America. Aztec legend says Quetzalcoatl journeyed east across the Atlantic to return to his land.

The authors of *Holy Blood, Holy Grail*[240] claim that Jesus settled down in southern France and raised a family. This family, they claimed, went on to be the Merovingian dynasty of kings, with the royal line blood-related to Jesus himself. This is the Holy Blood of European kings, and hence the book title, *Holy Blood, Holy Grail.*[240]

The Merovingian kings and the Visigoths were Cathars and Gnostic Christians who believed in reincarnation and the original Eastern Christianity taught at Alexandria, the Nestorian Heresy of the Council of Nicea in 431 A.D. When the Catholic Church was created in 431 A.D. it outlawed all other Christian sects. Thus, the Visigoths and the Merovingian kings were the enemies of the Church of Rome, yet they were devout Christians.

Two Christian armies fought for control over Europe, one from the Pyrenees and the other from Rome. For several centuries the

Merovingian kings had the upper hand until the Carolingian dynasty overthrew the last Merovingian king, Childeric III.

Pepin the Short, a mayor of the Palace, deposed Childeric III while he was away, and in 751 began the Carolingian dynasty. His son was Charlemagne, who was finally crowned Holy Roman Emperor in the year 800. In 771 Charlemagne and his brother Carloman invaded Italy to keep the Pope in power, thereby keeping the Merovingian kings from regaining the throne of France.

But the heresy of the Visigoths and their secrets still existed in the Languedoc region of France as well as in Cataluña. While the rest of Europe was plunged into the Dark Ages, a relative enlightenment remained in the Pyrenees. But eventually the forces of Rome reached out to crush the last of the heretics.

On March 16, 1244, Montségur was stormed by the forces of the Inquisition led by Simon de Montfort. Everyone inside the fortress was killed or burnt at the stake afterward.

Says David Wood in his book *GENISIS*,[227] "From 1209 for forty years, on the express orders of Pope Innocent I, an extermination occurred on so vast, so terrible a scale, it may well constitute the first case of genocide in modern European history. The agents of the massacre were an army of some 30,000 knights and foot-soldiers from Northern Europe. Their victims: almost the entire 'Cathari' or Albigensian population of the Languedoc region of what is today southern France. At that time it was a peaceful and cultivated population of independent people whose only crime seems to have been that it followed a religious way of life contrary to the one decreed by Rome.

"The Cathari, or Cathars as they are more popularly known, were Gnostics. To Rome they were infected, and therefore infectious. By the time the Crusade was over, the Languedoc had been utterly transformed, plunged back into the barbarity which characterized the rest of Europe. With that transformation came anonymity. And so it remained for 600 years—until the end of the nineteenth century."[227]

Atlantis and the Holy Grail

When Father Sauniere died in 1917, the mystery of the lost treasure of the Merovingian kings, a treasure reputed to contain relics from Atlantis, was still unsolved. Some of the treasure had been found by Sauniere, but the main treasure was still apparently unfound, or at least, unspent.

In the summer of 1931 (so the tale continues), 14 years after the death of Sauniere, a slender young man from Germany named Otto

Rahn came to the Languedoc area on a secret mission for Heinrich Himmler and the Nazi SS. His destination was the Cathar fortress of Montségur and his mission was to find the lost treasure from Solomon's Temple. Otto Rahn was to discover a cavern system beneath Montségur that was to lead him to discover (apparently) a portion of this treasure.

Otto Rahn was a fascinating person, an officer who was a scholar and a mystic. He believed in Atlantis, reincarnation and that he had been a Cathar in a previous life.

According to the former U.S. Army colonel Howard Buechner in his book *Emerald Cup, Ark of Gold,*[242] in February of 1944 the famous SS commando Otto Skorzeny recovered the treasure from the caverns beneath Montségur. Otto Rahn had died mysteriously the year before, apparently assassinated from within the Third Reich.

According to Buechner, the treasure that was so carefully guarded for thousands of years eventually went to the Berchtesgaden fortress high in the Bavarian Alps, Germany's famed Eagle's Nest. In a scene worthy of the Indiana Jones film *Raiders of the Lost Ark,* the treasure was taken aboard a Nazi transport plane and eventually flown to a secret destination.

Says Buechner, "In the very last days of April, 1945, eyewitnesses noted the mysterious takeoff, in the region of Salzburg, Austria, of a four engine aircraft believed to be a Heinkel 277 V-1. The destination of the plane has remained unknown, but some authors have proposed that it flew to the city of Katmandu in Nepal and then to some other location in the Himalayas or in Tibet. On board were five officers of the Black Order and in the cargo bay were the twelve stone tablets of the Germanic Grail which contained the key to ultimate knowledge."[242]

Buechner believes that the Holy Grail and the Ark of the Covenant, as well as other treasure, were taken to a secret hideaway somewhere in Tibet. This may seem far-fetched, but there is a great deal of literature supporting close associations between the Third Reich and certain remote areas of Tibet whose locations are unknown. Given the Nazis' obsession with the occult, a destination such as Katmandu or Tibet would not seem out of place.

Nevertheless, while it seems likely that large amounts of treasure were recovered by both Father Sauniere and by the Nazis, it has never been proven that the treasure included the Holy Grail or the Ark of the Covenant. One would think that such important treasures would never be "lost" but rather kept in secret custodianship by a group that knew the significance of the articles.

There is even the Priory of Sion, a secret group dedicated to preserving the "Holy Blood" and having the Merovingian dynasty control Europe once again. The secret of Sion or Zion is an ancient one. The search for Zion, as any Rastafarian from Jamaica will tell you, is the search for the Kingdom of God, the political paradise where all men are free, a nation in harmony with Gaia, the earth, and the karmic law of the universe: Do unto others as you would have them do unto you.

The ancient knowledge of Atlantis is said to have been passed down to the megalith builders of ancient France, as well as to Egypt.

David Wood in *GENISIS*[227] applies the geometry of Pythagoras onto the landscape of ancient France and finds that there was an astonishing correlation with the ancient sites of France, particularly on geometry based on Rennes-le-Château. Wood links various ancient churches in France together in a grid pattern that is similar to the work done by ley-line researchers in Britain.

Furthermore, Wood claims that the sacred knowledge preserved in this gigantic geomantic project came to a people who had a high knowledge of geometry, mathematics and the earth. These people, he claims, are the survivors of Atlantis. Where does Wood place the lost continent? He puts it where any good cataclysmist would, in the Atlantic Ocean with the mountaintops of Atlantis being the Azores.

And so Atlantis lives on in the mysteries of Rennes-le-Château and the Visigoths. The ancient power points of France were mapped out by ancient astronomers and geomancers to create a message for future generations. In Wood's second book, *GENESET*,[228] with Ian Campbell, he claims that the decoding of the geomantic landscape of France contained a warning to future generations of a comet catastrophe that was calculated to strike the earth.

From the hilltop village of Rennes-le-Château I looked out over the landscape at sunset. To the south was Montserrat and its caves, alleged to hold the Holy Grail in the Middle Ages. A few miles away was the Cathar fortress of Montségur. The shadow of Atlantis was cast out across the Pyrenees in the dying light. Were ancient secret societies from Atlantis struggling to recreate the ancient homeland in a new golden age of the future? The thought was intriguing.

> *Those who do not remember the past*
> *are condemned to repeat it.*
> —George Santayana (1863-1952)

The Great Pyramid of France

Atlantis and the World Grid were on my mind as I headed by train to Paris. Was France some ancient land with pyramids and obelisks designed as a marker for future man?

The French author on mysteries of the past, Robert Charroux, claims that there are a number of unrecognized pyramids and ancient sites in France.

Says Charroux in his book *The Gods Unknown*,[47] "The oldest civilized country in the world might be France, where flint tools and cave dwellings are found dating back at least 30,000 years before our era. It seems, however, that these facts are not enough to vouch for a civilization worthy of the name; that is to say, one which understood the uses of metals and wood and how to build stone houses. As though a house or a temple, an iron tool or a wooden bowl, could be expected to last for thirty or forty thousand years!

"But just try to make any reasonable being believe that the artists who painted the Montignac-Lascaux caves knew nothing about wrought iron and the mason's craft!

"Two separate laboratories have calculated that 25,000 years ago Africans in Malawi and Zambia worked haematite iron mines, with rich veins of copper. What did they do with these metals? We do not know; but the miners and the engineers who organized them must have had some idea!

"In 1964, some 125 miles north-east of Moscow, on the Sungir site, Otto Bader, the pre-historian, discovered burial-places which, from the strata in which they were found, must have been at least 30 to 40 thousand years old.

"The bodies, having been lying in frozen ground, were still in good condition. Beside them were found 7,500 bone ornaments and some kind of carved beads which had been sewn onto the garments. And the clothing, according to the discoverers, consisted of trousers, a pullover, and leather shoes.

"These prehistoric men, therefore, were not draped in indeterminate animal skins or bits of rag, but in actual properly-made, two-piece suits. They were, therefore, the report insists, quite modern—which should make some people revise their superficial, old-fashioned ideas."[47]

In his book *Masters of the World*,[60] Charroux writes about pyramids in France: "...in the village of Falicon, just above Nice, [an] invisible pyramid can be seen from a mile away. ...Nicholas Andréa, the mayor of Falicon, did me the honor of guiding me to Mont Cau, crossing a private estate that can be entered only by permission.

"A hundred yards from the top of Mont Cau stands the pyramid, made of stones joined by cement that is of better quality than Roman cement.

"Its sides are unequal because of its location on a steep slope and it is built over a fissure with an opening about eight feet wide. Its eastern side has a kind of doorway eight feet high. Until 1921 there was a carved swastika above the doorway, but it was then removed or destroyed by vandals. (The swastika was the sacred symbol of the Jains. It was also the sign of Manu...)

"Under the doorway is the entrance of the fissure. The pyramid stands over the cavity and cannot be entered. The orientation of the opening permits the sun, at ten o'clock on summer mornings to illuminate the white calcite pillar that supports the vault of the underground temple."[60]

Charroux says that the base of the pyramid is about 22 feet long and the capstone is missing. He says that the first known discoverer was an Italian named Rossetti in 1803. Charroux also says that the swastika or Jain cross that was once above the "entrance" to this pyramid is curious because "the oldest village in the region is called Jaïn or Jaïna on old maps. Its present name is Gaïna." Charroux then goes on to make the curious comment, "The Jains of India are said to have built pyramids as far away as Europe and South America."[60]

While it seems possible that this pyramid may be a natural hill and cavern system, Charroux mentions other pyramids in France. He claims that there is a pyramid near Autun, France, about a half mile from the town, halfway up the slope of Mount Briscou. He says the pyramid was originally higher than 80 feet with a quadrangular base of about 50 feet. Says Charroux, "The facing has been completely removed, but the masonry that remains is extremely solid."[60]

In Charroux's book, *Lost Worlds*,[10] he mentions two other pyramids in France, one at Plouézoch, in Brittany (six miles north of the town of Morlaix) and one at the town of Carnac, also in Brittany. The pyramid at Carnac is the well-known Saint-Michel mound near the center of town.

But the pyramid in France that Charroux champions the most is the Glozel pyramid. Says Charroux in *The Gods Unknown*, "Little is known about the Glozel civilization, except that it must have existed before the Flood, the great cataclysm which blocked the caves at Lascaux and swallowed up the necropolis or religious centre at Glozel, all the inhabitants having died in the disaster. By good fortune, some thousands of relics have been dug up and kept in a private museum—shingles, flints, jars, incised tablets, bone carvings, etc., which bear witness to a very fairly advanced culture, for the script of Glozel is the oldest known, and is undoubtedly the immediate ancestor of Phoenician writing."[10]

The Glozel civilization is known to the orthodox archaeologists of France, where it is largely thought to be an elaborate hoax. An article entitled "The Glozel Affair" appeared in the British journal *Nature* (257:355, 1975) by the archaeologist E.T. Hall.

Hall discusses the controversial nature of the Glozel discoveries: "In the world of professional archaeology of the 1920s and early 30s, the fact that you were a 'Glozelian' or 'Anti-Glozelian' determined who were your friends; this was particularly significant in an

academic discipline not unknown for acrimonious controversies. The
reason for this in-fighting was based on a reported discovery of
artifacts which to most archaeologists were—and to many still
are—unacceptable and were therefore labelled as fakes.

"The first pieces were reported in 1924 by a local farmer, Emile
Fradin, who is still very much alive living in the same farmhouse at
Glozel, an isolated village south of Vichy in France; these discoveries
were quickly followed by many more undertaken by a M. Morlet, a
doctor from Vichy. What caused the furor was the fact that these
objects were like nothing seen before anywhere in the world and
covered an amazing spectrum of different types. There were clay
tablets with mysterious incised inscriptions in an unknown
language, jars and other ceramics with and without inscriptions,
pottery phallic symbols, animals inscribed on bone and pebbles.

"None of these objects was recognizable archaeologically and even
if accepted as something new, many found it impossible to reconcile
the different periods represented apparently cheek by jowl; for
instance what might conceivably be neolithic incised stones were
apparently found in the same context as clay tablets with
inscriptions, which, some said, represented early Iberian scripts."[17]

The controversy about Glozel raged more or less continuously
until the War in 1939. During this time two international
commissions of inquiry sat and pronounced exactly opposite
decisions and some five lawsuits were fought with varying results. In
Britain the balance against the Glozelians was heavy although on
the continent such eminent archaeologists as Professor Reinach
were strongly opposed to the notion that deliberate forgery had
taken place.

Generally it was believed that Glozel was a fake and in 1974 Glyn
Daniel, Professor of Archaeology at Cambridge University, decided to
get final proof for his lecture on archaeological fakes and forgeries;
he would have a few pottery samples from Glozel tested using the
thermoluminescent (TL) technique in order to illustrate their
modern date. Professor Daniel was surprised at Cambridge when he
got the exact opposite result from what he had been expecting. As it
transpired, the TL measurements clearly indicated that the ceramics
were not modern, but seemed to have been manufactured in the
Gallo-Roman period. These results were published in the British
journal *Antiquity* in the December, 1974, issue.

According to Hall in his *Nature* article, "These results, which were
later more thoroughly confirmed by further measurements, have
again divided the archaeologists. To some the antiquity of the
ceramics in particular is no great surprise, although the admixture
of these ceramics in the same context as other less acceptable
material, such as engraved bone and pebbles of apparently Neolithic
date (which are less amenable to dating techniques), makes the

unravelling of the whole story very difficult. To other archaeologists the affair is still a distasteful hoax and TL dating must be in error; for them it is similar to telling a physicist that the laws of thermodynamics are no longer valid and, not surprisingly, they find it difficult even to listen."

Not surprisingly, modern science refuses to accept Glozel as an ancient site because the find would throw current theories on Europe's prehistory totally off. However, the experts in this case testify that Glozel is indeed an ancient site. Says Hall, "At the symposium on Archaeometry at Oxford University in March, details of the work undertaken by McKerrell at Edinburgh and Mejdahl in Denmark were given, and discussed at length by both physicists and archaeologists. There can now be little doubt that the ceramic material is not modern. ...The Glozel measurements would seem to show without doubt that the ceramics are not modern fakes, but it might be a little rash to differentiate with any complete confidence between, say, a Gallo-Roman and a medieval provenance."[17]

At least Charroux was vindicated concerning the authenticity of Glozel, a cause he championed for years. France was full of mysteries, and Charroux loved France.

Two other notable French authors on Atlantis are Jacques Bergier and Louis Pauwels. Their *Morning of the Magicians*,[251] published in the early '60s, was a milestone in occult investigations.

A letter to Bergier and Pauwels published in *INFO Journal* (No. 1, 1969) from a scientific lab in Caen, France, September 30, 1968, said: "As speleogists and investigators, we have studied for several years the Pays d'Auge region of Calvados. During the year 1968 we discovered some metallic nodules in a hollow in an Aptian chalk bed in a quarry being worked in Saint-Jean de Livet. These metallic nodules have a reddish brown color, a form absolutely identical (semi-ovoid), but are of different size.

"These nodules at first seemed to be fossils, but having examined them carefully we became conscious of their entirely metallic nature. Experiments at the forge showed that the carbon content was higher than castings of today. We were led to consider the hypothesis that they were meteorites, but five pieces were found all of the same nature, which led us to reject this hypothesis. There remains only an intelligent intervention in the Secondary Era (the end of the Cretaceous) of beings who could cast such objects. These objects, then, prove the presence of intelligent life on earth long before the limits given today by prehistoric archaeology."[17]

Another curious find of enigmatic ancient objects was made at Le Mas-d'Azil, 16 miles northwest of Foiz. During the course of excavations in the famous cave at Le Mas-d'Azil several thousand painted pebbles were discovered. They date from around 12,000 years ago, the period of transition between the Old Stone Age and the New Stone Age.

They are almost all oval-shaped, ringed by a line of paint and decorated on one side with an abstract sign—a cross, a circle, a stripe and so on. Some of the signs call to mind characteristics of Aegean, Phoenician and Cypriot writings, while others resemble signs that can be seen on some of the earliest cave paintings, which date back almost 20,000 years.[39]

What were these pebbles used for? Were they pieces of a game, coins, or stones endowed with magical power, like rune stones? The French prehistorian Edouard Piette, who discovered them at the end of the last century, believed that they were some sort of primitive writing. Perhaps a form of currency, like shells or tally sticks. More and more we have to revise our view on prehistory. For years we have excluded the facts instead of adjusting our perceptions.

〰〰〰〰〰🜚〰〰〰〰〰

Atlantis Rising...

It was a rainy September night when the train arrived in Paris. I took a taxi to a small hotel in the Latin Quarter. Paris is enjoyable, and I had been there before. At the Ile de la Cité I enjoyed going beneath the plaza near the Cathedral where one was in the ruins below modern Paris, in the Roman and pre-Roman streets of the small river island.

While staying in Paris, meeting with some French publishers, I met with a couple of old friends in a café in the Latin Quarter. They were Eric, a photographer friend of mine who lives in New York City, and Morrey, from the World Explorers Club in Illinois.

We talked of history, Atlantis and mysteries of the past. Paris had often been a haven for occultists, free-thinkers and the literary set. Atlantis was a topic that was popular and discussed by many.

For instance, in the short book *Prophecies of Great World Changes*[197] by George Brownell (1927), it was reported that a group met in Paris to pray that Atlantis not rise up from the ocean.

According to Brownell, who wrote on prophecies of World War II and Armageddon, "Jean Buvais, the sage of Notre Dame de Laguet, has invited penniless gamblers to a 40-day prayer meeting in the mountains just back of Monte Carlo. Buvais is organizing this meeting in the hope of saving Europe from a calamity which he thinks is on the way. This sage has great power over the peasants and shepherds for miles around. He has been foretelling the future for 40 years and his disciples claim for him a 90 per cent record of truthful predictions. The prayer meeting is called to prevent the lost continent of Atlantis from arising from the ocean bed, and causing the wickedest sections of the world to disappear."[197]

Since Atlantis hasn't risen from the ocean yet, we can presume that Buvais and his prayer group were satisfied with their success in keeping the lost continent from suddenly emerging.

Why did Buvais and his group want to keep Atlantis from rising? Most occult groups would probably want it to rise out of the ocean. Well, the reason was that a cataclysm would occur at the same time, destroying much of Europe, Africa and America. Indeed, the rising of Atlantis would be a cataclysmic disaster for millions of people. It is just such a disaster that is said to be looming on the horizon—a cataclysmic pole shift with its attendant earth changes.

Only 30 miles south of Paris is the mysterious Forest of Fontainebleau. This forest, which is now a popular recreation area, was an isolated region for thousands of years. It was a haunt of robbers, fringe dwellers and fugitives who sheltered in its caves and carved the walls with inscriptions, designs and abstract signs. More than 2,300 square yards of rock are decorated in this way.

Among the carvings are human figures with rectangular bodies, neck-less heads with sunken eyes and U-shaped noses. Their arms are outstretched, with the fingers spread like a fan, and often the legs are missing. A second group, in bas-relief, have their arms close to their bodies. In a third, the figures are dressed in skirts and have only three fingers on each hand.

Archaeologists are at a loss as to who made these rock carvings. The crosses, circles and hopscotch-like designs are almost impossible to date. They may be from prehistoric times, or they could have been carved a short time ago. All have been indexed and some are similar to designs which specialists have located elsewhere. However, there are some designs which are found only at Fontainebleau. These are the irregular latticed designs which have been deeply incised into the rock. They have been found in the most inaccessible places, in cavities where only an arm can reach. One can only wonder as to why these engravings were made under such obviously difficult conditions and what message their engravers wished to leave.

Chartres Cathedral and the Knights Templar

Nights of carousing through late-night Paris came to an abrupt halt the day I suddenly decided to rent a car. With a car, I had to be driving, so I offered Eric and Morrey a ride to Brittany if they wanted it. Eric had to go to his family's cottage in southern France, but Morrey was ready to go.

So, on a late September morning Morrey and I headed out of Paris, darting through downtown traffic and jumping on to the mass of freeways that encircled the sprawling city. I drove while Morrey navigated us to the road to Chartres, keeping the Eiffel Tower in the distance to our right.

Soon we were out of the city and shortly thereafter arrived at Chartres, one of the most famous cathedrals in France. We got rooms at a pension and explored the cathedral. It was dark inside, but this made it easier to view the fabulous stained-glass windows. We walked around the inside of the cathedral and I was particularly interested in the stained-glass window that held the zodiac. Chartres, it has been said, is an embodiment of ancient science and geometry in stone.

In his book *The Mysteries of Chartres Cathedral*[249] Louis Charpentier claims that Chartres is a repository for ancient wisdom that is equal to Stonehenge, the Temple of Solomon or the Great Pyramid of Egypt. He further claims that special knowledge about the Temple in Jerusalem was gained by a group of nine knights who lived at Solomon's Temple. Charpentier tells us it is historically recorded that in the year 1118 nine "French" knights presented themselves to King Baldwin II of Jerusalem and explained that they planned to form themselves into a company with a plan for protecting pilgrims from robbers and murderers along the public highways leading into Jerusalem. They also asked to be housed within a wing of the palace, a wing which happened to be adjacent to the Dome of the Rock mosque which was built on the site of Solomon's Temple.

The king granted their request and the legend of the Order of the Knights of Solomon's Temple or Knights Templar was born. Ten years later the nine knights presented themselves to the Pope, who gave his official approval to the Knights Templar. Although only nine mysterious knights existed, a tenth joined them, who was the Count of Champagne, an important French noble.

In fact, none of the "poor" knights was apparently poor, nor were they all French. Several came from important French and Flemish families. Of the ten original knights, four have not been identified, although their names are known. Furthermore, it seems unlikely that the Knights of the Temple of Solomon were formed to protect the pilgrims to Jerusalem because such an order of Knights already existed. They were the Knights Hospitallers or Knights of St. John, later to become the Knights of Malta, and a secret society for the Vatican.

Charpentier likens the original band of Knights Templar to a commando raid on the ancient Temple of Solomon in order to uncover its engineering secrets and possible lost treasure such as the Ark of the Covenant, possibly hidden deep in a strange cavern system beneath the temple.

With the help of the brilliant French abbot Bernard de Clairvaux, the nine knights, directed by the Count of Champagne, created the Knights Templar and built the cathedral at Chartres.

Incorporated into the cathedral are beautiful stained-glass windows, many of the colors difficult or impossible to duplicate today. Hidden within the cathedral are various ancient "cubits" of measure, plus such esoteric devices as the famous Chartres Maze and other visual tools such as sacred geometry, for personal transformation—a sort of personal alchemy of the soul. Included in the imagery was the quest for the Holy Grail.

All this was happening during the Dark Ages when knowledge and free-thinking were suppressed by the Church, the original "thought police." Within the confines of Chartres a special knowledge of the past was being preserved and literally engraved in stone for future generations. It was engineering knowledge (and much more) that went back to early builders of the pyramids in Egypt and, according to legend, to Atlantis itself.

The Sunken Temples of Carnac

Eventually our drive across France brought us to ancient Carnac in Brittany. Located on the south coast of Brittany, Carnac holds the greatest concentration of megaliths in the world. Conservative estimates claim that megaliths were being erected here by 5,000 B.C., nearly seven thousand years ago.

Morrey and I found a pension in the town of Locmariaquer, site of what may be the largest menhir in the world, and then set out to explore the Carnac region. Our first stop was a gigantic, broken menhir on the edge of town.

The Grand Menhir Brisé at Er Grah, Brittany, is said to be the largest menhir in the world and is situated on a promontory near the water. The problems of moving such a huge stone are illustrated in an article published in the *Journal for the History of Astronomy* (No. 2, pages 147-160, 1971) entitled "The Astronomical Significance of the Large Carnac Menhirs."[17] The astronomers, Mr. and Mrs. Thom, maintain that "Er Grah, or The Stone of the Fairies, sometimes known as Le Grand Menhir Brisé, is now broken in four pieces which when measured show that the total length must have been at least 67 ft. From its cubic content it is estimated to weigh over 340 tons.

"Hulle thinks it came from the Cote Sauvage on the west coast of the Quiberon Peninsula. His suggestion that it was brought round by sea takes no account of the fact that the sea level relative to this coast was definitely lower in Megalithic times; neither does he take account of the fact that a raft of solid timber about 100 x 50 x 4 ft.

would be necessary—with the menhir submerged. It is not clear how such a raft could be controlled or indeed moved in the tidal waters round the Peninsula.

"Assuming that the stone came by land, a prepared track (? of timber) must have been made for the large rollers necessary and a pull of perhaps 50 tons applied (how?) on the level, unless indeed the rollers were rotated by levers. It took perhaps decades of work and yet there it lies, a mute reminder of the skill, energy and determination of the engineers who erected it more than three thousand years ago.

"In Britain we find that the tallest stones are usually lunar backsights, but there seems no need to use a stone of this size as a backsight. If, on the other hand, it was a foresight, the reason for its position and height becomes clear, especially if it was intended as a universal foresight to be used from several directions. There are eight main values to consider, corresponding to the rising and setting of the Moon at the standstills when the declination was plus or minus. ...It has now been shown that there is at least one site on each of the eight lines which has the necessary room for side movement.

"We must now try to think of how a position was found for Er Grah which would have satisfied the requirements. Increasingly careful observations of the Moon had probably been made for hundreds of years. These would have revealed unexplained anomalies due to variations in parallax and refraction, and so it may have been considered necessary to observe at the major and minor standstills at both rising and setting. At each standstill there were 10 or 12 lunations when the monthly declination maximum and minimum could be used. At each maximum or minimum, parties would be out at all possible places trying to see the Moon rise or set behind high trial poles. At night these poles would have needed torches at the tops because any other marks would not be visible until actually silhouetted on the Moon's disc. Meantime some earlier existing observatory must have been in use so that erectors could be kept informed about the kind of maximum which was being observed; they would need to know the state of the perturbation.

"Then there would ensue the nine years of waiting till the next standstill when the other four sites were being sought. The magnitude of the task was enhanced by the decision to make the same foresight serve both standstills. We can understand why this was considered necessary when we think of the decades of work involved in cutting, shaping, transporting and erecting one suitable foresight. It is evident that whereas some of the sites, such as Quiberon, used the top of the foresight of Er Grah, others, such as Kerran, used the lower portion. This probably militated against the use of a mound with a smaller menhir on the top. Much has rightly been written about the labour of putting Er Grah in position, but a full consideration of the labour of finding the site shows that this may have been a comparable task.

"We now know that for a stone 60 ft. high the sighting is perfect. We do not know that all the backsights were completed. But the fact that we have not yet found any trace of a sector to the east does not prove that the eastern sites were not used because the stones may have been removed. Perhaps the extrapolation was done by the simpler triangle method or perhaps it was done at a central site like Petit Menec."[17]

Francis Hitching in *Earth Magic*[244] also agrees that this was a central sighting megalith for sighting moonrises and moonsets.

Much of this gigantic astronomical observatory is probably under water. Many of the megaliths along the Brittany coast are apparently submerged. Many famous sites actually lead into the water, and some megaliths can be seen at low tide when they are barely above the surface.

Many of the long lines of standing stones at Carnac and around the Morbihan Gulf were apparently built when the geography of Brittany was quite different.

We drove on to the town of Carnac and the famous alignment of hundreds of standing stones. They too are apparently part of some huge astronomical observatory. In another article by the Thoms entitled "The Carnac Alignments" for the *Journal for the History of Astronomy* (No. 3, pages 11-26, 1972),[17] they conclude that Carnac is also a lunar observatory of vast proportions. Say the Thoms about the Menec alignments at Carnac, "A remarkable feature is the great accuracy of measurement with which the rows were set out. It cannot be too strongly emphasized that the precision was far greater than could have been achieved by using ropes. The only alternative available to the erectors was to use two measuring rods (of oak or whale bone?). These were probably 6.802 ft. long, shaped on the ends to reduce the error produced by malalignment. Each rod would be rigidly supported to be level but we can only surmise how the engineers dealt with the inevitable 'steps' when the ground was not level.

"It may be noted that the value for the Megalithic yard found in Britain is 2.720 plus or minus 0.003 ft. and that found above is 2.721 plus or minus 0.001 ft. Such accuracy is today attained only by trained surveyors using good modern equipment. How then did Megalithic Man not only achieve it in one district but carry the unit to other districts separated by greater distances? How was the unit taken, for example, northwards to the Orkney Islands? Certainly not by making copies of copies of copies. There must have been some apparatus for standardizing the rods which almost certainly were issued from a controlling, or at least advising, centre."[17]

The Thoms see Carnac as part of an ancient and huge system that was used over much of Europe. In their article they conclude, "The organization and administration necessary to build the Breton alignments and erect Er Grah obviously spread over a wide area, but the evidence of the measurements shows that a very much wider area was in close contact with the central control. The geometry of the two egg-shaped cromlechs at Le Menec is identical with that found in British sites. The apices of triangles with integral sides forming the centres for arcs with integral radii are features in common, and on both sides of the Channel the perimeters are multiples of the rod.

"The extensive nature of the sites in Brittany may suggest that this was the main centre, but we must not lose sight of the fact that so far none of the Breton sites examined has a geometry comparable with that found at Avebury in complication of design, or in difficulty of layout.

"It has been shown elsewhere that the divergent stone rows in Caithness could have been used as ancillary equipment for lunar observations, and in our former paper we have seen that the Petit Menec and St. Pierre sites were probably used in the same way." The Thoms confess at the end of their article, "We do not know how the main Carnac alignments were used..."[17]

As I walked through the many rows of standing stones, I was amazed at the colossal scope of this prehistoric project 7,000 years ago. Clearly an organized effort by a learned and sophisticated population was necessary to achieve the result that is Carnac. But who were these people? Where did they go? Where was their capital city?

Carnac likens itself to the important Egyptian Temple of Karnak. The Egyptian Karnak is a huge building which also has long rows of megalithic columns which once supported a huge roof. The French Carnac reminded me of the rows of columns at the Egyptian Karnak. Had Carnac once had a roof? It seemed unlikely, I admitted as the sun began to set to the west. The stones stood tall against the orange sky. Would they ever tell their secrets?

The Sunken City of Ys

After a few days in the Carnac area we drove north along the coast, heading for Brest. Midway along the coast we came to Quimper, which some say is the lost land of Ys. Just 11 miles northwest of Quimper is the Bay of Douarnenez where the legend is told of the sunken land of Ys, an Atlantis-type story centered around this area of enigmatic megaliths.

The legend of Ys tells of a flourishing city that once stood on the

Bay of Douarnenez, with an embankment to protect it from high seas. A gate in the embankment was opened at low tide for the water from the river to flow out. It was then closed at high tide, and only the good King Gradlon of Ys had the key to it.

The king's daughter, beautiful Dahut, was dissolute and perverse and one day met the Devil in the form of a handsome young man. She had an affair with him and to test her love, the Devil asked her to steal the key to the sea gate from her father. When she gave him the key, the devil then opened the dike gate and the sea flowed in and Ys was submerged. All its inhabitants were drowned with the exception of the king, who raced for the mainland on horseback, his daughter riding behind him. The waves pursued him as he rode for higher ground and when he was about to be washed away, the celestial voice of St. Gwenole told him to cast off the demon who was sitting behind him into the sea. With aching heart he did so and immediately the waters receded.

His daughter became a mermaid who is known as Marie-Morgane. With her beauty she is said to still lure sailors to the bottom of the sea. She will remain cursed until the Good Friday when Mass is celebrated in one of the churches of the drowned city.

King Gradlon made it to the mainland and chose Quimper as his new capital. We stopped at the town square to see his statue between the two towers of the cathedral.

Was there once a city where the Bay of Douarnenez is now? Ancient structures have been reported in the bay at the beach of Le Ris, one and a half miles from Douarnenez. Some have reported seeing walls that have silted up. How old are they? The legend places the catastrophe in Christian times, but legends often modernize ancient events. It could possibly have been a Roman or Celtic town, or even built in the same period as were the megalithic monuments.

The presence of legendary sunken cities is a good indication that earth changes and a destruction of a civilization in the past has occurred. There are plenty of submerged and partially submerged megaliths throughout Brittany. The legend of Ys may be a folktale based on the actual submersion of the west coast of Brittany. This event may have happened only a few thousand years ago.

One example of a known submerged megalithic structure is the Covered Alleyway of Kernic in the District of Plousescat, Finistére, now submerged at high tide.[250]

Vitrified Forts of France
Among the many mysteries of Europe and the Mediterranean are the vitrified forts that are occasionally to be found. Vitrified forts in

France are discussed in the *American Journal of Science* (Volume 3, Number 22, pages 150-151, 1881), which had an article entitled "On the Substances Obtained From Some 'Forts Vitrifies' in France" by M. Daubree.

The author mentions several vitrified forts in Brittany and northern France whose granite blocks have been vitrified. He cites the "partially fused granitic rocks from the forts of Chateau-vieux and of Puy de Gaudy (Creuse), also from the neighborhood of Saint Brieuc (Cotes-du-Nord)."[17] Daubree, understandably, could not readily find an explanation for the vitrification.

Morrey and I stopped in Brest and then took in various megalithic sites along the north Brittany coast as we drove to Mont-Saint-Michel. We drove toward the tall spires of the ancient walled city and cathedral on the tiny rock in the bay.

"Wow, this is a photo opportunity," exclaimed Morrey, reaching for his ever-present camera. It was late afternoon when we walked up the winding street past restaurants and souvenir shops to the church.

It is thought that Mont-Saint-Michel was once connected to the continent, but today at high tide the water can be 15 meters deep. At low tide the jumble of buildings and church spires sits on a barren mud beach stretching many kilometers into the distance. Quicksand can be found in this treacherous tidal flat.

According to Celtic mythology Mont-Saint-Michel was one of the sea tombs to which the souls of the dead were conveyed. In 708 A.D. the Archangel Michael reputedly appeared to Aubert, Bishop of Avranches, and told him to build a devotional chapel at the top of the mount.

According to authors like John Michell in *The View Over Atlantis*[13] and other works, Mont-Saint-Michel is part of a system of ancient sacred sites that stretch all the way from Jerusalem to Greece, France and England. This is the so-called Michael Line, of which Mont-Saint-Michel is part. Across the English channel, on the same line, is Saint Michael's Mount in Cornwall.

In the late afternoon sun I looked up at the glittering gold statue of Michael and the Dragon that crowned the high spires of the church. It was an inspiring site. Mysteries lay all around us, and sometimes we must look upward to get the view we need.

As the sun set over the north coast of Brittany, I thought of how the land in Brittany, and indeed all of France, seemed alive with the past. The vibrancy of the present was in direct relationship with the energies of the past. Were the standing stones of Europe like crystal acupuncture needles used to geomance the living earth? Answers to these questions would have to wait until I got to Britain, another country still alive with the ancient past.

Stone avenue alignments at Carnac in Brittany.

The stones of Carnac in Brittany as depicted in an old print.

The stones of Carnac in Brittany as depicted in an old print.

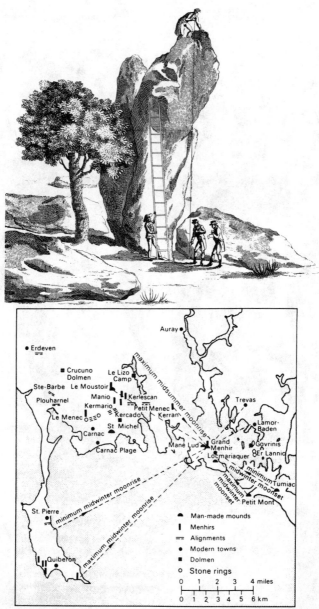

Top: Measuring a Carnac menhir in 1805. Bottom: The British astronomer A. Thom's map demonstrating how the great menhir of Er Grah could have been used as a universal lunar foresight for observations from various positions around it. Are other menhirs submerged in the surrounding bay?

One side of the "pyramid" of Plouézoch in Brittany.

The large megalithc dolmen at La Roche aux Fées à Esse, France.

Old print of a cross carved onto one of the Carnac megaliths.

A Doré engraving of the Brittany legend of the drowning of the Kingdom of Ys.

This 2-meter long engraving on the interior of the Labastide Cave in the Hautes-Pyrées Department of France. appears to depict a wild horse with a single horn on his forehead—a unicorn.

Chapter 10

GERMANY, HOLLAND & EASTERN EUROPE:

The Northern Atlantis

*Belief is not the beginning
but the end of all knowledge.*
—Johann Wolfgang von Goethe

It was a rainy afternoon when Morrey and I pulled into Amsterdam in our rented Peugeot.

I had been to Amsterdam before but it had been some years since I had visited this international city of travellers. As rain pounded the narrow streets and canals of the city, Morrey and I hopped from café to café, looking for some friends we had arranged to meet. Eventually we met up with Harry, my friend from Greece, and Herman, a publisher and crop circle researcher who lives in a small town outside of Amsterdam.

We all had a cold beer and sat at a table in Susie's Saloon to discuss Atlantis and the lost cities of the North Sea. Atlantis, many authors have suggested, was nearby.

Atlantis of the North

In 1954 a German archaeologist and minister named Jürgen Spanuth believed that he had found Atlantis in the submerged land north of Heligoland in the North Sea. He claimed that a huge sunken city lay five miles north of the Heligoland peninsula.

Spanuth, in his book *Atlantis of the North*,[237] claimed that he had explored a sunken, walled city that lay 50 feet beneath the shallow North Sea waters. He was convinced that this ancient city was from an advanced civilization linked to Atlantis.

Using Plato as his guide, Spanuth read that two of the principal

323

landmarks of Basilea, the capital of Atlantis, were the royal citadel and the great temple. According to Plato's account, the royal citadel was six miles from the coast and surrounded by a wall that was 3,035 feet in circumference.

Spanuth claimed in his book that his sunken city had a virtually undamaged wall surrounding it with a circumference of 3,956 feet. This was enough of a coincidence for Spanuth to believe his sunken city of the North Sea was the possible explanation for the Atlantis mystery. Everything seemed to fit: it was a sunken city beyond the Pillars of Hercules with a wall around it almost the same size as that described by Plato.

Spanuth claimed that the streets of the North Sea city were paved with molded slabs of firestone, and there was ample evidence to indicate that the forgotten inhabitants had mastered the craft of smelting ore.

However, Spanuth did not believe that Plato's date of 8000 B.C. was correct. He estimated that the submergence of the North Sea city was approximately 1200 B.C., only about 800 years before Plato's time.

Spanuth's lost Atlantis is in the submerged North Sea area around Heligoland and Denmark. He argues that a huge earthquake circa 1200 B.C. inundated the coastal area around Holland, Germany and Denmark and submerged the capital city, Basilea. With their capital destroyed, a flotilla of ships from "Atlantis" then invaded the Mediterranean.

Therefore, the mysterious Sea Peoples who attacked the eastern Mediterranean about 1200 B.C. were from the North Sea and Heligoland. According to Egyptian reliefs showing the defeat of the Sea Peoples, these invaders wore horned helmets exactly like those of the ancient Danes.[237]

〰〰〰〰〰🐟〰〰〰〰〰

The Oera Linda Book and Lost Atland

Similar to Spanuth's book are *The Other Atlantis*[253] and *Secrets of Lost Atland*[254] by Robert Scrutton. Scrutton also champions a proto-Viking Atlantis called Atland also located in the North Sea.

Scrutton uses the ancient Dutch manuscript, the *Oera Linda Book*, as a reference for his works. The *Oera Linda Book* is sometimes called the oldest book in the world and a number of authors believe that this ancient book holds a key to the Atlantis riddle.

In February of 1871 a Frisian antiquarian revealed the existence of a very strange manuscript which had apparently been in the possession of a local family for generations and had been handed down from father to son as a holy obligation. Originally the writing appeared to be in an unknown language, but eventually it was established that the writing was in the script and tongue of a very ancient dialect of Frisian.

The *Oera Linda Book* was immediately controversial because it spoke of a lost land called Atland that had existed in the North Sea. There was brief interest in the *Oera Linda Book* in Holland, Germany and England but because of the unusual content of the book, it was branded a hoax and forgery.

Dozens of articles and books appeared in Dutch, German and English discussing this. Most were critical of the *Oera Linda Book*, some saying it had been forged as recently as 1775. Yet, believers ask why a forger would write in old Frisian, a dead language since the 13th century. Most Dutch have heard of the *Oera Linda Book*; the original is still kept by the Linden family. To my knowledge, it is not on display.

The content of the *Oera Linda Book* is summed up by Scrutton as follows: "A large, semi-circular land mass, a sort of silhouette halo around the north and east of the British Isles, was contemporary with the conjectured Atlantis. It survived the traditional Atlantis, however, by many thousands of years.

"Its name was Atland, and there may be reason to suppose that Atland was the archetype of the Hyperborean tradition.

"Although situated between what are now the storm-striken Hebrides and the Greenland permafrost, Atland was no impoverished continent. On the contrary, its climate was subtropical, yielding abundance of everything for full and happy human existence. ...In the year 2193 B.C., some cosmic calamity struck Mother Earth; perhaps some imbalance of the kind suggested by Immanuel Velikovsky... perhaps an asteroid collided with the earth. At any rate, from descriptions in the *Oera Linda Book*, something consistent with a tilting of the earth's axis took place and, within about three days, climatic changes of overwhelming severity took place. Atland was submerged and her history lost ...or nearly so.

"According to the *Oera Linda Book*, the Atlanders were a maritime nation who had charted the seas of the world and sailed to the Mediterranean and colonists were already established in Scandinavia and Northern and Southern Europe, Africa and Greece."[253]

Scrutton goes on to say that the exact date of the catastrophe that destroyed Atland is 2193 B.C., according to the *Oera Linda Book*. "Was this the upheaval which sent an Atlantic tidal wave through the Pillars of Hercules and flooded the Middle East, giving rise to the legends of the Deluge, the Ark and Mount Ararat?" asks Scrutton.

In his second book, *Secrets of Lost Atland,* Scrutton went beyond his comet catastrophe scenario and the lost land of the North Sea. Scrutton devotes most of the book to the "Wisdom of the Ancients" and their knowledge of a coordinated system of "psycho-electric science or cosmology" that spanned the world. Evidence for this ancient "earth grid" of energy can be found in the stone circles, artificial hills, sacred sites, meditation chambers and altars. All of these were connected by ley lines and underground streams that formed an energy network that surrounded the globe.

Says Scrutton, "In pre-History times mental and biochemical energy were combined with telluric energies triggered into activity by Lunar and solar radiations, and used to give static charges to stratas of rock, key stones and sacred places. The ancient world had its astronomers, mathematicians, geologists and engineers with skills unheard of today. Neuro-electric energies were used for providing a strange form of illumination, to lighten heavy objects, to separate inertia from gravity, so that an object would hang in the air without physical support. Mass emotion and veneration were combined with life forces to speed the development of crops. Sometimes they were centered on a person to heal mind or body, or on a priest-scientist to enhance his intuitional faculties for the solving of various problems.

"The ancients used their psycho-electric science in order to discover many of Nature's secrets. Expensive equipment costing millions of dollars was totally unnecessary. All knowledge and wisdom were obtained intuitionally and applied with often small and simple artifacts of stone and metal fashioned into special geometric designs."[254]

Scrutton's "secret of Atland" seems a lot like the Vril power proposed by Bulwer-Lytton in the mid-1800s and later used as the name for a secret society in Germany at the turn of the century. In a similar way we can see the vortex patterns on ancient stones such as Newgrange and the use of granite standing stones and obelisks as acupuncture needles or antennas on the landscape. John Michell's landmark book *The View Over Atlantis*[13] is one of the original works proposing a planned, worldwide system of earth energies that can be viewed by looking at the geometry of megaliths and sacred sites on the landscape.

I liked Scrutton's books; they were an exciting mix of far-out archaeology, lost continents and speculative esoteric science. His Atland seemed analogous to the lost lands of Thule or Hyperborea. Another occult group in Germany, besides the Vril Society, was the Thule Group. Both delved into such topics as Vril-type earth energies and a lost continent of Nordic peoples: a Valhalla of the past, Asgard, home of the ancient gods, who were once men. Ignatius Donnelly's second book on the Atlantis theme was entitled

Ragnarok and it was about the Scandinavian myths of a cataclysm.

"Scrutton is on to something," I told Morrey, Harry and Herman around the table at Susie's Saloon.

"Do you think that Atland was a lost continent in the Arctic?" asked Herman, finishing an orange juice.

"Well, I think I prefer Jürgen Spanuth's explanation better," I answered. "His Atland is part of the continental shelf of Northern Europe, with the capital city near Heligoland. It seems likely that there is indeed a sunken city there."

"It shows that earth changes are happening all the time," said Morrey.

"Amsterdam is 40 meters below sea level," Harry pointed out.

"Is that right?" asked Morrey, astonished. "You mean we're already under water?"

"Yes, that's right," said Herman. "Many of the towns of Holland are below sea level."

"With a small shift of the North Atlantic tectonic plate," I mused, "Amsterdam and most of Holland could become inundated by a huge wave; a literal rushing of the Atlantic would occur."

"And Amsterdam would become a lost city!" exclaimed Herman. "You can write about it in one of your future lost cities books."

"If Amsterdam is going to be a lost city," said Morrey, "I'm going to have another beer." And with that, we all laughed.

~~~~~~~~~~⳨~~~~~~~~~~

Two days later I went down to the old Magic Bus company, now called Budget Bus, and bought a ticket across Germany to Budapest. The old Magic Bus company used to go from Amsterdam to Katmandu back in the '60s and '70s. Those days were gone, however. Once I got to Budapest, I decided I would spend a few weeks taking trains around Eastern Europe.

I spent a day on a bus rolling through Germany's forests and green, fertile land. As I viewed the countryside, I pondered on the whole Atlantis-of-the-North scenario and the Dutch connection to Atlantis. Like Atlanteans and the ancient people of yore, the Dutch were tall people. The Dutch, and possibly the Norwegians, are the tallest people in Europe.

The Dutch have a unique language, a language older than German, which is the closest relative to Dutch. They also have a history of fighting the sea to regain the lost land that was slowly being taken from them. It was certainly interesting to think of the Dutch and the Flemish as being derived from Atland or Atlantis.

One of the best authors on Atlantis was the German archaeologist Otto Muck who wrote the well-known book *The Secret of Atlantis*.[29]

Muck saw Atlantis as a great empire in the Atlantic as Plato had said, and believed that it was ultimately destroyed by a meteor shower.

Like Scrutton, Muck argues for a meteor cataclysm. Muck's Atlantis, however, is placed around the Azores and the mid-Atlantic ridge. The main theme in his book is that a comet hit the earth about 10,000 years ago and wiped out mankind's first civilization, "Atlantis." There followed two thousand years of darkness and severe weather conditions, a literal dark age. Eventually civilization returned with its dim memories of the "flood."

Cleverly, Muck is even able to come up with an exact day and year by using the beginning of the Mayan calendar. He theorizes that a catastrophic event of a meteor hitting the Atlantic would be important enough to start a new dating system. He reasons that the best calendar system to use for this is the ancient Mayan Tzolkin count, which begins on June 5, 8498 B.C. This date is known as Zero Day A to Mayanists, and Muck maintains that this is the exact same day that the comet hit the earth and Atlantis sank.[29]

The Amber Trade and Ancient Electricity

My first stop in Eastern Europe was Budapest, two cities, Buda and Pest, one on either side of the Danube. To the south of Hungary was the worsening war in the former Yugoslavia. The various ethnic groups were busy destroying each other's cities in fighting that seems to have no end. Warfare is creating modern ruins in these countries while ancient ruins are under water along the Adriatic coast.

One such lost city is in the Bay of Dubrovnik. In the clear water of the bay the remains of a long stone wall of a submerged town can be seen. According to legend, one of several towns named Epidaurus was in Illyria, at the very place where Dubrovnik now stands.

Tradition says, however, that the Epidaurians of Illyria settled on that spot after a first Epidaurus had been submerged by the waters of the bay. According to the same tradition, the founders of the vanished city came from Phoenicia.

Ancient Hungary was central to the major trade routes coming from Greece and the eastern Mediterranean. The area was controlled by the mysterious Scythians, and farther north were the Hyperboreans. The route through Eastern Europe was the Amber route, a river and overland route to Denmark where amber could be found. Amber was very valuable in the ancient world, and is still sought after in the Middle East today.

Jerry Zeigler in his book *YHWH: A Book On Ancient Electricity,*[113] proposes that many ancient shrines and sacred fires were actually electric lights or other simple electric phenomena. Zeigler says that amber is a key component to creating a simple static electrical display such as sparks from a metal ball or lighting effects. Impressive to someone who has never seen it before.

In fact, the Greek name for amber is elektron, and the modern words electricity and electronics are derived from it. Says my *Columbia Viking Desk Encyclopedia* (1968 edition) under Amber: "fossil resin exuded as gum by coniferous trees in past geologic time... Ancient Greeks knew that rubbing it with fur produced static electricity."

The Scythians controlled much of the amber trade and trade around the Black Sea as well. They are said to have spoken an "Indo-Aryan" language, though it is long dead and probably beyond classification. Scythian may well have been related to such oddball (unrelated to other) languages as Hungarian, Finnish or the Uiger language of the Gobi Desert and western Mongolia.

A Scythian burial from about 500 B.C. was discovered in Pazyryk, southern Siberia, in the early 1960s. The bodies of several men had been preserved by perpetual ice inside the mountainside tomb chambers. What is amazing about the find is the excellent preservation of the bodies and the elaborate tattoos over the men's arms and shoulders.

The men's entire arms, shoulders, and partial backs and chests were covered with finely made tattoos of rams, antelopes, lions, monkeys and other animal designs. The art of tattooing is widespread and it is curious to wonder what relationship the Scythians may have had with the Polynesians, a tall Caucasian race that covered their bodies with similar tattoos. One might wonder if the tall, red-haired mummies discovered in western China recently were once originally covered with tattoos.

Modern Atlantis lore such as that of the Lemurian Fellowship or the Theosophical Society holds that a portion of the "Right Thinking" population of Atlantis were air-lifted out of Atlantis onto the high plateau of Central Asia. Later these "Caucasians" spread north, west and to Asia Minor.

These same mysterious invaders were apparently the Aryan invaders of India, those "Caucasians" who brought the Vedas and Sanskrit with them. They mingled with the many original ethnic groups of India such as the Dravidians and Nagas. It was the ancient Dravidians and Nagas who had formed the legendary "Rama Empire," while the Aryan invaders from Central Asia came much later, circa 5,000 to 3,000 B.C.

The Scythians may have been descendants of Atlantis, though it is an idle thought. More interesting would be the suggestion that the

Polynesians, including the mysterious Easter Islanders, were the descendants of the Scythians.

No one seemed heavily tattooed as I walked through the streets of Budapest. I enjoyed the city, busy by Hungarian standards, but lazy compared to Western Europe. But it was a tour by train through the countryside of Scythia that I desired.

The Moon-shaft & Dr. Gurlt's Cube

Hungary is great for local trains making their way to small towns surrounded by vineyards and fields of paprika peppers. I climbed castle walls and visited wine cellars. Slowly I worked my way east to the Slovak Republic, which had been split away from Czechoslovakia.

Eastern Europe has its antediluvian mysteries too. Jacques Bergier, when he was the editor of Ivan T. Sanderson's *INFO Journal*, published two intriguing collections of anomalous data. One of the articles was on the mysterious Moon-shaft in a remote cave in Czechoslovakia (now two different countries).

According to Bergier, during the Slovak uprising in October 1944, towards the end of World War II, a Dr. Antonin T. Horak discovered an unusual cave near the villages of Plavince and Lubocna, in the Tatra Mountains of Slovakia. Horak crawled through a crack in a natural cave and came to a curious, rock-cut chamber in the shape of a crescent moon.[251]

This bizarre shaft had smooth walls and could only have been artificially made, Horak concluded. Another shaft went deep underground but Horak could not follow it. He shot several rifle shots into the long shaft and could not hear the bullets hit the end; they ricocheted down the shaft.

Horak eventually determined that the sides were not of the same stone as the rest of the cave and that it was some sort of gigantic artificial device that had somehow gotten inside this mountain, perhaps during some volcanic upheaval.

Dr. Horak later wrote about his explorations in the moon-shaft in the March, 1965, *Journal of the Czech National Speleological Society.* Said Horak about the strange cave, "What is this structure, with walls two meters thick and a shape that I cannot imagine of any purpose known nowadays? How far does it reach into the rocks? Is there more behind the 'moon-shaft'? Which incident or who put it into this mountain: Is it a fossilized man-made object? Is there truth in legends, like Plato's, about long lost civilizations with magic technologies which our rationale cannot grasp nor believe?"[251]

Bergier also tells the strange story of Dr. Gurlt's "cube," a strange object found in a German coal mine in 1865. Dr. Gurlt discovered the metallic cube himself; it was "deeply embedded in a layer (of coal) dating from the tertiary."

Dr. Gurlt went public with the find in 1886, convinced after long study that the cube was an artificial object that was tens of millions of years old. The object was nearly a perfect cube, with two opposing faces of the cube being rounded slightly. It measured about four centimeters by two centimeters and weighed about 28 ounces. Testing showed that it was made of hard carbon-and-nickle steel. It did not contain enough sulfur to be iron-pyrite, which sometimes takes cube-like geometric shapes.

Though some people suggested that it was a meteorite, it was generally thought that the cube was some sort of man-made puzzle from the past. Other strange artifacts like this are clearly manufactured objects, such as the bell-shaped metallic vessel that was blasted out of rock by workmen in Dorchester, Massachusetts, in June of 1851. It appears to be a vase of some fashion, but cannot be dated or identified. Geologists say that the rock that the vase was blasted from should be millions of years old by today's accepted geology.

One explanation for such anomalistic objects is that catastrophic geological change happens frequently and coal seams that are said to be millions of years old may only be tens of thousands of years old or hundreds of thousands of years old. If ancient civilizations existed 20,000 years ago and several cataclysmic pole shifts had occurred over time (maybe as often as every 6,000 years), one could have such "impossible" objects in coal seams, geodes, and solid rock.

From Slovakia, I headed north on a train full of schoolchildren to Krakow, Poland. Poland is the site of many early settlements and, in fact, the oldest boomerang in the world was found in Poland according to *Science News* in 1987. According to an article entitled "Prehistoric Tusk: Early Boomerang?" (*Science News* No. 132, 1987), "Scientists who found a curved piece of mammoth tusk in a cave in southern Poland have dubbed it the world's oldest known boomerang, dating to about 23,000 years ago.

"The claim is based on the artifact's shape, curvature and flattening at both ends, report Pail Valde-Nowak and his colleagues of the Polish Academy of Sciences in Krakow. It spans about 27 inches and is up to 2.3 inches wide and 0.6 inches thick. One side preserves the external, rounded surface of the tusk, while the other has been polished almost flat."

A 23,000-year-old boomerang in Poland? Indeed, other ancient boomerangs have been found in Florida (see *Lost Cities of North & Central America*[23]) and in Egypt as well as Australia. The ancient Egyptians were known to hunt with boomerangs and boomerangs were often found among the relics of ancient tombs, literally all over the world.

When the tragic young king Tutankhamen was entombed, an entire chest of boomerangs was part of his treasures. Many of these boomerangs can be seen today in a special display in the Tutankhamen section of the Cairo Egyptian Antiquities Museum.

I wondered whether ancient Poles slew dragons with their boomerangs as I walked through Krakow to the famous dragon statue. Krakow had an interesting legend about a dragon being slain in a cave beneath the castle, and I was amused by the statue that gave a burst of flame every few minutes.

It was a two-day train journey from Krakow to Prague. Walking through the elegant streets of the old city, I gazed at the wonderful architecture around me. The streets were lined with artists and street vendors and Prague was now the most popular city in Europe for foreign tourists. It was said that 20,000 Americans were living in Prague at any given time, and Prague even had an English-language weekly newspaper.

I enjoyed the beer halls of Prague for a few nights and then took off to Germany, deciding to hitchhike through the Black Forest, back to Amsterdam. In the chill air of autumn I walked down the local highways through the forest. I spent most nights at youth hostels, and one night I stayed with a family who had a spare room.

Germany certainly has its connections with Atlantis, from early archaeologists like Schliemann to the strange occult leanings of the Third Reich. Germany has its ancient traditions and links to occult societies in Central Asia. The Nazis studied every esoteric notion possible, including Hollow Earth theories, Atlantis, and lost treasures like the Holy Grail and the Spear of Destiny.

Germany is full of unusual mountain areas, and the western portions have megalithic remains similar to those in Holland, Belgium and Denmark. John Michell in his astro-archaeology book *Secrets of the Stones*[221] briefly describes a church at Elm in the Bernese Alps which is lit once a year by a sunbeam passing through a natural hole in a mountain above it. "This occurs on the feast day of the saint to whom the church is dedicated."[221]

As I looked out the window of a bus passing through Germany, I wondered how there could be a natural hole through a mountain that could pass a ray of light through it? Something of this sort seems suspiciously artificial to me. Some tunneling and mining from the ancient past?

Another curious rock formation in Germany is the Externsteine

Rocks, a group of tall spires of solid rock that have been turned into isolated rock-cut chapels. Michell implies in *Secrets of the Stones* that the Externsteine Rocks were an ancient astronomical site.

According to him, an ancient pagan symbol called the Irmensul tree once stood at the top of the highest pinnacle of Externsteine. This tree was a huge stone pillar similar to a Greek Doric column and it had been toppled by Christian priests in the Middle Ages. Michell informs us that the SS Ahnenerbe movement under Himmler planned to restore the symbolic Irmensul tree to Externsteine.

〰〰〰〰𓂀〰〰〰〰

Atlantis in Scandinavia

Approaching the Dutch border by train, I looked north and realized that I would have to miss Denmark and the rest of Scandinavia on this trip. Spanuth claims that Denmark with its many megaliths was part of Atland.

Going Spanuth one further, the 17th-century Swedish professor of medicine, Olof Rudbeck, proclaimed that Atlantis was actually located in Sweden. Rudbeck was the first person to write a medical treatise about the lymph glands, was a distinguished botanist, and designed the university gardens and dome of the anatomical theater.

Rudbeck was a professor at Uppsala University and was an acknowledged medical genius. Strongly patriotic, he pioneered the use of Swedish instead of Latin in academic papers. Rudbeck came to believe that ancient Sweden was the Hyperborea of ancient Greek geography.

Sweden, so he believed, was also the original land of the Druids, and ultimately, Sweden was Atlantis. In 1675 Rudbeck published *Atlantica*, one of a number of books in which he propounded his theory of a Scandinavian Atlantis. In the frontispiece of *Atlantica*, Rudbeck is shown peeling back the earth to uncover Atlantis in Scandinavia. He stands with a circle of his predecessors, including Plato, Aristotle and Herodotus, to show them the true location of the lost continent.[279]

Rudbeck based his theory of Sweden having been Atlantis by assuming that Plato's Atlantis was the same as Homer's Isle of Ogygia. Rudbeck used the sailing directions in the *Odyssey* to conclude that Ogygia lay between the latitudes of Mecklenberg, Germany, and Vinililand, Sweden. Rudbeck felt that the ancient Norse sagas vindicated his identification of Sweden as Atlantis. Its capital had been Uppsala, the very city Rudbeck lived in.[1]

Rudbeck's idea of Sweden as Hyperborea might have some truth to it. The ancient Scandinavian Runes, the tradition of Ragnarok, and a cataclysmic age of the gods all point to Sweden as having been an advanced civilization in the past. Sweden has many megaliths along the coastal area, and others may be submerged.

More likely than Uppsala being the capital of Rudbeck's sunken Hyperborean-Atlantis, we would probably find this capital city in the Baltic Sea, to either one side or another of the river that once flowed through this great valley.

Perhaps, as Rudbeck and Spanuth believe, the Scandinavians, like the Dutch, are the descendants of the survivors of Atland.

In 1937 the German history professor F. Gidon proposed that Atlantis had been in Scandinavia and the North Sea in the appendix to his translation of *L'Atlantide,* published as *Atlantis-Rätsel.* The French historian Alexandre Bessmertny had written *L'Atlantide* in 1935, probably the most important scholarly work on Atlantis to be written in French. Gidon translated Bessmertny's book into German and called it *Atlantis-Rätsel,* to which he added an appendix of his own theories. Gidon theorized that the separation of Britain from the mainland of Europe happened in relatively recent times, sometime in the Bronze Age, around 3,000 B.C. He bases his theory on the distribution of plants in northwest Europe and concludes that Plato's tale is based on a series of inundations in the Zuider Zee, plus other legends of Atlantic islands.

Curiously, Gidon suggests that Plato's Atlanto-Athenian war is but an echo of the great migrations and invasions of the ancient Celts and Germans, survivors of his Atlantis.[1]

Later these areas were connected via sea by the Phoenicians, who had trading establishments as far north as Scandinavia by the early Tyrian period. John Baldwin in his 1869 book *Pre-Historic Nations*[188] says, "The letters and literary culture of the ancient Scandinavians were incontestably Phoenician. It is freely admitted that the Runic letters of the Norsemen, 16 in number, found in the old inscriptions on the rocks and stone monuments of Denmark, Norway, Sweden, and the neighboring districts of Germany, and used in Norse literature, could have no other origin."

Runes, like the present-day Latin alphabet used worldwide, are taken from the early Phoenician writing which may have come from India or Atlantis. It replaced the pictographic scripts of Egypt, the Hittites and the Chinese.

Just as the Phoenicians had their "dragon ships" that ruled the Atlantic waves, the Viking dragon ships ruled the North Sea from Scandinavia to the Canadian Arctic. With their Phoenician-derived Runic (Punic?) script, the Vikings penetrated as far as Colorado and North Dakota in their voyages to America.

L. Sprague de Camp in his skeptical work, *Lost Continents,*[1] discounts the idea of a submerged Atlantis with his ultra-conservative notion of geological change, a notion that is very common. Says de Camp, "By normal movements of the earth's crust, like that of the Baltic region, or by a long series of terrific earthquakes, it might be possible to submerge a low flat island of good size in 100,000 years or so." This is the typical conservative geology of uniformitarianists, with major earth changes happening slowly over hundreds of thousands or millions of years.

The problem is, geological change can happen much faster than that, and Holland is proof of this. The inundation of the lowlands of Holland, Belgium, Germany and Denmark may have happened quickly, probably in a matter of days, rather than 100,000 years. Indeed, Amsterdam and much of Holland could be swallowed up by the ocean at any time. It could happen in a matter of days, and the struggle against the sea would begin again.

On a rainy evening in Amsterdam I looked across the table at my friend Herman, the editor of *Frontiers 2000* magazine.

"Well, here's to my last night in Amsterdam," I said, raising my glass. We had met at Susie's Saloon and were having a drink.

"Cheers," he said. "Where are you going next?"

"I'm off to England tomorrow evening," I said. "I'm heading for my ancestral homeland, Scotland."

"I'm going to England myself," he said. "Are you going there for the Crop Circle conference?"

"I really hadn't thought about it," I admitted.

Looking out at the rainy weather, I said, "Meanwhile, I hope that Holland doesn't drown in rain or a tidal wave."

"Well, you can relax for your last day," he said. "Amsterdam isn't going to go under water yet. But with the seedy atmosphere of the red light district, it does seem like the last days of Pompeii."

"Or Atlantis," I said.

This church in the Bernesse Alps of Germany is illuminated once a year by a sunbeam passing through a natural hole in a mountain above it. This occurs on the feast day of the saint to whom the church is dedicated. An ancient tunnel through the mountain or natural oddity?

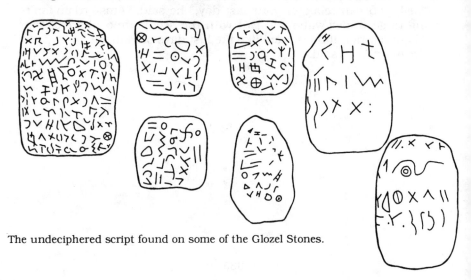

The undeciphered script found on some of the Glozel Stones.

Top: Pastor Spanuth, circa 1953. Bottom: One of his underwater photos showing what he said was pavement of fitted flint slabs, part of the capital city of Atlantis.

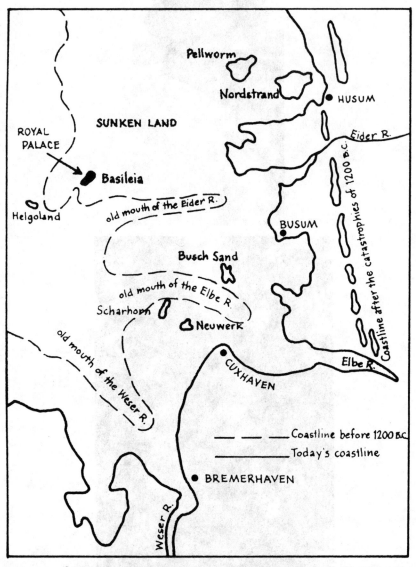

A map of Jürgen Spanuth's sunken Atlantis of the North off the coasts of Germany and Holland.

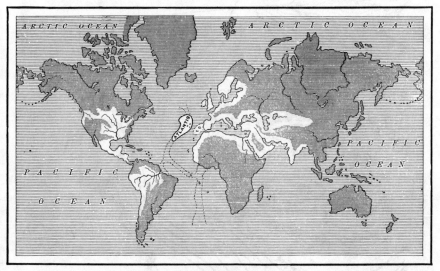

THE EMPIRE OF ATLANTIS.

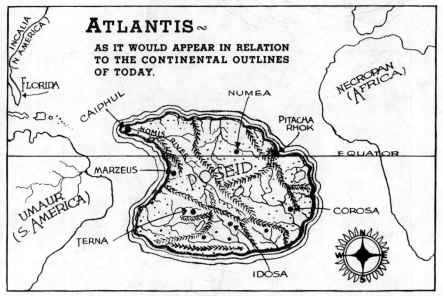

Top: Ignatius Donnelly's 1882 map of Atlantis from his book *Atlantis, The Antediluvian World*. Bottom: A 1946 map of Atlantis from the Lemurian Fellowship of California.

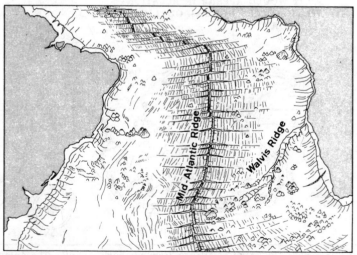

Top: A map of Atlantis and its capital city by Paul Schliemann, who claimed to be the grandson of Heinrich Schliemann. Bottom: A diagram of the midatlantic ridge in the South Atlantic.

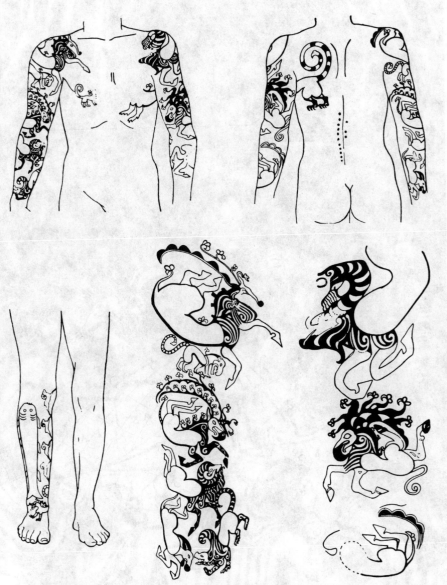

"Scythian" animal art in tattooing. Fantastic tattoo designs found on the bodies of men of 2,400 years ago, preserved in perpetual ice in the tomb chambers of Pazyryk, southern Siberia.

Engraved frontispiece of Olof Rudbeck's Atlantica first published in 1657. The engraving depicts Rudbeck, a professor of medicine at Uppsala University in Sweden, peeling back the globe and revealing to his predecessors who had missed it that Sweden was Atlantis.

Chapter 11

ENGLAND & WALES:

Stonehenge & the Holy Grail

What know they of England,
who only England know?
—Rudyard Kipling

Dawn was just breaking as I looked up from the deck of the ferry at the white Cliffs of Dover. Moments later the ferry horns sounded to warn passengers to get back in their cars and buses and be ready for departure to British immigration and customs.

Despite the fact that Great Britain was now part of the European Union and I was coming from Holland, everyone from the ferry had to go through a brief customs and immigration check before we got back on the bus and headed out on the motorway to London.

I smiled to myself as I looked out the window at the small, thatched roof cottages that lined the road in Dover. They were pleasant and neat with their gardens and hedges. There was something simple and cultured about the English, a polite people who had managed to spread their language and culture around the world. Were they the inheritors of Atlantean civilization as some authors claimed?

〰〰〰〰𓂀〰〰〰〰

Atlantis In Britain

Once in London I called Nicholas, an old friend from Katmandu, whom I had met many years before while trekking in the Himalayas.

Nicholas graciously invited me to stay at his apartment for a few days while I arranged my trip through the United Kingdom. Nicholas is an English teacher at a private school for the many foreign students who have temporarily moved to London to learn advanced English.

Sitting in his apartment in the West End area of London, I told him over a cup of tea that I was in search of Atlantis.

"Atlantis?" he said, raising an eyebrow. "Do you expect to find Atlantis here in England?"

"Well, not exactly," I answered, "but many authors claim that there is a strong connection between Atlantis and the British Isles. Some authors do in fact claim that Atlantis was in Britain itself. How about that?"

"Atlantis in Britain?" he scoffed. "Now that seems far-fetched to me. I suppose they think that Stonehenge is something from Atlantis? Maybe the Loch Ness Monster as well."

"It's not as farfetched as you might think," I said, pulling a well-worn book out of my daypack and putting it on his coffee table. It was a copy of a recent book published in England entitled *The Atlantis Researches*[212] by Paul Dunbavin.

Dunbavin's book is a thick and scholarly treatise on myths and legends of the world and their relating of devastating floods, famines and geological catastrophes. Dunbavin analyzes Plato's account in detail and then concludes that a great catastrophe occurred about 3,000 B.C., during Britain's Neolithic Age.

Dunbavin ascribes this catastrophe to a pole shift or crustal slippage, altering the earth's rotation and submerging large portions of continental Europe and other areas. In conclusion, he suggests that the capital city of Atlantis lies submerged in the Irish Sea between Wales, Scotland and Ireland.

Dunbavin essentially argues that with sea levels considerably lower 5000 years ago, the now submerged shelf around the British Isles can be made to fit the description of Plato's lost island continent. In Dunbavin's reconstruction, Britain remains cut off from the European continent by a narrow strait and becomes a much larger island linked together with Ireland. In the center of this "super-Britain" is a flat rectangular plain where broad river estuaries flow across what is now the bed of the eastern Irish Sea. He believes this submerged plain to be the plain of Atlantis.

Dunbavin spends much of his book discussing submerged forests and raised beaches around Britain and Ireland. Says Dunbavin, "Current theories of when the Irish Sea basin was flooded and the link between Britain and Ireland severed, centre upon the raised beaches found around Scottish coasts. The so-called 50-foot beach is thought to date from a cold period at the end of the last glaciation and is noted as far south as Islay and the Galloway Peninsula. It has been destroyed in places by the younger 25-foot beach, upon which several dug-out canoes have been found. Neither beach can be traced south of Lancashire; but corresponding beaches do occur in Northern Ireland, particularly around Rathlin Island. These beaches are often cited as evidence that the rise of the sea had cut off Ireland from Britain at least as long ago as the Boreal Period." (The Boreal Period was about 8,000 B.C.)

Dunbavin then shows that a radiocarbon date for one of these raised beaches was approximately 4400 B.C. He also cites evidence such as submerged forest deposits that have been found during the course of tin mining work in the Pentewan Valley in Cornwall and around Cardigan Bay in Wales.

Dunbavin describes his Atlantis in the Irish Sea thusly: "A sea level drop of about 35-40m is all that would be required to expose the floor of the eastern Irish Sea. A further fall to say, 65 meters would make little difference to the overall shape of the shoreline created. Somewhere between these limits, an irregular concave shoreline would be created starting from a point west of Holyhead, to a point south-west of the Calf of Man. The shoreline would then continue more or less directly north to a point only a few miles from the Mull of Galloway, then continuing on beyond Ailsa Craig to the Mull of Kintyre. To the west of this shoreline, between Anglesey and the Isle of Man, there would also be a small low-lying triangular island, of about the same area as the Isle of Man."

Dunbavin then says that the submarine features of the Irish Sea fit remarkably well into the description of Atlantis by Plato if used at about a ratio of three to two.

I set my cup of coffee down on Nicholas' coffee table and asked him what he thought of the Atlantis-in-Britain theory.

"Is that the crux of this theory?" he asked. "What about other elements of Plato's story, the wars, the huge city, the strange *orichalcum* metal and the elephants?"

"Well, Dunbavin claims that the city of Atlantis, on a three-to-two scale, is beneath the Irish Sea near the Isle of Man. He says that there were huge forests all over Britain and even the Orkneys in those days, just as Plato says. However, Plato says that Atlantis had an abundance of elephants and it does not seem that ancient Britain was an island of elephants.

"Dunbavin does have an interesting explanation for the mysterious orichalcum of Atlantis," I went on, as Nicholas watered the flowers on the balcony of his penthouse apartment. "Orichalcum is often translated as 'mountain copper,' but Dunbavin says that it may actually be red gold, a naturally occurring alloy of copper and gold. The Egyptians only knew white gold, which has small amounts of silver in it. Therefore the red, copper variety of gold was very rare to them."

"So what do you think?" asked Nicholas.

"Well, *The Atlantis Researches* is a fascinating book and has a great deal of interesting information on ancient Britain and Atlantis. There may be a lost city beneath Cardigan Bay, but I don't think it was Atlantis. Dunbavin himself admits that the area is not large enough to be Plato's Atlantis. Therefore, he must scale the city down to make it fit, much like theorists do when they argue that Thera or Santorini are Atlantis, making the island one tenth the size."

Nicholas then showed me a book recently published in Britain called *Where Troy Once Stood*[226] by the Dutch author Iman Wilkens. "In a similar fashion," he said, handing me the book, "this author claims that the Trojan War of Homer's *Iliad* and the *Odyssey* was fought here in England, not in Turkey and Greece. How about that!"

I looked at the book and then turned to a chapter on the location of Troy. Wilkens says that from ancient times the ruins of the famous city of Troy were believed to be located near the town of Bunar-Bashi in western Turkey. Wilkens says that the site, excavated by Schliemann, does not fit the descriptions in Homer's work and cannot be the site of the Trojan Wars.

Wilkens says the site is far too small, and because of the mountainous terrain it is impossible to go around the city walls as Achilles did when pursuing Hector in the *Iliad*. Furthermore, Schliemann himself admitted that this fortress could not have held more than 5,000 people and probably much less. However, Homer's Troy held an army of 50,000.

Homer describes Troy as having broad streets and King Priam's palace as huge with over 60 rooms. Wilkens says that Schliemann's site of Hissarlik is now less than five kilometers from the sea, and was less than two kilometers in ancient times. Homer says an army of 65,000 men and their attending forces occupied the coast between Troy and the ocean. They then destroyed seven towns around an area with 14 different rivers before finally defeating Troy with their Trojan horse trick. Wilkens says, logically, that there is not enough room around Schliemann's city to fit this huge army around the walls.

"If Troy is not in Turkey, where is it then?" I asked, putting down the book.

"Well, Troy is located in England. Essentially, Wilkens takes the Trojan War and the subsequent travels of Odysseus out of the Mediterranean and supplants the entire story as taking place in France, Holland, Germany and England.

"He places Troy at Cambridge in East Anglia," Nicholas said with a smile of amusement.

"Cambridge? Just north of London? That's amazing," I said. "It looks like both Atlantis and Troy might be located in Britain."

"This is our wonderful island. We rule the world from it," laughed

Nicholas.

I studied *Where Troy Once Stood* for the remainder of the afternoon and was impressed by the argument presented.

Essentially Wilkens claims that King Priam of the *Iliad* was the king of England at the time, whose fortress was the Gog-Magog Hills near Cambridge. This huge prehistoric earthworks fortress commands the great East Anglia plain, and could have held a huge army of 50,000.

Wilkens cites as evidence for his theory the two huge "war dikes" running parallel to each other to the northeast of Cambridge. One is 12 kilometers long and the other is 15 kilometers long. The massive earthworks are known as the Fleam Dyke and the Devil's Dyke. No one knows who built them or what their purpose was.[226]

Wilkens claims that the ditches built in front of these dikes are on the side facing inland, not towards the sea, which means that they were built by those invading the territory, not defending it. Homer mentions the building of such dikes.

Says Wilkens, "It is obvious that the invader was preparing for a long war (the Trojan War lasted for 10 years) and must have had a very large army to be able to shift the huge volume of earth needed for building the dikes, which are 20 m. high and 30 m. wide at the base. The estimate put forward that the Achaean army numbered between 65,000 and 100,000 would seem no exaggeration..." [226]

Wilkens says that midway between the two dikes is the ancient fortress now called the Gog-Magog Hills. This was ancient Troy, sieged for ten years by Mycenae.

But this Mycenae is not in Greece but in France! Wilkens places the city of Achilles up the Seine past Paris near to the town of Troyes, which he says was Mycenae. In Wilkens' whole scenario, the entire Trojan War including the voyage of Odysseus out into the Atlantic takes place in England, Holland, Belgium and France. After the Trojan War, Odysseus journeys out into the Atlantic to the Azores, Homer's "Ogygia in the Ocean Stream," and eventually returns to Europe.

It is a fascinating concept worth considering. Could Troy, or Holy Ilium, have been prehistoric England, a sophisticated and civilized area that had built Stonehenge and other great monuments? I noted the similarity between the name for the mystic world of ancient Britain, Albion, with the city of ancient Troy, Ilium.

Perhaps the Trojan War involved a war between the Mediterranean and the North Atlantic—where Troy was indeed at Cambridge and Mycenae was in ancient Greece.

Indeed, the mystery of England's ancient heritage was growing greater, not smaller, as I looked for answers.

Crop Circles and the View Over Atlantis

During my days in London I visited the British Museum and the many bookstores in the vicinity. One bookstore, down a narrow cobblestone backstreet, was appropriately named *The Atlantis Bookstore*. Inside were shelves to the ceiling stacked with books on Atlantis, ancient wisdom, psychic phenomena and arcane knowledge. I soon found myself in the basement browsing through the used books on lost cities and ancient mysteries.

"Well, hello, David!" said a voice above me.

I looked up from the floor, where I was sitting with stacks of books around me, and there was my old friend from Australia, Duncan Roads, the publisher of NEXUS magazine.

"Duncan, it's good to see you!" I cried, getting up from the floor. "You said you would be in London."

"Don't let me disturb your book search," he said, picking up a stack of books.

"Not at all," I said, taking the stack from him. "I was just about to buy these books. I'd better do it now before you buy them instead."

"Ha, ha," he laughed, following me upstairs to the cash register. Afterwards we went out for a cup of tea and Duncan told me he was going to a crop circle conference in Glastonbury.

"A crop circle conference? That sounds great," I said. "Are crop circles still happening?"

"Oh, yeah," said Duncan. "It's still happening in a big way. We'll learn about the latest cryptograms at the conference. Glastonbury is a super place. Very mystical."

I told him that I had been planning on renting a car and suggested that I give him a ride to Glastonbury. He agreed to share gasoline expenses with me.

I picked him up one afternoon after I had gotten the small Fiat hatchback from the rental agency in Portobello Road. We were soon speeding down the motorway on our way to the great plain of Salisbury where many of the mysterious crop circles are found.

In the afternoon sun we saw several giant chalk horses etched into the green hills. At Bratton in Wiltshire is carved the figure of a horse nearly 180 feet long. There are other figures of the same type in the area.

The Bratton horse was actually re-cut in the 18th century, and looks quite different from its predecessor of earlier days. According to popular tradition, the original Bratton horse was created to commemorate the victory of Alfred the Great over the Danes in A.D. 878.

However, it is now thought to date back to Celtic times when horses—animals much loved by the Celts—were worshiped and represented in various ways. Such large-scale representations as the Bratton horse are now thought to have been acts of veneration and pleas for protection, possibly to the Celtic horse goddess, Epona.[96]

"Here's a bed-and-breakfast," said Duncan, pointing to a farm along the road. "It's near a special pub I've heard about. Let's stay here."

I agreed, and after renting our room from a young family of four, we were able to head down the road to the pub Duncan was talking about.

"It's called the Barge Inn," Duncan said. "I think it's just up here."

We walked down a dark country road past a few houses and around a corner by a creek. It was dark and lonely. We got further and further from the houses we had passed.

"Are you sure that there's a pub down this road?" I asked.

"Well, I think it's down here. This pub is a mecca for crop circle buffs and skeptics alike, from all over the world," said Duncan. "I bet it's just around this next corner."

Just then we came around a corner and could see the lights of a building through the trees. A few more minutes of walking and we came to a parking lot with quite a few cars in it.

"Wow, I didn't expect this," I said.

"There are a lot of people here," said Duncan as we walked past vans and even a camera crew that was putting away video equipment.

Inside, the bar was packed with people, including a busload of tourists on their way to the same crop circle conference. Michael Hesseman, a well-known German crop circle expert, was being interviewed by German television, or maybe it was British television.

"Hey, there's our friend Herman," I said. There sitting at a table was tall Herman, whom both Duncan and I knew from Holland. Sitting with him was Filip Coppens from the *Frontier 2000* offices in Belgium.

"What are you doing here?" I laughed as we sat at their table.

"We are going to the crop circle conference," said Herman.

"So are we," said Duncan. "Are you staying here at the Barge Inn?"

"We are camping in tents in the back," said Filip. "There are three of us and we have three tents."

Soon we were talking about crop circles and drinking beer. The pub was a lively place and quite unusual as pubs go. Here were the hard-core crop circle types who camped out all summer looking for the latest manifestations. They climbed hills to look out over the countryside during the day and then came back to this pub to tell their stories at night.

There was a great camaraderie among the researchers, and many seemed to devote their entire summers to looking for crop circles. It was a good quest as well, I thought—a quest for the mysteries of man and nature.

England's largest military base was nearby. What did they know about the mysterious formations—happening in the immediate vicinity of their highly secured military test area?

Indeed, I thought, as we walked down the dirt road and stared at the starry sky, crop circles may run the entire spectrum from psychological manifestations, UFOs and special technology to the power of ancient earth energies.

Perhaps it is the earth herself that is making these enigmatic markings. After a night at the Barge Inn, anything seemed possible.

〰〰〰〰〰👁〰〰〰〰〰

The Great Pyramid of Britain

The next day we drove immediately to Silbury Hill, near the megalithic structures of Avebury. Silbury Hill is the largest artificial hill in Europe. It is conical, more than 130 feet high, and measures 550 feet across the base. Being conical, it could be considered a pyramid structure, as pyramids can be step-shaped, three-, four- or five-sided, or conical, as in the Comacalco Pyramid near Mexico City. Therefore, it might be said that Silbury Hill is the largest pyramid in Europe.

In ancient times, the "Silbury Pyramid" could be reached by boat because the pyramid was part of a huge earthworks project that included a canal to the site. A ditch surrounding the Silbury site was originally more than 120 feet wide and about 30 feet deep. The ditch continues towards the west in the form of a canal. Perhaps this canal gives us some indication of the method that the ancient engineers used to build the conical pyramid.

Excavations carried out in 1968 have established the fact that Silbury Hill was built in three stages around 2100 B.C., a time when classical Egyptian civilization was at its height. The builders first constructed a foundation of clay and gravel, topped with earth supported by stakes. On this foundation they piled up materials from the nearby river and the entire structure was then covered with chalk.

A wide, deep ditch was hollowed out next to Silbury Hill and though it is often thought by archaeologists to have been constructed after the pyramid, it seems more likely that the canal was constructed first. It has been calculated that these great works would have occupied 500 men for ten years.[96]

350

Artificial hills, just like pyramids, are generally thought to have served as burial places. But when the center of Silbury Hill was investigated nothing was found. It is generally believed that ancient mounds, like the pyramids of Egypt, were built as tombs for megalomaniac rulers. Yet, no Egyptian mummy was ever found in an Egyptian pyramid. Most kings and queens were buried in rock-cut vaults deep underground at the Valley of Kings or Valley of Queens. Was Silbury Hill, as were the Egyptian pyramids, built for some other reason than as tombs?

In an article on Silbury Hill published in *Antiquity* (Number 41, 1967),[17] the British archaeologist R. J. Atkinson had this to say about the massive structure: "Silbury forms a regular truncated cone, with a flat top 100 ft. (30.5 m.) in diameter and 130 ft. (40 m.) high above the surrounding meadows. The base covers about 5.25 acres (2.1 hectares). A little below the top the profile is broken by a marked step or terrace; and there are traces of what may have been similar terraces lower down, on the north and east sides. It may be that the mound was built originally in the form of a stepped cone. Here we see that the Silbury Mound may have originally been very similar to a stepped pyramid from the Middle East or Mesoamerica.

"Excavations have been made in the mound or ditch on five previous occasions. In 1776 a shaft 8 ft. square was sunk from the centre of the top to the old ground surface, but apparently found nothing apart from a fragment of oak. In 1849 the Archaeological Institute, as an adjunct to its Salisbury meeting, sponsored the driving of a tunnel along the base of the mound to the centre. This revealed at the centre a primary barrow of chalk, clay-with-flints and turf, which was at least 80 ft. in diameter and 8.5 ft. high, and may be larger if the section then recorded proves to lie on a chord and not a diameter. Short lateral galleries showed that a part of the interior of this barrow was surrounded, and perhaps capped, by a convex layer of sarsen boulders. Apart from animal bones, nothing was found except some fragments of string, apparently made of grass. This and other indications suggest that organic material is exceptionally well preserved beneath the mound."[17]

From the top of Silbury Hill we could see a crop circle in a field to the south.

"Look, there's a crop circle," said Duncan.

"That one is said to be a fake," Herman commented, pulling out his camera.

Not one to miss a photograph of a crop circle, fake or real, I too got out my camera and took a couple of photos.

"How do they know the fake crop circles from the real ones?" I asked.

"They have ways of testing them," Herman said, smiling. "But I admit that no one is really sure."

We took a photograph of the flattened circle of wheat in the field and then followed the trail that wound down Silbury Hill in a spiral fashion. From the hill we drove a few miles further down the road to the megalithic site of Avebury.

Avebury is the largest of the many stone circles in Britain and it contains some of the largest megaliths in the country. They have stood for thousands of years just inside the earthbank that surrounds the site. The Christian clergy built a church outside the earthbank in 634 A.D. but the older beliefs continued to attract people to the ancient stones. Early in the 14th century the church took drastic action by taking a portion of the stone circle and throwing it into a nearby section of the Avebury ditch. Some of the megaliths were toppled and thrown into the ditch and buried.

This served to preserve some of the stones, which were re-erected in the last century. Ironically, the ancient stones claimed vengeance on at least one of their desecrators as recent excavations revealed the skeleton of a "barber surgeon" who was killed when a large monolith that he was helping to bury toppled over on him.

As Duncan, Herman, Filip and I walked among the awesome stones in the late morning, I was amazed at the size of the stones and the great expanse of the site. In the 17th century the amateur archaeologist John Aubrey said, "Avebury doth as much exceed Stonehenge in grandeur as a Cathedral doth an ordinary parish church."[209]

Looking at the huge scope of the structure, I could only speculate on what it could have been used for and by whom it was made. According to Aubrey Burl, the two gigantic stones at the south entrance are over 15 feet (5 meters) high, they each weigh about 60 tons and "must have demanded incredible efforts to erect them."[209]

Avebury is believed to be even older than Stonehenge (circa 1500 B.C. by conservative estimates) and is usually said to have been an ancient Sun Temple. Dr. William Stukeley, a British antiquarian, studied Avebury in the early 18th century and was probably the first to discover that from the great central stone circle there extended two avenues of standing stones that were 50 feet wide and a mile and a half long. One avenue reaches out southeast and terminates in another stone circle that is 130 feet in diameter on top of Overton Hill. This stone circle, called the Sanctuary, is thought to represent a serpent's head.

The other avenue makes a sinuous double curve towards the southwest, though little evidence remains. Like other parts of Avebury it was destroyed shortly after Stukeley made drawings of it. Stukeley theorized that this double avenue of stones represented the Solar Serpent which passed through the Avebury Circle, and symbolized the Sun.[208]

Stukeley was a scholar of ancient Egyptian, Hebrew and Greek teachings and recognized that the solar disc and the serpent were often used together to represent the supreme creative force and the wisdom of inner truths. For example, Egyptians frequently used a winged solar disc and a serpent to symbolize Ra or Aton, the supreme deity.

John Michell says that one of the longest and most impressive ley lines in England cuts through the southern edge of the Avebury Circle. This "Dragon Line" stretches from Land's End to Burrow Mump and Glastonbury Tor, on to Avebury and eventually to Bury St. Edmunds in Suffolk. En route it touches on many hills and churches that are dedicated to Saint Michael (the Archangel). Perhaps the "Serpent Power" or "Dragon Power" of this ley line is somehow captured at Avebury, making it the ritual-religious center that it was in remote antiquity.

The well-known British archaeologist, Aubrey Burl, author of *Prehistoric Avebury*,[208] is critical of the ley line theories, however. "Theodolites wink towards every skyline notch where the sun once set or moon rose where Arcturus for a brief year or two shimmered dimly down into the mists of a prehistoric evening. Ley-liners draw impossibly accurate alignments from Avebury through Silbury Hill to a random barrow or church or mile-wide hill that God happened to place in the correct position. There are even those who believe that the rings were landing-bases for flying saucers."[208]

I couldn't help wondering, as I walked among the massive stones, whether the Avebury Temple had always been an open-air temple, or if it had ever had solid walls and a roof. Perhaps the smaller stones had long since been carried away for other building projects, leaving only the largest megaliths still in place. Exactly such a thing has taken place at the megalithic ruins of Tiahuanaco in Bolivia.

That the megalithic site of Avebury might have been even larger and enclosed by a roof was mind-boggling. Such a structure would put Avebury in the same category as the largest modern buildings. Were Avebury and Stonehenge ancient temples from Atlantis? Maybe John Michell and Paul Dunbavin were right: England was Atlantis.

Stonehenge: A Neolithic Computer

After lunch at the pub in Avebury, we headed for nearby Stonehenge, England's most famous monument. Only 18 miles away from Avebury, Stonehenge sits alone on the Salisbury plain, flanked by a parking lot and gift shop for tourists.

In 1964 the British astronomer Gerald S. Hawkins first published his now famous treatise on Stonehenge as an astronomical computer. His article, entitled "Stonehenge: A Neolithic Computer," appeared in issue 202 of the prestigious British journal *Nature*. In 1965, Hawkins' famous book *Stonehenge Decoded* was published.[247]

Hawkins upset the archaeological world by claiming that the megalithic site was more than just a circular temple erected by some egocentric kings but rather a sophisticated computer for eclipses and astronomical data.

He begins his *Nature* article with a quote from Diodorus on prehistoric Britain in his *History of the Ancient World*, written about 50 B.C.: "The Moon as viewed from this island appears to be but a little distance from the Earth and to have on it prominences like those of the Earth, which are visible to the eye. The account is also given that the god [Moon?] visits the island every 19 years, the period in which the return of the stars to the same place in the heavens is accomplished....There is also on the island, both a magnificent sacred precinct of Apollo [Sun] and a notable temple...and the supervisors are called Boreadae, and succession to these positions is always kept in their family."

Hawkins' basic theory was that "Stonehenge was an observatory; the impartial mathematics of probability and the celestial sphere are on my side." Hawkins' first contention was that alignments between pairs of stones and other features, calculated with a computer from small-scale plans, compared their directions with the azimuths of the rising and setting sun and moon, at the solstices and equinoxes, calculated for 1500 B.C.

Hawkins claimed to have found thirty-two "significant" alignments, and his second contention was that the fifty-six Aubrey holes were used as a "computer" (that is, as tally marks) for predicting movements of the moon and eclipses, for which he claims to have established a "hitherto unrecognized 56-year cycle with 15 percent irregularity; and that the rising of the full moon nearest the winter solstice over the Heel Stone always successfully predicted an eclipse. It is interesting to note that no more than half these eclipses were visible from Stonehenge."

Says Hawkins in *Stonehenge Decoded*, "The number 56 is of great significance for Stonehenge because it is the number of Aubrey holes set around the outer circle. Viewed from the centre these holes are placed at equal spacings of azimuth around the horizon and therefore, they cannot mark the Sun, Moon or any celestial object. This is confirmed by the archaeologist's evidence; the holes have held fires and cremations of bodies, but have never held stones. Now, if the Stonehenge people desired to divide up the circle why did they not make 64 holes simply by bisecting segments of the circle—32, 16, 8, 4 and 2? I believe that the Aubrey holes provided a system for counting the years, one hole for each year, to aid in predicting the movement of the Moon. Perhaps cremations were performed in a particular Aubrey hole during the course of the year, or perhaps the hole was marked by a movable stone.

"Stonehenge can be used as a digital computing machine. ...The stones at hole 56 predict the year when an eclipse of the Sun or Moon will occur within 15 days of midwinter—the month of the winter Moon. It will also predict eclipses for the summer Moon."[247]

The critics of Hawkins, the ruling academic minds of their time, immediately jumped on his discoveries and denounced them. In 1966 an article by the British astronomer R. J. Atkinson appeared in *Nature* (volume 210, 1966), entitled "Decoder Misled?",[220] in which Atkinson criticized Hawkins for many of his statements about Stonehenge being an astronomical computer.

Said Atkinson of Hawkins' book *Stonehenge Decoded*, "It is tendentious, arrogant, slipshod and unconvincing, and does little to advance our understanding of Stonehenge.

"The first five chapters, on the legendary and archaeological background, have been uncritically compiled, and contain a number of bizarre interpretations and errors. The rest of the book is an unsuccessful attempt to substantiate the author's claim that 'Stonehenge was an observatory; the impartial mathematics of probability and the celestial sphere are on my side.' Of his two main contentions, the first concerns alignments between pairs of stones and other features, calculated with a computer from small-scale plans ill-adapted for this purpose."

Atkinson's scathing criticism of Hawkins is revealing because it shows how resistant to new ideas established academics can be. Atkinson's reluctance to believe that Stonehenge was some sort of astronomical computer is probably largely due to the popular belief that ancient man simply didn't have a state of civilization that allowed him to pursue such topics of higher knowledge.

But these critics are heard from no more, and there seems little doubt to even the most conservative archaeologist that Stonehenge is some sort of astronomical temple. There are a number of simple astronomical truths that can be discerned from Stonehenge. For instance, there are 29.53 days between full moons and there are 29 and a half monoliths in the outer Sarsen Circle.

There are 19 of the huge 'Blue Stones' in the inner horseshoe which has several possible explanations and uses. There are nearly

19 years between the extreme rising and setting points of the moon. Also, if a full moon occurs on a particular day of the year, say on the summer solstice, it is 19 years before another full moon occurs on the same day of the year.

Finally, there are 19 eclipse years (or 223 full moons) between similar eclipses, such as an eclipse that occurs when the sun, moon and earth return to their same relative positions. Other planets' positions may vary in even larger cycles.

It is also suggested that the five large trilithon archways represent the five planets visible to the naked eye: Mercury, Venus, Mars, Jupiter and Saturn.

The British writer on antiquities, John Ivimy, makes a stirring suggestion at the end of his popular book on Stonehenge, *The Sphinx and the Megaliths*.[217] He spends the bulk of the book trying to prove his thesis that Stonehenge was built by a group of adventurous Egyptians who were sent to the British Isles to establish a series of astronomical sites at higher latitudes in order to accurately predict solar eclipses, which the observatories in Egypt could not do, because they were too close to the equator.

Ivimy gives such evidence as the megalithic construction, keystone cuts in the gigantic blocks of stone, the obvious astronomical purpose, and most of all, the use of a numbering system that is based on the number six, rather than the number ten, as we use today. Ivimy shows that the Egyptians used a numbering system based on the number six, and that Stonehenge was built using the same system. He then suggests that the Mormons used a number system based on six when building their temples, especially the great temple in Salt Lake City.

In the end, Ivimy's thesis is quite controversial: he believes that Brigham Young and the original Mormon settlers in Utah are the reincarnation of the same Egyptian group of settlers who were sent to Britain to build Stonehenge. Says Ivimy, "Reference has already been made to the vast wooden dome, built entirely without metal, that roofs the Mormon Tabernacle. Could its construction have been inspired by a dim recollection of how the same people, in another incarnation some centuries earlier, had built a dome over what had then become the Temple of Hyperborean Apollo?"[217]

It is a fascinating idea that the Egyptians came to Britain to build a megalithic observatory to accurately predict lunar eclipses. It is recorded that about 2,000 B.C. a Chinese emperor put to death his two chief astronomers for failing to predict an eclipse of the sun.[204] Asks ancient astronaut theorist Raymond Drake, "Today, would any king care?"

The Egyptians, Chinese, Mayans and many other ancient cultures were obsessed with eclipses as well as other planetary-solar phenomena. It is believed that they associated catastrophes, including the sinking of Atlantis, with planetary movements and eclipses. Perhaps the ancient Egyptians, Mayans or other civilizations thought they could predict the next cataclysm by monitoring lunar eclipses and the positions of the planets in relation to the earth.

Richard Noone in his book *5-5-2000: Ice, The Ultimate Disaster*[19] says something to this effect. He claims that cataclysms have wiped out many of mankind's ancient civilizations, including Atlantis. These catastrophes can be predicted, Noone claims, and, because of a rare planetary alignment, the next cataclysm is due on May 5, 2000, hence the title of his book.

Herodotus writes about ancient Egyptian astronomy and cataclysms in *Book Two*, chapter 142: "...Thus far the Egyptians and their priests told the story. And they showed that there had been three hundred and forty-one generations of men from the first king unto this last, the priest of Hephaestus. ...Now in all this time, 11,340 years, they said that the sun had removed from his proper course four times; and had risen where he now setteth, and set where he now riseth; but nothing in Egypt was altered thereby, neither as touching the river nor as touching the fruits of the earth, nor concerning sicknesses or deaths."

If Herodotus is to be believed, then the earth has shifted around its axis in what is called a pole shift. The sun then appears to rise in a different direction than normal. Pole shifts are accompanied by a wide variety of devastating earth changes and severe weather phenomena. Therefore, if the Egyptians were familiar with this sort of occurrence, they may well have gone to great length to improve their astronomical knowledge, including the colonization of England and the building of Stonehenge.

Glastonbury and the Neo-Druids of Arthur

Duncan and I arrived in Glastonbury while following Herman and Filip to the town. They turned into the campground off the road near Glastonbury Tor. Duncan and I continued to the center of town where I let Duncan off at a bed-and-breakfast he had booked.

I asked them if they had a room for me but was directed to a private home down the road. I arranged to meet Duncan later and found a room just down the street. Shortly, I met up with Duncan and he suggested we walk to Glastonbury Tor.

"One of the trails to the Tor starts at the end of this street," he said as we began walking uphill. It was a pleasant path that wound up the hill to the west side of the Tor, through several farmers' fields to the odd, rounded hill with a solitary tower looking out across the enchanted landscape of Glastonbury.

The British occultist Dion Fortune said in *Avalon of the Heart*,[283] "The Tor is a strange hill, and it is hard to believe that its form is wholly the work of Nature. Round it winds a spiral way in three great coils, which was beyond all question a processional way. When did the Christians worship upon high places? Never. But such mounts as this were always sacred to the sun."

Was Glastonbury Tor an artificial pyramid mound such as Silbury Hill? Legend indicates that it is hollow. In her book *Albion: A Guide To Legendary Britain*,[223] Jennifer Westwood tells the story of St. Collen, a friar who overheard two men speaking of Gwyn, the king of the fairies that lived on the Tor. The friar, who lived in a hermitage at the base of the hill, forbade them to speak about fairies, which he said were actually devils.

The men warned him that the king of the fairies would not overlook such an insult and eventually a messenger came to the saint and told him that the King of the Tor had invited him to visit. As a precaution St. Collen carried a flask of holy water beneath his cloak. Says Westwood, "He entered the hill by a secret door and found himself in a wonderful palace, where Gwyn sat in a golden chair. The king offered him food, but Collen refused it, no doubt because he knew that fairy food was perilous. 'I do not eat the leaves of a tree,' he said, and after further boorish remarks sprinkled his holy water about him."[223] Suddenly the king and palace vanished and Collen found himself standing alone on the cold, windy hillside.

This legend is reminiscent of the modern myths of people being taken inside such sacred places as Mount Shasta in northern California or the Great Pyramid in Egypt. Was Glastonbury part of a secret and ancient network of caverns where Atlantean knowledge was kept?

Glastonbury Tor can also be directly related to Atlantis studies. Janet and Colin Bord in their excellent book *Mysterious Britain*[134] recount a curious 1945 incident in which the British antiquarian John Foster Forbes brought a psychic named Iris Campbell to record psychometric impressions of the Tor.

The psychometrist gave Forbes some interesting impressions which he recorded for posterity. According to the Bords, these impressions indicated that "rites being practiced there were designed to restore bird and flower life forms to a more complete condition. They had become greatly impaired due to the succession of natural calamities that had befallen the earth. The ritual involved a dance of circular motion, moving sunwise and upwards round the spiral path. A tremendous vortex of power was produced which, on an etheric level, created a canopy of a 'glazed substance'. This could act as a receiving centre for the absorption and refraction of regenerative forces to which the bird and flower life could respond."[134] The natural calamities that befell the earth would likely be the collapse of an ecological system in the sort of cataclysm that is associated with the destruction of Atlantis and the worlds before our own.

Duncan and I sat on the grass at the top of the Tor for the remainder of the afternoon and watched the sun set over the village of Glastonbury. In the distance we could see the coast and it reminded me that, according to legend, Glastonbury was originally an island which was separate from the mainland of Britain. Today it is about 15 miles from the ocean.

I was told that there is even a zodiac built into the landscape. According to John Michell, there were seven hills around Glastonbury which symbolized the Great Bear constellation which made Glastonbury the "Crown Chakra" of planet Earth. Glastonbury is similarly said to have a geomanced zodiac built in the hills around the Tor. This was presumably done at about the same time as the early megaliths were being built around southwest England.[13]

Looking out from the top of Glastonbury Tor, I could see how the ocean could come up the broad coastal-river plain and make Glastonbury an island. Glastonbury was the Isle of Avalon and the center of the Arthurian world of early Britain.

Most ancient authors on Glastonbury point out that the sea came much further inland 2,000 years ago and that Glastonbury was an island reached by boat along the coast. The Isle of Avalon was then thought to be an island in the river delta of the Brue River. The present delta town of Burnham was in an area submerged at that time.

It is popular tradition that the abbey at Glastonbury was the first Christian church in Britain and the burial place of both the Holy Grail and of King Arthur. A number of books claim that in 63 A.D. Joseph of Arimathea landed in Britain and brought with him the Holy Grail.

According to these writers, Joseph of Arimathea came to Glastonbury and thrust his staff into the ground where it immediately took root—a sign from Heaven that this was where he was to create a new kingdom based on harmony between the earth and heaven.

For safekeeping, he hid the Holy Grail at "Montsalvat" which, the *Columbia Desk Encyclopedia* (1968 version) says, "was thought to have been the site of the castle of the Holy Grail." Apparently Joseph of Arimathea, after founding the church at Glastonbury, then left for the Pyrenees, probably going by boat to the ancient Phoenician port of Barcelona.

From Barcelona, Joseph brought the Holy Grail, plus other important artifacts and treasures, to either Montserrat in Cataluña or Montségur in France. The Welsh history scholar R. F. Treharne in his book *The Glastonbury Legends*[260] shows how the Grail legend, which originated in France, had the knights of King Arthur searching Europe for the Holy Grail, now hidden at "Montsalvat."

Arthurian legend is fascinating and ultimately steeped in Atlantis lore. Treharne quotes from the historian "Gerald of Wales" in his *De Instructione Principis* written in 1193 A.D.: "Now the body of King Arthur ...was found in our own days at Glastonbury, deep down in the earth and encoffined in a hollow oak between two stone pyramids erected long ago in the consecrated graveyard, the site being revealed by strange and almost miraculous signs..."[260]

It seemed fitting that reincarnated Grail Knights along with King Arthur should be buried between two pyramids, I thought as I browsed through one of the bookstores at Glastonbury. I bought a number of books on the theme of Arthurian legends and the Holy Grail including *St. Joseph of Arimathea At Glastonbury*,[261] a 1922 book by a former vicar of Glastonbury, Lionel Smithett Lewis; the Reverend C. Dobson's *Did Our Lord Visit Britain As They Say In Cornwall and Somerset?*[262]; and *Celt, Druid and Culdee*[263] by Isabel Hill Elder.

In the book *Celt, Druid and Culdee*[263] Isabel Elder maintains that the Glastonbury Culdee church was the first Christian church outside of Jerusalem, having been founded only a few years after the crucifixion by Joseph of Arimathea. The Culdee or Culdich church was founded by Saint Columba, who came from Donegal in Ireland. The original Culdee church was made up largely of converted Druids.

Elder also maintains that the Druids were already descended from priests of ancient Egypt and Israel, such as those associated with the *Stone of Destiny* in the next chapter.

Taliesen, a bard of 6th-century Wales, is quoted by Elder in *Celt, Druid and Culdee*: "Christ, the word from the beginning, was from the beginning our teacher, and we never lost His teaching. Christianity was a new thing in Asia, but there never was a time when the Druids of Britain held not its doctrines."[263] These doctrines, presumably, would have included reincarnation.

In other words, early Christians and Druids were one and the same. In his 1927 book *The Druids*,[264] T. D. Kendrick points out how the Druids virtually vanished when Christianity came to the islands. But this Christianity was not the Christianity that we are familiar with today.

Kendrick postulates that the Druids are connected with the Phoenicians and Etruscans and that they were the keepers of knowledge of the solar temples that had been built in England thousands of years before by scientists from the Mediterranean.

Though Roman historians did not realize it, the ancient Celts of Ireland, Britain, and Europe were closely allied to the Phoenician ports of the eastern Mediterranean. That someone might journey from Palestine to England immediately after the crucifixion becomes a very plausible scenario. It is quite possible that Jesus and Mary Magdalene were also on this voyage. Jesus and Mary may have set up house in the Pyrenees as suggested by the authors of *Holy Blood, Holy Grail*.[240]

Joseph went on to Glastonbury with the Holy Grail, something to help start the faith back home, and a few hundred years later, the idyllic Camelot of Glastonbury's King Arthur was to send its Grail Knights in search of the Grail. In this way, the Holy Grail is not only a legendary physical cup but it is also the jewel of perfect peace and inner wisdom that comes to the seekers of arcane truths. The Grail Knights themselves are the inheritors of the Druidic tradition.

In his book *The Druids*,[264] Stuart Piggott shows us not only the ancient world of the Druids but also the modern world of neo-Druids. These neo-Druids of the last few centuries have been an eccentric group whose origins, as they themselves often claim, go back to Atlantis.

Piggott goes on for pages about modern neo-Druid priests like the Archdruid of the Welsh Eisteddfod or Dr. William Price of Llantrisant who typically wore a "suit of scarlet merino wool with green silk lettering." This magical lettering in green silk was apparently keeping up with some Druidic tradition.

The mystic William Blake would qualify as a neo-Druid according to Piggott. Blake with his neo-Druid hymn to Jerusalem and illustrations of Stonehenge was an early popularizer of neo-Druid ideas, including the belief that Jesus had been to England.

~~~~~~~~~≈~~~~~~~~~

I spent several days wandering about the town of Glastonbury and relaxing. One day, to my delight, I was introduced to the well-known author John Michell who has written *The View Over Atlantis, Megalithamania, Living Wonders,* and many other books mentioned in these pages. I told him that I had read quite a few of his books and would like to take him to lunch. We found a table in a café and were soon talking about Atlantis, Glastonbury and ancient Britain.

"I've enjoyed your books on Fortean phenomena like strange rains, anomalistic objects and strange people," I told him as I stirred a cup of mint tea. "But probably my favorite topic is flying cats."

"Oh yes, flying cats," said John, "a fascinating subject."
I laughed. John was the master of the understatement, and I knew he was well informed about flying cats. In his classic book on animal mysteries, *Living Wonders*,[129] written with *Fortean Times* editor Bob Rickard, John Michell included an entire chapter, with photos, on "Cats with Wings."

Michell and Rickard begin by relating an account of a flying cat that was kept in the Oxford Zoo during the 1930s. They report that this cat apparently actually flew with the aid of its furry wings. The London *Daily Mirror* sent a special correspondent to Oxford to inspect it, and he reported (June 9, 1933):

"A few days ago neighbors of Mrs. Hughes Griffiths of Summerstown, Oxford, saw a strange black and white cat prowling round their gardens.

"Last evening Mrs. Hughes Griffiths saw the animal in a room of her stables.

"'I saw it move from the ground to a beam—a considerable distance which I do not think it could have leaped—using its wings in a manner similar to that of a bird,' she said to me."

The cat was captured in a net and taken to the Oxford Zoo, where Mr. W. E. Sawyer, the curator, was to later state, "I carefully examined the cat tonight, and there is no doubt about the wings. They grow just in front of its hindquarters."[129]

Michell and Rickard published a photograph (see photo section at the end of the chapter) of the Oxford flying cat and reported that this was all they could find out as the zoo is now defunct. Plenty of other flying cats have been reported, particularly in England, and they reproduce four photos of winged cats. One photo from 1939 is of a winged cat named Sally which belonged to Mrs. M. Roebuck of Attercliffe, Sheffield. Another photo is from *The Strand* magazine of November, 1899. The last photo is from the *Manchester Evening News* of December 23, 1975.[129]

A flying cat terrorized Ontario in 1966 according to John Keel in his book *Strange Creatures from Time and Space*[122].

He recounts how two black "flying cats" were shot near Ottawa and another near Montreal. Then in June of 1966 a large, black flying cat was said to be swooping down on terrified pets and farm animals at Alfred, Ontario. On 24 June it was shot by Mr. Jean J. Revers of Alfred as it sailed in, howling and screeching, to attack a local cat, "making gliding jumps of 50 to 60 feet—wings extended."

The police were called, and Constable Argall later gave his description of the dead predator: "Its head resembled a cat's, but a pair of needle sharp fangs five eighths of an inch long protruded from the mouth. It had a cat's whiskers, tail and ears, and its eyes were dark, greenish and glassy. I never saw anything like it in my life."[122, 129]

Michell and Rickard point out that at least some "winged cats" are genuinely able to use their wings in a sort of "flying leap."

"I suppose a similar mammal to these cats," I said, "would be the North American flying squirrel."

"Well," said John, "I've wondered whether housecats could have winged ancestors? The earthbound ostrich and penguin had winged ancestors; why not cats?"

"So," I said, a smile growing across my face, "are flying cats from Atlantis? Or rather, do you think that they had flying cats in Atlantis?"

John laughed. "Well, I suppose that's possible. They had to come from somewhere."

The crop circle conference went on for several days and I paid one day to get in and see the proceedings. Several presenters demonstrated how "Sacred Geometry," as at Chartres Cathedral, was being used in the crop circle formations.

The general thrust of the conference was that crop circles are an ongoing phenomenon that demonstrates that a higher intelligence is creating the different designs. There are some hoaxers involved in the crop circles, but these hoaxers are now well known and could only have made a few of the circles.

No one seemed to think that the British military were involved, such as possibly testing a microwave beam or chemical laser from space.

"Why would the government want to create crop circles?" I asked our group that night in a pub. We were discussing the subject with some friends.

"Well, maybe they started out as simple tests and when people noticed them, they decided to make them into symbols and designs to confuse the issue," Duncan suggested.

"Someone once told me that they had seen a crop circle formed and claimed that it was done by the military," said Marcus, a British friend of ours. "I didn't believe him though, it just seemed too fantastic."

"Do you think the government has technology that can create crop circles?" I asked.

"Well, no, I don't," said Marcus.

"But what about the Star Wars programs?" asked Duncan. "That is supposed to be a strike from space. Could crop circles be made in a similar way?"

"I must admit that if extraterrestrials are coming to earth to make these things, you would think the British military would know about it, since it happens next to their largest military base," I said.

"Maybe it's the earth mother coming alive and making these symbols spontaneously," suggested Marcus.

"Or trying to communicate with us," said Duncan.

"There is another explanation that you've all overlooked," I said with a smile. "Time travellers from Atlantis!"

Everyone laughed. Still, I thought it was as good an explanation as any.

The Ley Lines of Atlantis

After several days in Glastonbury I said my farewells to Duncan, Marcus and friends and headed for Cornwall and Land's End at the southern tip of England.

It was a pleasant drive through the fields and small towns of rural England on my way south. I picked up a hitchhiker on the way to Penzance. He was a pipe-fitter who was out of work. He had just been to another town looking for a job.

"No jobs to be had; maybe I'll go to South Africa," he said.

"South Africa?" I asked.

"I've been promised a job if I can get myself down there," he said. "They need pipe-fitters. What do you do?"

I told him that I was a writer and wrote books about archaeological mysteries, lost cities and such.

"Wow, cool job," he said. "I've always been interested in Stonehenge, ley lines and all that. They say that a special ley line goes from Saint Michael's Mount near Penzance to Glastonbury and beyond," said my hitchhiker.

We talked for a time about ley lines and how these straight lines of energy are thought to run across the English landscape from megalithic site to sacred well and so on.

Probably the first person to popularize the phrase "ley lines" was Alfred Watkins, who wrote a book called *The Old Straight Track*[284] in 1925. Others have come after him: John Michell and *The View Over Atlantis*,[13] Francis Hitching with *Earth Magic*,[244] Paul Devereux with his *Shamanism and the Mystery Lines*[205] or even the skeptical book, *Ley Lines in Question*,[206] by Tom Williamson and Liz Bellamy.

Peter Lancaster Brown wrote about Watkins in his book, *Megaliths, Myths and Men*,[245] noting that "The cult of the leys via Watkins' theories had its genesis one hot summer's day in the early 1920s. On that afternoon, Watkins recalled, he was riding across the

Bredwardine hills some 19 km west of Hereford and stopped on a crest for a moment in order to take in the sweep of the panorama before him. It was then he noticed something which he believed no one in Britain had seen for thousands of years: it was as if the more recent surface of the great landscape had been stripped away, revealing an unambiguous web of lines linking the ancient sites of antiquity that stretched out before him. Each fell into place in the whole scheme of things; old stones, holy wells, moats, mounds, crossroads, and pagan sites obscured by Christian churches stood in exact alignments that ran on for as far as the eye could trace."

Watkins maintained that the so-called old straight tracks which crossed the landscape of prehistoric Britain had decided the site of many of Britain's churches, shrines, villages and town squares.

John Michell's *The View Over Atlantis*[13] was the first book to put forward the theory that ley lines were not paths for normal travels but rather marked the course of a mysterious form of energy which was known by ancient man but is now lost.

Ley lines and straight tracks have long been a mystery and seem to relate to earth energies. Straight lines across the landscape are found in Bolivia, at Nazca in Peru, as well as in France, England and Ireland. The respected French scientist Amie Michel wrote a book in 1958 entitled *Flying Saucers and the Straight Line Mystery.*

F. W. Holiday, who wrote the classic Loch Ness monster book *The Great Orm of Loch Ness*,[216] also wrote a book entitled *The Dragon and the Disc*[215] in which he discussed such diverse topics as ley lines, the Loch Ness monster and UFOs. He went on, in his book *The Goblin Universe*,[213] to further relate paranormal phenomena to power points and energy grids.

Essentially, Holiday argued that different dimensions exist simultaneously and that an electromagnetic web of energy interlocks all things. The megalithic standing stones seek to warp this grid and therefore a great deal of paranormal phenomena is associated with ancient power spots and megalithic alignments. He theorized that prehistoric critters like a plesiosaur or a Bigfoot might materialize briefly into our time-space continuum for a period of time and then return to its own time.

The Lost Land of Lyonesse

I let my hitchhiker off a few miles before Penzance and then drove into the center of town. I parked by the harbor and began walking through the streets looking for a bed-and-breakfast. I spied into a courtyard with a bed-and-breakfast sign and procured a room.

Next I was off to the Land's End cliffs a few miles away from Penzance. It was a short drive along the rocky cliffs of the southwest shore of Cornwall to a tourist center and pub called Land's End.

I parked the car and walked around on the paved sidewalks around the cliffs. Below me the cold ocean surf crashed against the rocky cliffs. Beneath these waves was the lost land of Lyonesse.

The legendary lost land of Lyonesse lay between Land's End and the Isles of Scilly, which are to be found out in the English Channel between France and Cornwall. According to legend, in a single night 140 towns were inundated and it is said that their church bells can still be heard beneath the sea.

In a story similar to that of the lost land of Ys in Brittany, it is said that there was but one survivor, Trevilian, who fled on a white horse to dry land at Perranuthnoe on Mount's Bay (present-day Penzance). One version says that he was the last governor of Lyonesse and a member of the Vyvyan family of Trevelyan. The family crest is "a white horse saddled proper."

The Isles of Scilly which lie 28 miles (45 km) southwest of Land's End consist today of around 100 islands of which only the largest five are inhabited. The islands can be reached via a daily boat or helicopter flight from Penzance.

All of the islands are granitic with cliffs and white sand beaches. Says Peter Stanier in his book *Cornwall and the Isles of Scilly*,[209] "There has been a long history of human occupation on Scilly. There may have been only one or two main islands before a rise in sea level in post-Roman times. This is evidenced by drowned houses, field walls and graves which can be traced at very low tides. The islands may have taken their present form as late as the sixteenth century A.D."

The Scilly Isles have a large number of megalithic remains including chamber tombs and standing stones. Many more must be under water at the present time.

Similarly, Saint Michael's Mount near Penzance was known to be several miles from the coast and is now an   island. The Mount's Bay where Michael's Mount now stands was once a thick forest surrounding the mount, now submerged.

Nigel Pennick in his book *Lost Lands and Sunken Cities*[46] says that the entire southwestern promontory of Britain shows evidence of submergence and submarine forests. This area was once known as Dumnonia or West Wales. Says Pennick, "In his Report on Cornwall, Sir Henry de la Beche remarked that 'submarine forests are so common that it is difficult not to find traces of them in the district at the mouths of all the numerous valleys which open upon the sea and are in any manner silted up.'"

Pennick says that during Roman times the Scilly Isles were

probably one large island and, writing in 240 A.D., the Roman historian Solinus called it *Siluram Insulam*—the Scilly Isle—indicating that it was one large island. Pennick asserts that if the sea level were lowered by 60 feet then the many isles of Scilly would be one island.

One mystery of history has been the identity of the fabled island of Ictis of Roman tradition. Ictis was an island, somewhere along the south coast of England, from which the valuable cargoes of tin and lead were loaded onto Roman ships for the journey to the Mediterranean.

Some historians suggest that the Isle of Wight, which was known in Roman times as Vectis, was the Island of Ictis, with ancient Hurst Castle as the main fortification for the important port. Others have claimed that Saint Michael's Mount was Ictis, as suggested by tourist literature in Penzance.

A tourist brochure I obtained in Penzance said that the mount "was widely known as a port by prehistoric traders and was probably the island of Ictis from which Cornish tin was exported to Greek trading communities around the 4th century B.C." However, as we have pointed out, St. Michael's Mount was not even an island during those times, but was miles from the sea, so it was certainly not Ictis.

Perhaps Lyonesse itself was Ictis, separated from the mainland by a narrow channel like the Isle of Wight. Or perhaps Ictis, like Lyonesse, is under water.

Conservative archaeologists in the last century were skeptical of walls that were discovered underwater, but as Pennick says, there seems to be no doubt that these walls, which often start above water and then head under the sea, are the submerged remains of farmers' walls marking their (former) fields.

Pennick mentions other official discoveries of stone huts off the island of Tean that were seven feet underwater. Official estimates were that the water must have been at least 14 feet lower in ancient times.[46]

The ancient capital of Lyonesse was the "City of Lions" which according to tradition was situated about midway from Land's End to the Scilly Isles at a site known as the Seven Stones Reef. It is interesting to think about this City of Lions, and the famous Lion Gates at Mycenae in Greece and Hattusas in Turkey. Is there some connection between these ancient kingdoms?

Lest we start to see Lyonesse as the potential candidate for Atlantis, the earthquake that probably sank the land occurred many hundreds of years after Plato. It is estimated that a sudden inundation of Lyonesse occurred sometime after the Christian era.

Says Nigel Pennick in *Lost Lands and Sunken Cities*, "The date of the inundation of Lyonesse is usually reckoned at sometime in the sixth century of our era, perhaps concurrently with the similar destruction along the Coast of Wales, where the lost Lowland Hundred known as *Cantref y Gwaelod* was over-whelmed by the sea. It is possible that the Breton coast also suffered a similar fate, with the destruction of Caer Ys (Ker Ys), for to this day the stone circle at Er Lanic in Brittany is partially submerged by the tide."[46]

Certainly the lesson of the lost land of Lyonesse is that inundations and large earthquakes swallowing entire states and kingdoms has been happening regularly for thousands of years. Surely Lyonesse is not the only Atlantic kingdom suddenly swallowed up by the sea? Perhaps Caer Ys in Brittany was swallowed up in the same earthquake circa 500 A.D. that submerged Lyonesse. One thing that is agreed is that it was not a slow eating away of the coast by the sea.

Perhaps Paul Dunbavin's thesis gains some credibility. Dunbavin's Atlantis in the Irish Sea may have been destroyed in the first of a series of earthquakes that kept taking large bites out of coastal Wales, Ireland and England until the present time. The loss of Lyonesse was just the latest of these cataclysmic inundations. Is England due for another cataclysmic inundation in the near future as the geological clock goes?

〰〰〰〰〰𓂀〰〰〰〰〰

After several days in Cornwall, going to megalithic sites and looking for Arthurian legendary spots (there are many), I drove north to Wales.

Along the way I stopped at the famous Bodmin Moor which has a number of odd spots for the archaeologist in quest of mysteries. The small town of Camelford claims that it is the site of King Arthur's Camelot. I was to find while touring Britain that claims for King Arthur ranged from Cornwall all the way north to southern Scotland.

Located in western Cornwall, the Camel river and the Camelford may or may not have something to do with King Arthur's Camelot. The foundations of a huge building are to be seen nearby and these are said to be the remains of Arthur's Hall in which the Round Table stood. Also in Bodmin Moor is Dozmary Pool, where legend says that King Arthur's sword was thrown after his death.[210]

Bodmin Moor is truly a lost-world landscape with huge megalithic monuments, odd rock formations, stone circles and hilltop forts. All of this in a windswept land of stark hills and empty grasslands—sort of an English Badlands. Clearly, in the past, a much larger

368

population lived in the now sparsely populated country.

One fascinating rock formation is called the Cheesewring, a bizarre megalithic rock formation that is said to be natural, but also has stacked stones balanced on walls that are clearly artificial. Curiously, the Cheesewring is located on the St. Michael's Ley Line that runs through Britain, according to John Michell, Hamish Mill and other ley line enthusiasts.[267]

Another similarly bizarre "natural" rock formation is that of the Bowerman's Nose, a huge megalithic stack of squared rocks on the top of a hill near Dartmoor. The formation has every appearance of being the extremely weathered remains of a megalithic wall such as one would find in Greece, Turkey, Egypt or Peru. As I looked at it I couldn't help thinking that this was something from another time, ruins that were perhaps 10,000 years old. It made me wonder if some of the dolmens were also the replaced blocks of even earlier ruins, now re-erected as memorials to a world before our own.

Also in Bodmin Moor is Trethevy Quoit, one of the largest and finest chamber tombs in England, usually dated about 2,000 B.C. Trethevy Quoit consists of five cut and dressed slabs with a huge roof slab placed on top. The stones are particularly large and well shaped, with several of them giving the impression that they had originally been cut by stone masons for something other than a rough tomb. Trethevy Quoit was originally covered with earth to form a large mound.

I drove that night up to Wales and stayed with two of the investigators of the Rennes-le-Château mystery, Lionel and Patricia Fanthorpe. Together they had written the book *The Secrets of Rennes-le-Château*,[243] among others. They graciously allowed me to spend the night at their home and that night we sat up drinking a bottle of wine and talking about lost Wales.

"Cornwall and Lyonesse are fascinating," said Lionel, "but Wales probably has more lost lands and legends than the rest of England put together."

Lionel was familiar with Pennick's book on sunken cities. One of these cities is the lost Lowland Hundred of Cantref y Gwaelod which was devastated by the sea at about the same time as Lyonesse. Pennick quotes from manuscript number 3514 in the library of Exeter Cathedral, dated at about 1280: "There are three kingdoms that were submerged by the sea: The Kingdom of Tewthi, son of Gwynnon, King of Kaerrihog between Mynwy (St. David's) and Ireland. No one escaped from it, neither man nor beast, except Teithi Hen and his horse, and for the rest of his life he was sick with fright. The second kingdom was that of Helig, son of Glannawg that was between Cardigan and Bardsey Island and as far as Mynwy. And that land was extremely good and fruitful and flat... and stretched from Aber (Aberystwyth) to Lleyn and as far as Aberdyfi. The sea submerged a third, the kingdom of Rhedfoe, son of Rheged…"

All along the coast of Wales are submerged forests, submerged walls, ancient roads apparently going into the ocean and other indications of a sunken land. These inundations probably have taken place in the last few thousand years, during the time of recent folk memory. Paul Dunbavin's Atlantis theories place similar earthquakes and inundations about 3,200 B.C.

"Do you think that Wales and the Irish Sea were Plato's Atlantis as Paul Dunbavin suggests?" I asked Lionel.

Lionel leaned back and took a sip of wine. "Atlantis is a mystery," he said, "but I doubt if it will be found here in Wales." We all agreed to drink to that.

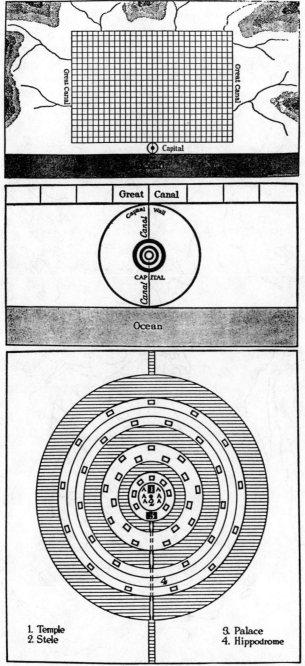

1. Temple
2. Stele

3. Palace
4. Hippodrome

Top: The great coastal plain of Atlantis as described in Plato's *Critias*, with its capital, plots of land and canal system. Center: The city of Atlantis with is Great Canal, City Wall and link to the ocean. Bottom: Inside the capital of Atlantis. 1. Temple. 2. Inscription column. 3. Palace. 4. Horse-racing track.

Paul Dunbavin's map of the Irish Sea and the Isle of Man as the area for the Great Plain of Atlantis. The present day shoreline is shown by the dotted line. Note the presence of the small central island opposite the central plain.

The Westbury white horse on Bratton Down, near Westbury, Wiltshire.

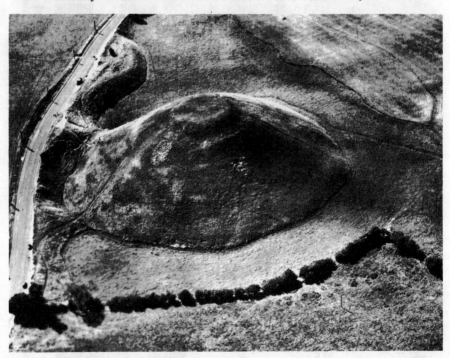

An aerial photo of Silbury Hill, the largest "pyramid-mound" in Europe.

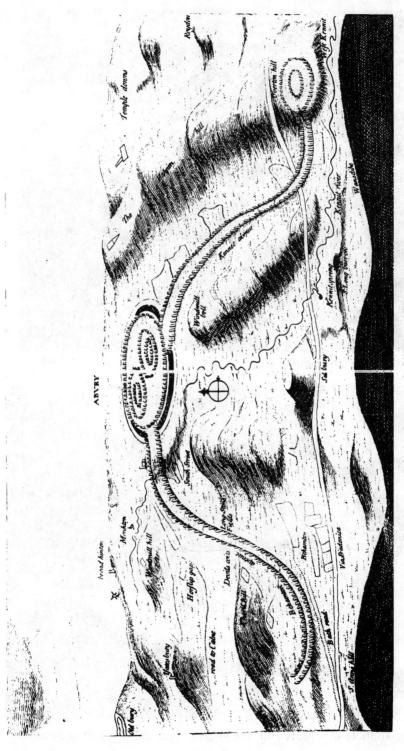

Region round Avebury and Silbury Hill depicting the West Kennet and Beckhampton Avenues restored according to Stukeley's ideas.

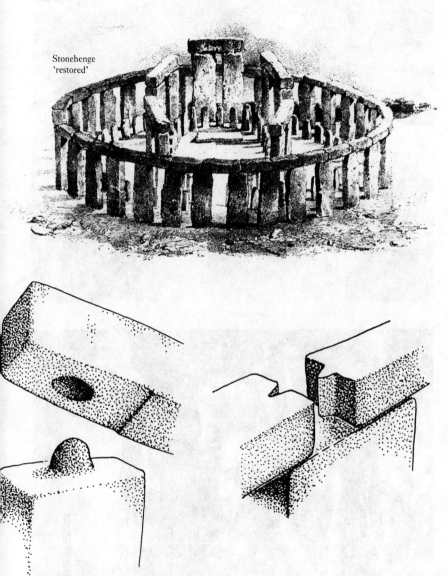

Stonehenge 'restored'

Top: Stonehenge restored as it may have originally looked. Bottom: Upright stones were attached to the lintel stones with mortise and tenon joints. The lintel stones at Stonehenge were dovetailed together.

The Glastonbury Tor, Somerset

The Quest for the Holy Grail: a tapestry by William Morris and Co., from a design
by Sir Edward Burne-Jones

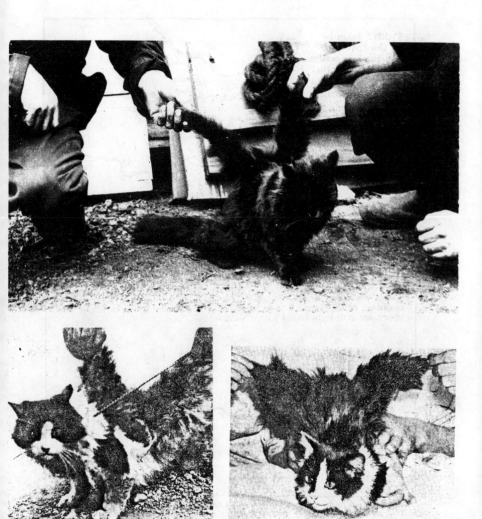

Winged Cats of Britain. Top: This photo of a winged cat appeared in the Manchester Evening News on December 23, 1975. Bottom Left: The winged cat formerly in the Oxford Zoo. Bottom Right: 1939 photo of a winged tomcat belonging to Mrs. M. Roebuck of Attercliffe, Sheffield which had a two-foot wingspan. He could not fly but used his "wings" to help him take long leaps. From Michell and Rickard's book, *Living Wonders*.

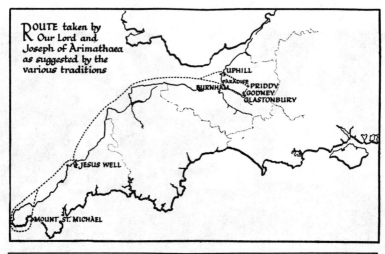

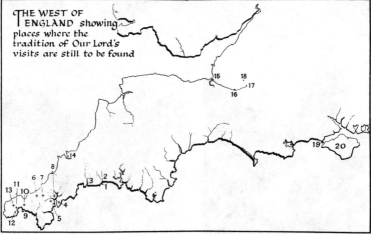

Top: The traditional route to Glastonbury said to have been taken by Joseph of Arimathea and Jesus. Bottom: Various places in the west of England where Jesus is said to have visited. 1. Lammana or Looe Island. 2. Looe. 3. Polruan by Fowey. 4. St. Just-in-Roseland Here Jesus is said to have come in a boat and landed in St. Just Creek. A stone with strange markings is pointed out as that on which He stepped. 5. Falmouth. The tradition says that Jesus landed at the Strand, crossed the stream and went up Smithwick Hill. 6 and 7. Redruth and St. Day. The tradition states that Jesus visited the ancient mines of Creeg Brawse. 8. Carnon Downs. A mining district. 9. St. Michael's Mount. 10. Nancledra. 11. Penzance. 12. Mousehole. 13. Ding Dong, an ancient mine. 14. Jesus Well. 15. Burnham, mouth of the Brue. 16. Glastonbury. 17. Pilton at the foot of the Mendip Hills. 18. Priddy, center of the lead mines. 19. Hurst Castle. 20. The Isle of Wight, which in Roman times was called Vectis and was thought by some to be the Ictis of Roman tradition.

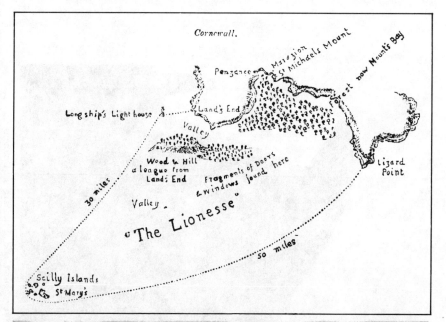

Top: A map of the lost land of Lyonesse from Beckles Willson's book *The Story of Lost England* (1902). Bottom: A stone wall in the Scilly Isles, revealed during a low spring tide in 1925.

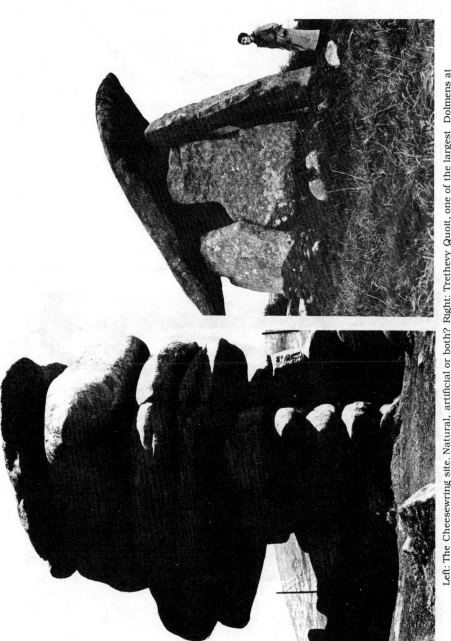

Left: The Cheesewring site. Natural, artificial or both? Right: Trethevy Quoit, one of the largest Dolmens at Bodmin Moor. These slabs may have been part of another structure originally.

Top: The Cheesewring Hill in Cornwall, an ancient fort. Bottom: An old picture postcard of the "Bowerman's Nose," in Dartmoor. Thought to be natural, this may be an ancient megalithic wall.

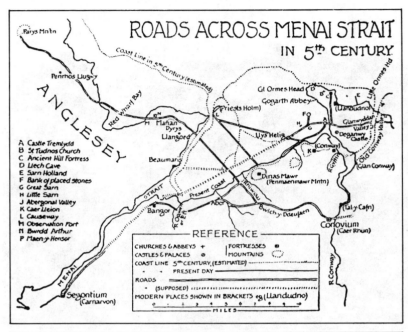

ROADS ACROSS MENAI STRAIT
IN 5th CENTURY

Parys Mn'tn

Penrhos Llugwy

Coast Line in 5th Century (estimated)

Gt Ormes Head

Gogarth Abbey

Little Ormes Hd

(Llandudno)

ANGLESEY

Red Wharf Bay

H Mathan Dyrys

Llangoed

(Priests Holm)

Llys Helig

Glanwddyn Valley

Deganwy Castle

(Conway)

Old Conway

A   Castle Tremlydd
B   St Tudnos Church
C   Ancient Hill Fortress
D   Llech Cave
E   Sarn Holland
F   Bank of placed stones
G   Great Sarn
H   Little Sarn
J   Abergonal Valley
K   Caer Lleion
L   Causeway
M   Observation Fort
N   Bwrdd Arthur
P   Maen-y-Hensor

Beaumaris

STRAIT

Present Coast

(Glan Conway)

Dinas Mawr
(Penmaenmawr Mntn)

Bangor

Aber

Bwlch-y-Ddeufaen

(Tal-y-Cafn)

Conovium
(Caer Rhun)

R Conway

MENAI

Segontium
(Carnarvon)

REFERENCE

CHURCHES & ABBEYS   +   FORTRESSES   ⊞
CASTLES & PALACES   ⊙   MOUNTAINS
COAST LINE 5TH CENTURY. (ESTIMATED) - - - - -
               PRESENT DAY ——————
ROADS
      (SUPPOSED) ·················
MODERN PLACES SHOWN IN BRACKETS eg (Llandudno)

0   1   2   3   4   5   6   7   8   9   10
——— MILES ———

Top: A 1920 map of some of the now submerged roads along the Welsh coast. Bottom: An 1893 sketch of a submerged wall in Cardigan Bay, Wales.

Chapter 12

SCOTLAND:

The Vitrified Forts of Atlantis

*I am told that there are people who do not care for maps,
and find it hard to believe. The names, the shapes of the
woodlands, the courses of the roads and rivers, the
prehistoric footsteps of man still distinctly traceable up hill
and down dale, the mills and the ruins, the ponds and the
ferries, perhaps the Standing Stone or the Druidic Circle on
the heath; here is an inexhaustible fund of interest for any
man with eyes to see, or tuppence worth of imagination to
understand with.*
— Robert Louis Stevenson

I drove from Wales up to the Lake Country of northwest England
and the next day entered into the green glens of Scotland. Scotland
was the land of my ancestors and I was particularly keen to see this
northern land of deep, narrow lakes, windswept islands and vast
forests. As I drove north to Glasgow I thought about the mysterious
origins of the Scots.

According to the book *The Search For the Stone of Destiny*[268] by
Pat Gerber, the Scots came originally from Ireland where the word
Scot meant "raider." Furthermore, the famous Stone of Scone at
Westminster Abbey came from ancient Israel!

Gerber's fascinating theory begins in 585 B.C. when the prophet
Jeremiah of Israel was imprisoned by his own people for
prophesying bad times for the country. Jeremiah was tragically
proved correct when Nebuchadnezzar of Babylon besieged Jerusalem
for two years and eventually captured the city. King Zedekiah
escaped over his garden wall with some of his family, but
Nebuchadnezzar's men caught up with him, killed his sons in front
of him, put out his eyes and took him captive.

Things were bad for ancient Israel. The days of the glory of King Solomon were gone and now there were no male descendants to inherit the throne of Israel. However, King Nebuchadnezzar freed the prophet Jeremiah from prison and Jeremiah was able to rescue several important items from the great Temple of Solomon which held the Ark of the Covenant and other holy relics sacred to the Hebrews.

He also rescued one of the daughters of Zedekiah, Princess Tea, and together with a small band escaped from Israel to Egypt, an ally of Israel at the time. Jeremiah hid some items in a cave near Mount Pisgah and then his scribe Baruch wrote down his last prophecy—that Nebuchadnezzar would soon attack Egypt.

Jeremiah and Princess Tea were now refugees from the eastern Mediterranean and together they disappeared from recorded history—or did they?

≈≈≈≈≈≈≈≈ 𓂀 ≈≈≈≈≈≈≈≈

The Stone of Destiny and the Tuatha de Danann

Gerber in *The Search For the Stone of Destiny* claims that Jeremiah, Princess Tea and their entourage left Egypt with the remnants of the Phoenicians, those seafarers who were a mixture of the Hebrews and Philistines, the tribe of Dan. Gerber quotes from *Judges* 5 where the prophetess Deborah asks, "Why did Dan remain in ships?"

The tribe of Dan, says Gerber, sailed with the Phoenicians, then allegedly took Jeremiah and Princess Tea to their northernmost trading outposts, which were in Northern Ireland. According to the old Irish book, *Chronicles of Eri,* at some time around 580 B.C. a ship landed at Ulster and on board was the Prophet Ollamh Fodhla, the Princess Tara and a scribe named Simon Brech. These, says Gerber, were none other than Jeremiah, Princess Tea and the scribe Baruch.

According to Irish tradition these people, the Tuatha de Danann, or Tribe of Dan, brought with them a magic cauldron, a magic sword, a magic spear and a magical stone called the Stone of Destiny. Princess Tara also brought with her a harp—once the emblem of the House of David—and this harp is said to have been buried at Tara. This harp of David is now the symbol of Ireland, and can be seen on every bottle of Guinness, the national drink. More on Tara in the next chapter.

Princess Tea/Tara married the local Irish King Eochaid the Heremon and the kingdom of the Tuatha de Danann was set up. The Stone of Destiny, kept for a time at Tara, was believed to be the same stone that the Biblical patriarch Jacob had used as a pillow when he dreamed and had the vision of "Jacob's Ladder" which angels used to move up and down from Heaven.

It was believed by ancient peoples that stones held the "vibrations" of historical events in them. As a result, many ancient civilizations held their coronations on a slab of stone that all the former kings had been coronated on as well. In certain societies, it was believed that the stone would "cry out" if the king to be crowned was not the rightful heir to the throne. An interesting parallel here is the legend of King Arthur and the sword in the stone. Only the rightful heir to Camelot's throne could draw the sword from the stone.

In the case of the Stone of Destiny, it was said that when a king of the royal blood sat on it, it would cry out. If an impostor sat on the throne, it would remain silent.

The Princess Tea became known in Irish mythology as Scota, Queen of the Raiders. Irish tradition says that 1,000 years of prosperity and peace existed in Ireland following the arrival of the Tuatha de Danann. Then, in the 5th century A.D., the northern Irish, known as the Scotti, began to colonize the Argyll region of western Scotland. They brought with them Ogam writing and the Stone of Destiny, or a portion of it.

The Scots then used this stone as the coronation stone for Scottish kings. Scotland was inhabited by the Celtic Picts prior to the invasion of the Scotti. The Picts did not use a written language but communicated by the use of illustrated scenes, much like cartoons. With steady expansion and absorption, the Scotti, with the help of St. Columba, subdued the Picts and converted them to the new religion of Christianity, a gentle religion of peace and goodwill toward neighbors.

At one point St. Columba even subdued a monster in Loch Ness, circa 568 B.C., and so impressed the local Pictish king, that the first united Scotland was created when St. Columba crowned Aidan king of the independent kingdom called Scotch Dalriada. King Aidan was crowned on the Stone of Destiny.

Later the Scottish chieftain Kenneth Mac Alpin was to bring the sacred stone from Argyll to the castle at Scone, where the ancient relic became known as the Stone of Scone. The stone remained in Scone until 1296 A.D. when Edward I of England conquered Scotland and took the stone to Westminster Abbey.

Later, in July of 1324, Robert the Bruce of Scotland with 6,000 Scots miraculously defeated 20,000 English soldiers. In 1326 the Pope recognized Robert the Bruce as King of Scotland and sent a stern letter to Edward II of England concerning the independence of Scotland. Eventually, in 1603, Scotland and England were united under the Scottish King James I (who started out as James IV of

Scotland), son of Mary, Queen of Scots.

So here, in the familiar relic of the Coronation throne of Westminster Abbey, we have an intriguing tale that takes us back to the turbulent history of the eastern Mediterranean in the sixth century B.C. Invading armies sent refugees to Ireland, who eventually founded a dynasty in Scotland. As we have seen with the submerged areas of Wales and Cornwall, much of this former territory is now apparently under water. The lost cities of the Tuatha de Danann may be discovered by archaeologists in the future beneath the Irish Sea.

~~~~~~~~🙙~~~~~~~~

The Stones of Callanish

It was late in the afternoon when I pulled into the lively Scottish port town of Oban. The sun shone brightly on the ferries and ships in the port as I drove downhill into the center of town. Oban was awash in German and French tourists, and all places were fully booked up. After hours of searching for a hotel, hostel or bed-and-breakfast, I finally realized that there was not a room to be had.

With a full moon rising above the island of Iona in the distance, I walked the late night streets of Oban. Iona was a mysterious island of sacred relics and has a famous monastery founded by St. Columba. He was from Donegal, a Druid center, like Tara, of Ireland. St. Columba was of a royal family, but became a priest instead. He was exiled from Ireland after causing a dreadful intertribal battle and came to Iona with twelve companions. The Stone of Destiny, according to some legends, is said to have been brought to Scotland at this time. St. Columba was also said to use the stone as his pillow, in a manner similar to the Biblical Jacob.

I slept that night in my rented Fiat and decided in the morning I would have to get up into northern Scotland if I was to find a room. I was back on the road, my destination the Isle of Skye and the famous stone circle of Callanish in the Outer Hebrides.

I reached the Isle of Skye by ferry and drove further north to the town of Uig where I got the late afternoon ferry to Stornoway on the Island of Lewis in the Outer Hebrides. The next day I drove from Stornoway to the ancient megaliths of Callanish.

The stone circle at Callanish is one of the most famous antiquities of Scotland. When it was first discovered by science in the mid-1800s the stones were more than half buried in peat. They were dug out of the peat in 1867 and in those times the mark of where the stones had been buried could still be seen at a height of ten feet or more above the ground. The stones were so old that ten feet of turf had accumulated around them.

Since the stones of Callanish are thousands of years old, it's not surprising they would have such an accumulation of soil. Curiously, the great statues of Easter Island on the slopes of the volcanic quarry of Rano Raraku were also discovered buried up to their necks in the local volcanic soil, but they are only thought to be a few hundred years old, built around 1400 A.D. By the Callanish standards, the Easter Island statues should be thousands of years old.

Callanish is more than a stone circle, it is a circle with a cross intersecting it, forming a huge Celtic cross. Today, Callanish is believed to be an astronomical computer for predicting eclipses, as is Stonehenge. It was possibly even built by the same people.

Gerald S. Hawkins compared Stonehenge with Callanish in *Science* (No. 147, 1965) as follows: "On the basis of the stone record it appears that the Callanish people were as precise as the Stonehengers in setting up their megalithic structure, but not as scientifically advanced. Callanish is, however, a structure that could have been used much as Stonehenge was. It would be interesting to obtain a date by the radiocarbon method from the peat in the area of Callanish, to determine how much older, or more recent, than Stonehenge this structure is. Perhaps the knowledge gained at Callanish was later used in the design of Stonehenge."[17]

Hawkins maintains that both structures are at critical latitudes. Callanish is at the latitude where the moon skims the southern horizon. Says Hawkins, "If Stonehenge and Callanish are related, then the builders may have been aware of some of the fundamental facts which served later as the basis of accurate navigation and led to a knowledge of the curvature of the earth."

These stone circles could be used to measure the earth's surface as well as used in astronomy and the ancients' study of solar eclipses. In his book *Prehistoric Stone Circles*,[207] Aubrey Burl says that there are more than 50 such megalithic circles to visit. He gives a full account of the circles, their location and size in his guidebook. Callanish, like Stonehenge, is proof of a highly sophisticated civilization having occupied these northern isles at some point in prehistory, say 2,000 to 4,000 B.C.

A Stonehenge at the Bottom of Loch Ness
The sky was overcast as I pulled into the town of Inverness, the capital of the Highlands. I had wisely booked ahead and carefully drove through the narrow streets looking for my hotel.

Soon I was settled into my hotel on the shallow Inverness River and ready to go out and see the town. Ever since I had been a kid, Inverness and Loch Ness were places that fascinated me. The Loch Ness monster was one of the first mysteries I had been exposed to and the idea of some sort of ancient sea monster trapped in a lake was very intriguing to me.

My teachers had told me that prehistoric monsters such as this had been dead for 65 million years, yet here was a critter that had supposedly survived up to modern times.

The lore on the Loch Ness monster, and other lake monsters, goes back to the Pictish-Celtic times of early Scotland.

The lake is deceptively small if viewed on a map or from the bank, as the opposite shore is easily seen. However, it is the largest lake in Great Britain, containing more than three times as much water as Loch Lomond, which is considerably wider than Loch Ness and covers approximately the same area.

Scientists have estimated that the loch holds about 263 billion cubic feet of water when its surface is at its average height of 52 feet above sea level. When compared to the English Channel or North Sea, both have a larger surface area but are less than half as deep. The deepest part of Loch Ness is about 754 feet while the average is about 433 feet deep. The total volume of water contained in the loch would be enough to flood an area of approximately 9,400 square miles to a depth of one foot.[218]

The loch is part of a great geological fault that stretches across the entire length of Scotland, from Oban on the west coast to Inverness on the northeast coast. This fault and its waters are affected by earthquakes thousands of miles away. When an earthquake destroyed Lisbon and parts of Morocco in 1775, huge waves crashed against the shores of the loch.[218]

Though Loch Ness is at the same latitude as Kodiak, Alaska, it has never been known to freeze over. The water at the bottom of the loch never grows colder than 42 degrees Fahrenheit. Cold water at the surface of the loch sinks to the bottom as warmer water rises to the top. It has been estimated that the amount of heat sent into the atmosphere by Loch Ness during the winter is equivalent to that which would be generated by burning about two and a half million tons of coal. Because of the tremendous amount of heat given out by the loch, snow rarely lies around the glen for more than a few hours while 20 miles north, severe winters occur with snowdrifts up to 15 feet deep.[218]

For this reason, it is thought that the lake could hold several families of large marine animals feeding in deep water on the many schools of salmon and other plentiful fish.

I drove out to the loch town of Drumnadrochit where the "Official

Loch Ness Monster Exhibition Centre" is located at a large hotel-restaurant-gift shop complex. I had a leisurely lunch looking out over the calm waters of the loch. Tourists peered intently at waves out on the loch. Was the monster there?

Afterwards I paid five quid and took the tour through the 40-minute audio-visual exhibition about the loch and the monster. The presentation was impressive and scientific, and if evidence was to be believed, there seemed little doubt that there was some sort of family of large animals living deep in the loch.

It is said that the very first recorded sighting was by Scotland's patron saint, St. Columba, around the year 565 A.D. This was when St. Columba subdued the monster (possibly with a Druid incantation) and thereby impressed a local Pictish king. Peter Costello in his book *In Search of Lake Monsters*[219] records a sighting published in *The Times* in March of 1856 and taken from the Inverness Courier of the same month.

The rash of modern sightings began in 1933 when a new road, the A82, was being built along the northern side of the loch. One explanation for the sudden series of sightings and photos was that blasting with dynamite along the edge of the loch was disturbing the large animals deep in the water and they were coming to the surface with more regularity than normal. At the same time tall trees that lined the edge of the loch were being cut down, which allowed for a better view of the loch.

A number of famous photos were taken, including one by a British surgeon in 1934 of a head appearing out of the water. The "MacNab photo" taken in 1955 clearly shows a huge undulating object in the loch with Urquart Castle in the foreground. NASA computers enhanced the area around the humps in the photo and concluded that it was a real object in the water and not a photographic effect.

In 1960 Tim Dinsdale took movie film of a large object on the lake and millions of pounds were later spent on underwater searches and photographs of the monster. In 1972 Dr. Robert Rines and his team from the Academy of Applied Science took underwater photographs of a moving object and came up with at least one good photograph of a large plesiosaur-type flipper. Finally, in 1975 an underwater photograph of an entire long-necked animal was obtained by Dr. Rines and his team.

Other photos of the monster have proven to be hoaxes, including a recent confession to forgery by one famous monster hunter, and the controversy continues to this day. The "Official Loch Ness Monster Exhibition Centre" assures us, however, that there is indeed a monster in the loch.

Even stranger than a large prehistoric animal in the loch is the surprise discovery of ancient structures at the bottom of the deep lake. In 1976 it was reported that structures were discovered at the bottom of the lake by sonar.

In an article published in *Science News* (Number 110, 1976) entitled "Ancient Stoneworks Found in Loch Ness," it was reported that "Scientists searching for the Loch Ness monster have stumbled upon several large, prehistoric manmade stoneworks submerged in the Loch. The structures include a stone wall, several ancient mounds (locally called cairns) and possibly an ancient fortified island (called a crannog). Though such cairns and crannogs are common in the area, the discovery of such structures some 30 feet below the Loch's surface indicates the water level has risen sharply over the centuries. Also, since most cairns have long since been pillaged of whatever remains they might have contained, the discovery of several apparently intact structures may allow archaeologists to learn more about the area's ancient inhabitants.

"The cairns are made of piled stones, varying in size from nearly one foot diameter down to pebbles. Such structures were presumably built as burial and religious mounds three or four thousand years ago. The mounds are generally laid out in a series of concentric circles, as much as 100 feet in diameter, but one complex series stretches 250 feet."[17]

Other ruins may be at the bottom of Loch Ness, apparently an area of serious earth changes over the last 15,000 years. Loch Ness was connected to the ocean but then sealed shut by an earthquake, preserving the deep loch with its ruins and sea monsters.

As I headed out of Loch Ness for the vitrified fort of Craig Phadrig one autumn morning, I wondered whether my teachers had been wrong and not all prehistoric monsters became extinct 65 million years ago.

The Vitrified Forts of Scotland

I arrived at Craig Phadrig, parked the car and began to walk around the stone rubble of the ancient fortress. One of the great mysteries of classical archaeology is the mystery of the many vitrified forts of Scotland. There are said to be at least 60 of them in central and northeastern Scotland. Among the most well-known are Tap O'Noth, Dunnideer, Craig Phadrig (near Inverness), Abernathy (near Perth), Dun Lagaidh (in Ross), Cromarty, Arka-Unskel, Eilean na Goar, and Bute-Dunagoil on the sound of Bute on Arran Island.

A good example of a vitrified fort is that of Tap O'Noth which is near the village of Rhynie in northeastern Scotland. This massive fort from prehistory is on the summit of a mountain of the same name, Tap O'Noth (1,859 ft.; 560 m.), which commands an impressive view of the Aberdeenshire countryside.

At first glance it seems that the walls are made of a rubble of stones, but on closer look it is apparent that they are made, not of dry stones, but of melted rocks! What were once individual stones are now black and cindery, fused together by heat that must have been so intense that molten rivers of rock once ran down them. Huge blocks of stones are fused with smaller rubble in a hard and glassy mass that scientists call "vitrified."

Explanations for this vitrification are few and far between, and none of them universally accepted. One early theory was that these forts are located on ancient volcanoes (or the remains of them) and that the people used molten stone ejected from eruptions to build their settlements.

This idea was replaced with the theory that the builders of the walls had designed the forts in such a way that the vitrification was purposeful, in order to strengthen the walls. This theory postulated that fires had been lit, and flammable material added, to produce walls strong enough to resist the dampness of the local climate or the invading armies of the enemy.

It is an interesting theory, but one that has several problems. For starters, there is really no indication that such vitrification actually strengthens the walls of the fortress; rather, it weakens them. In many cases, the walls of the forts seemed to have collapsed because of the fires. Also, since the walls of many Scottish forts are only partially vitrified, this would hardly have proved an effective building method.

Julius Caesar described a wood-stone fortress known as a *murus Gallicus* in his account of the Gallic Wars. The *murus Gallicus* was interesting to those seeking solutions to the vitrified fort mystery because these forts were made of a stone wall filled with rubble with wooden logs inside and throughout the walls for stability. Since logs were part of the construction of these *murus Gallicus* forts, it seemed logical to suggest that perhaps the burning of such a wall might create the phenomenon of vitrification.

A Scottish archaeologist, Helen Nisbet, believes that the vitrification was not done on purpose by the builders of the forts. In a thorough analysis of rock types used, she reveals that most of the forts were built of stone easily available at the chosen site and not chosen for their property of vitrification.[131]

Other researchers are sure that the builders themselves caused the vitrification. Arthur C. Clarke quotes one team of chemists from the Natural History Museum in London who were studying the many forts: "Considering the high temperatures which have to be produced, and the fact that possibly sixty or so vitrified forts are to be seen in a limited geographical area of Scotland, we do not believe that this type of structure is the result of accidental fires. Careful planning and construction were needed."[131]

However, the vitrification process itself, even if purposely set, is quite a mystery. A team of chemists on Arthur C. Clarke's *Mysterious World* subjected rock samples from eleven forts to a rigorous chemical analysis, and stated that the temperatures needed to produce the vitrification were so intense—up to 1,100°C—that a simple burning of walls with wood interlaced with stone could not have achieved such temperatures.[131]

Nevertheless, experiments carried out in the 1930s by the famous archaeologist V. Gordon Childe and his colleague Wallace Thorneycroft showed that forts could have been set on fire by invaders piling brushwood against the walls and that a sufficient amount of wood plus a correct technique could indeed generate enough heat to vitrify the stone.

In 1934 these two created a test wall that was 12 feet long, 6 feet wide and 6 feet high which was built for them at Plean Colliery in Stirlingshire. They used old fireclay bricks for the faces, pit props as timber, and filled the cavity between the walls with small cubes of basalt rubble. Finally, they covered the top with turf. Then, they piled about four tons of scrap timber and brushwood against the walls and set fire to them. Because of a snowstorm in progress, a strong wind fanned the blazing mixture of wood and stone so that the inner core did attain some vitrification of the rock.

In June of 1937 Childe and Thorneycroft duplicated their test vitrification at the ancient fort of Rahoy in Argyllshire, using rocks found at the site.

Their experiments did not resolve any of the questions surrounding vitrified forts, however, because they had only proven that it was theoretically possible to pile enough wood and brush on top of a mixture of wood and stone to vitrify the mass of stone.

One criticism of Childe is that he seems to have used a larger portion of wood to stone than many historians believe made up the wood-stone fortress known as a *murus Gallicus*. An important part of Childe's theory was that it was invaders who were assaulting the forts and then setting fire to the walls with brush and wood; however, it is hard to understand why people would have repeatedly built defenses that invaders could destroy with fire, when great ramparts of solid stone would have survived unscathed.[131]

Furthermore, critics of this theory maintain that in order to generate enough heat by a natural fire, the walls would have to have been specially constructed to create the heat necessary.

Therefore, the problem with the assault theory is that it seems unreasonable to suggest the builders would create forts to be burned or that such a great effort would be made by invaders to create the kind of fire it would take to vitrify the walls—at least with traditional techniques.

If one were to believe in the great Indian epic of the *Mahabharata*, fantastic battles were fought in the past with airships, particle beams and chemical warfare. Just as battles in this century have been fought with incredibly devastating weapons, it may well be that battles in the latter days of Atlantis were fought with highly sophisticated and high-tech weapons. The "Greek fire" of the eastern Mediterranean was one form of chemical warfare that may have had the means to vitrify walls.

As I stood looking at the walls of Craig Phadrig, it occurred to me that the problem with all the many theories is their assumption of a primitive state of culture associated with ancient Scotland.

It is astonishing to think of how large the population or army must have been that built and inhabited these ancient structures. Janet and Colin Bord in their book *Mysterious Britain*[134] speak of Maiden Castle to give an idea of the vast extent of this marvel of prehistoric engineering. "It covers an area of 120 acres, with an average width of 1,500 feet and length of 3,000 feet. The inner circumference is about 1-1/2 miles round, and it has been estimated, as mentioned earlier, that it would require 250,000 men to defend it! It is hard, therefore, to believe that this construction was intended to be a defensive position.

"A great puzzle to archaeologists has always been the multiple and labyrinthine east and west entrances at each end of the enclosure. Originally they may have been built as a way for processional entry by people of the Neolithic era. Later, when warriors of the Iron Age were using the site as a fortress they probably found them useful as a means of confusing the attacking force trying to gain entry. The fact that so many of these 'hillforts' have two entrances—one north of east and the other south of west—also suggests some form of Sun ceremonial."

With 250,000 men defending a fort, we are talking about a huge army in a very organized society! This is not a bunch of fur-wearing Picts with spears defending a fort from marauding bands of hunter-gatherers.

The evidence of the vitrified forts is clear: some hugely successful and organized civilization was living in Scotland, England and Wales in prehistoric times, circa 1,000 B.C. or more, that was building gigantic structures, including forts. This apparently was a maritime civilization that prepared itself for naval warfare as well as other forms of attack.

Hilltop Forts of Western Scotland

I walked around the fort and looked carefully at the melted mass of granite rock. Craig Phadrig is a sort of oval granite fort which looks like a citadel with a basin-shaped depression at the center. The enclosure is constructed from granite blocks which have been vitrified and granite requires temperatures of at least 1,300 degrees C., far beyond the means of a normal fire.

Reports on vitrified forts were made as far back as 1880 when Edward Hamilton wrote an article entitled "Vitrified Forts on the West Coast of Scotland" in the *Archaeological Journal* (Number 37, pages 227-243, 1880). Hamilton writes about several vitrified forts on the west coast of Scotland.

At the entrance to Loch Ailort are two islands, one of which is called Eilean na Goar. Says Hamilton, "At the point where Loch na Nuagh begins to narrow, where the opposite shore is about one-and-a-half to two miles distant, is a small promontory connected with the mainland by a narrow strip of sand and grass, which evidently at one time was submerged by the rising tide. On the flat summit of this promontory are the ruins of a vitrified fort, the proper name for which is Arka-Unskel.

"The rocks on which this fort are placed are metamorphic gneiss, covered with grass and ferns, and rise on three sides almost perpendicular for about 110 feet from the sea level. The smooth surface on the top is divided by a slight depression into two portions. On the largest, with precipitous sides to the sea, the chief portion of the fort is situated, and occupies the whole of the flat surface. It is of somewhat oval form. The circumference is about 200 feet, and the vitrified walls can be traced in its entire length... We dug under the vitrified mass, and there found what was extremely interesting, as throwing some light on the manner in which the fire was applied for the purpose of vitrification. The internal part of the upper or vitrified wall for about a foot or a foot-and-a-half was untouched by the fire, except that some of the flat stones were slightly agglutinated together, and that the stones, all feldspatic, were placed in layers one upon another.

"It was evident, therefore, that a rude foundation of boulder stones was first formed upon the original rock, and then a thick layer of loose, mostly flat stones of feldspatic sand, and of a different kind from those found in the immediate neighborhood, were placed on this foundation, and then vitrified by heat applied externally. This foundation of loose stones is found also in the vitrified fort of Dun Mac Snuichan, on Loch Etive."[17]

Hamilton describes another vitrified fort that is much larger, situated on the island at the entrance of Loch Ailort. "This island, locally termed Eilean na Goar, is the most eastern and is bounded on all sides by precipitous gneiss rocks; it is the abode and nesting place of numerous sea birds. The flat surface on the top is 120 feet from the sea level, and the remains of the vitrified forts are situated on this, oblong in form, with a continuous rampart of vitrified wall five feet thick; attached at the S.W. end to a large upright rock of gneiss. The space enclosed by this wall is 420 feet in circumference and 70 feet in width. The rampart is continuous and about five feet in thickness. At the eastern end, is a great mass of wall in situ, vitrified on both sides. In the centre of the enclosed space is a deep depression in which are masses of the vitrified wall strewed about, evidently detached from their original site."[17]

Hamilton naturally asks a few obvious questions about the forts: Were these structures built as a means of defense? Was the vitrification the result of design or accident? How was the vitrification produced?

He concludes that the forts were intended as places of defense. "The regular design of these walls, their great extent and uniformity, the large area enclosed, all lead to prove that these early people had a design in their construction; and it is a curious circumstance that many of the most important of these works were re-occupied by the conquerors of the original designers, as places of defense."

He discounts the idea that beacon fires or feasting caused the vitrification. He says the fire was applied externally and on all sides, this being proved by the internal part of the wall being unvitrified. The questions remain though as to what huge army might have occupied these cliffside forts by the sea or lake entrances? And what massive maritime power were these people unsuccessfully defending themselves against?

These forts on the western coast of Scotland are reminiscent of the mysterious clifftop forts in the Aran Islands on the west coast of Ireland. Here we truly have shades of the Atlantis story with a powerful naval fleet attacking and conquering its neighbors in a terrible war. Was Dunbavin correct in his *Atlantis Researches* that the Atlantis story took place in Wales, Scotland, Ireland and England? However, in the case of the Scottish vitrified forts it looks as if these were the losers of a war, not the victors.

Perhaps the vitrified forts are part of Iman Wilkens' theory of the Trojan War being fought in England and Scotland. Here, at least, we have the ancient British as the losers of the war. And defeat can be seen across the land: the war dikes in Sussex, the vitrified forts of Scotland, the utter collapse and disappearance of the civilization that built these things. What long-ago Armageddon destroyed ancient Scotland?

In ancient times there was a substance known through writings as "Greek fire." This was some sort of ancient napalm bomb that was hurled by catapult and could not be put out. Some forms of Greek fire were even said to burn under water and were therefore used in naval battles. The actual composition of Greek fire is unknown, but it must have contained chemicals such as phosphorus, pitch, sulfur or other flammable chemicals.

Could a form of Greek fire have been responsible for the vitrification? While ancient astronaut theorists may believe that extraterrestrials with their atomic weapons vitrified these walls, it seems more likely that they were a man-made apocalypse of a chemical nature. With siege machines, battleships and Greek fire, did a vast flotilla storm the huge forts and eventually burn them down in an unnatural blaze?

The Orkney Islands and the Holy Grail

One of the most interesting and mysterious of Scottish characters was Prince Henry Sinclair, the last king of the Orkney Islands. Henry Sinclair, like many other nobles of the Middle Ages, held many titles and he was many things. He was king of the Orkney Islands, although they were officially an earldom granted to Prince Henry by the King of Norway. At the same time Prince Henry held other territories as a vassal of the Scottish king. Prince Henry Sinclair was also a Grand Master of the Knights Templar, a veteran of the crusades and, according to some sources, the possessor of the Holy Grail.

In the year 1391 A.D. Prince Henry Sinclair met with the famous explorer and mapmaker Nicolo Zeno at Fer Island, a lonely island between the Orkneys and the Shetlands. The Zeno brothers were well known for their maps of Iceland and the Arctic. Prince Henry contracted with them to send an exploratory fleet to the New World.[258]

With the aid of funding from the Knights Templar, who had now been banished by the Pope, Prince Henry gathered a fleet of twelve ships for a voyage to establish a safe haven for the order of Knights and their treasure. The party was led by Prince Henry under the guidance of Antonio Zeno, the mapmaker from Venice.

The fleet left the Orkneys in 1398 and landed in Nova Scotia, wintered there and later explored the eastern seaboard of the United States. It is said that the effigy of one of Henry's close companions, Sir James Gunn, who died on the expedition is to be found carved upon a rock-face at Westford, Massachusetts.

The party is said to have built a castle and left a portion of their navy in Nova Scotia. As we shall see, the famous Oak Island just off the mainland of Nova Scotia is to become part of the mystery surrounding Prince Henry Sinclair.[257, 258]

Prince Henry and his fleet returned to the Orkneys but shortly afterward Prince Henry was murdered. The year was 1400 and it was 92 years before Cristobal Colón, known to us as Columbus, was to use his knowledge of Iceland and the Zeno Brothers' maps to make his famous voyage across the Atlantic.

In his book *Holy Grail Across the Atlantic*,[257] Michael Bradley attempts to show that the ancient treasure from the Temple of Solomon was kept at Montségur in the French Pyrenees, the Cathar region of France. This mountain fortress was besieged by the forces of Simon de Montfort and the Inquisition on March 16, 1244, but it is believed that the secret treasure escaped.

The treasure probably included both ancient treasure from the Middle East but also gold, silver and jewelry of more modern manufacture. The Knights Templar were well funded in secret by various royalty; after all, the Merovingian kings were of the Holy Blood of Jesus—so it was claimed.

Bradley asserts that Prince Henry took over as many as 300 colonists to the New World and a literal "Grail Castle" was built in Nova Scotia—the New Scotland.

While Buechner claims the German S.S. retrieved the sacred relics such as the Holy Grail during World War II, it does seem more likely that the most important parts of the treasure like the Holy Grail and the Ark of the Covenant had already been rescued by the Merovingian kings during or after the siege. Other treasure left by the Cathars in the vicinity of Montségur may well have been discovered by the priest Sauniere as well as the Nazis.

So strong is the evidence for Prince Henry Sinclair's voyage across the Atlantic with the Knights Templar that his distant relative Andrew Sinclair wrote a book entitled *The Sword and the Grail*[258] in which he claimed much the same as Bradley in *Holy Grail Across the Atlantic.*

The Templars may have also come into the possession of some highly accurate maps made by the Moors and Turks, and in so doing, inherited the secret sea knowledge once guarded so carefully by the Carthaginians and their allies.

Bradley and Sinclair claim that a special Grail Castle was built in an area of central Nova Scotia called "The Cross." This spot could be reached via river from either side of the Nova Scotia peninsula and at the mouths of both rivers was an island called "Oak Island." Curiously, one of these Oak Islands has the famous "Money Pit" which is a man-made shaft hundreds of feet deep with side tunnels. It is believed that there is a treasure in this pit and millions of dollars have been spent in attempts to reach the submerged bottom of the pit.[257]

It has been traditionally believed that the Oak Island Money Pit was built by pirates to hide a treasure, but Bradley and Sinclair claim that it was built by Sinclair and the Knights Templar. Furthermore, they claim, Canada was settled as a direct result of the Holy Grail being taken there. Sinclair and the Templars were attempting to create the prophesied "New Jerusalem" in the New World.

The French explorer and founder of the Quebec colony Samuel de Champlain (1567-1635) was a secret agent for the Grail Dynasty, says Bradley, and the Grail was moved to Montreal just before Nova Scotia was attacked by the British Admiral Sedgewick in 1654. A mysterious secret society called the Compagnie du Saint-Sacrement carried the Grail to Montreal. Its whereabouts today are unknown, Bradley says.

The fascinating concept of the Knights Templar taking the Holy Grail to the New World in order to found the New Jerusalem takes us directly into Atlantis studies. It is possible that the exploits and desires of Prince Henry influenced Sir Francis Bacon who, around the year 1600, published his unfinished utopian romance entitled *The New Atlantis.*

Bacon's *The New Atlantis* tells how, on a voyage from Peru to China, the narrator's ship was blown off course to an undiscovered South Sea land where a turbaned population have a perfect society that is a democratic state with an enlightened king, much as Britain was to eventually aspire to.

The people had come to their country which they called "Bensalem" from Plato's Atlantis, which was actually in America. This Atlantis was an empire that stretched from Mexico to Peru and into the Pacific. The area was devastated by a great flood, changing the geography, and the Pacific island was the last remnant of the original Atlantean population. In some ways, Bacon's lost remnant of Atlantis was similar to Easter Island, an island that was not to be officially discovered until 200 years later.

Bacon's Atlantis-in-America utopia is a very scientific land with submarines, airplanes, microphones, air-conditioning and a great research foundation. The folk of Bensalem are Christians, of course, having received the gospel from Saint Bartholomew.

Bacon's *The New Atlantis* is similar to Sir Thomas More's *Utopia,* published in 1516, and Saint Augustine's *City of God. The New Atlantis* was published 200 years after Prince Henry's tragic murder in the Orkneys in 1400 A.D.

The history of the Orkneys may well go back to Atlantis, as some of the most well-known prehistoric ruins in Scotland are to be found in the island group. The lost city of Skara Brae, 11 miles northwest of Kirkwall, is in the Orkneys.

Prince Henry would have been ignorant of Skara Brae as it was only in the middle of the last century that the wind shifted the dunes and revealed stone houses with stone furniture under the sand. Excavations and fresh storms have revealed a perfectly preserved Stone Age village at least 4,000 years old!

Built by master craftsmen, the village was extremely well organized. Paved paths linked the houses, and a sewer collected the dirty water piped from the dwellings. All the structures, made from unmortared stone, have been well protected by the sand dunes, with the exception of the roofs, which have disappeared.

The village consisted of a group of seven or eight houses all of the same design: one room with rounded corners, a very low entrance (3 ft. 10 in.) which could be closed by means of a large flat stone, and a hearth in the middle, where peat ashes were found. There was no wood on the island and the various vessels unearthed were made from stone, whales' vertebrae and pottery. Color pigments, no doubt used in body painting, were in bowls made from the vertebrae of marine animals. The inhabitants, who were sheep breeders, lived on milk, meat, fish, shellfish and whatever they could catch by hunting. One house, isolated from the others, seems to have served as a workshop where flint was shaped into tools and weapons.[225]

Says *Readers Digest* about the mystery of Skara Brae, "What is unclear is why people capable of building such houses came to settle on such a remote island in a very severe climate, while Europe offered so many more hospitable places. It seems as if the inhabitants fled there suddenly, because of some threat."[39]

Indeed, Skara Brae was inhabited by a sophisticated population in 2,000 B.C., an impressively old date for these remote islands. The Orkney Islands would have been important links in the North Atlantic sea route to the Great Lakes region of North America for the Hittites and other precursors of the Phoenicians in 2,000 B.C., just as they were in the days of Prince Henry. Hittites may well have used the Orkneys as a stopping place on their way to the open quarries of pure copper in Lake Superior.

At the Stones of Stennes in Orkney, a circular henge similar to Callanish, it was shown that the builders had quarried through three feet of solid sandstone when they were digging out the ditch that surrounds the standing stones.

The Orkneys even have their pyramids! In 1861 a conical pyramid mound, similar to Silbury Hill, was excavated in the Orkneys. Called the Tumulus of Maes-Howe, it was written up in the *Archaeological*

Journal of 1861 as "the most remarkable tumulus in Orkney, a very large mound of a conical form, 36 feet high and about 100 feet in diameter, and occupies the center of a raised circular platform which has a radius of about 65 feet. This is surrounded by a trench 40 feet in breadth.

"The mound was excavated from the top down where a large megalithic rock chamber with a vaulted roof was discovered, but little else." Continued the article, "With the exception of a quantity of bones and teeth of the horse, and a small fragment of a human skull, of unusual thickness, which were found in the debris in the chambers, no other relics were noticed."

The unusual thickness of the human skull fragment found might also indicate a larger skull and therefore a larger person, say, someone seven or eight feet tall. Certain ancient races were literal giants by today's standards and in my book *Lost Cities of North & Central America*[23] I discuss the many cases of giant skeletons found inside some of the pyramid mounds throughout the Midwest of the United States. Were the builders of Maes-Howe giants?

The inner chamber of Maes-Howe is made of naturally splitting red sandstone which is easily obtainable in the Orkneys. Elegantly tapering buttresses in each corner help support the weight of the roof, one is decorated in chevrons, and rune inscriptions (carved at a later period) appear on the stones. Some of the stones have been dressed and the naturally oblique fracture of the stones is used to create a smooth, inwardly curving face on the upper part of the walls.

Though it is thought to have been a tomb, it may well have been a fortified dwelling, much like the brochs that appear around Scotland. Indeed, master builders were at work here, as we shall see with the Scottish brochs.

One of the many mysteries of Scotland is the age and purpose of the many round towers that are found in the northern part of the country. A 1927 article in the British journal *Nature* (issue 120) described the typical Scottish broch as "consisting of a circular tower surrounding an open court, built of dry masonry without mortar or other binding material, and of which the height originally in some cases must have been as much as 60 feet. The walls at the base are usually 15 feet thick and contain a series of superimposed galleries."[17]

A ledge near the top, on the inside, provided support for wooden posts that supported a roof. These high, thick towers had a closed colonnade around a central hearth that was open to the sky. The tower was thus a fortress, a kitchen, and a lookout tower to see out into the ocean.

Brochs are found in the north and west of Scotland, and in the

Orkney and Shetland Islands. Says the 1927 *Nature* article, "Roman coins, and other objects, indicate that they were occupied at the time of the Roman invasion and in the second century A.D., though probably they date back some hundreds of years before that time. They probably were occupied for some time later, but from the absence of wheel-made pottery and Viking relics, it cannot be asserted that they survived to the eighth century."

Farther north of the Orkneys in the Shetland Islands is the island of Mousa, 11 miles south of Lerwick, which has the largest of all these mysterious towers. The Mousa broch stands 43 feet high, with 20-foot-thick walls. A long narrow passage, along which men and small livestock would have been able to worm their way, goes through the wall, leading to an interior courtyard 33 feet in diameter. A stairway is built inside the wall to spiral to the top of the tower.

A study of the soil in the courtyard of the Mousa broch confirms the fact that this construction would have served as a shelter for pastoral peoples. Livestock may have been kept briefly on the island and then transported elsewhere, possibly to North America.

The Mousa broch has survived intact partly because of its remote location on a promontory and partly because it was probably the tallest and largest of the brochs.

As with Skara Brae, history has not left us the identity of these builders. It has been suggested that the Shetland brochs were built by the descendants of the builders of Skara Brae, who themselves, are a mystery. Is it possible that they were watch towers for the North Sea trade route?[39]

But why should these brochs, especially at such a remote spot as the Shetlands, have to be so massive with walls 20 feet thick? These brochs were protective towers that were similar to those in Sardinia and elsewhere. Apparently they guarded an important north sea route to somewhere—but to where? Spitzbergen? Not likely. Probably they guarded the important North Sea route to Iceland, Greenland, and Vinland. It was these very sea routes that Henry Sinclair was to inherit as the last King of the Orkneys and Shetlands.

In the fascinating book *Sailing to Paradise*,[281] author Jim Bailey maintains that by 7,000 B.C. voyagers were making transatlantic trips to the copper mines in Michigan via the northern sea route. He claims that the Shetland Islands are the Set-Lands of the ancients, named after the Egyptian god Set, brother of Osiris.

The Shetlands, or Set-lands, had forests on them circa 6,000 B.C., though no tree will grow there today because of the high winds blowing from the North Atlantic. Bailey theorizes that the land of Set was the final jumping-off spot for Iceland and the New World for the sailors of 7,000 B.C.

The Final Stand of the Knights Templar

I drove south to Edinburgh, where I hoped to see the graves of some of my ancestors. For several days I enjoyed walking through the city, visiting the museums and soaking up Scottish history.

Of particular interest to me was the association of the Knights Templar, the Masons, the lost fleet of the Templars and the connections with the Holy Grail and Atlantis.

The lost Templar fleet is discussed in Michael Baigent and Richard Leigh's book *The Temple and the Lodge*.[241] They point out that the Templars had a huge fleet at their disposal, a fleet that was stationed out of ports in Mediterranean France and Italy as well as ports in northern France, Flanders and Portugal.

"On the whole, the Templar fleet was geared towards operation in the Mediterranean—keeping the Holy Land supplied with men and equipment, and importing commodities from the Middle East into Europe. At the same time, however, the fleet did operate in the Atlantic. Extensive trade was conducted with the British Isles and, very probably, with the Baltic Hanseatic League. Thus Templar preceptories in Europe, especially in England and Ireland, were generally located on the coast or on navigable rivers. The primary Atlantic port for the Templars was La Rochelle, which had good communication with Mediterranean ports. Cloth, for example, could be brought from Britain on Templar ships to La Rochelle, transported overland to a Mediterranean port such as Collioure, then loaded aboard Templar ships again and carried to the Holy Land. By this means, it was possible to avoid the always risky passage through the Straits of Gibraltar, usually controlled by the Saracens."[241]

When the order was persecuted by Philip IV of France starting in 1307 and culminating in the burning at the stake of Jacques de Molay in 1314, the Knights Templar became an outlawed organization. Philip IV of France persecuted them because of their financial and political power, but to many historians the persecution was part of a continued campaign against early Christian heretics like the Cathars. Indeed, there is a great deal of evidence to show that the Knights Templar and the Cathars were strongly allied.

The Knights Templar were apparently part of a secret movement to restore the Merovingian kings, who had the Holy Blood of Jesus in their veins. The question is, what happened to the Templar Fleet after they were outlawed? Traditional history has no answer to this question.

Baigent and Leigh in *The Temple and the Lodge*[241] claim that the Templar fleet escaped en masse from the various ports in the Mediterranean and northern Europe and left for a mysterious destination where they could find political asylum and safety. This destination was Scotland.

The Mediterranean fleet had to sail through the dangerous Straits of Gibraltar and then probably stopped at various Portuguese ports that were sympathetic to the Templars such as Almourol castle, near the town of Abrantes. The fortress of Almourol was constructed by Gualdim Pais, Master of the Order of the Templars in 1171.

Baigent and Leigh go on to say that the Templar Fleet sailed up the west coast of Ireland to the safe ports in Donegal and Ulster, where Templar properties were located and arms smuggling to Argyll was common.

The Templar fleet then landed in Argyll by sailing to the south of the islands of Islay and Jura into the Sound of Jura where the Templars unloaded men and cargo at the Scottish Templar strongholds of Kilmory, Castle Sweet and Kilmartin.

Robert the Bruce controlled portions of Scotland, but not all of it. Significant portions of the northern and southern Highlands were controlled by clans that were allied with England. Robert the Bruce had been excommunicated by the Pope in 1306, one year before the persecution of the Templars began. Essentially, the Papal decree that outlawed the Knights Templar was not applicable in Scotland, or at least the parts that Robert the Bruce controlled.

The turning of the tide for Robert the Bruce, Scotland and the Knights Templar was the famous Battle of Bannockburn which took place on June 24, 1324.

I drove out of Edinburgh looking for the site of the Battle of Bannockburn. I headed for Stirling Castle to the south of Edinburgh, and although the actual site of the battle is not known, it is known to have taken place within two and a half miles of Stirling Castle.

On June 24 of 1324, Robert the Bruce of Scotland with 6,000 Scots miraculously defeated 20,000 English soldiers. But exactly what took place has never really been recorded. It is believed by some that he did it with the help of a special force of Knights Templar. June 24 was also a special day to the Knights Templar; it was St. John's Day.

Say Baigent and Leigh: "Most historians concur that the Scottish army was made up almost entirely of foot soldiers armed with pikes, spears and axes. They also concur that only mounted men in the Scottish ranks carried swords, and that Bruce had few such men..."[241]

Suddenly in the midst of the battle, with the English forces engaged in a three-to-one battle against the Scottish soldiers, there was a charge from the rear of the Scottish camp.

A fresh force with banners flying rode forth to do battle with the English. The English ranks took one look at the new force and in sheer terror of the new combatants, they literally fled the field. Say Baigent and Leigh in *The Temple and the Lodge*, "...after a day of combat which had left both English and Scottish armies exhausted... Panic swept the English ranks. King Edward, together with 500 of his knights, abruptly fled the field. Demoralized, the English foot-soldiers promptly followed suit, and the withdrawal deteriorated quickly into a full-scale rout, the entire English army abandoning their supplies, their baggage, their money, their gold and silver plate, their arms, armour and equipment. But while the chronicles speak of dreadful slaughter, the recorded English losses do not in fact appear to have been very great. Only one earl is reported killed, only 38 barons and knights. The English collapse appears to have been caused not by the ferocity of the Scottish assault, which they were managing to withstand, but simply by fear."[241]

In fact, what happened was a charge in full regalia by the remaining forces of Knights Templar against the English host. These crusade veterans were like the Green Berets or Special Forces of the Middle Ages. All combatants suddenly stopped to witness the charging army of Knights Templar, white banners with red cross insignias flying high above these mounted Grail Knights. This sight evidently frightened the English forces so much that even though they still had a superior force, they fled, rather than fight.

The probable strategy behind the Templars' charge into battle would have been to ride through the thick of the battle and attempt to reach King Edward and his personal guards. Once engaged with the commanding officers of the English foe, these seasoned war veterans would have easily defeated King Edward's knights and possibly killed the king himself. As noted, King Edward and his special knights immediately fled upon witnessing the Templar charge.

My friend Lionel Fanthorpe back in Wales had told me that I should visit Rosslyn Chapel while I was near Edinburgh, so I headed south from the Bannockburn battle area. It was just about noon when I arrived at Rosslyn Chapel in the Lothian Hills south of Edinburgh.

I parked the car and walked around the small but ornate chapel. It was a Sunday and there was a church service going on inside, so I looked at some of the graves on the cemetery of the west side of the building.

When the service finished, a tall, thin man in a tweed sport coat came out of the chapel and stood in the courtyard for a moment.

"Excuse me," I said to him, "but isn't Rosslyn Chapel associated with the Knights Templar?"

"Oh, yes indeed," the man said. "This chapel was built by William St. Clair, Grand Master of the Templars."

We stood there for a moment talking about the chapel and the Knights Templar, when he told me he had written several books on Rosslyn, the Knights Templar, the Holy Grail and the Spear of Destiny. "I co-wrote *Mark of the Beast* with Trevor Ravenscroft," he said, "plus these other books for sale at the chapel gift shop."

"I've read *The Mark of the Beast*," I said. "Are you Tim Wallace-Murphy?"

"Indeed I am," he acknowledged, a bit surprised that I knew who he was and had read one of his books.

"It's a pleasure to meet you," I said, and we talked a bit about the Battle of Bannockburn, since I had just come from the area of the battlefield. "The charge of the Knights Templar at Bannockburn must have been quite a sight," I said. "Were any of the knights killed?"

"No, not a one," he said. "The English fled in total fear of the seasoned warriors. Not even one Knights Templar was killed."

"Well, that's the kind of statistic I like," I said. Privately, I wondered if this battle was the reciprocal battle to the last stand of the Cathars at Montségur. At Montségur everyone had been killed; at Bannockburn the Grail Knights had triumphed and not a man was lost.

Dr. Tim Wallace-Murphy took me into the gift shop where he showed me his other books on Rosslyn Chapel and its history. He also told me the story of Rosslyn, which is connected to the Orkneys and the taking of the Holy Grail to North America.

The builder of Rosslyn Chapel, William St. Clair, was the last Sinclair 'Jarl' of Orkney, who lived in the middle of the fifteenth century. After Earl William, the 'Jarldom of Orkney' passed from the family to the Scottish crown as part of the dowry of Margaret of Denmark on her marriage to King James III of Scotland. William was not only the grandson of Prince Henry and the last Jarl of the Orkneys, he also had the somewhat peculiar title of Knight of the Cockle and the Golden Fleece.

As Dr. Wallace-Murphy points out in his book, *The Templar Legacy & the Masonic Inheritance within Rosslyn Chapel*,[259] Sir

William St. Clair was a member of a secret group that preserved important knowledge concerning the Holy Grail, the Holy Blood of the Merovingian kings, and the destiny of the new continent across the Atlantic. Wallace-Murphy speculates that the Knights of the Cockle and the Golden Fleece was the current Grail Order, of which Sinclair was possibly Grand Master.

I thanked Tim for his personal tour of Rosslyn and got back in my car, my head full of new concepts about secret societies.

The ancient capital of Atlantis, according to Plato, was the very pinnacle of stone masonry and was laid out to specific geometric patterns. The citadel of Atlantis was a circular structure and nearly all of the Knights Templar churches and buildings were circular.

The Knights Templar, and later the Masons, put a great deal of importance into the story of Hiram, the king of Tyre and builder of Solomon's Temple. Neo-Templar orders such as the "Knights Templar of Aquarius" in London maintained that Solomon's Temple was a reconstruction of the sacred measurements and geometry of Atlantis. The Great Pyramid of Egypt was likewise thought to have been built by these master builders.

The "Knights Templar of Aquarius" existed in the 1940s and 50s in England, based in Canfield Gardens, London, and the Island of Jersey. The head of the order was an Englishman named H. C. Randall-Stevens. Randall-Stevens wrote several curious books, including one entitled *The Chronicles of Osiris*, and another entitled *Atlantis To the Latter Days*,[266] which was published in 1954. In this rare book, Randall-Stevens discusses various topics including Atlantis, the Great Pyramid, King Solomon's Temple and the Knights Templar.

In *The Temple and the Lodge*,[241] Baigent and Leigh say that, "...by the Middle Ages, the architect or builder of Solomon's Temple had already become significant to the guilds of 'operative' stonemasons. In 1410, a manuscript connected with one such guild mentions the 'king's son of Tyre', and associates him with an ancient science said to have survived the Flood and been transmitted by Pythagoras and Hermes. A second, admittedly later, manuscript, dating from 1583, cites Hiram and describes him as both the son of the King of Tyre and a 'Master.' These written records bear testimony to what must surely have been a widespread and much older tradition."[241]

Clearly, the Knights Templar saw themselves as the inheritors of ancient knowledge that went back to Atlantis. They struggled for hundreds of years against the Vatican and the reign of terror known as the Inquisition. To the Templars, the true church, one that taught mysticism, reincarnation and good works, was being suppressed by a dark power that called itself the one true faith. Oppression of these other faiths was done with the familiar devices of torture, terror and extermination.

Did the Templars seek to rediscover and recreate Atlantis in America? Henry Sinclair of Orkney had risked all to make his voyages across the North Atlantic. Had he taken the Holy Grail and possibly even the Ark of the Covenant to America? Had these sacred relics helped spur on the creation of the United States, a land which Masonic founding fathers like George Washington, Thomas Jefferson and Benjamin Franklin were to create partially on the Templar ideals of religious freedom?

According to Templar historians like Michael Baigent, Richard Leigh, Andrew Sinclair and Tim Wallace-Murphy, the Knights Templar had helped create an independent Scotland, then a "New Scotland" and finally an independent United States.

It was interesting as well that the Stone of Destiny had also come to Scotland. Scotland had at one point possibly been the location of this stone, the Holy Grail and the Ark of the Covenant. Did Scotland's history go back to King Solomon's Temple and ultimately, Atlantis?

As I headed southwest through the Lothian Hills towards England and Wales, I wondered if the United States was the New Atlantis of the Templars. Or perhaps the New Atlantis was yet to come.

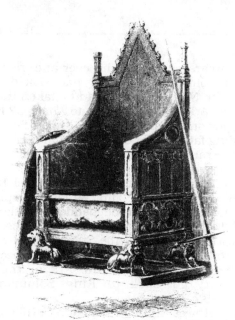

The Stone of Destiny, or Stone of Scone, in Westminster Abbey.

There where the spreading consecrated Boughs
Fed the sage Mistletoe, the holy DRUIDS
Lay rapt in moral Musings — Mason's Elfrida.

These mighty Piles of Magic-planted Rock,
Thus ranged in mystic order, mark the Place
Where, oft at times of holiest festival
The DRUID leads his train — Mason's Caractacus.

Druid in a grove with sickle, mistletoe, and Stonehenge, vignette from
title-page of Francis Grose, *Antiquities of England and Wales*, 1773–87, vol. IV.

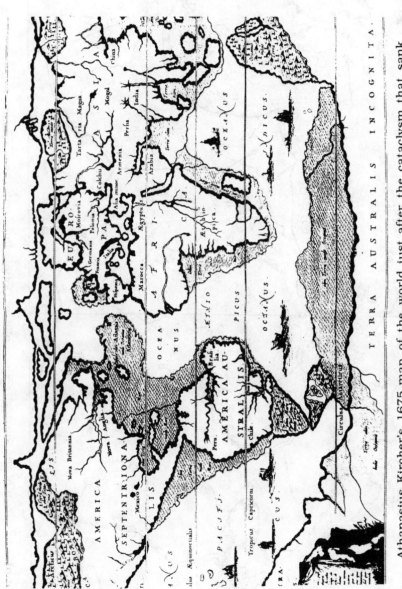

Athanasius Kircher's 1675 map of the world just after the cataclysm that sank Atlantis. Shaded areas, as around Ireland and Britain, indicate land that has been submerged after Atlantis.

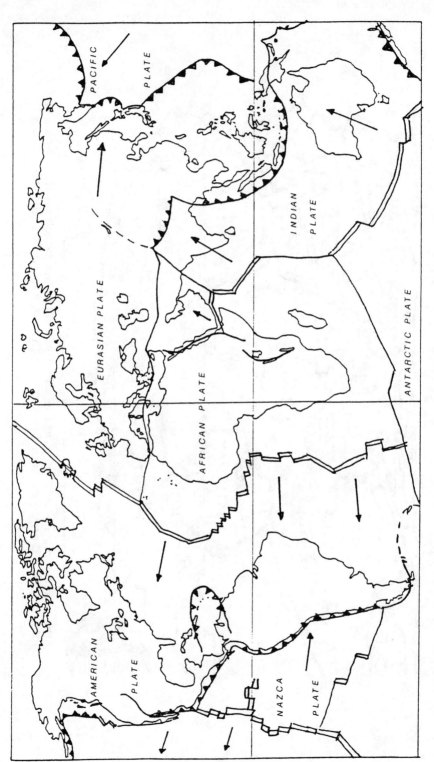

Paul Dunbavin's map of the earth's tectonic plates. Double lines indicate spreading ridges. Serrated lines show subduction zones.

An aerial view of the Callanish stone circle on the island of Lewis in the Outer Hebrides. Callanish seems to have been built in the form of a Celtic cross.

A drawing of Callanish made in 1867, soon after the stones were dug out from the peat which had formed around them. Their former height above ground is shown by the change in color.

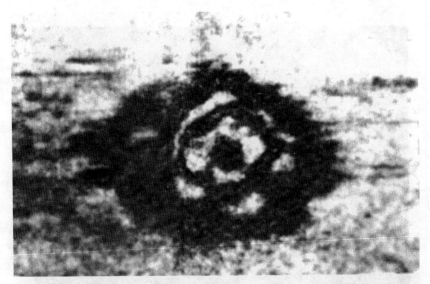

Martin Klein's side-scan sonar image of stone structures on the bottom of Loch Ness.

P.A. MacNab

The MacNab photo of a large object in Loch Ness with Urquhart Castle in the foreground. The Loch is 600 feet deep at this point and the castle walls 50 feet high.

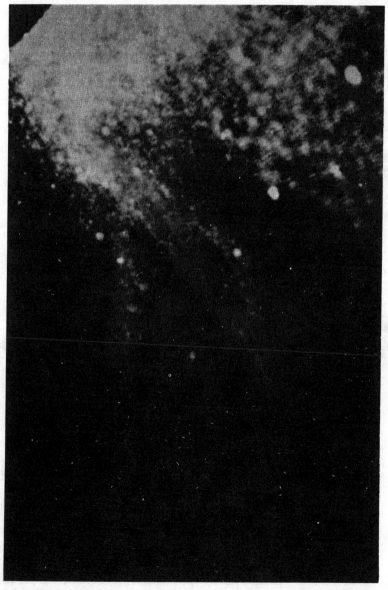

A 1972 underwater photo of what appears to be the flipper of a large animal.

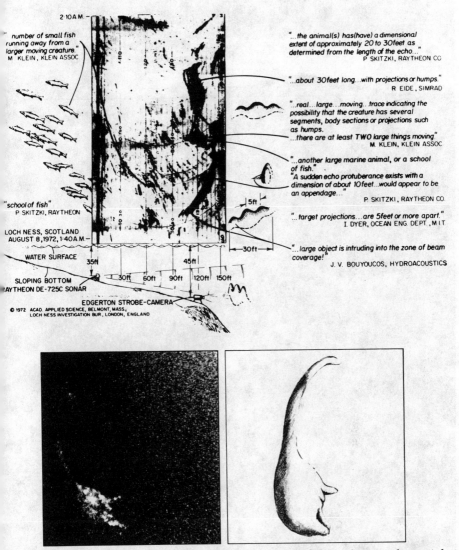

2:10 A.M.

"...number of small fish running away from a larger moving creature."
M. KLEIN, KLEIN ASSOC

"...the animal(s) has(have) a dimensional extent of approximately 20 to 30 feet as determined from the length of the echo..."
P. SKITZKI, RAYTHEON CO

"...about 30 feet long...with projections or humps."
R. EIDE, SIMRAD

"...real...large...moving...trace indicating the possibility that the creature has several segments, body sections or projections such as humps."
...there are at least TWO large things moving"
M. KLEIN, KLEIN ASSOC

"...another large marine animal, or a school of fish."
"A sudden echo protuberance exists with a dimension of about 10 feet...would appear to be an appendage..."
P. SKITZKI, RAYTHEON CO.

"school of fish"
P. SKITZKI, RAYTHEON

5ft

"...target projections...are 5 feet or more apart."
I. DYER, OCEAN ENG. DEPT., M.I.T.

LOCH NESS, SCOTLAND
AUGUST 8, 1972, 1:40 A.M.
WATER SURFACE

30ft

"...large object is intruding into the zone of beam coverage!"
J. V. BOUYOUCOS, HYDROACOUSTICS

35ft   45ft
SLOPING BOTTOM   30ft 60ft 90ft 120ft 150ft
RAYTHEON DE-725C SONAR

EDGERTON STROBE-CAMERA
© 1972 ACAD. APPLIED SCIENCE, BELMONT, MASS.,
LOCH NESS INVESTIGATION BUR., LONDON, ENGLAND

Top: A 1972 sonar trace taken at the same time that the flipper photograph was taken. Bottom: A 1975 underwater photo which appears to show part of the body, neck and fin of the "monster." On the right is an artist's impression of the photograph.

The broch tower and island stronghold in Clickhimin Loch, near Lerwick, Shetland—as it was in the 1st century A.D., in a reconstruction drawing by Alan Sorrell.

The Ring of Brodgar at Stenness in the Orkneys.

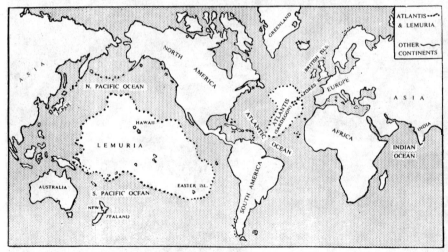

A map of Atlantis and "Lemuria" by neo-Templar H. Randall-Stevens.

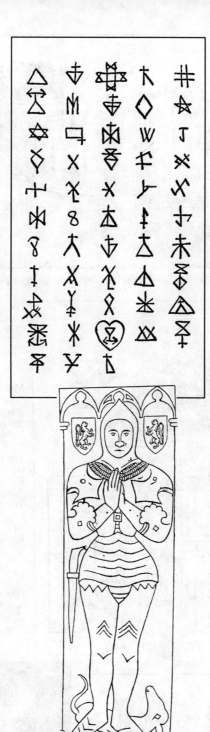

Top: Mason's marks, similar to Norse Runes.
A Knights Templar grave at Rosslyn Chapel.

Rossyln Castle, home of the Knights Templar in Scotland.

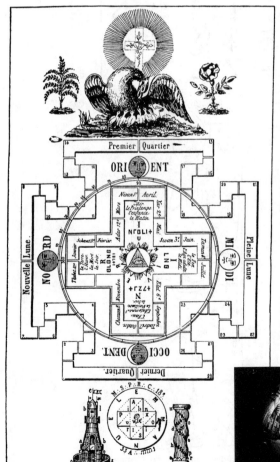

Mystical diagram of Solomon's Temple, as prophesied by Ezekiel and planned in the building scheme of the Knights Templar. The two pillars represent Jachin and Boaz from the original Temple of Solomon. The pillar on the right resembles the Apprentice Pillar at Rosslyn.

BELOW: The sacred rock within the Dome of the Rock in Jerusalem.

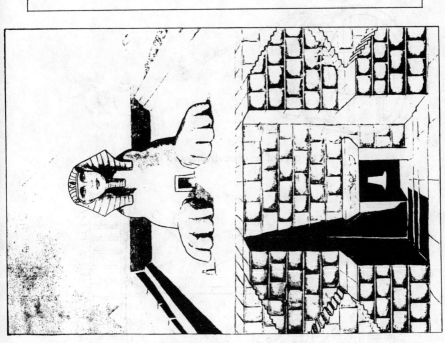

ATLANTIS

TO

THE LATTER DAYS

Inspirationally Dictated

to

H. C. RANDALL-STEVENS

(EL EROS)

*By the Masters Oneferu and
Adolemy of the Osirian Group*

Second Edition

THE KNIGHTS TEMPLARS OF AQUARIUS
LONDON
1957

Left: Randall-Stevens' illustration of the secret temple yet to be discovered beneath the Sphinx at Giza. Right: Title page to Randall-Stevens' book *Atlantis To the Latter Days*.

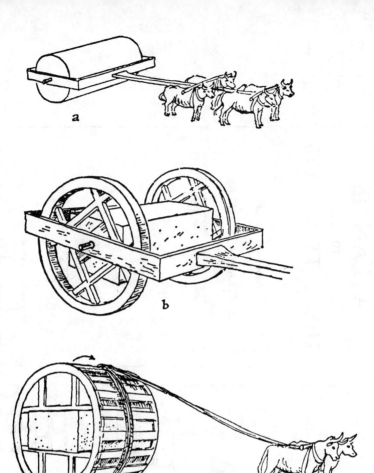

Transport of column drums and stone blocks.

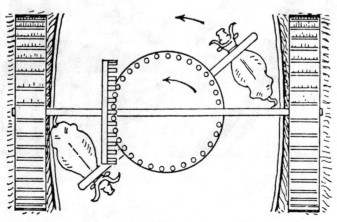

Oxen used to propel a ship.

Chapter 13

IRELAND:

The Lost Land of Tir na n'Og

*The Deathless Ones will waft you instead to the world's end,
the Elysian Fields, where yellow-haired Rhadamanthus is.
There indeed men live unlaborious days. Snow and tempest
and thunderstorms never enter there, but for men's
refreshment Ocean sends out continually the high-singing
breezes of the west.*
—Homer, The *Odyssey*

From Scotland, I drove back to Wales, where I turned in my rental car and got a bus to Holyhead at the westernmost portion of Wales. From there I took a night crossing over the Irish Sea to Dublin.

It was dawn as the ferry began to pull into the port of Dublin, the lights of the city glittering along the horizon as far as I could see. Soon I was in downtown Dublin, crossing the Half Penny Bridge and eating lunch at the Bad Ass Cafe down the street from the Guinness brewery.

To me, Ireland was the Emerald Isle, the Elysian Fields of ancient Greek mythology, a land that was pleasant, fruitful and without extremes of temperature, either hot or cold. What is more, Ireland is a land whose roots go back to the very dim mists of history.

We know more of Irish Celtic mythology than we do of other Celtic countries. Because of its remoteness, Ireland has managed to preserve more of its ancient history than Scotland, Wales or England. Yet what we know is still confusing and mysterious. Much of the imagery in the old Irish sagas has what one might call "Atlantean" overtones.

423

The Tuatha de Danann and The Book of Invasions

A mythological history of Ireland has been preserved in an ancient manuscript called *The Book of Invasions*. It chronicles the various races that have invaded and settled in Ireland. The history begins just after the legendary flood that drowned the world when the tribe of Partholon arrives in Erin, fleeing the flood.

Partholon and his tribe are said to have come from the west, across the Atlantic, to an Ireland that was quite different from today. There were just nine rivers, three lakes and one plain, called the Old Plain. Partholon and his people cleared away some of the forests and fought against a people called the Fomorians. Partholon and his group are eventually wiped out by a terrible plague and Ireland is deserted for 30 years.

A tribe called the Nemed, or Nemedians, then arrive in Ireland. *The Book of Invasions* says that they came from Greece, via Scythia and the Northern Sea. They followed what was the ancient amber trade route; amber came from Denmark, Germany and Scandinavia and was sold in the eastern Mediterranean.[212]

While Nemed and his 34 ships were wandering the ocean, according to the story, they saw a golden tower on the sea. When the tide was in ebb, the tower appeared above it, but when the tide rose the tower was submerged. They set a course for the tower, hoping to plunder it, but in their greed failed to notice that the sea was rising about them. A great wave overcame the fleet of ships and most of them were drowned. The survivors then wandered about on the sea for a year and a half until they eventually reached Ireland.

They settled in Ireland, where their descendants still live today, but soon another catastrophe overtook them, the bursting of four lakes in the mountains which flooded large areas of the land.

Meanwhile Nemed fought three battles against the Fomorians and successfully fought them off until Nemed died of the plague. The Fomorians returned and their chief, Conann, built a great tower on Tory Island, off the north-west coast of Donegal, where he ruled over Ireland. His rule was oppressive and harsh, extracting from his subjects a tribute each year of two-thirds of their wheat, milk and children.

The Nemedians asked for a three-year period of grace from the taxes during which time they sent messengers back to their homeland, which the old Irish chronicles say was Greece. The king of Greece, who was related to Nemed by marriage, set out for Ireland with a great army of Druids and Druidesses. The Greeks brought with them venomous animals (probably snakes or scorpions) which they used to penetrate the walls of Conann's tower.

The Fomorians were driven out and had to fight. The Nemedians defeated the Fomorians and killed every one, including Conann himself. But no sooner had they defeated the Fomorians, then a further host of Fomorians came to reinforce Conann. The Nemedians then began to fight the new Fomorian fleet, when suddenly a giant tidal wave swept into the harbor and killed nearly everyone.

Only 30 of the Nemedians and a single ship of the Fomorians survived the tidal wave. The survivors divided into three bands, one remaining in Ireland to become subjects of the Fomorians, one band returning to Greece and the third band moving to Scotland under their leader, a man named Briton Mael. The name of Britain has its origin with Briton Mael according to the old Irish sagas.

Ireland was virtually deserted for 200 years, says *The Book of Invasions,* until the Nemedians returned from Greece, calling themselves the Firbolgs or "Men of Bags." The Firbolgs were conquered by the legendary Tuatha de Danann, with their magical weapons, the magic cauldron and the Stone of Destiny.

Paul Dunbavin in *The Atlantis Researches*[212] speculates that the Fomorians were Norwegian raiders or early Vikings. The Fomorians were giants with yellow hair, and figure in the long history of Ireland, as well as all the northern islands.

Dunbavin identifies the Tuatha de Danann as "another branch of the Nemedians." We have seen in the last chapter that there is quite a bit of evidence that the Tuatha de Danann was the Tribe of Dan with the Prophet Jeremiah and the Princess Tea arriving from Israel and Egypt.

Many different theories have circulated concerning the Tuatha de Danann, however. Robert Charroux, the French author who wrote a series of ancient astronaut and Atlantis-type books in the late '60s, theorizes in his book *Lost Worlds*[10] that the Tuatha de Danann were Mayans from Central America. Says Charroux, after describing the invasion of Ireland by the Sons of Nemed and later by the Firbolgs, "from beyond the ocean river came the Tuatha de Danann tribe, who were undoubtedly Quiché Mayans from South America."

Since the Tuatha de Danann were from beyond the ocean river, they must be Mayans, thought Charroux. Charroux sees the Mayans as Celts who had previously left Europe and were now returning to Ireland, red hair, freckles and all, as the Tuatha de Danann. The French-American Masonic archaeologist Augustus Le Plongeon also believed that the Mayans had a strong influence on ancient Europe and that the last words spoken by Christ while on the cross were in Mayan.

While the Mayans, Toltecs, Mixtecs and other Mesoamerican cultures may well have had an influence on ancient Europe, and in an older sense, a connection with Atlantis, it seems somewhat premature to assert, on little evidence that the Tuatha de Danann were "undoubtedly Quiché Mayas from South America."[10] The

Quiché Mayas, anyway, live in Central America, not South America (though it is possible that they are originally from South America). The French-American UFO investigator Jacques Valleé theorized in his book *Dimensions*[282] that the Tuatha de Danann were interdimensional fairy-folk that arrived in glowing UFOs. They are responsible for many modern UFO sightings as well, Valleé theorizes. While the Tuatha de Danaan have been mythicized into Irish folklore, Valleé's theories are even more far-out than Robert Charroux's.

Historian N.L. Thomas says this about the Tuatha de Danann in *Irish Symbols of 3500 B.C.*[130]: "The followers of the Bolg were some time later subjected to an invasion from the north by the Tuatha de Danann, the 'Peoples of the Goddess Danann.' The Tuatha were a people possesed of magic wonders, the supreme artists of wizardry, who came to Ireland, not by ship, but descended from the northern sky. They dwelt in a timeless land of everlasting festivities, a supernatural realm, the domain of the gods. Their mythological sites of the Otherworld, the 'Brú', were magic places not inhabited by humans. The Brú na Boinne (Newgrange by the river Boyne) was the most important of these places."[130]

It is fascinating to think that the Tuatha de Danann arrived via airships, rather than boats. This may be merely a legend, or perhaps it actually chronicles the landing of ancient airships in Ireland. It is said that the Tuatha de Danann landed first in Northern Ireland, so that might be one explanation for their arriving from the north, rather than the south, which is the direction of Mediterranean.

As we have seen, a great deal of tradition and associated evidence shows us that the Tuatha de Danann probably migrated from the eastern Mediterranean at the time of Nebuchadnezzar's attack on Jerusalem. Still, it is interesting to consider the connection between ancient Israel, Egypt, Phoenicia and the Mayans. Diffusionist historians are certain of such contacts, and such Mayan cities as Comacalco have been cited as transcultural Mayan-Phoenician universities. (See my book *Lost Cities of North & Central America*[23] for more information on Comacalco and ancient Mayan contacts with China, Europe, Africa and other countries.)

As mentioned in the last chapter, the Tuatha de Danann were said to come from Egypt and Israel with the Stone of Destiny. The Irish version of this story can be found in the old Irish book, *Chronicles of Eri*, which says that at some time around 580 B.C. a ship landed at Ulster and on board were the prophet Ollamh Fodhla, the Princess Tara and a scribe named Simon Brech. These three were apparently the prophet Jeremiah, Princess Tea and the scribe Baruch.[268]

The magical items possessed by the Tuatha de Danann were probably various items of machinery and electrics as were known to still exist in those days. Such simple but effective devices as a crossbow would seem like "magic spears" to people who had never seen one, and similarly an electrical device, as the Ark of the Covenant was said to be, would seem magical to any primitive observer.

Another simple invention that could be described as a "magic spear" is small field rockets. The Chinese and Hindus used small rockets, similar to modern fireworks, in warfare. A barrage of exploding rockets into a fort or onto a battlefield could cause havoc and even death.

The Hill of Tara and the Ark of the Covenant

I contacted some friends in Kilkenny, south of Dublin, and they came to the city to meet me. Michael is a ceramicist who works for a local pottery manufacturer and Thérèse is an artist who works in ceramics and other mediums.

The three of us drove out to Tara in Michael's car. We drove through busy Dublin and out into the lush green countryside northwest of the city and into the narrow country lanes of County Meath. After several wrong turns and missing road signs, we eventually found the legendary Hill of Tara.

The Hill of Tara today is a high hill covered in green pasture with sheep grazing on it. Yet, it commands a tremendous view of the countryside in four directions, and in ancient times people came from all over Ireland to Tara, for celebrations, coronations, or simply pilgrimage.

Tara, two and a half thousand years ago, was a huge palace with a great wooden tower and a Druidic college. James Bonwick, in his 1894 book *Irish Druids and Old Irish Religions*[269] says: "The palace of Teamair, or Tara, was held by the Tuatha. The chief college of the Druids was at Tara. At Tara was held the national convention of the Teamorian Fes. It was associated with the marriage sports of the Tailtean. The foundation is attributed to the wise Ollam Fodhla."

The tenth-century Irish poet O'Hartigan spoke of Tara in the *Book of Ballymote*:

> Fair was its many-sided tower,
> Where assembled heroes famed in story;
> Many were the tribes to which it was inheritance,
> Though decay lent a green grassy hand.

The story of Tara goes back to Princess Tea and her marriage to the local Irish King Eochaid the Heremon, forming the Kingdom of the Tuatha de Danann. It didn't last long, with the Tuatha de Danann having to fight the Firbolgs for control of Ireland. The Tuatha de Danann defeated the Firbolgs, but then Nuada, the first Tuatha de Danann king, lost a hand in the battle. Since kings had to be perfectly whole, in a magnificent gesture of reconciliation, he abdicated in favor of Bress, son of the Fomorian king.[268]

Bonwick quotes from various Irish historians and tells how the Irish *Csalacronica,* dated 1355, declared that it was Simon Brec "who brought with him a stone on which the Kings of Spain were wont to be crowned, and placed it in the most sovereign beautiful place in Ireland, called to this day the Royal Place; and Fergus, son of Ferchar, brought the Royal Stone before received, and placed it where it is now, the Abbey of Scone."

Bonwick cites another 14th-century version from Baldred Bisset: "The stone which had first served Jacob for his pillow, was afterwards transported to Spain, where it was used as a seat of justice by Gathalus, contemporary with Moses." Bonwick then says that the historian Boece declares that Gathalus was the son of Cecrops of Athens, and married "Scota, daughter of Pharaoh."[269]

This shows some understanding of the truth by historians but also a general confusion about ancient history. Moses lived some 500 years earlier than Scota and Simon Brec.

Were the kings of Spain and Tartessos also crowned for a time on the Stone of Destiny? Princess Tea, or Scota, probably came to Ireland via Spain, and may have stopped in Spain for several years. It is also possible that her Irish husband-to-be may have also lived in Spain for a time. Ireland, apparently, has always had a close connection with Spain and North Africa. Spain, of course, would be a natural stopping place for any ships coming from the eastern Mediterranean to Ireland.

In a chapter on Tara, Bonwick says, "Other stories connected with the preacher at Tara are narrated elsewhere in the present work, and relate to a period subsequent to the institution of the Ollamh Fodhla college at Tara... *Heber* of *Heber of the Bards* is to them Hebrew. Tara is named for Terah (Torah). Jeremiah fled thither after the siege of Jerusalem, carrying away the treasures of the temple; as, the ark, the scepter of David, the Urim and Thummin, and others. Some persons at this day affect to believe that in the hill of Tara might yet be found these memorials of Judaism, and hope to recover thence David's harp, carried to Ireland by Jeremiah and the Princess Scota, daughter of Pharaoh."

Bonwick also mentions the Reverend F. R. A. Glover, M.A., who says the Stone of Destiny, or Liag Phail, was taken from the sanctuary in 588 B.C. and "brought thither by Hebrew men in a ship of Dan, circa 584."[269]

Reverend Glover goes on to say that Jacob's pillar was taken to Tara. "In Ireland, in the royal precincts of Tara, circa B.C. 582-3, there was a Hebrew system and a transplanted Jerusalem..." Bonwick comments, "Some pious friends of the Anglo-Israel movement have desired a digging search over Tara, now a wilderness region, to discover the missing treasures from Solomon's temple."[269]

The question that historians continually wonder about is whether or not the Ark of the Covenant was part of the sacred and magical items of the Tuatha de Danann.

But what was the Ark of the Covenant and why was it so important? Was it a relic from Atlantis as some have claimed?

The Biblical Ark of the Covenant is well known to most of us from Sunday school class and the popular film *Raiders of the Lost Ark*. It is mentioned approximately 200 times in the Old Testament and was said to be a chest of metal and wood sandwiched together. The Ark of the Covenant first appears in the Old Testament story of the Exodus. Moses is said to have placed a copy of the Ten Commandments inside the Ark, which was a nesting of three boxes one inside the other.

Descriptions of the Ark in the Bible are brief and scanty, but it seems that the box, or "Ark," was something between four and five feet long and two to three feet in both height and width. The three boxes were a sandwiching of gold, a conducting metal, and acacia wood, a non-conductor.

There are reports in the Bible of persons touching the box, and being struck dead. This is probably quite true, because such a sandwiching of a conductor and a non-conductor creates what is known as an electrical condenser. A condenser such as the Ark would accumulate static electricity over a period of days (or months) until it suddenly discharged onto a person, or was grounded by means of a conductor, like a wire or metal rod touching the ground.

If the Ark had not been grounded for some long period of time, the electrical charge built up in it could give a very nasty and fatal shock to someone who touched it. If the shock itself was not fatal, then the surprise of the shock could well be. After the Ark had been discharged, however, it would be quite safe to touch, as many of the Temple Priests did.

Another part of the Ark of the Covenant was a golden statue, whose importance is often missed. Indeed, in esoteric literature, it is the most significant part of the Ark. It is described in the Bible as the Holy of Holies. It was a solid gold statue of two cherubim (angels) facing each other, their wing tips touching above them. With their outstretched arms, they hold between them a shallow dish. This was known as the Mercy Seat.

It is upon this Mercy Seat that an esoteric flame called in Hebrew the *Shekinah Glory* rests. The Shekinah Glory is supposedly a kind of "spirit fire" which was maintained from a distance, originally by Moses and later by an Adept of the Temple. If the person viewing the Holy of Holies was able to detect the Shekinah Glory, that showed psychic talent, as it could only be perceived by a person with clairvoyant ability.

This statue, along with the Ark, is first referred to in the Biblical book of *Exodus,* and it is usually believed that the Hebrews manufactured them both, while they were out in the desert. This seems unlikely, especially the manufacturing of the solid gold statue of the angels. Rather, it is more likely that the Holy of Holies, and the Ark, were relics from an earlier time, and were being taken out of Egypt by the fleeing Israelites. Indeed, it is quite possible that this is the reason the Egyptian army decided to pursue the Israelites, even after they had given them permission to depart.

According to some of the esoteric "Atlantis" schools, the golden statue of two angels facing each other, holding a bowl together, was a relic from Atlantis that was well known to the Initiates of ancient times.

According to Eklal Kueshana in his book *The Ultimate Frontier,*[270] in which he quotes other sources, the golden statue, or Holy of Holies, was originally created tens of thousands of years ago in a time even before Atlantis. Kueshana claims it was originally created on what is today a lost continent in the Pacific. (For more information see my book *Lost Cities of Ancient Lemuria & the Pacific*[59]). This lost continent, a controversial subject among geologists and mystics, then reportedly sank in a cataclysmic pole shift circa 22,000 B.C.

According to Kueshana, with the downfall of the Pacific civilization, the Holy of Holies and plans for rebuilding the Tabernacle were removed to Atlantis. Prior to the supposed destruction of Atlantis circa 10,000 B.C., the Holy of Holies was taken to Egypt, which was part of the Osirian Empire at that time. According to *The Ultimate Frontier,*[270] the relic was first kept in the Temple of Isis and then secreted in the large stone box which occupies the King's Chamber of the Great Pyramid at Giza. For 3,400 years it remained there, until the time of Moses.

The box, or Ark, within which the Holy of Holies was kept, was probably constructed in Egypt. Electricity was used by the Egyptians, as evidenced by electroplated gold objects and electrical lighting reportedly being used in the temples. Because many persons still knew the significance of the gold statue, it was important that the Holy of Holies and the Ark be kept away from the evil Amon priests who fostered mummification in Egypt and controlled the country for thousands of years.

Graham Hancock in his bestselling 1992 book *The Sign and the Seal*[235] says that the nested sarcophagi of the young Pharaoh Tutankhamen was apparently a similar type of box as that described as the Ark of the Covenant. According to Hancock, this sort of special construction for a box was relatively common in ancient Egypt. He too is a believer in ancient Egyptian electrics and other special knowledge left over from ancient civilizations.

Therefore, secret Mystery Schools supposedly operated in Egypt and kept the ancient traditions of Atlantis alive. The Holy of Holies and possibly the Ark were sealed in the King's Chamber of the Great Pyramid, and the entrance to the inside was a carefully guarded secret, known only to a select few.

The story of Moses is a familiar and fascinating tale. Abandoned child of a Hebrew family living in Egypt, he was raised by the inner court of the royal family and taught the ancient mysteries in the secret Mystery Schools, a heritage from the days of Atlantis and Osiris. With Egypt slipping deeper and deeper into the grip of the evil and powerful priesthoods, the Mystery Schools decided that Moses should take the Holy of Holies to his "Promised Land" where a Temple would be built for it, and mankind would again have access to the important relic from the dawn of civilization.

In theory, Moses and a companion were able to gain entry into the Great Pyramid, which had been sealed thousands of years before in early Egyptian history. Opening the main door from the inside, Moses and his companion removed the Holy of Holies from the King's Chamber of the pyramid and took it with them during their Exodus from Egypt to their Promised Land.

The Holy of Holies, apparently the golden statue of two angels, may have already been placed inside a condenser box similar to Tutankhamen's, according to Hancock.

The 25th chapter of *Exodus* says that while on Mt. Sinai, Moses received instruction as to the rebuilding of the Tabernacle and its furnishing. We may presume that "sacred geometry" of one sort or another was to be used in the building of the Temple, much as at Chartres Cathedral in France or Karnak Temple at Thebes.

The Ark of the Covenant within the Tabernacle was kept in Jerusalem until, during Solomon's reign, a permanent home was built for it in Solomon's Temple. Also placed in the Ark is a copy of the ten commandments, a golden pot of manna, and Aaron's rod that budded. That the statue of the angels was sometimes kept in the box, rather than being merely part of the lid, is evidenced by the fact that the statue was not always seen by persons who viewed the Ark.

While Hancock claims that the Ark of the Covenant can be found at an Ethiopian temple in Axum, this Ark is usually said to be a replica of the original Ark. The Ark of the Covenant was still at Solomon's temple when Babylon attacked Jerusalem. (For more information see my book *Lost Cities & Ancient Mysteries of Africa and Arabia.*[58])

Hancock's second book, *Fingerprints of the Gods,*[234] attempts to prove that an advanced civilization existed in 15,000 B.C. Call these advanced ancient civilizations Atlantis or whatever you want. Hancock's books are scholarly and well researched, and he accepts the idea that the Egyptians and other early civilizations had knowledge of electrical devices.

In *Maccabees* 2:1-8, we read that Jeremiah the prophet, "being warned of God, commanded the Tabernacle and the Ark to go with him, as he went forth into the mountain, where Moses climbed up, and saw the heritage of God. And when Jeremiah came thither, he found a hollow cave, wherein he laid the tabernacle, and the ark, and the altar of incense, and so stopped the door."

What the Bible is speaking about is Jeremiah removing the Ark to Mount Nebo (now in Jordan, across from the Dead Sea), hiding it in a cave, and then concealing the entrance.

Did Jeremiah return to get the Ark, or did the Tuatha de Danann return to get it with instructions from the dying Jeremiah? There are also stories that the original knights of the secret Templar order did the excavation at the Temple in Jerusalem to free the Ark. Did they have a secret manuscript that had come down to them from the Tuatha de Danann?

It has been said that the Ark was taken via ship to the Phoenician port of Cataluña, where it is allegedly kept in secret by the Essene Brotherhood. At the monastery of Montserrat in the Pyrenees Mountains outside of Barcelona, there is a tradition that the Ark of the Covenant is kept in a secret cave. Indeed, the symbol for the monastery is three mountain peaks with a box on the top of the center peak. Is this the Ark of the Covenant?

Most important to us here is the tradition that says that the Ark of the Covenant was taken to Ireland by Jeremiah himself. He fled to Egypt when the Babylonians invaded Israel, and then to Ireland with Queen Tamar Tephi (Tea), who married King Eochaid of Ireland. She died only a short time after her marriage and was buried at Tara. Buried with her was a great chest said to contain relics from Palestine. Some believe that this chest was the Ark of the Covenant!

It is also interesting to note that Jeremiah is buried on Devenish Island in Loch Erne in western Ireland, according to local tradition.

If the Ark was not removed to Ireland or Spain, then it might still be in the Middle East, perhaps beneath the Dome of the Rock mosque in Jerusalem or in a cave somewhere. Even today, Biblical scholars and professional "Ark Raiders" search for the Ark of the Covenant in various places around the world.

In 1911 the Captain Parker expedition attempted to break through an ancient wall beneath the Dome of the Rock mosque which they believed led to an ancient tunnel. But, there were riots in the streets as rumors spread that Englishmen had discovered and stolen the Crown and magical ring of Solomon, the Ark of the Covenant, and the Sword of Mohammed! Parker's group escaped to the Mediterranean coast where Parker's yacht was waiting. He was further banned from ever entering Jerusalem again, and the local Turkish governor and commissioners were replaced.

In more recent times, various Ark hunters claim to have discovered the Ark in a cave in the Middle East or in Jerusalem somewhere. It seems unlikely though that such an important relic as the Ark of the Covenant would be left unattended or buried with a queen, no matter who she was.

Indeed, like the Holy Grail, the Spear of Destiny, or the Stone of Destiny—even more so—the Ark of the Covenant is such an important relic that whole armies would be moved if need be to keep it safe. Secret societies would swear blood-oaths not to reveal its location, and its possessor would have to be an Initiate of the highest degree.

The Ancient Laser Show at Newgrange

Newgrange was our next stop after Tara. The three of us, in Michael's car, drove from Tara directly to Newgrange, about an hour north of Dublin. It is Ireland's best known prehistoric monument, and is said to be one of the finest megalithic monuments in all of Europe.

According to legend, the kings of Tara were buried at Newgrange. Newgrange is one of many mounds in the pagan cemetery of Brug-Na-Boinne, which also has associations with the Tuatha de Danann.

While Newgrange may well be one of the most amazing megalithic monuments in Europe, it is unlikely that it was a tomb. It was built at least 2,000 years before the era of the kings of Tara, and is now generally believed to have been some sort of astronomical observatory. It is an almost heart-shaped mound about 36 feet high and about 300 feet in diameter. Standing upright in the earth outside the base of the mound are large boulders up to 8 feet high. Of the original 38 gigantic boulders, only 12 survive.

The most famous of the stones at Newgrange are the entrance

stones which are marked with a triple spiral pattern, said to be unique to Newgrange. Yet the spirals are similar to those in Malta, Crete and other places.

Michael, Thérèse and I waited until an hourly tour into the mound was conducted by a government guide. We were the only ones there so we followed her in single file through the low entrance.

We went along a passage 62 feet long with massive roof slabs above us. At the end we came to a chamber where we could stand upright again. Here, the guide told us, was the center of the mound.

Newgrange has been open to the public since it was first excavated in 1699 A.D. Charcoal samples obtained from the caulking of the roof slabs were dated at 3100 B.C. according to the archaeologist J. Patrick in an article that appeared in the British journal *Nature* (No. 249, 1974) entitled "Midwinter Sunrise At Newgrange."[17]

Because a 1967 excavation of the tomb floor revealed the burnt bone fragments of five people, it has generally been assumed that Newgrange was a tomb. Says Patrick, "At the base of the mound is a continuous kerb of large slabs. It is believed that dry-stone walling was built on top of the kerb to a height of 3 m. and that this wall was made of quartz for about 30 m. on each side of the entrance. The sun on the glistening white quartz would have presented a spectacular sight from the surrounding countryside. Most of this wall collapsed soon after completion of the monument, and the kerb stones became completely buried and remained hidden until uncovered again at the start of this century. Outside the kerb, there are 12 large standing stones that may form part of a circle, but their true relationship with the mound is not known for certain. They may be older than the passage-grave.

"One of the most outstanding features of Newgrange is the decoration on the stones. The Entrance Stone, set in front of the passage, is regarded as one of the most impressive pieces of Megalithic art in Europe. The artist who executed this piece of work has succeeded in using the shape of the stone to the utmost advantage in creating its aesthetic appeal. Another small but remarkable design is the three-spiral figure in the rear recess. There are many other decorations within the passage and chamber, and on the kerbstones, virtually making Newgrange a Megalithic art gallery."

Patrick, in his *Nature* article, goes on to mention that during the winter solstice in 1969 Professor M. O'Kelly observed that 4 minutes after sunrise the Sun's rays shone through the roof box, along the passage, and up to the rear recess of the burial chamber, which became fully illuminated. The spectacle lasted for 17 minutes before the sun moved out of alignment. Patrick surveyed the tomb in 1972 and found that light shone directly into the central chamber on a number of days before and after the winter solstice. He therefore theorized that the mound was part of some sort of winter solstice festival.

The answer to the mystery of Newgrange may be found in *The Mysterious Chequered Lights of Newgrange*,[278] by Hugh Kearns. Kearns says that the ancient chamber was part of a laser light show that involved crystals, golden discs and the jumping of salmon in the river nearby.

Kearns maintains that the sun-worshipping culture of 3,000 B.C. created a spectacular light show for the illumination and inspiration of the people. They did it with simple but effective means. Kearns maintains that the alignment of Newgrange to the summer solstice is so that on that day a great sun ceremony and laser light display could take place.

Kearns theorizes that a highly polished mirror was suspended by a tripod in the main chamber of the tomb and as the sun rose on the winter solstice, a shaft of light came deep into the tomb to the central chamber. This beam of light then struck the mirror and was bounced back down the shaft to the outside.

The focused shaft of brilliant light (Kearns likens it to a laser show) comes out of the mound at a slight decline and was so positioned to strike the Boyne River, which makes a meandering curve in front of Newgrange. Since Newgrange was originally covered with crushed white quartz, when the sunlight hit the mound itself, it sparkled and glowed in the early morning sun.

Kearns also says that vast numbers of salmon spawn in the Boyne River at the time of the winter solstice. With the combination of the jumping salmon and the laser beam hitting the river, the winter solstice sun ceremonies created an awe-inspiring spectacle of glittering, flashing lights, a laser beam and a sparkling mound of white quartz in the early morning sun. Kearns suggests that a large choir and band were on hand as well to sing and play music at the occasion. No doubt people came from all over Ireland to witness the sacred event—a true salutation to the sun.

Kearns created a 1:24 scale model of Newgrange to test his various theories and found that what he proposed would have worked perfectly. Newgrange was a masterpiece of ancient ingenuity and technology, he says, and suggests that other similar light displays were set up in other parts of Ireland and continental Europe.

I found it a fascinating theory myself, and one that made a lot of sense. As I stood outside the entrance of Newgrange and looked out at the waters of the Boyne, I tried to imagine the scene. Musicians playing, a choir singing, a shaft of brilliant light emerging from the mound and striking the salmon in the river.

I asked the government guide at the site what she thought of

Kearns' light-show theory.

"It is an interesting book," she admitted. "But I don't think that it is true."

"Why do you say that?" I asked her.

"Well, Kearns says that they probably used a large gold disc as a mirror to project the laser beam," she said, "and Ireland does not have any gold. They could not have made a metal disc here in Ireland to use as a mirror."

I thought about what she said for a moment and then responded by saying the gold disc could easily have been imported from Europe or the Mediterranean. "Ireland wasn't isolated from the rest of the world back then," I pointed out. "They could have imported many gold sun discs and other objects."

She was unconvinced, and I walked back to the gate where Michael and Thérèse were waiting. In the great Inca Sun Temple in Cuzco there had once been a large golden sun disc. Gold was thought by the Incas to be the tears of the sun. Was the sun disc used at Newgrange related to the sun discs of the Americas? It seemed quite possible to me, I thought as the sun set over the Irish hills in the distance.

~~~~~~~~~~⬦~~~~~~~~~~

The Mystery of the Round Towers

From Newgrange we drove south to Michael's house in the country outside of Kilkenny. Michael was building his own house, and he invited me to stay in a guest room for a few days. We went down to the local pubs and drank pints of Guinness. Kilkenny was an artist's town and had ancient sites, including dolmens, standing stones, menhirs and round towers.

I was fascinated by the mysterious round towers, so one day Michael and Thérèse took me to see the ancient round tower in Kilkenny. Like other round towers, the tower in Kilkenny was tall and narrow, built out of finely cut stones held together by both mortar and their interlocking placement.

It is generally believed by historians that the famous round towers of Ireland were built by the early Christians, and in some cases quite late in Ireland's history. Yet, curiously, other historians have claimed just the opposite, that the round towers were built long before the Christian era by the Tuatha de Danann or some earlier race. There are arguments for both sides.

The mystery deepens as we realize that we have no idea who built the towers, or why. In his 1894 book *Irish Druids and Old Irish Religions*[269] James Bonwick says, "One has affirmed that a celebrated tower was built by the devil in one night. To this, Latocnaye says, 'If the devil built it, he is a good mason.' Others may still ask 'Who erected the rest?' While over a hundred are known to us now, their number must have been much greater formerly, if, as that ancient *Chronicler Annals,* declares, 75 fell in the great Irish earthquake of 448 A.D."

Bonwick goes on to say that the towers have been variously described as "fire-towers, belfries, watch-towers, granaries, sepulchers, forts, hermit dwellings, purgatorial pillars, phallic objects of worship, astronomical marks, depositories of Buddhist relics, Baal fire-places, observatories, sanctuaries of the sacred fire, Freemason lodges, etc, etc. They were Pagan and Christian, built long before Christ, or a thousand years after."

One early authority on Irish round towers was Dr. G. Petrie who wrote the mid-1800s book, *Ecclesiastical Architecture of Ireland.* Dr. Petrie makes the conservative statement that the towers "are of Christian ecclesiastical origin, and were erected at various periods between the fifth and thirteenth centuries."[269]

Basically, Dr. Petrie is saying that the towers were built by the Norman conquerors as belfries, starting around 400 A.D. Yet, in the great earthquake of 448 A.D., 75 of the towers fell down. Says Bonwick, "Petrie and others point to the fact of skeletons being found in some, and these lying east and west, as a proof of Christian origin. Yet, as is replied, all this existed under paganism. Christian emblems, found only in three out of 63, have been regarded as modern alterations. The silence about the Towers in Irish hagiography, as the *Acta sanctorum,* etc., would seem to indicate a non-Christian origin, as early monkish authors forbore reference to paganism."

Bonwick and others ask, if this is a Christian monument, then where are the prototypes for such a building and why are they only found in Ireland? Bonwick goes on to say, "If an Irish style of Christian building, why did it not appear in countries known to have been under Irish missionary influence—as in Cornwall, Isle of Man, Scotland, France, Germany, etc.? Why did not Culdees leave such memorials in the Hebrides, in Lindisfarne, and other localities?"[269]

Bonwick quotes the Irish historian Gradwell who says, "There are weighty authorities on both sides, but there are sufficiently high names who maintain they were already in existence when the Saint was brought to Ireland. If they belong to a later period, when Ireland was Christian, it seems strange that the architects of those times should have displayed such surpassing skill in the construction of these Towers, for which it is difficult to assign any adequate purpose; and yet, on the other hand, have left us no monuments whatever of more useful kind."[269]

Indeed, it is a good point to make that in many cases, the amazing towers stand by themselves, the churches having long passed into rubble. Why were not the churches constructed in the same indestructible manner as these towers? The early Irish churches were constructed of wood, not stone. Says Bonwick, "St. Patrick and his followers almost invariably selected the sacred sites of paganism, and built their wooden churches under the shadow of the round towers, then as mysterious and inscrutable as they are today."[269]

Bonwick quotes the Irish historian H. O'Brien, who wrote the book *Round Towers,* and claimed that Irish tradition held that they were built by the Tuatha de Danann. The Towers "were specifically constructed for the twofold purpose of worshiping the Sun and Moon, as the authors of generation and vegetable heat..."[269]

The linking of the towers to the Tuatha de Danann is important, and Bonwick mentions that the great battle between the Tuatha de Danann and the Firbolgs took place on a battlefield that became known as the "Field of the Towers."

One Irish authority, Kenrick, believes that the towers have a Phoenician origin, which as we have seen, is the same as saying the Tuatha de Danann were the builders. Bonwick indicates a Phoenician origin as well when he likens the round towers to similar towers in the Mediterranean: "...they may be likened to the Nurhaghs or Giants' Towers of Sardinia, Gozo Island, Balearic Isles, etc., though these towers are much more complicated in structure, and rather conical. Like our Towers, they are splendid specimens of masonry."[269]

~~~~~~~~~𝕽~~~~~~~~~

The Chinese Connection

Some writers on the round towers ascribe them to Buddhism, and it is said that the closest structures resembling Irish round towers are to be found in India. Says Anna Wilkes in *Ireland, Ur of the Chaldees* (quoted by Bonwick), "There can be no doubt the Towers in the interior of Hindustan bear more than a striking likeness to those remaining in Ireland. These resemblances are to be found in such great quantities in the latter place, that it is impossible but to believe that Ireland was the centre from which a great deal of the religion of Budh developed."[269]

Bonwick then tells us of the Irish Tree of Life or Aithair Faodha, or Tree of Budh. "In Irish we read of the Danann King Budh the red; of the Hill of Budh, Cnox Buidhbh, in Tyrone; of other Budh hills in Mayo and Roscommon; and in the Book of Ballymote, of Fergus of the Fire of Budh."[269]

The idea of ancient Ireland being a Phoenician state as well as influenced in early times by Buddhism is fascinating. Perhaps we can see some explanation for the discovery in the mid-1800s of a cache of Chinese seals and coins as reported by Charles Fort in his first collection of anomalous material, *The Book of the Damned*.[271]

Fort quotes from the *Proceedings of the Royal Irish Academy* (1852, 1-381) that a paper by Mr. J. Huband Smith describes a dozen ancient Chinese seals discovered in various places in Ireland, each a cube with an animal carved in it and "inscriptions upon them of a very ancient class of Chinese characters." Fort goes on to say that many more seals have been found in Ireland. "In 1852, about 60 had been found. Of all the archaeological finds in Ireland, none is enveloped in greater mystery."

The seals had been discovered in various places around Ireland: three in Tipperary, six in Cork, three in Down, four in Waterford, and one or two in other counties. Comments Fort dryly, "(There is) agreement among archaeologists that there were no relations, in the remote past, between China and Ireland."[271]

The evidence says, however, that there was indeed a connection between ancient Ireland and China. Were special ambassadors and consultants from an ancient court in China sent to Ireland on some important mission? How would a group, or several groups of Chinese visitors have arrived in Ireland and why would they have wanted to go?

The Chinese had a large and sophisticated navy and might have arrived in Ireland by several different ways. We know that the Chinese traded via large sailing vessels into the Indian Ocean area. There is evidence that Chinese explorers reached Madagascar and East Africa. Chinese vessels may have sailed around the African Cape and arrived in Europe via West Africa but it would have been easier, and presumably safer, for them to have sailed the familiar Indian Ocean around Arabia into the Red Sea. A short land crossing from either Eilat or Port Said to a Phoenician port on the eastern Mediterranean coast would have brought them from one common transportation network to another.

If the theories of a close connection between the eastern Mediterranean and Ireland are correct, it would have been easy for several ships to have been hired to take our Chinese ambassadors to Ireland. In light of this theory, it is interesting to note some curious facts that have surfaced in the past few decades such as Chinese characters discovered in some of the Dead Sea Scrolls, written by the Essenes. The Essenes were a secret sect with centers in Israel, Egypt, southern France and possibly Ireland and Britain. It is believed by some Biblical scholars that Joseph, Mary, Jesus and their relatives, like John the Baptist, were all members of the Essenes.

It is known that the Essenes had connections to France, Spain and western Europe, but did they also have close connections with China? And if yes, then why so?

In esoteric lore there are many tales of secret retreats of "Masters" and "Adepts" who keep at least one hidden city somewhere in Central Asia. Chinese legends tell of the land of "Hsi Wang Mu" in the area of northern Tibet and the Gobi Desert. It was to this legendary Land of the Immortals that the great Chinese philosopher Lao Tsu disappeared in his old age. His book, the *Tao Te Ching*, was written at a frontier border post in western China, before he disappeared forever to the Land of the Immortals, Hsi Wang Mu.

There are Central Asian legends of King Solomon journeying in an aerial craft to Tibet, according to the Russian-American explorer Nicholas Roerich. Ethiopian records also corroborate the far journeys of King Solomon in an aerial car, known in ancient Hindu texts as a Vimana. King Solomon had many wives and several of them were reputedly from the Far East.

Looking at the Round Tower at Kilkenny, I wondered if Ireland was at one time the "Promised Land" for Utopian seekers of 1000 B.C., the Elysian Fields of Homer. With the cruel military despots of history like Nebuchadnezzar marching their armies through country after country, peaceful, loving sorts would be driven to farther and farther lands in search of a haven from enslavement, death and destruction. Ireland would certainly be a good place for such an end-of-the-world retreat.

Even during the Dark Ages, Ireland was blissfully apart from a great deal of the wars, plagues and suppression of thought by the Vatican. Ireland was raided by Vikings and invaded by the Normans, but the royalty of Europe still sent their children to be educated in Ireland. Several Irish bishops were excommunicated, like St. Brendan, for claiming a contact with a transatlantic world.

At a later time, also looking for safe refuge from the long arm of repression, Sir Henry Sinclair of the Orkneys and the fleet of the Knights Templar attempted to settle "New Scotland."

The Megalithic Crosses of the Tuatha de Danann

Thérèse was going from Kilkenny north to the west coast of Ireland and I was able to get a ride with her up the cliffs of County Mayo in the province of Connaught. Along the way we stopped at several ancient sites to look at round towers and high crosses. The megalithic high crosses of Ireland, often found near round towers, are also a subject of controversy because they too may have been built before Christianity. It seems a radical thought to think of these megalithic crosses as pre-Christian, but many ancient civilizations used the cross as a symbol, including the ancient Mystery Schools of Egypt. Bonwick in *Irish Druids and Old Irish Religions*[269] says, "When the Christians assaulted the Osirian temple in Alexandria, and with destructive force entered its sacred precincts, they saw a huge cross occupying the marble pavement."

Bonwick quotes Dr. Graves, Bishop of Limerick in the early 1800s, who was comparing Egyptian Coptic crosses with Irish crosses: "These were brought into both Egypt and Ireland from Palestine, Syria, Asia Minor, Byzantium." Bonwick mentions that Bishop Graves had found oriental-type crosses on many Ogham Irish monuments. Bonwick then quotes the archaeologist W. E. Wakeman's book *Irish Inscribed Crosses,* saying that Wakeman believes the huge crosses "were used by the people of Erin as a symbol of some significance, at a period long antecedent to the mission of St. Patrick."

Comments Bonwick, "Pre-Christian crosses he identifies at Dowth and Newgrange upon the Boyne, Knockmany of Tyrone, Deer Park of Fermanagh, Cloverhill of Sligo, Slieve-ha-Calliagh near Lough Crew of Meath. These are like the heathen inscriptions in Scotia Minor or Lesser Ireland, which we know now as Scotland.

"Tuatha de Danann crosses are associated with snakes, and are not likely to be Christian ones. The Tuatha ones resemble those of Buddhist countries. That at Killcullen, county Kildare, bears the figures of nine Buddhist priests in oriental garb, and even with a sort of Egyptian beard."

Bonwick quotes M. Keane's early 1800s book, *Towers and Temples of Ancient Ireland*: "Gobban-Saer means the sacred past, or the Freemason sage, one being on the Tuatha de Danann Cross of Clonmacnoise. The latter was adorned with birds and other animals."[269] Keane is saying, rather cryptically, that certain Irish crosses are pre-Christian and connected to the Masons, Knights Templar, and the Tuatha de Danann. Modern Masons claim that they are descended from the Knights Templar, ancient Phoenicians and the builders of King Solomon's Temple, hence Keane's reference to the "Freemason sage."

According to Bonwick, Clonmacnoise was a sacred spot before Christianity. It is ten miles from Athlone in County Offaly and has a number of mysterious ancient monuments. "The North Cross, thirteen feet, has some splendid figures of birds, deer, etc. There are staves, with bunches of leaves. A dog appears among the animals. That would have no meaning with a Christian cross, but the sacredness of that friend of man in Zend (Zoroastrian) books, classes

441

that cross among those of oriental origin.

"The human figure has an eastern look, fully clothed and crowned. It holds two sceptres crossed in the arms, with crosses at the top. That Clonmacnoise was a sacred spot is evidenced by the two remaining round towers there. Its sanctity was continued, though in a Christian channel. Besides the cathedral, there are remains of nine churches." Clonmacnoise has so many ancient monuments, that within two acres "we have condensed more religious ruins of antiquarian value, than are to be found in a similar space in any quarter of the habitable world."269

The crossing of the arms is the gesture of Osiris, and one often used in Egyptian depictions. The cross with a circle on top is of Egyptian origin and is called an ankh. Its origin goes back many thousands of years, possibly as far back as Atlantis. While the Egyptian ankh looks a great deal like a person standing with his arms outstretched, the Celtic cross may have a different origin.

Some of the crosses even have Atlantean-type motifs, says Bonwick. "The base of the cross at Kells, County Meath, has the figure of a centaur with the trident, another centaur behind armed with a bow and arrows, birds, fishes, and a sacred hare."269 Here we have the Greek symbols of the centaur along with the trident, the symbol of Poseidon. The actual name of Atlantis was said to be Poseid.

Some of the early interpreters may have been carried away a bit. O'Brien, in his book *Round Towers* (circa 1880), declares the Virgin and St. John figures on one of the Round Towers "to be Rama and Buddha's mother." While this is a bit far-fetched, it would seem possible that they are Isis and Osiris, if the cross is pre-Christian.

Bonwick concludes his chapter on the great stone crosses by saying that the "so-called Druidical temple of Newgrange, one of the most wonderful monuments of old Ireland, is in the form of a Latin cross. There are four angled crosses or fylfots within a circle. The emblem, seen also on cromlechs, may be a reminiscence of Baal, or of the Scandinavian Thor, both being associated with crosses. The pyramidal cross, observed at Newgrange, was known in countries as far apart as India and the Tonga Isles. Every one knows that the several deities of ancient Egypt are recognized by the cross they hold in their hands."

According to Donald Cyr and the archaeologists who write for his *Stonehenge Viewpoint* book series, the origin of Celtic crosses has to do with ancient atmospheric effects. Cyr's theory is that in the ancient past there was more water vapor in the atmosphere and at extreme latitudes there was a large quantity of ice crystals suspended in the atmosphere. As a result of the ice crystals in the sky, the natural phenomenon of "Sun Dogs" and "Sun Crosses" will appear in the sky.

As the sun shines down at certain angles, huge crosses of light are created in the sky and these crosses have a circular halo around them. This phenomenon of Sun Dogs and Sun Crosses is still seen today in the polar regions as well as occasionally in mountains and other areas where ice crystals may be present. In the past, this phenomenon was more common, and ancient man saw these crosses in the sky more often.

Donald Cyr theorizes that a canopy of moisture, a thick greenhouse veil, once existed around this planet. This canopy of moisture once sheltered the Earth from harmful rays from the sun and preserved a hot, humid environment in the middle latitudes of the planet at a more or less constant temperature.

Some 10,000 years ago or so, Cyr theorizes that this canopy of moisture surrounding the earth burst, causing the Biblical flood and 40 nights of rain. After the flood, there were large quantities of ice crystals in the air, more than today, and the Cross and Circle designs were seen commonly in the sky.

This sign of a cross and circle in the sky was one of reassurance and inspiration to ancient people and, like the rainbow, indicated God's desire not to inflict more cataclysms on his children.

By the evidence, it appears that ancient Ireland was a blessed and sacred island of initiation and higher education. Truly, Ireland was the Elysian Fields of Mediterranean mythology, a land of even temperature, of lush fields and a peaceful life away from the problems of the Middle East or mainland Europe. It was on the far edge of the "known" world, and from Ireland, one could voyage to lesser Ireland, which was Scotland, and on to the Orkneys and Set-Lands (Shetlands).

When "Pharoah's daughter Scota" came to Ireland, it was not by chance. Ireland was a special land used by the ancients as their university for higher studies, a refuge away from the wars and power struggles of the Mediterranean world. Ireland was not a savage place but an island carefully nurtured by its mother countries: ancient Egypt, Phoenicia and Israel.

While the mighty armies of Babylon threatened to break down the great gates at the megalithic temple of Thebes, far-away Ireland was safe and serene. Unlike Egypt, it had no gigantic temples, but was able to preserve its basic technology and "sacred way."

Ancient Ireland was a special world of learning, with an idyllic lifestyle, and the round towers were apparently an important part of that world. The round towers of Ireland seemed to have served a variety of purposes; they were solid refuges in times of invasion and could have been granaries in times of peace. And, according to researchers like Christopher Bird and Philip S. Callahan, they are also antennas for receiving electromagnetic rays from the sun and transmitting them into the ground.

Callahan in his fascinating 1984 book *Ancient Mysteries, Modern Visions*[272] maintains that the Irish round towers are agricultural antennas for helping to energize the soil. He claims that the round towers are all built of paramagnetic rocks which help channel natural earth energies into the soil and energize it for greater fertility.

Callahan spent a great deal of time in Ireland and studied many of the towers. He draws a distinction between the many round towers and the many square towers scattered about Ireland. The square towers were built by the Normans in the 12th century, a time often ascribed to the building of round towers.

Callahan says that every single round tower he tested (fifteen in number) was made of a paramagnetic stone, such as the Glendalough tower, which is built of mica schist, one of the most paramagnetic varieties of stone. Farmhouses and other later structures were usually made of diamagnetic stone.

Despite the popular belief that the towers were either fortresses or bell towers, Callahan believes they are neither. He says, "I have always considered both explanations to border on the ludicrous. Large bells were not cast until the Middle Ages (except China), and the Viking attacks began long after the tower-building seventh century. ...According to Professor G.L. Barrow, in his book *The Round Towers of Ireland*, the Irish themselves attacked the monasteries more often than Vikings did in the later centuries. The round towers are like huge smokestacks. A few fire spears or arrows through the lower door or windows would burn the wooden floors and smoke the monks out in no time at all. The towers were not built over springs and could not possibly hold enough food for a long siege. Starvation was the main siege technique in warfare, and we may be assured neither the Vikings nor the Irish attackers were too impatient that they would not camp in place for a couple of weeks until the hungry monks crawled out."

Callahan's theory is that the tower is a resonant cavity that is tuned by piling up soil inside. This is the reason for the door being partially up the tower, to allow a portion of the base to be filled in with dirt, as many were.

Further, he believes that a paramagnetic, crystalline rock outcrop would serve as a "lens" or antenna to focus and direct the sun's "monopole" signal into the ground where the roots of plants pick up this energy and grow faster.

Callahan does not seem to question the date of the towers, and generally believes them to have been built in the 7th century. He does, however, ultimately attribute the concept and technology to the

Egyptians. In Egypt, Callahan points to the crystalline antennas and antenna headdresses worn by the Pharaohs. He also likens these antenna, including round towers, to the antenna of insects.

The whole subject seems to indicate that Ireland was a special center for esoteric sciences and agricultural work. The round towers may be from before the Christian era and may have their origins in Egypt, the round towers being a version of a solid stone obelisk. This is basically what Callahan is implying. Until some sort of accurate dating is done on the towers themselves, and not on charcoal or bones found within the tower (which may be hundreds or thousands of years younger), the Round Towers of Ireland will remain a mystery of the past.

St. Brendan and the Search For Hy-Brazil

From Foxford in County Mayo, I was fortunate to catch a lift up to Belfast in Northern Ireland with Thérèse's sister Eimear. Eimear was driving to Scotland where she was going to school and would take an afternoon ferry from just outside of Belfast.

The violence between Protestants and Catholics was still going on in Northern Ireland, and as we passed the frontier I looked with wide eyes at the soldiers in black ski masks with their automatic rifles poised for an attack.

Soon, I was on the streets of Belfast, pack on my back, looking for a hotel. In was early on a rainy Sunday evening and the streets were deserted. On certain street corners were soldiers standing patrol. I found a small hotel in the university district and was soon out on the street.

Ancient Ireland was on my mind as I walked down the backstreets of the university area. Fast-food places, video arcades, pubs and movie theaters were open. I passed by a discotheque and the sounds of Van Morrison singing *Here Comes the Night* came wafting through the chill evening air. There was a slight drizzle beginning; I turned up my collar to the wind. The north winds were blowing in from the Atlantic, somewhere over the Giant's Causeway, a huge formation of crystalline basalt that runs into the sea.

At a pub in Belfast I began talking to the man next to me, an older gentleman with a trench coat and plaid hat. He was a teacher at one of the business colleges in Belfast.

When he learned that I had been to South America, he began to tell me the story of Saint Brendan and the Inca Empire.

"Irish monks used to sail up and down both North and South America," he told me over a Guinness. "They sailed in leather boats called currahs."

"So you think that Saint Brendan and other Irish monks sailed to South America in their currahs?" I asked him.

"Irish monasteries were quite unusual," he replied. "Ireland didn't suffer through the turmoil and invasions that beset the rest of Europe. Irish monks were about the best-educated people in Europe in the first millennium A.D. Irish monasteries also had a great deal of wealth, but they were continually raided by Vikings and local Irish kings who stole their gold. The monks wanted the gold for the glory of God, not for trade, and zealously sought for more with their boats.

"One land in Irish legend was Hy-Brazil, thought to be a wealthy kingdom full of gold across the Atlantic. This land would seem to be South America. Irish monks probably reached Peru from Columbia, having heard of the fabulous gold artifacts and endless gold mines in the Andes."

"The first Inca king was called Manco Capac and he was said to have red hair and a beard," I mentioned.

"Yes," he agreed. "The Inca Manco Capac may have been an Irish missionary who introduced himself as *Manko Catholic*. Saint Brendan, or another monk, may have actually founded the Inca empire in the fourth century A.D. He taught them to live as monks did in Ireland, which is a unique system. All property was held in common, belonging to a small city-state which the monks founded, probably at ancient Cuzco. Work, not gold or other metals, was the medium of exchange, just as in an Irish monastery. For a certain number of hours' work, a person received food for his family and a place to live. Gold and silver were used for ornaments and decorations."

"You know," I said, "I have seen red-haired mummies in the museums of Peru."

"Foreign people with light hair and beards abound in ancient American legend and literature," he agreed, nodding. "But not all of them were necessarily Irish. Many were probably Vikings or even Iberian Celts. Brazil was supposedly named by the Portuguese because dye-wood, or brazil-wood was found there. However, this may not be the case, as the name Hy-Brazil was used by the ancient Irish. As a matter of fact, an Irish priest told Pope Zacharias in 780 A.D. that the old Irish habitually communicated with a transatlantic world! The Pope had him excommunicated for saying this.

"When St. Brendan sailed for Hy-Brazil with 50 monks over 1,500 years ago from the Abbey of Clonfert, he was gone for seven years. When he returned, he wrote about '...the fairest country a man might see; clear and bright, neither hot by day, nor cold by night, the trees laden with fruit, the herbage glorious with blooms and gay flowers...' It's not likely that St. Brendan was speaking of Labrador or even New England; he was probably speaking of Central and South America."

Taking a train north to the Giant's Causeway, I thought of Hy-Brazil and the lost islands of the Atlantic. Robert Fuson in *Legendary Islands of the Ocean Sea*[147] says that there are over 20 name variations on Hy-Brazil or O'Brasil, one of the oldest references being from the Voyage of Maelduin dated 1100 A.D. Fuson says that there is even a book in the Library of the Royal Academy (Dublin) with the title, *The Book of O'Brasil.*

The name Brazil appeared on many early charts of the Atlantic. Later, Brazil became associated with the east coast of Canada, either Newfoundland or Nova Scotia. Eventually the name was applied to Portugal's domain in South America. Sometime in the 16th century, the Portuguese dominion called Terra de Vera Cruz became known as Brazil, a name possibly derived from old Irish.

In the 16th century, "Four Masters" compiled a mass of very ancient material on the history of Ireland and its many traditions. Hy-Brazil is mentioned by them as Breasail, a demigod like Chronos, who rules the Atlantic.

The legendary island of Hy-Brazil may have been the Azores, and in fact, a section of one of the Azores was later named Brasil. Says Bonwick, "The Spanish Bay of Souls lies west of Cape Finisterre. Ogygia was thought by Plutarch to be five days' sail west of Brittia. The ancient Egyptian ritual spoke of the Happy West. The home of Calypso was in the west. Bailly, writing to Voltaire, in 1778, said, 'The giant Gyges inhabited the island of Atlantis, which is the same as Ogygia.'"

Central American legend says that there were several bearded messengers who visited Mexico and each of these was given the Nahuatl name of Quetzalcoatl. St. Brendan may have been one of the Quetzalcoatls of Mexican legend. One of the Quetzalcoatls was said to have built himself a boat of alligator skins and sailed it east across the Atlantic, back to his 'Holy Island.' Since Irish monks built their currahs out of oxhide, it makes sense that in Mexico, lacking oxen or other large animals, they would have made a boat from the skins of alligators.

~~~~~~~~~⚜~~~~~~~~~

I continued via train from the Giant's Causeway across the north coast of Ireland into the Donegal region. I hitchhiked along the narrow country roads of Donegal, catching rides with farm trucks and delivery vans down the highway. This northwest coast of Ireland is a legendary area of mountains, rough coasts and impressive castles. Donegal was an ancient Druid center and from Tory Island, Conann, the chief of the Fomorians, ruled over Ireland.

Tory Island is off the north coast of Donegal and has some of the strangest ruins in all of Ireland. On this island, which is still inhabited by a small population, there exists a number of curious megalithic monuments of uncertain age, plus the scanty remains of an old monastery from the 6th century A.D.

Along with the remains of several megalithic buildings and a round tower, probably the strangest of all the ruins on this tiny island is the huge T-cross that stands over seven feet high on a platform of rectangular megalithic stones. It is a unique, undecorated T-cross that is similar to the pre-Christian crosses in the Balearics or Corsica.

It is curious that all that is left of the ancient settlement are the cross, the remains of a round tower standing about 57 feet high, and a few "cursing stones." These cursing stones were said to have been used effectively in 1884 when a gunboat was sunk during its effort to land troops on the island to collect taxes owed by the islanders.

Was Tory Island a sacred maritime port for the journey farther north to Iceland and North America? Tory Island once ruled ancient Ireland, yet today it is an isolated island of ruins, situated off the far northwest coast, absolutely the closest point in Ireland to Iceland, Greenland and Newfoundland. Why else would a megalithic port with tower be found on a small, barren island in northwest Ireland?

Jim Bailey in *Sailing to Paradise*[281] maintains that the first kings of Europe and the Mediterranean in 7,000 B.C. were the navigators of the earliest seafarers. Tory Island was clearly a center for the ancient Sea Kings, the fortress from where Conann, a navigator king, ruled Ireland. Today Tory Island is a remote, windswept isle of ancient walls and piles of stones. A solitary cross maintains vigil for the return of the ancient mariners.

~~~~~~~~~~~~~~~~~~~~~~~~~~~~~

The Lost Land of Tir na n'Og

My last stop in Ireland would be Galway, a wonderful city with narrow streets and many cafés and bookstores. After a day's visit I took a bus from Galway to the port of Rossaveal. The scenery was bleak and rocky; huge rocks had fallen along the limestone tablelands of Rossaveal Point and were scattered about the rocky coast. The scenery was bleak and angular, looking like another planet.

As a winter rainstorm pelted the small ferry, the passengers boarded by walking over a wooden plank. It was a rough and stormy crossing to the Aran Islands. We landed at the small port of Kilronan on the main island of Inishmore. At a rocky jetty I jumped off the old ferry and walked through the rain to a small boardinghouse within the cluster of houses that was the main town on Aran.

The next day I rented a bicycle and peddled around the island. The Aran Islands are an amazing wealth of strange archaeological sites. Massive Iron Age forts such as Dún Aengus and Dún Dúchathair on Inishmore and Dún Conchuir on Inishmaan can be found overlooking the ocean. Says my *Lonely Planet* guidebook to Ireland, "Almost nothing is known about the people who built these structures, partly because their iron implements quickly rusted away. In folklore, the forts are said to have been built by the Fir Bolg, a Celtic tribe who invaded Ireland from Europe in prehistoric times."

I peddled my bicycle up and down the narrow road that works its way westward to the tip of the island. I left my bicycle at a stone wall and then walked up the stony path to Dún Aengus, the mighty fort on the edge of a sheer cliff over the sea.

The fort is formed as a half-circle around the cliff, and there is some speculation as to whether the fort was at one time completely circular, as other forts on the Aran Islands are, or originally built as a semicircle. If it was originally built as a circular fort, as some authors suggest, then portions of it have fallen into the sea as the cliffs collapsed.

The fort consists of three rows of defenses forming concentric semicircles. The innermost one has wall-walks and wall-chambers, and a massive entrance tunnel through the main wall. Beyond the third wall is the 'chevaux-de-frise' defensive measure, a remarkable field of sharp pointed stone spikes placed closely together in the ground. This 'chevaux-de-frise' would certainly make it difficult for a charging army to reach the walls of the fort, and this sort of defensive measure can be found at some forts in France, hence the French name.[273]

Says Peter Harbison in his guide, *Monuments of Ireland*,[273] "The earliest inhabitants are said to have been the Firbolgs, who, having escaped after the Battle of Moytura, fled first to Meath. But they were not prepared to pay the exorbitant rents imposed upon them there by Cairbre-Nia-Fer, King of Tara in the first century, A.D., and retired to Connacht were they were granted lands along the western seaboard, including the Aran Islands. They fortified themselves on the Islands, and called their fortresses after their chiefs, Aengus, Eoghanacht and Eochla. The Firbolgs later lost the islands to the Eoghanacta of Munster."

One thing is clear when looking at Dún Aengus; it was built in anticipation of some attack by large forces. A massive effort had been made to create this fort, yet we do not know who has built it, or against whom it was fortified in such a spectacular way. Today the Aran Islands are barren, sparsely populated, rocky islands, barely able to support a small fishing population, yet in prehistory they were apparently an important and strategic military base.

Were the Aran Island forts built to protect the northern sea routes to America? Like Tory Island off Donegal, the Aran Islands were apparently far more important in ancient times than they are today. Atlantis authors such as Charles Berlitz in his book *Atlantis, The Eighth Continent*[3] claim that the Aran Islands and their forts are linked to the lost continent, possibly as outposts of the mid-Atlantic empire.

<center>~~~~~~~~~~〜⚲〜~~~~~~~~~~</center>

Later that night at a pub in Kilronan I talked to the bartender. It was a slow night and he asked what I was doing in the Aran Islands. I told him that I was researching a book on Atlantis and was interested in the mysteries of Ireland.

"Sure, and we have our own Atlantis here on Aran," he said in a melodious Irish brogue.

"Really?" I asked.

"Here on the Aran Islands we have many stories about the lost land of Tir na n'Og, a legendary island now beneath the ocean."

I slowly drank my Guinness as he continued his story. "Tir na n'Og is the land of eternal youth," he said. "On a misty day, when the light is just right, legend says, you can see the towers of Tir na n'Og beneath the sea from the southern cliffs of Inisheer."

Later, when I returned to my guesthouse, I got out my copy of Bonwick's *Irish Druids and Old Irish Religions*[269] to read about the lost land to the west. Bonwick says an account of Tir na n'Og was given to St. Patrick by the heathen Fenian Oisin: "...when a hero was carried off from the field of battle by the golden-haired fairy Niamh, the region was divided into states under sovereigns, as in the Land of the Living. It lay beneath the waves in the West, in a lovely climate." After spending three months in Tir na n'Og, the hero returns to Ireland but finds that instead 300 years have passed.

Similarly, there is the story of a King Porsuma who was "carried off by a Zephyr (gentle wind)—the princess taking him for a phoenix, and conveying him to Thierna-na-Oge, the paradise of eternal youth."[269]

The Lost Land of Tir na n'Og (spelled various ways including Tiro na n-Og, Thierna-na-Oge, Tir-nan-Og, and others) was a lost land to the west, a glorious land beneath the sea where the souls of the departed journeyed in the afterlife similar to the way in which the Egyptians departed on a boat down the River Styx to an eternal land in the West.

Paul Dunbavin in *The Atlantis Researches* tells of the old Irish saga of Cormac. "A great mist was brought upon them in the midst of the plain, and Cormac found himself alone. There was a large fortress in the midst of the plain with a wall of bronze around it. In the fortress was a house of white silver, and it was half-thatched with the wings of white birds... Then he saw another royal stronghold, and another wall of bronze around it. There were four palaces therein. He entered the fortress and saw the vast palace with its beams of bronze, its wattling of silver, and its thatch of the wings of white birds."[212]

In this story we see a strong parallel with Plato's Atlantis and a hall of bronze and pillars of bronze. Perhaps Tir na n'Og was the capital city of Atlantis itself, now beneath the waves.

Says Bonwick, "Chronos slept in his palace of glass in Ogygia, Isle of the West. The Hesperides and its apples lay in the happy West. The Teutones went to the glass Isles of the West, as did the Norsemen and Celtiberians. Arthur was rowed to Avalon in the West. The Sacred Isles of Hindoos were to the West. Christian hymns still speak of crossing the waters to Heaven."[269]

Bonwick quotes from the early Irish saga *Battle of Gabhra* about the "mysterious realm of Tethra, beyond the sea, that the fabled Fomorian race of Irish retreated to, when finally vanquished by the next comers."

From the *Battle of Gabhra*: "The Firbolg and Fomorian races, being more or less sea-faring men, placed their Elysium far out in the sea, and called it by various names, such as Island of the Living, Island of Breasal, Island of Life, etc. The Firbolgs are said to have lived under the waters of our lakes. The Tuatha de Dananns, being devoted to civil and literary pursuits, and their Druids having held their seminaries in caves and other secluded subterranean abodes, fancied their Elysium placed under the earth, while the Milesians steered, as it were, a middle course between both, and made their Elysium in a sort of indescribable locality to which a subterranean passage led. This they called Tir-na-n'Og, the country of perpetual youth."[269]

Bonwick relates the Irish Land of Youth or Land of the Blessed to the Egyptian *Book of the Dead* and the Hymn to Osiris. "Renouf, in his translation of the *Book of the Dead*, has this Egyptian prayer—'Let me have my heart, that it may rest within me. I shall feed on the food of Osiris. Hail to you, O ye Lords of everlasting Time and Eternity! Let not my heart be torn from me. I shall not surrender to thee this heart of the Living. Come forth to the bliss towards which we are bound.'" This bliss is the Isles of the Blessed in the West, says Bonwick, in both Irish and Egyptian tradition.

The sun sets in the west, so there are many reasons for legends and religions to involve a journey to the west. Yet, Atlantis did exist to the west of Egypt and Europe, and of Ireland as well.

Says Bonwick, "Ireland was associated with the west by the old Welsh... Taliesin, the great Welsh Druid, was stolen by an Irish pirate vessel of the period, but he escaped in a magic coracle (boat) before reaching Erin. The Land Beneath the Sea was beyond Cardigan Bay, the Annwn of the old Sun. The Welsh Avalon, or Island of Apples, the everlasting source of the Elixir of Life, the home of Arthur and other mythological heroes, was in the Irish direction."

Continues Bonwick on Tir na n'Og, "it was the western Arranmore Isle of the Bay of Galway (Inishmore), from which the quicksighted, upon a fine day, could discern *Hy-Braefailth*, or the Enchanted Isle."[269] Here we see how Tir na n'Og is confused with another legendary land, the Island of Hy-Brasil.

Bonwick mentions the legend of a lost city that can be seen just off the Aran Islands in Liscannor Bay: "The white breaking waves are said to be caused by the shallowness of the water over this enchanted little city, which is believed to be seen once in seven years, and of which, it is observed, that those who see it shall depart this world before the lapse of seven years to come."

In ancient times, warfare was man's favorite sport [now, too, it seems], and the Irish, like their relatives, the Norse and Germans, loved to fight. The Mayans and other cultures staged ritual battles between city-states, and the Romans took their battles into the opulent and "civilized" world of the Roman coliseum, where they even staged naval battles.

And so it was in the Land of Youth, these immortals amused themselves with battles and clan fighting. Says Bonwick, "War was, with the Irish, as with other people of German or Norse descent, a most pleasant way of beguiling time in the world beyond. Even Cuchulainn was induced to undertake his perilous voyage, that he might gain a goddess for a wife, by promising to help her family in a fight."[269]

Was Tir na n'Og and its legends based on Atlantis? It would seem that the story of Tir na n'Og is based on a mixture of topics, including a sunken land in the Atlantic that may well have been Atlantis. The story also contains Egyptian-type mythology of the dead going west as well as the localized legends of a disaster that struck the Aran Islands and Galway Bay. In antiquity, the Aran Islands may have been one large island off the mainland of Ireland with a larger population. An earthquake, perhaps around 1200 B.C., may have devastated the islands and large parts of the south coast literally dropped into the Atlantic. This may have happened during the same earthquake that sank the lost land of Lyonesse in Cornwall.

Perhaps a sudden change in the North Sea around Ireland, Britain and Holland devastated a thriving sea culture that had built these large forts and walled cities. When their homeland was destroyed, these people took to their many boats and invaded the Mediterranean. This invasion circa 1200 B.C. could have been the sudden invasion of the mysterious Sea Peoples that destroyed the Hittites and other eastern Mediterranean nations.

~~~~~~~~~ 🜚 ~~~~~~~~~

Ancient Ireland may have been the Elysium Fields of Homer, but the forts of the Aran Islands indicated that there was fighting as well as long periods of peace.

L. Sprague de Camp in *Lost Continents* tells the story briefly of Tir na n'Og and the lost land in the Irish Sea: "Cardigan Bay in Wales and Lough Neagh in Ireland also have stories of (a sudden sinking) connecting with them. The Irish of Connemara tell a tradition of a sunken city offshore that will one day come up again, at which time Galway will in its turn be submerged. One stormy night in 1946 these folk were shocked to see a host of lights twinkling over the water where the city should be. Their fears were confirmed when a man who tried to telephone Galway was told by a fresh operator: 'There's no reply; they must be all dead in there.' At dawn, however, the Connemarans were relieved to see the 'city,' a fleet of Spanish trawlers riding out the storm in the lee of the Aran Islands, hoist anchor and sail away."[1]

The next day I peddled my bike out to the megalithic structure generally known as the oratory of St. Benan. It is a one-room building constructed with exceptionally large stones on its sidewalls. The walls consist of massive blocks of stone, perfectly cut to intersect and create a nearly indestructible structure.

The oratory was meant to have a straw roof. In many ways it was very similar in style to the megalithic houses built in the Andes, also thatched with straw.

The Teampall Bheanain, or St. Benan Oratory, may have been occupied by the saint himself at one time, but it was probably not built by him. It is likely that this megalithic structure was built by the same people who built Dún Aengus and the other Aran forts. These people, I believe, are best identified with the ancient Sea Kings of 2000 B.C.

One can only gaze at such megalithic structures in wonder and ask, why were they built? Why build using such gigantic, highly dressed slabs of stone? Such astounding megalithic building can be seen in Peru, Bolivia, Greece, Malta, Mexico and many other places. Even such remote localities as Easter Island and Tonga display a type of megalithic perfection that amazes modern engineers.

There would seem to be a number of different answers to the question as to why megalithic structures are built. The first answer would be that megalithic buildings will last for thousands of years. Proof of this are the many ancient structures still standing, from 6,000 B.C. or more in the case of Malta and other sites.

Structures built out of interlocking blocks of hard stone can withstand even large earthquakes, as the Andes Mountains of South America are known to have every few hundred years or less.

Another reason for building on a megalithic scale is that invading armies will have a more difficult time attacking and destroying a megalithic structure. A megalithic wall of interlocked blocks of stone weighing many tons will hold up longer to an onslaught than a wall made of bricks or timber.

Another interesting idea along these lines is the megalithic fortress protecting against huge wild animals and giant reptiles. Ancient man had to deal with more wild animals than we must worry about today.

The last reason for megalithic construction would be for the simple demonstration of the mason's art. Every carpenter and engineer wants to design and build the best structure possible. Megalithic structures, especially perfectly constructed ones, are an amazing showcase for the master mason or architect.

〜〜〜〜〜〜〜〜☞〜〜〜〜〜〜〜

Later, at sunset, I stood on the edge of the southern cliffs of Inishmore at the fort of Dún Duchathair. Like Dún Aengus, Dún Duchathair is a semicircular fort on the edge of a 200-foot cliff. I looked out at the cold, gray Atlantic. Waves shook the cliffs below and sometimes the spray reached nearly to the tops of the cliffs.

As I looked out over the fathomless deep of the ocean, I thought about Atlantis and the lost lands to the West.

My guide to ancient Ireland, Bonwick, sums up the spiritual element in the legends of a lost land of the west: "We may fancy some white-haired sage of Erin, feeling the sands of life slowly but surely sinking, who could seat himself on the tempest-tossed cliffs beside the Atlantic, watching a sunset in those western waters, where the gradually lessening glow foreshadowed his own departure."[269]

Tir na n'Og was more than just a mythical land to the west. Was it the remembrance of a lost land and a golden age now gone?

In my own mind, I was now satisfied that Atlantis, an ancient civilization of seafarers in prehistory, did in fact exist. If this lost land had existed in history, then where was it? Was Atlantis a Mediterranean island or off the coast of North Africa? Did Atlantis exist in the North Sea or Scandinavia? Perhaps Atlantis was in the Irish Sea or off the Aran Islands? These areas certainly had their lost cities, but while they may have been associated with Atlantis, they were probably not Atlantis itself.

Many authors had proposed that the continent of North or South America, lost to history after an early discovery by seafarers, was the true Atlantis. It is true that the Americas had their lost cities, but Atlantis was clearly said to have sunk beneath the ocean.

On this day, looking out at an orange and red sunset in the distance, I decided that, after all, Atlantis was pretty much when and where Plato, Solon and the Egyptian priests said it was. Atlantis, I believe, is beneath the mid-Atlantic in the vicinity of the Azores. Although it was a small continent, its influence reached across the water to the Americas and to what are now Britain, Ireland and parts of the European continent. This Atlantic island civilization was contemporary with other civilizations such as the Osirian civilization and the Rama Empire.

Around 10,000 B.C., geological upheavals, perhaps both natural and manmade, sank the small continent. Effects of this disaster reached other areas of the Atlantic and the Mediterranean. The Mediterranean was apparently flooded at this time, creating the various islands and unique megalithic cultures discussed in this book.

A thousand years after the destruction of Atlantis and upheavals in other empires, the Hittites and Egyptians began to explore the newly created Mediterranean Sea area and the Atlantic. In the Americas, early groups such as the Tiahuanaco culture and the Mayans began to recreate their civilizations. Seafarers of the legendary Atlantean League began to cross the Atlantic again by about 6,000 B.C. These same Mediterraneans colonized areas of northern Europe, including the British Isles as far north as the Shetlands (Set-lands).

North Sea earthquakes finished off the coastal civilization that was described in Jürgen Spanuth's *Atlantis of the North*. This civilization was much later than Atlantis, probably reaching its height about 1500 B.C. At about this time or shortly thereafter, the Sea Peoples with their horned helmets came from Denmark, England, Holland, Germany and France to the Mediterranean to invade Greece, Egypt and the Hittite empire.

We have seen the fantastically huge building projects of

prehistory, at Ba'albek, Hattusas and the submerged megalithic harbors at Alexandria and Phoenicia. Mysterious megaliths lie abandoned on Malta, Sardinia and the Balearic islands.

A strange world existed in the Sahara some 10,000 years ago, and meanwhile, Carthage built its capital city as a miniature version of the capital city of Atlantis. Like today, powerful nations fought wars that spanned entire continents. Secret societies like the Knights Templar turned ancient Phoenician ports into their own strongholds, and the Templars even reopened the ancient Phoenician trade routes for a brief time.

The megalithic buildings in the British Isles were abandoned and later occupied again, as in the case of many Irish antiquities. Meanwhile the cataclysmic forces of nature continued to cause upheavals and earth changes. The lost lands of Lyonesse, Wales, Tartessos, Brittany and Frisia were lost to the sea in relatively recent times, reminding us of the great destruction that befell Atlantis many thousands of years previously. More earth changes are likely to happen in the near future.

There is an old saying, "what goes around, comes around." Mankind's love for warfare has both fueled his technology and created much destruction and woe. Great teachers incarnate from time to time to try to teach man to love his neighbor and to live in a peaceful, helpful manner with others.

Yet our history is one of non-stop warfare and invasion. Man slaughters man, and the gods look down in pain and sorrow at what we have created for ourselves. Plato and the Egyptian priests have given us the story of one ancient civilization that waged war on the rest of the world with disastrous results.

As the sun set in the distance I resolved to dedicate my life to the peaceful betterment of mankind. But what could I do?

Sir Francis Bacon wrote *The New Atlantis* in 1600, a utopian novel of a new world to be. Secret societies, good and bad, had sought to create their own domains. Who was who in the elaborate game for the creation of the New Atlantis? The Knights Templar had fought against the power of the Vatican, a battle that was for the very hearts and minds of the people themselves.

Perhaps the greatest battle of Atlantis was happening in the hearts of mankind. This battle between good and evil, right and wrong, harmony and destruction has waged its war across the centuries. From Atlantis to Armageddon, modern man stands on the brink of more cataclysms and wars. Will the New Atlantis emerge from the ashes of world destruction like a phoenix from its dying body?

As a chill wind blew in from the sea, I resolved to do what I could to build the New Atlantis, a nation where man will finally learn to live in harmony with nature and his fellow man.

1910 photograph taken at the entrance to Newgrange. Note the massive entrance stone with the spiral carvings, similar to those at Tarxien on Malta.

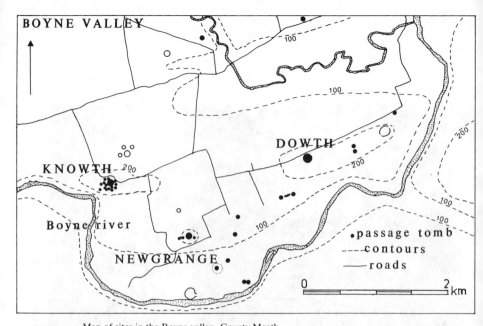

Map of sites in the Boyne valley, County Meath.

Pre-Christian crosses found at Polvorin, near Coruña, Spain.

1914 photo of the Cross of the Scriptures in Clonmacnoise, one of the finest high crosses in Ireland. Many of these high crosses may be pre-Christian, like the round towers.

A reconstructed round tower at Clondalkin, Co. Dublin.

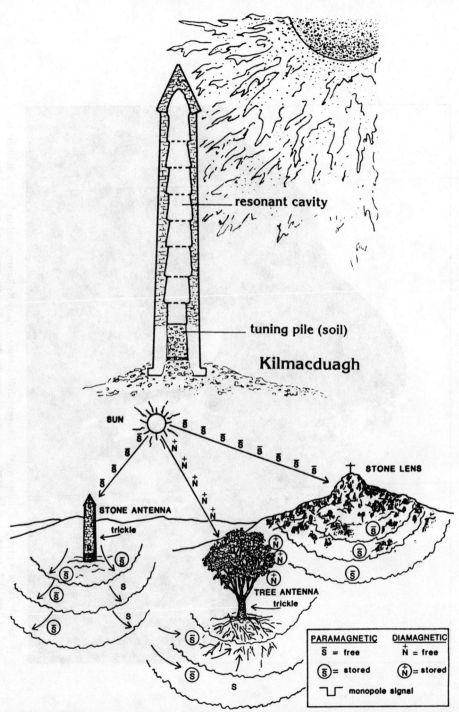

resonant cavity

tuning pile (soil)

Kilmacduagh

SUN

STONE LENS

STONE ANTENNA
trickle

TREE ANTENNA
trickle

PARAMAGNETIC	DIAMAGNETIC
$\bar{S}$ = free	$\overset{+}{N}$ = free
$\textcircled{\bar{S}}$ = stored	$\textcircled{\overset{+}{N}}$ = stored
⊓⊔ monopole signal	

Philip Callahan's diagrams of how the round towers of ancient Ireland were used as magnetic antennas to bring earth energies to the soil. The tower could be "tuned" by partially filling it with dirt.

An old photo of a group of ladies at the Browneshill Dolmen near Kilkenny, Ireland. This dolmen is said to have the largest and heaviest capstone of any dolmen in Europe, weighing over 100 tons.

1908 photo of the west door of the West Church at Killevy in Co. Armagh. This massive linteled doorway was once part of a 10th century church, but may have been part of an earlier structure.

Early photo of the *Grianan of Aileach* fort in Co. Donegal. Similar in construction to the forts on the Aran Islands, legend says that this tall, circular structure was built by the ancient gods.

Top: A 1907 photo of the megalithic cross on Tory Island on the north coast of Donegal. Bottom: An early print of ruins on Tory Island, including the cross, megalithic wall and stub of a round tower. Tory Island was said to rule Ireland in early times. Compare this megalithic cross to those on the Balearic Islands of Spain.

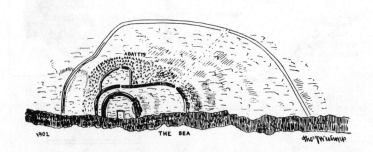

Opposite: An aerial photo of Dun Aengus on Inishmore. This spectacular fort is on the edge of a 200-foot cliff. Top: A map of Dun Aengus. "Abattis" is the "Chevaux-de-frise" defensive spikes. Bottom: A close-up photo of the "Chevaux-de-frise" razor-sharp rock-spikes with the walls of the fort in the background.

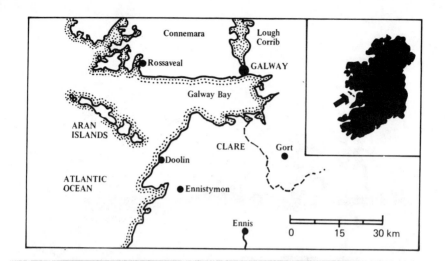

Top: A map of Galway Bay and the Aran Islands. Bottom: The outer defenses of the Dun Aengus fort.

An 1897 photo of the megalithic building called St. Benan's Oratory on the Aran Island of Inishmore.

An 1899 photo of Rev. D. Murphy and Dr. George Stokes at the Gallarus Oratory, Dingle, Co. Kerry. This boat-shaped structure is highly similar to structures on the Balearic and other Mediterranean islands.

And this the form of mighty Hand sitting on Albions cliffs
Before the face of Albion: a mighty threatning Form.

His bosom wide & shoulders huge overspreading wondrous
Bear Three strong sinewy Necks & Three awful & terrible Heads
Three Brains in contradictory council brooding incessantly.
Neither daring to put in act its councils, fearing each other.
Therefore rejecting Ideas as nothing & holding all Wisdom
To consist in the agreements & disagreents of Ideas.
Plotting to devour Albions Body of Humanity & Love.

Such Form the aggregate of the Twelve Sons of Albion took; & such
Their appearance when combind: but often by birth pangs & loud groans
They divide to Twelve: the Key-bones & the chest dividing in pain
Disclose a hideous orifice; thence issuing the Giant-brood
Arise as the smoke of the furnace, shaking the rocks from sea to sea.
And there they combine into Three Forms, named Bacon & Newton & Locke.
In the Oak Groves of Albion which overspread all the Earth.

Imputing Sin & Righteousness to Individuals; Rahab
Sat deep within him hid: his Feminine Power unreveald
Brooding Abstract Philosophy, to destroy Imagination, the Divine-
Humanity A Three-fold Wonder: feminine: most beautiful: Three-fold
Each within other. On her white marble & even Neck, her Heart
Inorbd and bonified: with locks of shadowing modesty, shining
Over her beautiful Female features, soft flourishing in beauty
Beams mild, all love and all perfection, that when the lips
Recieve a kiss from Gods or Men, a threefold kiss returns
From the pressd loveliness: so her whole immortal form three-fold
Three-fold embrace returns: consuming lives of Gods & Men
In fires of beauty melting them as gold & silver in the furnace
Her Brain enlabyrinths the whole heaven of her bosom & loins
To put in act what her Heart wills; O who can withstand her power
Her name is Vala in Eternity: in Time her name is Rahab

The Starry Heavens all were fled from the mighty limbs of Albion   His

A Mythological Trilithon, from William Blake's *Jerusalem*, Chap. 3, 70.

An imaginary photo collage of London under water. Thanks to Nigel Pennick.

BIBLIOGRAPHY. & FOOTNOTES

1. **Lost Continents**, L. Sprague de Camp, 1954, Gnome Press, New York.

2. **American Genesis**, Jeffrey Goodman, 1981, Summit Books, New York.

3. **Atlantis, The Eighth Continent**, Charles Berlitz, 1984, G.P. Putnam's Sons, New York.

4. **Serpent In the Sky**, John A. West, 1979, Harper & Row, New York.

5. **Atlantis The Antediluvian World**, Ignatius Donnelly, 1882, New York.

6. **The Problem of Atlantis**, Lewis Spence, 1924, Rider & Co., London.

7. **Megaliths and Masterminds**, Peter Lancaster Brown, 1979, Charles Scribner's Sons, New York.

8. **The God-Kings & the Titans**, James Bailey, 1973, St. Martin's Press, New York.

9. **Mysteries of Forgotten Worlds**, Charles Berlitz, 1972, Doubleday, New York.

10. **Lost Worlds**, Robert Charroux, 1973, Collins, Glasgow, Great Britain.

11. **Chariots of the Gods**, Erich Von Daniken, 1969, Putnam, NY.

12. **The History of Atlantis**, Lewis Spence, 1926, London, reprinted 1995, Adventures Unlimited Press, Stelle, IL.

13. **The View Over Atlantis**, John Michell, 1969, Ballantine Books, NY.

14. **The Occult Sciences In Atlantis**, Lewis Spence, 1943, Rider & Co., London.

15. **Lost Atlantis**, James Bramwell, 1938, Harper & Brothers, New York.

16. **Lost Cities of China, Central Asia & India**, David Hatcher Childress, 1991, Adventures Unlimited Press, Stelle, Illinois.

17. **Ancient Man: A Handbook of Puzzling Artifacts**, William Corliss, 1978, The Sourcebook Project, Glen Arm, MD.

18. **The Atlas of Archaeology**, 1982, St Martin's Press, NY.

19. **Ice, The Ultimate Disaster**, Richard Noone, 1982, Crown Publishers, New York.

20. **Atlantis In Andalucia**, E.M. Whishaw, 1928, Rider, London. Reprinted as *Atlantis In Spain* by Adventures Unlimited, Stelle, IL.

21. **Atlantis & the Giants,** Denis Saurat, 1957, Faber & Faber, London.

22. **We Are Not the First,** Andrew Tomas, 1971, Souvineer Press, London.

23. **Lost Cities of North & Central America,** D.H. Childress, 1992, Adventures Unlimited Press, Stelle, IL.

24. **Atlantis: From Legend to Discovery,** Andrew Tomas, 1972, Robert Laffont, Paris. (Sphere Books, 1973, London).

25. **The Shadow of Atlantis,** Colonel A. Braghine, 1940, London (Dutton, NY).

26. **The Subterranean Kingdom,** Nigel Pennick, 1981, Turnstone Press, Wellingborough, Northamptonshire, GB.

27. **The Ancient Atlantic,** L. Taylor Hansen, 1969, Amherst Press, Amherst, WI.

28. **Legends of the Lost,** Peter Brookesmith, ed., 1984, Orbis, London.

29. **The Secret of Atlantis,** Otto Muck, 1976, Collins, Glasgow.

30. **The Mediterranean Was A Desert,** Kenneth J. Hsü, 1983, University of Princeton Press, Princeton, NJ.

31. **Plato Prehistorian,** Mary Settegast, 1990, Lindisfarne Press, Hudson, NY.

32. **Voyage To Atlantis,** James W. Mavor, Jr., 1969, Putnam, NY. (reprinted 1990, Park Street Press, Rochester, VT).

33. **Lands Beyond,** L. Sprague de Camp & Willy Ley, 1952, Gnome, NY.

34. **The Cyclades In the Bronze Age,** R.L.N. Barber, 1987, University of Iowa Press, Iowa City.

35. **Cataclysms of the Earth,** Hugh A. Brown, 1967, Twayne Pubs., NY.

36. **Maps of the Ancient Sea Kings,** Charles Hapgood, 1970, Chilton Publishers, Philadelphia.

37. **Pole Shift,** John White, 1980, Doubleday, NY.

38. **Strange Artifacts,** William Corliss, 1974, The Sourcebook Project, Glen Arm, MD.

39. **The World's Last Mysteries,** Reader's Digest, 1976, Reader's Digest Association, Inc., Pleasantville, NY.

40. **The Stones Of Atlantis,** David Zink, 1978, Prentice-Hall, Englewood Cliffs, NJ.

41. **The Lost Continent of Mu,** James Churchward, 1931, Ives Washburn, New York.

42. **The Children of Mu**, James Churchward, 1931, Ives Washburn, NY.

43. **The Search For Atlantis**, Edwin Björkman, 1927, Alfred Knopf, NY.

44. **Lost Tribes & Sunken Continents**, Robert Wauchope, 1962, University of Chicago Press, Chicago.

45. **Strange Life**, Richard Corliss, 1976, Sourcebook Project, Glen Arm, MD.

46. **Lost Lands & Sunken Cities**, Nigel Pennick, 1987, Fortean Tomes, London.

47. **The Gods Unknown**, Robert Charroux, 1972, Berkley Books, (1969, Robert Laffont). Published in the U.K. as *The Mysterious Unknown*.

48. **Flood From Heaven**, Eberhard Zangger, 1992, William Morrow, NY.

49. **Enigmas**, Rupert Gould, 1945, University Books, New York.

50. **Lost Outpost of Atlantis**, Richard Wingate, 1980, Everest House, NY.

51. **Strange World**, Frank Edwards, 1964, Bantam Books, New York.

52. **Stranger Than Science**, Frank Edwards, 1959, Bantam Books, NY.

53. **Voyage To Atlantis**, James W. Mavor, Jr., 1969, Park Street Press, Rochester, VT.

54. **Technology In the Ancient World**, Henry Hodges, 1970, Marboro Books, London.

55. **Unearthing Atlantis**, Charles Pellegrino, 1991, Random House, NY.

56. **Along Civilization's Trail**, Ralph M. Lewis, 1940, AMORC, San José, CA.

57. **Lost Cities & Ancient Mysteries of South America**, David Hatcher Childress, 1987, Adventures Unlimited Press, Stelle, Illinois.

58. **Lost Cities & Ancient Mysteries of Africa & Arabia**, David Hatcher Childress, 1990, Adventures Unlimited Press, Stelle, Illinois.

59. **Lost Cities of Ancient Lemuria & the Pacific**, David Hatcher Childress, 1988, Adventures Unlimited Press, Stelle, Illinois.

60. **Masters of the World**, Robert Charroux, 1974, Berkley Books, New York (1967, Robert Laffont, Paris).

61. **Atlantis, The Lost Continent Revealed**, Charles Berlitz, 1984, Macmillan, London.

62. **Timeless Earth**, Peter Kolosimo, 1974, University Press, Seacaucus, NJ.

63. **Mysteries of Time & Space**, Brad Steiger, 1974, Prentice Hall, Englewood Cliffs, NJ.

65. **Sacred Mysteries Among the Mayas & the Quiches**, Augustus LePlongeon, 1886, Kegan Paul (Agent), London & New York.

66. **Queen Moo & the Egyptian Sphinx**, Augustus LePlongeon, 1900, Kegan Paul (Agent), London & New York.

67. **The Babylonian Genesis**, Alexander Heidel, 1942, University of Chicago Press.

68. **The Secret of the Hittites**, C.W. Ceram, 1956, Alfred A. Knopf, New York.

69. **Mysteries of the Ancient World**, National Geographic Society, 1979, Washington, D.C.

70. **Atlas of Ancient Archaeology**, Jacquetta Hawkes, 1974, McGraw Hill, NY.

71. **Atlas of Ancient History**, Michael Grant, 1971, Macmillan, London.

72. **Shanidar, The First Flower People**, Ralph Solecki, 1971, Alfred Knopf, New York.

73. **Atlantis Rising**, Brad Steiger, 1973, Dell Publishing, New York.

74. **Popul Vuh**, Translated by Dennis Tedlock, 1985, Simon & Schuster, NY.

75. **The Chalice & the Blade**, Riane Eisler, 1987, HarperCollins, NY.

76. **In Quest of the White God**, Pierre Honoré, 1963, Hutchinson & Co., London.

77. **The 12th Planet**, Zechariah Sitchin, 1976, Avon Books, New York.

78. **The End of Atlantis**, J.V. Luce, 1969, Thames & Hudson, London.

79. **Fair Gods & Stone Faces**, Constance Irwin, 1963, W. Allen, London.

80. **Megalithomania**, John Michell, 1982, Thames & Hudson, London.

81. **Legends of the Lost**, Peter Brookesmith, ed., 1984, Orbis Publishing, London.

82. **Archaeology Under Water**, George F. Bass, 1966, Praeger Publishers, New York.

83. **Diving Into the Past**, Hanns-Wolf Rackl, 1968, Scribner, New York.

84. **Under the Mediterranean**, Honor Frost, 1963, Prentice-Hall, Englewood Cliffs, NJ.

85. **Archaeology Beneath the Sea**, George F. Bass, 1975, Walker & Co., New York.

86. **Cities In the Sea**, Nichols C. Fleming, 1971, Doubleday & Co., Garden City, NJ.

87. **4,000 Years Under the Sea**, Philippe Diolé, 1952, Julian Messner, Inc, NY.

88. **Did the Phoenicians Discover America?**, Thomas Johnston, 1913, James Nesbit & Co., London.

89. **Marine Archaeology**, edited by Joan du Plat Taylor, 1965, Thomas Crowell Co., New York.

90. **Secrets of the Bible Seas**, Alexander Flinder, 1985, Severn House Publishers, London.

91. **The Sea Gods After Atlantis**, Bonwick & Bigras, 1986, Intaglio Publishing, Vancouver, Canada.

92. **Secrets of the Lost Races**, Rene Noorbergen, 1977, Barnes & Noble Publishers, New York.

93. **Lost Worlds**, Alistair Service, 1981, Arco Publishing, New York.

94. **The World's Last Mysteries**, Readers Digest, 1976, Pleasantville, NY.

95. **Not of This World**, Peter Kolosimo, 1971, University Books, Seacaucus, NJ.

96. **World Almanac of the Strange**, 1977, Signet Books, New York.

97. **Doomsday 1999 A.D.** Charles Berlitz, Doubleday, Garden City, NJ.

98. **Gods of Air and Darkness**, Richard Mooney, 1975, Stein & Day, NY.

99. **From Earthquake Fire and Flood**, R. Hewitt, 1958, Scientific Book Club, London.

100. **The Bible As History**, Werner Keller, 1965, Hodder & Stoughton, London.

101. **Mysteries of Time & Space**, Brad Steiger, 1974, Prentice-Hall, NY.

102. **Info Journal**, No. 55, "Unbelievable Baalbek," by Jim Theisen, 1988.

103. **Investigating the Unexplained**, Ivan T. Sanderson, 1972, Prentice-Hall, New York.

104. **The World's Last Mysteries**, Nigel Blundell, 1980, Octopus Books, London.

105. **Searching For Hidden Animals**, Roy Mackal, 1980, Doubleday, NY.

106. **Atlantic Crossings Before Columbus**, Frederick Pohl, 1961, Norton, New York.

107. **They All Discovered America**, Boland, 1961, Doubleday, New York.

108. **Vanished Cities**, Hermann & Georg Schreiber, 1957, Alfred Knopf, New York.

109. **Calalus**, Cyclone Covey, 1975, Vantage Press, New York.

110. **Mexican Cities of the Gods**, Hans Helfritz, 1968, Praeger, NY.

111. **Hidden Worlds**, Van der Veer & Moerman, 1974, Souvenir Press, London,

112. **The Birth & Death of the Sun**, George Gamow, 1940, Viking, NY.

113. **YHWH**, Jerry Ziegler, 1987, Next Millennium Publishers, Stamford, CT.

114. **Indra Girt by Maruts**, Jerry Ziegler, 1994, Next Millennium Publishers, Stamford, CT.

115. **The Ancient Stones Speak**, Dr. David Zink, 1979, E.P. Dutton, NY.

116. **Engineering In the Ancient World**, J.G. Landels, 1978, U. of California Press, Berkley.

117. **The Oxford Illustrated Prehistory of Europe**, edited by Barry Cunliffe, 1994, Oxford University Press, Oxford & New York.

118. **The Atlas of Archaeology**, K. Branigan, consulting editor, 1982, St. Martin's Press, New York.

119. **Atlantis: The New Evidence**, Martin Ebon, 1977, Signet Books, NY.

120. **Edgar Cayce on Atlantis**, Edgar Evans Cayce, 1968, Warner Books, NY.

121. **Nicaraguan Antiquity**, Carl Bovallius, 1886, Swedish Society of Anthropology & Geography, Stockholm.

122. **Strange Creatures from Time & Space**, John Keel, 1970, Fawcett, New York.

123. **Extraterrestrial Intervention: The Evidence**, Jacques Bergier, 1974, Henry Regnery, Chicago.

124. **Mysteries of Ancient South America**, Harold Wilkins, 1946, Citadel Press, NY.

125. **Secret Cities of Old South America**, Harold Wilkins, 1952, Library Publications, Inc., NY.

126. **Exploration Fawcett (Lost Trails, Lost Cities)**, Brian Fawcett, 1953, Hutchinson & Co., London.

127. **A Dweller On Two Planets**, Frederick Spencer Oliver, 1884, Borden Publishing, Alhambra, CA.

128. **The Lost Realms**, Zechariah Sitchin, 1990, Avon Books, NY.

129. **LIving Wonders**, John Michell & Bob Rickard, 1982, Thames & Hudson, London.

130. **Irish Symbols of 3500 B.C.**, N.L Thomas, 1988, Mercier Press, Dublin.

131. **Arthur C. Clarke's Mysterious World**, Simon Welfare & John Fairley, 1980, Wm. Collins & Sons, London.

132. **Crete: The Traveller's Guide**, Eberhard Fohrer, 1990, Springfield Books, Huddersfield, U.K.

133. **The Ancient Greek Computer From Rhodes**, Victor J. Kean, 1991, Efstathiadis Group, Athens.

134. **Mysterious Britain**, Janet & Colin Bord, 1972, Granada Publishing, London.

135. **The Secret Country**, Janet & Colin Bord, 1976, Granada Publishing, London.

136. **On the Trail of the Sun Gods**, Marcel Homet, 1965, Neville Spearman, London.

137. **Crete: New Light On Old Mysteries**, Victor J. Kean, 1993, Efstathiadis Group, Athens.

138. **Vimana Aircraft of Ancient India & Atlantis**, Childress, Sanderson, Josyer, 1991, AUP/Publishers Network, Stelle, IL.

139. **Men Who Dared the Sea**, Gardner Soule, 1976, Thomas Crowell, NY.

140. **Michigan Prehistory Mysteries**, Betty Sodders, 1990, Avery Studios, Au Clair, MI.

141. **Michigan Prehistory Mysteries II**, Betty Sodders, 1991, Avery Studios, Au Clair, MI.

142. **The Unexplained**, William Corliss, 1976, Bantam Books, New York.

143. **Riddles in History**, Cyrus H. Gordon, 1974, Crown Publishers, NY.

144. **The Secret of Crete**, Hans Georg Wunderlich, 1972, Macmillan, NY.

145. **Enemy of Rome**, Leonard Cottrell, 1960, Evans Brothers, London.

146. **Daily Life In Carthage**, Gilbert Charles-Picard, 1961, Macmillan, NY.

147. **Legendary Islands of the Ocean Sea**, Robert H. Fuson, 1995, Pineapple Press, Sarasota, FL.

148. **Egyptian Myth & Legend**, Donald Mackenzie, 1907, Bell Pub., NY.

149. **The Phoenicians**, Donald Harden, 1962, Praeger Publishers, NY.

150. **Cities In the Sea**, Nicholas C. Flemming, 1971, Doubleday, NY.

151. **The Alexandria Project**, Stephen Schwartz, 1983, Dell Books, NY.

152. **Alexandria: A History & a Guide**, E.M. Forster, 1922, Morris, Alexandria.

153. **The Phoenicians**, Gerhard Herm, 1975, William Morrow & Co. NY.

154. **Baalbek**, Friedrich Ragette, 1980, Chatto & Windus, London.

155. **Mystery Religions In the Ancient World**, Joscelyn Godwin, 1981, Thames & Hudson, London.

156. **The Sea Peoples**, N.K. Sandars, 1978, Thames & Hudson, London.

157. **Atlantis Illustrated**, H.R. Stahel, 1982, Grosset & Dunlap, New York.

158. **The World of Megaliths**, Jean-Pierre Mohen, 1989, Facts on File, New York.

159. **The Standing Stones of Europe**, Alastair Service & Jean Bradbery, 1979, Orion Publishing, London.

160. **Mysterious Places: The Mediterranean**, Wilkinson, Dineen, & Ingen, 1994, Chelsea House Publishers, New York.

161. **Mysteries In the Human World & Mind**, Konstantinos Zissis, 1992, Sirena AB, Vaxjo, Sweden.

162. **The Once & Future Star**, George Michanowsky, 1977, Sphere Books, London.

163. **Psychic Archaeology**, Jeffrey Goodman, 1977, Berkley Books, NY.

164. **Holy Grail Across the Atlantic**, Michael Bradley, 1988, Hounslow Press, Willowdale, Ontario.

165. **The Sword & the Grail**, Andrew Sinclair, 1992, Crown, NY.

166. **The Ancient Sun Kingdoms of the Americas**, Victor von Hagen, 1957, World Publishing Co. Cleveland, OH.

167. **Guide To Cretan Antiquities**, Costis Davaras, 1976, Eptalofos, Athens.

168. **The Palaces of Crete**, James Walter Graham, 1962, Princeton

University Press, Princeton, NJ.

169. **The Bull of Minos**, Leonard Cottrell, 1953, Holt, Rinehart & Winston, New York.

170. **The Archaeology of Greece & the Aegean**, Stewart Perowne, 1974, Viking Press, New York.

171. **Malta's Prediluvian Culture**, Joseph Ellul, 1988, Printwell, Malta.

172. **Malta's Ancient Temples & Ruts**, Roland Parker & Michael Rubinstein, 1988, ICR Monograph Series, Tunbridge Wells, Kent.

173. **Malta: An Archaeological Guide**, D.H. Trump, 1972, Faber & Faber Ltd., London.

174. **Gozo—A Historical & Tourist Guide**, Dr. Anthony Gauci, 1966, St. Joseph's Press, Malta.

175. **An Illustrated Guide to Prehistoric Gozo**, Anthony Bonanno, 1986, Gaulitana Books, Malta.

176. **Malta**, Insight Guides, 1993, APA Publications, Singapore.

177. **Undiscovered Islands of the Mediterranean**, Moyer & Willes, 1990, John Muir Publications, Sante Fe, NM.

178. **Oceans Magazine**, "Wild Ocean Tales," Jerry Leblanc, August, 1986.

179. **The Disc From Phaistos**, Victor Kean, 1985, Efstathiadis, Athens.

180. **Earth's Shifting Crust**, C.H. Hapgood, 1958, Pantheon Books, NY.

181. **The Secret: America In World History Before Columbus**, Joseph Mahan, 1983, ISAC Press, Columbus, GA.

182. **Man: 12,000 Years Under the Sea**, Robert F. Burgess, 1980, Dodd, Mead & Company, New York.

183. **Pale Ink**, Henriette Mertz, 1953, Swallow Press, Chicago.

184. **Atlantis, Dwelling Place of the Gods**, Henriette Mertz, 1976, Swallow Press, Chicago.

185. **The Wine Dark Sea**, Henriette Mertz, 1964, Swallow Press, Chicago.

186. **The Mystic Symbol**, Henriette Mertz, 1986, Global Books, Chicago.

187. **Bronze Age America**, Barry Fell, 1982, Little, Brown & Co., Boston.

188. **Pre-Historic Nations**, John Baldwin, 1869, Harper & Brothers, New York.

189. **"Ancient Roman Shipwreck Found In Brazil,"** Robert Marx, *Fate*, Sept. 1983.

190. **Atlantis: Mother of Empires**, Robert Stacy-Judd, 1939, DeVorss & Co., Santa Monica, CA.

191. **The Berumuda Triangle Mystery—Solved**, Lawrence Kusche, 1975, Warner Books, New York.

192. **Who's Who in Non-Classical Mythology**, Egerton Sykes, 1952, 1993, Oxford University Press, New York.

193. **World of the Odd & Awesome**, Charles Berlitz, 1991, Fawcett, NY.

194. **No Longer On the Map**, Raymond H. Ramsay, 1972, Viking, NY.

195. **Legendary Islands of the Atlantic**, William Babcock, 1922, American Geographical Society, New York.

196. **Across the Ocean Sea**, George Sanderlin, 1966, Harper & Row, NY.

197. **Prophecies of Great World Changes**, George Brownell, 1927, The Aquarian Ministry, Santa Barbara, CA.

198. **Un Continent Perdu: L'Atlantide**, Otto Silbermann, 1930, Genet, Paris.

199. **The Bermuda Triangle**, Charles Berlitz, 1974, Doubleday, NY.

200. **Atlantis: The Autobiography of a Search**, Robert Ferro & Michael Grumley, 1970, Doubleday & Co., Garden City, NY.

201. **They All Discovered America**, Charles Boland, 1961, Doubleday, Garden City, New York.

202. **Saga America**, Barry Fell, 1980, New York Times Books, New York.

203. **La Vérité sur l'Atlantide**, René-Maurice Gattefossé, 1923, Legendre, Lyon, France.

204. **Gods & Spacemen In the Ancient East**, W. Raymond Drake, 1968, Sphere Books, London.

205. **Shamanism and the Mystery Lines**, Paul Devereux, 1992, Quantum Books, London.

206. **Ley Lines in Question**, Williamson & Bellamy, 1983, World's Work, Kingswood, Surrey, England.

207. **Prehistoric Stone Circles**, Aubrey Burl, 1979, Shire Publications, Buckinghamshire, U.K.

208. **Prehistoric Avebury**, Aubrey Burl, 1979, Yale University Press, London & New Haven.

209. **Cornwall and the Isles of Scilly**, Peter Stanier, 1987, Shire Publications, Buckinghamshire, U.K.

210. **The Atlas of Occult Britain**, Charles Walker, 1987, Hamlyn Publishing Group, Twickenham, Middlesex.

211. **Smara: The Forbidden City**, Michel Vieuchange, 1932, Dutton, New York. Reprinted 1987, Ecco Press, New York.

212. **The Atlantis Researches**, Paul Dunbavin, 1995, Third Millenium Publishing, Nottingham, UK.

213. **The Goblin Universe**, Ted Holiday, 1979, Futura, London.

214. **The Dictionary of Imaginary Places**, Alberto Manguel & Gianni Guadalupi, 1980, Macmillan Publishing Co., New York.

215. **The Dragon and the Disc**, Ted Holiday, 1973, Futura, London.

216. **The Great Orm of Loch Ness**, Ted Holiday, 1973, Futura Publications, London.

217. **The Sphinx and the Megaliths**, John Ivimy, 1974, Abacus, London.

218. **The Great Monster Hunt**, David Cooke, 1969, Norton Co., NY.

219. **In Search Of Lake Monsters**, Peter Costello, 1974, Berkley, NY.

220. **"Decoder Misled?"** R. J. Atkinson, *Nature*, No. 210, 1966.

221. **Secrets of the Stones**, John Michell, 1989, Inner Traditions, Rochester, Vermont.

222. **The Origins of Britain**, L. & J. Laing, 1982, Paladin Books, London.

223. **Albion: A Guide to Legendary Britain**, Jennifer Westwood, 1987, Paladin Books, London.

224. **Magical and Mystical Sites**, E. Pepper & J. Wilcock, 1993, Phanes Press, Grand Rapids, Michigan.

225. **Ancient Britain**, James Dyer, 1990, B.T. Batsford Ltd., London.

226. **Where Troy Once Stood**, Iman Wilkens, 1990, St. Martin's Press, New York.

227. **GENISIS**, David Wood, 1985, Baton Press, Tunbridge Wells, Kent.

228. **GENESET**, David Wood & Ian Campbell, 1994, Bellevue Books, London.

229. **The Azores: Fairy-Tale Islands of the Atlantic**, Robert B. Silverman, 1990, Phoenix Press, Rotterdam, Netherlands.

230. **São Miguel, Azores**, Mauricio Abreu, 1992, Praceta, Lisbon.

231. **Those Mysterious Etruscans**, Agnes Carr Vaughn, 1964, Doubleday, New York.

232. **The Buried People**, Sibylle Von Cles-Reden, 1955, Rupert Hart-Davis, London.

233. **The Search For the Etruscans**, James Wellard, 1973, Sphere Books, London.

234. **Fingerprints Of the Gods**, Graham Hancock, 1995, Crown, NY.

235. **The Sign and the Seal**, Graham Hancock, 1992, Crown, NY.

236. **Ancient Mysteries**, Rupert Furneaux, 1977, McGraw Hill, New York.

237. **Atlantis of the North**, Jurgen Spanuth, 1979, Van Nostrand Reinhold Co., New York.

238. **The Mystery of Atlantis**, Charles Berlitz, 1969, Grosset & Dunlap, New York.

239. **The Balearic Islands**, L. Pericot Garcia, 1972, Thames & Hudson, London.

240. **Holy Blood, Holy Grail**, Michael Baigent, Richard Leigh & Henry Lincoln, 1982, Johnathan Cape, London (published in the U.K. as **The Holy Blood and the Holy Grail**).

241. **The Messianic Legacy**, Michael Baigent, Richard Leigh & Henry Lincoln, 1985, Johnathan Cape, London.

241. **The Temple and the Lodge**, Michael Baigent & Richard Leigh, 1989, Johnathan Cape, London.

242. **Emerald Cup—Ark of Gold**, Col. Howard Buechner, 1991, Thunderbird Press, Metairie, LA.

243. **The Secrets of Rennes-le-Château**, Lionel & Patricia Fanthorpe, 1991, Bellevue Books, London.

244. **Earth Magic**, Francis Hitching, 1976, William Morrow Co, New York.

245. **Megaliths, Myths and Men**, Peter Lancaster Brown, 1976, Harper & Row, New York.

246. **Stonehenge Complete**, Christopher Chippindale, 1983, Thames & Hudson, London.

247. **Stonehenge Decoded**, Gerald S. Hawkins, 1965, Doubleday, Garden City, NY.

248. **Beyond Stonehenge**, Gerald S. Hawkins, 1973, Dorset Press, NY.

249. **The Mysteries of Chartres Cathedral**, Louis Charpentier, 1975, Avon Books, New York. 1966, Robert Lafont, Paris.

250. **Megalithic Brittany**, Aubrey Burl, 1985, Thames & Hudson, London.

251. **The Morning of the Magicians**, Jacques Bergier & Louis Pauwels, 1960, Stein & Day Publishers, New York.

252. **Extraterrestrial Visitations From Prehistoric Times To the Present**, Jacques Bergier & the editors of INFO, 1973, Signet Books, New York.

253. **The Other Atlantis**, Robert Scrutton, 1977, Neville Spearman, Jersey.

254. **Secrets of Lost Atland**, Robert Scrutton, 1978, Neville Spearman, Jersey.

255. **Prince Henry Sinclair**, Frederick Pohl, 1974, Clarkson Potter Publisher, New York.

256. **Scotland B.C.**, Anna Ritchie, 1988, Historic Scotland Books, Edinburgh.

257. **Holy Grail Across the Atlantic**, Michael Bradley, 1988, Hounslow Press, Willowdale, Ontario.

258. **The Sword and the Grail**, Andrew Sinclair, 1992, Crown, New York.

259. **The Templar Legacy & the Masonic Inheritance Within Rosslyn Chapel**, Tim Wallace-Murphy, 1993, Friends of Rosslyn, Rosslyn, Scotland.

260. **The Glastonbury Legends**, R. F. Treharne, 1967, Sphere Books, London.

261. **St. Joseph of Arimathea At Glastonbury**, Lionel Smithett Lewis, 1922, James Clark & Co., Cambridge.

262. **Celt, Druid and Culdee**, Isabel Hill Elder, 1962, Covenant, London.

263. **Did Our Lord Visit Britain**, Rev. C. C. Dobson, 1936, Covenant, London.

264. **The Druids**, T. D. Kendrick, 1927, Methuen & Co., London.

265. **The Druids**, Stuart Piggott, 1967, Thames and Hudson, London.

266. **Atlantis To the Latter Days**, H.C. Randall-Stevens, 1957, The Knights Templars of Aquarius, London.

267. **The Sun and the Serpent**, Hamish Miller & Paul Broadhurst, 1989, Pendragon Press, Launceston, Cornwall.

268. **The Search For the Stone of Destiny**, Pat Gerber, 1992, Canongate Press, Edinburgh.

269. **Irish Druids and Old Irish Religions**, James Bonwick, 1894, reprinted by Dorset Press, 1986.

270. **The Ultimate Frontier**, Eklal Kueshana, 1961, Stelle Group Publications, Stelle, IL.

271. **The Book of the Damned**, Charles Fort, 1919, Fortean Society (1941).

272. **Ancient Mysteries, Modern Visions**, Philip S. Callahan, 1984, Acres USA Publications, Kansas City, MO.

273. **Guide to National and Historic Monuments of Ireland**, Peter Harbison, 1970, Gill and Macmillan, Dublin.

274. **A World of Stone**, Paul O'Sullivan, 1972, O'Brian, Dublin.

275. **Pre-Christian Ireland**, Peter Harbison, 1988, Thames & Hudson, London.

276. **Sun and Cross**, Jakob Streit, 1984, Floris Books, Edinburgh. Original edition 1977 in German.

277. **Mythic Ireland**, Michael Dames, 1992, Thames & Hudson, London.

278. **The Mysterious Chequered Lights of New Grange**, Hugh Kearns, 1993, Elo Publications, Dublin.

279. **Atlantis, Lost Lands, Ancient Wisdom**, Geoffrey Ashe, 1992, Thames & Hudson Ltd., London.

280. **Science Frontiers**, compiled by William Corliss, 1995, Sourcebook Project, Glen Arm, MD.

281. **Sailing To Paradise, The Discovery of the Americas by 7000 B.C.**, Jim Bailey, 1994, Simon & Schuster, New York.

282. **Dimensions**, Jacques Valle, 1988, Ballantine Books, New York.

283. **Avalon of the Heart**, Dion Fortune, 1971, Aquarian Press, Wellingborough, England.

284. **The Old Straight Track**, Alfred Watkins, 1925, Methuen, London.

ADVENTURES UNLIMITED

(ISBN prefix 0-932813-)

In David Hatcher Childress's Lost Cities series:

LOST CITIES & ANCIENT MYSTERIES OF AFRICA & ARABIA

Maverick archaeologist/ adventurer Childress discovers lost cities in the Empty Quarter, Altlantean ruins in Egypt, a port city in the Sahara, King Solomon's mines, and antediluvian ruins in the Kalahari.

LOST CITIES OF ANCIENT LEMURIA & THE PACIFIC

Was there once a lost continent in the Pacific? Who built the mysterious megaliths that appear throughout the region? Childress examines the theories and legends surrounding Mu and comes to some surprising conclusions.

LOST CITIES OF CHINA, CENTRAL ASIA & INDIA

Like a real-life Indiana Jones, Childress has some hair-raising adventures in the world's oldest and most remote countries. Amazing tales of mysterious tunnels leading to supernatural realms, hidden monasteries high in the Himalayas, and the fabulous Rama Empire of India.

LOST CITIES & ANCIENT MYSTERIES OF SOUTH AMERICA

Childress searches windswept mountains for cities of gold, deadly jungles for living dinosaurs, and scorching deserts for Egyptian gold mines. Translated into both Spanish and Portuguese: a best seller in Brazil and Cuzco, Peru.

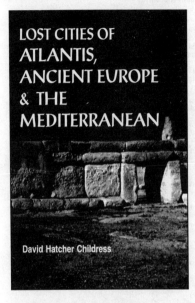

NEW!

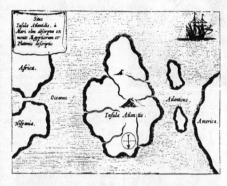

LOST CITIES OF ATLANTIS, ANCIENT EUROPE & THE MEDITERRANEAN

by David Hatcher Childress

Atlantis! The legendary lost continent comes under the close scrutiny of maverick archaeologist David Hatcher Childress in this sixth book in the internationally popular Lost Cities series. Childress takes the reader on a quest for the lost continent of Atlantis in search of sunken cities in the Mediterranean; across the Atlas Mountains in search of Atlantean ruins; and to remote islands in search of megalithic ruins, living legends, and secret societies. From Ireland to Turkey, Morocco to Eastern Europe, or remote islands of the Mediterranean and Atlantic, Childress takes the reader on an astonishing quest for mankind's past. Ancient technology, cataclysms, megalithic construction, lost civilizations, and devastating wars of the past are all explored in this amazing book. Childress challenges the skeptics and proves that great civilizations not only existed in the past but that the modern world and its problems are reflections of the ancient world of Atlantis. Join David on an unforgettable tale in search of the solutions to the mysteries of the past.

524 pp. ♦ 6x9 paperback ♦ Illustrated with hundreds of maps, photos & diagrams ♦ Footnotes & bibliography ♦ $16.95 ♦ code: MED

ATLANTIS

ATLANTIS IN SPAIN
A Study of the Ancient Sun Kingdoms of Spain
by E.M. Whishaw

First published by Rider & Co. of London in 1928, this extremely rare, classic book—a study of the megaliths of Spain, ancient writing, cyclopean walls, sun worshipping empires, hydraulic engineering, and sunken cities—is now back in print after 60 years. Learn about the Biblical Tartessus, an Atlantean city at Niebla, the Temple of Hercules and the Sun Temple of Seville, Libyans and the Copper Age, more.
284 pp. ♦ 6x9 paperback ♦ Illustrations, maps & photos ♦ Epilogue with tables of ancient scripts ♦ $15.95 ♦ code: AIS

VIMANA AIRCRAFT OF ANCIENT INDIA & ATLANTIS
by David Hatcher Childress with an introduction by Ivan T. Sanderson

Did the ancients have the technology of flight? In this incredible volume on ancient India, authentic Indian texts such as the Ramayana and the Mahabharata are used to prove that ancient aircraft were in use more than four thousand years ago. Included in this book is the entire Fourth Century B.C. manuscript *Vimaanika Shastra* by the ancient author Maharishi Bharadwaaja translated into English by the Mysore Sanskrit professor G.R. Josyer. Also included are chapters on Atlantean technology and the incredible Rama Empire of India and the devastating wars that destroyed it. Also an entire chapter on mercury vortex propulsion and mercury gyros, the power source described in the ancient Indian texts. Not to be missed by those interested in ancient civilizations or the UFO enigma.
334 pp. ♦ 6x9 paperback ♦ 104 rare photographs, maps & drawings ♦ $15.95 ♦ code: VAA

HOW DID THE ATLANTEANS
TAP THE FREE ENERGY
OF THE UNIVERSE?

ATLANTIS IN WISCONSIN
New Revelations About Lost Sunken City
by Frank Joseph

During the 1950s, scuba divers, using the latest high-tech search instruments, verified Indian legends of an ancient City of the Dead at the bottom of a small lake about 50 miles due west of Milwaukee. After Frank Joseph's original book on Rock Lake was released, he was presented with startling evidence to show that the real mystery of Rock Lake is far more bizarre than anyone realized: evidence that Rock Lake is a sacred vortex where time is bent; that other holy lakes in Japan, Bolivia, and Ireland hide similar structures; that the lost civilization was connected with Rock Lake; that the alleged "monster" of Rock Lake really exists; and that a worldwide natural catastrophe, not some local event, inundated the City of the Dead. Atlantis in Wisconsin will change your perspective not only of America's past but of the human mind's capacity to transcend time itself.
224 pp. ♦ 6x9 paperback ♦ Illustrations & photos ♦ $12.95 ♦ code: AIW

ATLANTIS: A DEFINITIVE STUDY
by George Firman

This book includes a study of Plato's texts, Phoenicians, dolphins, and an exhaustive study of ancient maps. Also included are chapters on plate tectonics, the Ursula Theory of Magnetic Accumulation, Edgar Cayce, and Pole Shifts, and more.
125 pp. ♦ 5x8 paperback ♦ 45 diagrams, maps & photographs ♦ $9.95 ♦ code: ADS

BLINDSIDED

THE LOST MILLENNIUM
How Did Atlanteans Tap the Free Energy of the Universe?
by Walt & Leigh Richmond

Back in print after many years, this book, written as a novel, delves into the topic of Atlantean power sources, known as "solar taps." Did Atlantean science cause their destruction? Was the Great Pyramid built as one of the Atlantean Solar Taps? The back cover of the book asks "Did the Ancient Atlanteans have Free Energy?" "Why did Velikovsky place the last earth upheaval at about 5,200 years ago?" and "What made the continents break apart á la the Continental Drift theory?" Students of unusual science, free energy, and Atlantis will not want to miss this classic book.
172 pp. ♦ 6x9 paperback ♦ $12.95 ♦ code: LOM

BLINDSIDED
A Novel of Coming Earthchanges
by Dick & Leigh Richmond-Donahue

Leigh Richmond's earlier novel, *The Lost Millennium* (published in 1969 by Ace books as *Shiva*) was about the collapse of Atlantis and the fantastic technology that ultimately destroyed those who used it. This sequel is a prophetic story of the end of our current civilization—a worldwide war coupled by famine and earth-changes. As the Chinese and their allies take over the world, small survival communities with free energy struggle to survive...
171 pp. ♦ 6x9 paperback ♦ $10.95 ♦ code: BLS

VIMANA AIRCRAFT OF ANCIENT INDIA & ATLANTIS
DAVID HATCHER CHILDRESS
INTRODUCTION BY IVAN T. SANDERSON

Did the ancients have the technology of flight? In this incredible volume on ancient India, authentic Indian texts such as the Ramayana and the Mahabharata are used to prove that ancient aircraft were in use more than four thousand years ago. Included in this book is the entire fourth century BC manuscript Vimaanika Shastra by the ancient author Maharishi Bharadwaaja, translated into English by the Mysore Sanskrit professor G.R. Josyer. Also included are chapters on Atlantean technology, the incredible Rama Empire of India and the devastating wars that destroyed it. Also an entire chapter on mercury vortex propulsion and mercury gyros, the power source described in the ancient Indian texts. Not to be missed by those interested in ancient civilizations or the UFO enigma. 334 pages, 6x9 paperback, 104 rare photographs, maps and drawings. $15.95. (code: VAA)

Vimana Aircraft
of
Ancient India
&
Atlantis

By DAVID HATCHER CHILDRESS

INTRODUCTION BY IVAN T. SANDERSON.
THE COMPLETE VIMAANIKA SHASTRA TEXT.
SECRET LIBRARIES & ANCIENT SCIENCE.
ATLANTEAN AIRCRAFT & TECHNOLOGY.
SANSKRIT SCHOLARS & VIMANA TEXTS.

MEN AND GODS IN MONGOLIA
HENNING HASLUND.

First published in 1935 by Kegan Paul of London, this rare and unusual travel book takes us into the virtually unknown world of Mongolia, a country only now, after seventy years, is opening up to the west. Haslund, a Swedish explorer, takes us to the lost city of Karakota in the Gobi desert. We meet the Bodgo Gegen, a God-king in Mongolia similar to the Dalai Lama of Tibet. We meet Dambin Jansang, the dreaded warlord of the "Black Gobi". There is even material in this incredible book on the Hi-mori, an "airhorse" that flies through the air (similar to a Vimana) and carries with it the sacred stone of Chintamani. Aside from the esoteric and mystical material, there is plenty of just plain adventure: caravans across the Gobi desert, Haslund's being kidnapped and held for ransom, initiation into Shamanic societies, warlords and the violent birth of a new nation. 358 pages, 6x9 paperback, illustrated, 57 photos, illustrations and maps, $15.95 (code: MGM)

IN SECRET TIBET
THEODORE ILLION.

Reprint of a rare 30's travel book. Illion was a German traveller who not only spoke fluent Tibetan, but travelled in disguise through forbidden Tibet when it was off-limits to all outsiders. His incredible adventures make this one of the most exciting travel books ever published. Includes illustrations of Tibetan monks levitating stones by acoustics. 210 pages, 6x9 paperback, illustrated, ISBN 0-932813-13-5. $15.95 (code: IST)

IN SECRET TIBET
T. Illion

MYSTIC TRAVELLER SERIES

DARKNESS OVER TIBET
THEODORE ILLION.

In this second reprint of the rare 30's travel books by Illion, the German traveller continues his travels through Tibet and is given the directions to a strange underground city. As the original publisher's remarks said, this is a rare account of an underground city in Tibet by the only Westerner ever to enter it and escape alive! 210 pages, 6x9 paperback, illustrated, ISBN 0-932813-14-3. $15.95. (code: DOT)

ANTI-GRAVITY

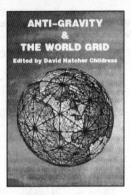

THE ANTI-GRAVITY HANDBOOK Revised/Expanded Edition
edited by David Hatcher Childress with Arthur C. Clark, Nikola Tesla, T.B. Paulicki, Capt. Bruce Cathie, Leonard G. Cramp & Albert Einstein

The book that blew minds and had engineers using their calculators is back in print in a new expanded compilation of material on Anti-Gravity, Free Energy, Flying Saucer propulsion, UFOs, Suppressed Technology, NASA Cover-ups and more. Highly illustrated with patents, technical illustrations, photos, and more, this revised and expanded edition has more material, including photos of Area 51, Nevada, the government's secret testing facility, Australian Secret Facilities, plus a rare reprint of Space, Gravity & the Flying Saucer by Leonard G. Cramp. This classic on weird science is back in a 90s format!
- How to Build a Flying Saucer;
- Read about Arthur C. Clark on Anti-Gravity;
- Learn about Crystals and their Role in Levitation;
- Secret Government Research and Development;
- Nikola Tesla on how Anti-Gravity Airships could Draw Power from the Atmosphere;
- Bruce Cathie's Anti-Gravity Equation;
- NASA, the Moon and Anti-Gravity, & more.

230 pp. ♦ 7x10 paperback ♦ Bibliography, index, appendix ♦ Highly illustrated with 100s of patents, illustrations & photos ♦ $14.95 ♦ code: AGH

ANTI-GRAVITY & THE WORLD GRID
edited by David Hatcher Childress

Is the earth surrounded by an intricate electromagnetic grid network offering free energy? This compilation of material on the earth grid, ley lines, and world power points contains chapters on the geography, mathematics, and light harmonics of the earth grid. Learn the purpose of ley lines and ancient megalithic structures located on the grid. Discover how the grid made the Philadelphia Experiment possible. Explore Coral Castle and many other mysteries including acoustic levitation, Tesla Shields and Scalar Wave weaponry. Browse through the section on anti-gravity patents and research resources.

274 pp. ♦ 7x10 paperback ♦ 150 rare photographs, diagrams & drawings ♦ $14.95 ♦ code: AGW

ANTI-GRAVITY & THE UNIFIED FIELD
edited by David Hatcher Childress

Is Einstein's Unified Field the answer to all of our energy problems? Explored in this compilation of material ARE how gravity, electricity, and magnetism manifest from a unified field around us; why artificial gravity is possible; secrets of UFO propulsion; free energy; Nikola Tesla and anti-gravity airships of the 20s and 30s; Flying saucers as superconducting whirls of plasma; anti-mass generators; vortex propulsion; suppressed technology; government cover-ups; gravitational pulse drive; spacecraft; and more.

240 pp. ♦ 7x10 paperback ♦ 30 rare photographs, diagrams & drawings ♦ $14.95 ♦ code: AGU

THE FANTASTIC INVENTIONS OF NIKOLA TESLA
by Nikola Tesla with additional material by David Hatcher Childress

This book is a virtual compendium of patents, diagrams, photos, and explanations of the many incredible inventions of the originator of the modern era of electrification. The book is a readable and affordable collection of his patents, inventions, and thoughts on free energy, anti-gravity, and other futuristic inventions. Covered in depth, often in Tesla's own words, are such topics as:
• His Plan to Transmit Free Electricity into the Atmosphere;
• How Anti-Gravity Airships could Draw Power from the Towers he was Building;
• Tesla's Death Rays, Ozone Generators, and more...

342 pp. © 6x9 paperback © Highly illustrated © Bibliography & appendix © $16.95 ©
code: FINT

EXTRATERRESTRIAL ARCHAEOLOGY
by David Hatcher Childress

With hundreds of photos and illustrations, Extraterrestrial Archaeology takes the reader to the strange and fascinating worlds of Mars, the Moon, Mercury, Venus, Saturn, and other planets for a look at the alien structures that appear there. This book is non-fiction! Whether skeptic or believer, this book allows you to view for yourself the amazing pyramids, domes, spaceports, obelisks, and other anomalies that are profiled in photograph after photograph. Using official NASA and Soviet photos, as well as other photos taken via telescope, this book seeks to prove that many of the planets (and moons) of our solar system are in some way inhabited by intelligent life. The book includes many blowups of NASA photos and detailed diagrams of structures—particularly on the Moon. Extraterrestrial Archaeology will change the way you think.

224 pp. © 8¹/2x11 paperback © Highly illustrated with photos, diagrams & maps! © Bibliography, index, appendix © $18.95
code: ETA

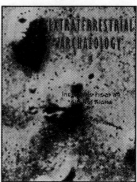

LOST CITIES OF ANCIENT LEMURIA & THE PACIFIC
by David Hatcher Childress

Was there once a continent in the Pacific? Called Lemuria or Pacifica by geologists, and Mu or Pan by the mystics, there is now ample mythological, geological and archaeological evidence to "prove" that an advanced and ancient civilization once lived in the central Pacific. Maverick archaeologist and explorer David Hatcher Childress combs the Indian Ocean, Australia, and the Pacific in search of the astonishing truth about mankind's past. Contains photos of the underwater city on Pohnpei, explanations on how the statues were levitated around Easter Island in a clockwise vortex movement, disappearing islands, Egyptians in Australia, and more.

379 pp. ♦ 6x9 paperback ♦ Photos, maps, & illustrations ♦ Footnotes & bibliography ♦ $14.95
code: LEM

MAN-MADE UFOS: 1944-1994
50 Years of Suppression
by Renato Vesco & David Hatcher Childress

A comprehensive and in-depth look at the early "flying saucer technology" of Nazi Germany and the genesis of early man-made UFOs. From captured German scientists, escaped battalions of German soldiers, secret communities in South America and Antarctica to today's state-of-the-art "Dreamland" flying machines, this astonishing book blows the lid off the "Government UFO Conspiracy." Examined in detail are secret underground airfields and factories; German secret weapons; "suction" aircraft; the origin of NASA; gyroscopic stabilizers and engines; the secret Marconi aircraft factory in South America, and other secret societies, both ancient and modern, that have kept this craft a secret, and much more. Not to be missed by students of technology suppression, UFOs, anti-gravity, free-energy conspiracy, and World War II. Introduction by W.A. Harbinson, author of the Dell novels Genesis and Revelation.

440 pp. 6x9 paperback ♦ Packed with photos & diagrams Index & footnotes ♦
$18.95 ♦ code: MMU

Renato Vesco &
David Hatcher Childress

THE FREE-ENERGY DEVICE HANDBOOK
A Compilation of Patents & Reports
by David Hatcher Childress

Large format compilation of various patents, papers, descriptions, and diagrams concerning free-energy devices and systems. The Free-Energy Device Handbook is a visual tool for experimenters and researchers into magnetic motors and other "over-unity" devices with chapters on the Adams Motor, the Hans Coler Generator, cold fusion, superconductors, "N" machines, space-energy generators, Nikola Tesla, T. Townsend Brown, the Bedini motor, and the latest in free-energy devices. Packed with photos, technical diagrams, patents, and fascinating information, this book belongs on every science shelf. With energy and profit a major political reason for fighting various wars, free-energy devices, if ever allowed to be mass-distributed to consumers, could change the world. Get your copy now before the Department of Energy bans this book!

306 pp. ♦ 7x10 paperback ♦ Profusely illustrated ♦ Bibliography & appendix ♦ $16.95 ♦
code: FEH

THE HISTORY OF ATLANTIS
by Lewis Spence

Lewis Spence's classic book on Atlantis is now back in print. Lewis Spence was a Scottish historian (1874-1955) who is best known for his volumes on world mythology and his five Atlantis books. The History of Atlantis (1926) is considered his best. Spence does his scholarly best in such chapters as The Sources of Atlantean History, The Geography of Atlantis, The Races of Atlants, The Kings of Atlantis, The Religion of Atlantis, The Colonies of Atlantis, more. Sixteen chapters in all.

240 pp. ♦ 6x9 paperback © Illustrated with maps, photos & diagrams ♦ $16.95
code: HOA (Autumn '95)

Adventures Unlimited Press
One Adventure Place
Kempton, Illinois
60946
24 Hour Telephone Order Line
815 253 6390
24 Hour Fax Order Line
815 253 6300
EMail orders
adventures_unlimited
@mcimail.com

816 - 8335
LARRY

ADVENTURES UNLIMITED

303 Main Street
P.O. Box 74
Kempton, Illinois 60946
USA
Tel.: 815-253-6390 ♦ Fax: 815-253-6300
Email: adventures_unlimited@mcimail.com

ORDERING INSTRUCTIONS

➤ Please Write Clearly
➤ Remit by USD$ Check or Money Order
➤ Visa/MasterCard Accepted
➤ Call ♦ Fax ♦ Email Any Time

SHIPPING CHARGES

United States

➤ Postal Book Rate { $2.00 First Item / 50¢ Each Additional Item
➤ Priority Mail { $3.50 First Item / $1.50 Each Additional Item
➤ UPS { $3.50 First Item / $1.00 Each Additional Item
NOTE: UPS Delivery Available to Mainland USA Only

Canada

➤ Postal Book Rate { $3.00 First Item / $1.00 Each Additional Item
➤ Postal Air Mail { $4.00 First Item / $2.00 Each Additional Item
➤ Personal Checks or Bank Drafts MUST BE USD$ and Drawn on a US Bank
➤ Canadian Postal Money Orders OK
➤ Payment MUST BE USD$

All Other Countries

➤ Surface Delivery { $5.00 First Item / $2.00 Each Additional Item
➤ Postal Air Mail { $10.00 First Item / $8.00 Each Additional Item
➤ Payment MUST BE USD$
➤ Personal Checks MUST BE USD$ and Drawn on a US Bank
➤ Add $5.00 for Air Mail Subscription to Future *Adventures Unlimited* Catalogs

SPECIAL NOTES

➤ RETAILERS: Standard Discounts Available
➤ BACKORDERS: We Backorder all Out-of-Stock Items Unless Otherwise Requested
➤ PRO FORMA INVOICES: Available on Request
➤ VIDEOS: NTSC Mode Only
  PAL & SECAM Mode Videos Are Not Available

Thank you for your order
We appreciate your business

Please check: ☑

☐ This is my first order ☐ I have ordered before ☐ This is a new address

Name		
Address		
City		
State/Province		Postal Code
Country		
Phone day		Evening
Fax		

Item Code	Item Description	Price	Qty	Total
CAT	Adventures Unlimited Catalog	N/C		N/C

Please check: ☑

☐ Postal-Surface
☐ Postal-Air Mail (Priority in USA)
☐ UPS (Mainland USA only)

Please Use Item Codes!

Subtotal ➤	
Less Discount-10% for 3 or more items ➤	
Balance ➤	
Illinois Residents 7% Sales Tax ➤	
Previous Credit ➤	
Shipping ➤	
Total (check/MO in USD$ only) ➤	

☐ Visa ☐ MasterCard

#_____ Exp. _____

Comments & Suggestions

Share Our Catalog with a Friend